THE ORIGINS OF WORLD WAR TWO

THE DEBATE CONTINUES

Edited by

Robert Boyce
London School of Economics

and

Joseph A. Maiolo
King's College London

First published 2003 by
PALGRAVE MACMILLAN
Houndmills, Basingstoke, Hampshire RG21 6XS and
175 Fifth Avenue, New York, N.Y. 10010
Companies and representatives throughout the world

PALGRAVE MACMILLAN is the global academic imprint of the Palgrave Macmillan division of St. Martin's Press LLC and of Palgrave Macmillan Ltd. Macmillan® is a registered trademark in the United States, United Kingdom and other countries. Palgrave is a registered trademark in the European Union and other countries

ISBN 0–333–94526–3 hardback
ISBN 0–333–94539–5 paperback

This book is printed on paper suitable for recycling and made from fully managed and sustained forest sources.

A catalogue record for this book is available from the British Library.

Library of Congress Cataloging-in-Publication Data

The origins of World War Two : the debate continues / edited by Robert Boyce, Joseph A. Maiolo.
    p. cm.
  Includes bibliographical references and index.
  ISBN 0–333–94526–3 (hard.) – ISBN 0–333–94539–5 (pbk.)
  1. World War, 1939–1945 – Causes. I. Boyce, Robert W. D., 1943 – II. Maiolo, Joseph A.

  D741.O76 2003
  940.53'11–dc21   2003042968

10   9   8   7   6   5   4   3   2   1
12   11   10   09   08   07   06   05   04   03

Typeset in Great Britain by
Aarontype Ltd, Easton, Bristol

Printed and bound in Great Britain by
Creative Print and Design (Wales), Ebbw Vale

Contents

The Small European Powers and China

List of Maps

List of Figures

Acknowledgements

The editors wish to thank the contributors. Without their hard work, cooperation and expertise this collection would not have been possible. We are in debt to our editor at Palgrave Macmillan, Terka Acton, who showed great enthusiasm for the project when it was proposed, and superhuman patience while it was being produced. Her editorial team, Felicity Noble and Sonya Barker, were always prompt and helpful. We are grateful to Penny Simmons for copy editing the typescript and Jane Ashley for compiling the index. Permission to reproduce the maps was granted by Margaret Lamb and Nicholas Tarling.

This book is dedicated to our students, from whom we have learned much about the origins of the Second World War.

Note on Chinese and Japanese names

Chinese spellings have been rendered in Pinyin, except for Chiang Kai-shek, which has been kept in its most familiar form. Japanese names have been rendered with the family name last in order to avoid confusion, thus Hideki Tōjō, rather than Tōjō Hideki.

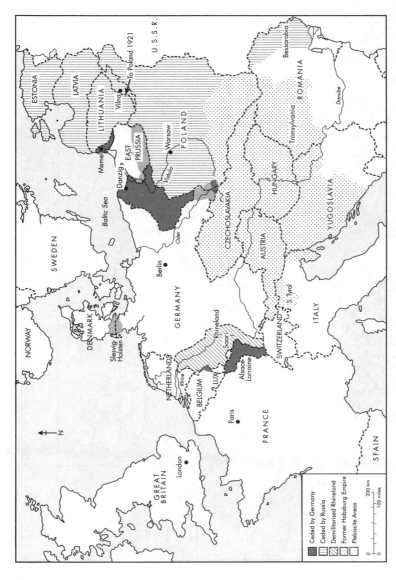

Map 1   Europe 1921–35 from Margaret Lamb and Nicholas Tarling, *From Versailles to Pearl Harbor: The Origins of the Second World War in Europe and Asia*; Basingstoke: Palgrave Macmillan (2001), p. xii.

Legend:

- Ceded by Germany
- Ceded by Russia
- Demilitarised Rhineland
- Former Habsburg Empire
- Plebiscite Areas

Scale: 0 — 200 km / 0 — 100 miles

Labels on map:

NORWAY, SWEDEN, GREAT BRITAIN, London, DENMARK, Slesvig-Holsten, NETHERLANDS, BELGIUM, LUX., Paris, FRANCE, SPAIN, GERMANY, Berlin, Rhine, Rhineland, Saar, Alsace-Lorraine, SWITZERLAND, ITALY, S. Tyrol, AUSTRIA, Baltic Sea, Memel, Danzig, EAST PRUSSIA, Oder, Vistula, Warsaw, POLAND, Vilna, To Poland 1921, LITHUANIA, LATVIA, ESTONIA, U.S.S.R., CZECHOSLOVAKIA, HUNGARY, YUGOSLAVIA, Transylvania, ROMANIA, Bessarabia, Danube

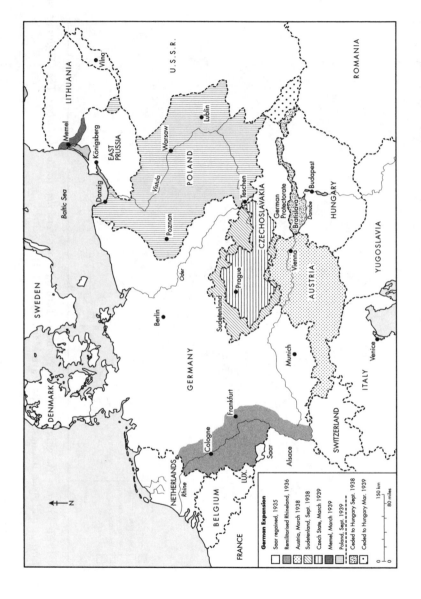

Map 2 Europe 1935–39 from Margaret Lamb and Nicholas Tarling, *From Versailles to Pearl Harbor: The Origins of the Second World War in Europe and Asia*; Basingstoke: Palgrave Macmillan (2001), p. xiii.

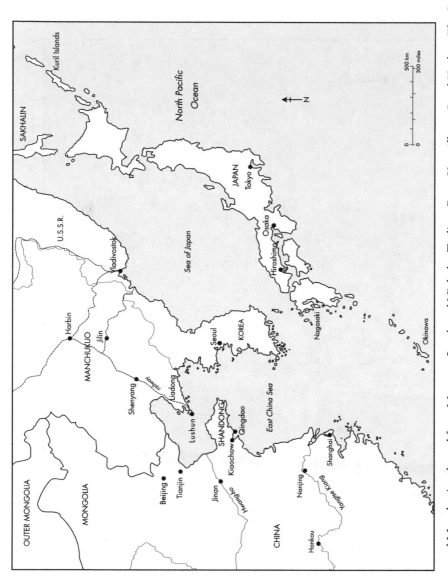

Map 3 Japan and Manchuria adapted from Margaret Lamb and Nicholas Tarling, *From Versailles to Pearl Harbor: The Origins of the Second World War in Europe and Asia*; Basingstoke: Palgrave Macmillan (2001), p. xiv.

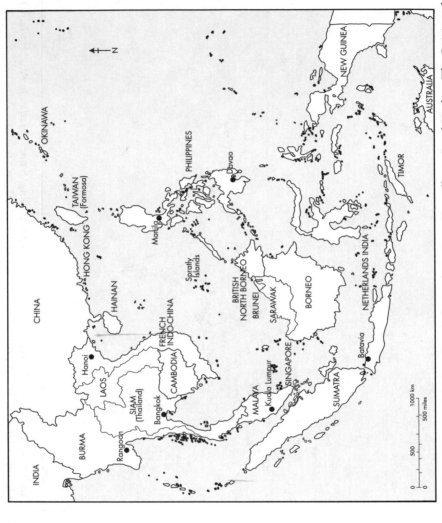

Map 4 Southeast Asia from Margaret Lamb and Nicholas Tarling, *From Versailles to Pearl Harbor: The Origins of the Second World War in Europe and Asia*; Basingstoke: Palgrave Macmillan (2001), p. xv.

Introduction: The Debate Continues

Robert Boyce and Joseph A. Maiolo

Why continue to study the origins of the Second World War? Few of us today (and fewer with each passing year) have direct experience of the war. For sheer horror, it is the First World War that retains the greater fascination among students of the twentieth century, while the Cold War offers the only recent experience of global conflict. Yet with the events of 1989–91 even the Cold War has ended,[1] and arguably none of the three global conflicts of the twentieth century has much relevance to contemporary security problems. Today's security nightmare has become global terrorists operating outside the nation-state system and armed with weapons of mass destruction. As E. H. Carr observes in *What is History?*, the present determines what each generation finds most significant in the past.[2] Perhaps therefore interest in the Second World War will fade, and popular and scholarly attention will turn instead to the Crusades (1095–1291) and the pre-national forms of order and conflict in the medieval world.

The editors of this collection of essays do not think so. For one thing, the consequences of the Second World War will continue to be felt well into this century and beyond. Its direct effects are evident everywhere: in the altered urban landscapes of Europe and Japan; in scientific and technological advances including jet propulsion, liquid-fuel rockets and atomic weapons; in surgical techniques and the treatment of psychological trauma; in the adoption throughout the developed world of national income accounting and the use of operations research methodologies for complex management problems; in military tactics and strategy; in institutions such as the United Nations, the International Monetary Fund and the World Bank; in literature, film and so on. The indirect effects of what was after all the most extensive and lethal war in history are no less evident. Among other things, it

abruptly ended Europe's long imperial, economic and cultural predominance in the world. It created the conditions for the Holocaust, with its
consequential effects on the future of Palestine and relations in the Middle
East. It accelerated the rise of the Superpowers and helped to create the
political vacuum in Europe and East Asia that led to their long confrontation
during the Cold War. The rise of the United States, if anticipated by Alexis
de Tocqueville, Friedrich Gentz and others a century or more earlier, and
made possible by its continental expansion and industrial growth, was
decisively provoked by the events of 1939–41. Russia extended its sway over
much of Central Europe and its influence into other continents. China
emerged from the chaos left by the war in East Asia as a Great Power in its
own right. Europe was transformed, the institutions that make up the core of
the present-day European Union coming into being under the chastening
effect of the war and the uncertain demarcation of the victorious armies that
soon hardened into the Iron Curtain. No less important, the vast British,
French and Dutch empires were shaken to their roots by the war, which
awoke subject peoples to a new level of national self-consciousness and
brought on their collapse within barely 15 years. As for the human
and moral impact of the war: the part played by ordinary Germans in the
'Final Solution'; the conduct of Japanese soldiers and bureaucrats in the
conquered territories of East Asia and the Pacific; the legality of the Vichy
regime and its responsibility for extending the Holocaust to France; the large
but ambiguous role of Communists within the national liberation movements of Italy, France, Greece and Yugoslavia; London's decision to accept
or reject asylum seekers escaping the ravages of Nazism; Washington's decision to drop atomic bombs on Japanese population centres; Moscow's
indifference to the systematic rape and abuse of ethnic Germans by Soviet
troops – these and other dimensions of the war still spark intense public
controversy and academic debate.[3]

As mythology, the Second World War and its origins have had a profound
and enduring influence on the conduct of international relations and, as
Robert Jervis reminds us in his chapter, on the discipline of political science.
Despite the efforts of historians to explain the considerable constraints upon
British and French governments in their confrontation with the Fascist and
militarist powers in the 1930s, 'appeasement' seems likely to remain a term
of political derision throughout the English-speaking world. Consequently,
when statesmen or journalists perceive the threat of aggression from Colonel
Nasser or Ghadaffi, Slobodan Milosovic or Sadam Hussein, allusions to
Hitler, Munich and appeasement can be expected to follow. Whatever the
merits of the historical analogy, President George W. Bush's description
of Iran, Iraq, North Korea and their 'terrorist allies' as an '*axis of evil*'
illustrates the continuing currency of the 'lessons' of the Second World
War.[4] One of the features of the international system today is that the
powers with the capacity to mount a massive conventional military and

nuclear challenge to the *status quo* now have little reason to do so. The era of Great Power and Superpower rivalry has, at least for the time being, closed. Yet defenders of the liberal, capitalist international system are still confronted by challengers who seek a radical, and in some cases violent, restructuring of the global order. While, to be sure, the world has changed, the ideological battle lines of the present 'war on terror' resonate powerfully with the great power clashes of the 1930s and 1940s.

The fact that the coming of the Second World War is an important element in the collective memory of the contemporary world sustains the urge to understand it. The task is not a simple one. The events of the 1930s and the onset of war continue to present a remarkable challenge to students of history. The same, of course, may be said of the First World War and the Cold War, but the editors contend that the road to global war from 1931 to 1941 presents a more complex problem. The Great War originated in a general crisis in the Great Power system that might have passed without world war. Even in June 1914, no statesman anticipated or desired four years of mass industrial killing. Unfortunately, the crisis sparked by the assassination of the Austrian archduke, Franz Ferdinand, and his wife was allowed to escalate because key decision-makers miscalculated that the potential gains of a localised Balkan war outweighed the risks of a general European one. Arguably no power actively sought the larger war or looked forward to a vast smash-up in order to take advantage of it. The Cold War, if decades long and vastly expensive in money and lives, was also paradoxically limited in other ways. In retrospect, the crisis years between 1947 and 1953 may be seen as the formative stage in the establishment of a relatively stable international system founded on two competing socio-economic and alliance blocs. It was above all an ideological contest, and while the stakes were high, particularly for those caught up in the small wars on the periphery of the two blocs, most of the key decisions remained in the hands of statesmen in Washington and Moscow, where the key watchwords became control and order. In contrast, the origins of the Second World War constitute a different order of magnitude. Not only was open aggression on two continents a feature of the decade preceding the war, there were also at least three – some say four – determined aggressors vying for the opportunity to upset the *status quo*. The diversity of players and the loose bonds between them meant that the game was very fluid, fast-paced and intricate. Making sense of the world crisis of 1931 to 1941, as it was played out on different continents by different powers, may be likened to playing racket ball, chess or poker simultaneously against several opponents. So complex was this crisis that historians have disagreed on when the Second World War began and even whether it was initially two separate wars, the first in East Asia starting perhaps as early as 1931, and the second in Europe, which merged into a single global conflict only in December 1941. To be sure, powerful lines of continuity may be drawn between the great calamities of the twentieth century, including the world depression. But a case can be made for saying that the Second World War constituted a sharp break from the continuum. As the German-American historian, Gerhard Weinberg, writes, 'it was [Hitler's] concept of a demographic revolution in the world that made World War II not a continuation of World War I but an entirely different type of conflict.'[5]

The purpose of this book is to provide an up-to-date and comparative textbook on the origins of the Second World War in Europe, Asia and the Pacific. It was commissioned with several different readers in mind. The editors hope the volume will provide undergraduate students with a wide-ranging and lively source for their studies. They hope that postgraduates and scholars in the fields of international history, European history and international relations will find it a useful starting-point for their research. They also hope to serve the wider reading public who may wish to know the state of knowledge among academic specialists. The collection is divided into two parts. The first part examines the role of the major and minor powers in the coming of war; the second part explores important themes that do not fit properly within a national context. The editors deliberately set out to include aspects of the subject that are not treated extensively in other texts. Readers will therefore find chapters not only on Germany, Britain, France, Italy, the United States, Japan and the Soviet Union, but also on several of the lesser powers such as Poland, Czechoslovakia and China. The collection includes – paradoxically some might say – a chapter by Neville Wylie on the role of the neutral states and another by Philip Bell on international peace movements. John Ferris synthesises research into the secret world of intelligence and evaluates the influence of intelligence on the international system of the 1930s. Philip Taylor does the same for the instruments of propaganda and persuasion that governments deployed to bolster public support behind foreign and domestic policies. Other chapters by Alan Cassels, Joseph Maiolo, Robert Boyce and Donald Cameron Watt deal respectively with the themes of ideology, armaments competition, economic crisis and doctrine, and diplomacy. Each of these topics requires separate treatment, the editors believe, because they shed light on the nature of international politics in the period as a whole, and because they affected statesmen in ways that cannot be properly understood by restricting analysis to any single country. Lastly, in an acknowledgement of the important contribution of the social sciences, which has always distinguished international history, Robert Jervis examines the ways in which political scientists use the 1930s as evidence in their theoretical inquiries. Our hope is that readers will find his chapter a fascinating insight into how another discipline treats the subject and adopts a systemic approach to the international problems of the inter-war period.

The present book originated in conversation between the editors in early 1999 about the state of the debate. We agreed that the time had come for a follow up to the two earlier collections published by Macmillan: Esmonde M. Robertson's *The Origins of the Second World War: Historical Interpretations* (1971) and Esmonde Robertson and Robert Boyce's *Paths to War: New Essays on the Origins of the Second World War* (1989). At the time the first volume appeared, historians were preoccupied with the controversy provoked by A. J. P. Taylor's *The Origins of the Second World War*. Few collections of historical essays could be more brilliant or disputatious, but it must be said that the narrow and unselfconsciously Eurocentric focus of the debate, on German intentions and British appeasement, even then invited challenge. The second collection was published when the tide of academic revision had transformed the debate on British and French appeasement, and the appraisal and integration of the sources that became available in the 1970s and 1980s had reached the historiographical high-water mark. The scope was widened to include, among other things, Francoist Spain, the United States and the impact of the world depression. One essay, by Sidney Aster, on Neville Chamberlain and the 'guilty men' of Britain, pointed towards, or rather back to, a negative assessment of British appeasement policy, based on the view that alternatives were available had statesmen possessed the political enlightenment required to appreciate the looming danger. By and large, however, the contributors, drawing heavily upon recently opened official sources, were more impressed by the practical constraints upon statesmen and the rational, if sometimes shortsighted, character of their decision-making. Since 1989, historians have turned their attention to new themes and new sources of evidence in the former Soviet and eastern European as well as in various western archives. For his chapter on the Soviet Union and Spain, for instance, Jonathan Haslam draws not only on newly released Russian sources, but also British transcripts of secretly intercepted communications between the Communist International and member parties, which the Public Record Office in London has recently opened to scholars. Interestingly, even with the fresh sources and the prospect of a post-Cold War perspective on the 1930s, the most striking trend in the 1990s in the historiography of the European war has been a partial revival of the orthodoxy of the 1940s and 1950s. If the appeasers are no longer represented as merely cowardly and corrupt, a number of highly regarded scholars have again advanced the thesis that they pursued wilfully misconceived policies and squandered the chance to stop Hitler and Mussolini before it was too late. The military historian, Williamson Murray, takes up this theme in his chapter on British statesmen and their strategic thinking. This is complemented by analyses of the impulses behind Nazi and Italian Fascist foreign policy. Few historians now support the 'functionalist' argument that Hitler was driven into aggression by forces beyond his control; most accept the 'intentionalist' argument that Hitler himself consistently aimed at a racially inspired revolution within the Third Reich and wars of racial annihilation abroad. Christian Leitz underlines the case in his chapter on Hitler's readiness for war despite Germany's relative unreadiness for a long conflict. The military historian John Gooch confirms the relevance of a similar intentionalist argument in the case of Mussolini and Fascist Italy.

What prevented the formation of an anti-German coalition of France, Britain and the Soviet Union? It was almost certainly not the *realpolitik* thinking of Stalin and the Soviet leadership, who until the spring of 1939 looked to collective security and the League of Nations as vehicles for the containment of Nazism. As chapters by Peter Jackson, Anita Prazmowska and others illustrate, the explanation is to be sought elsewhere, in fear of the domestic economic, political and social consequences of war, in continuing uncertainty over Soviet intentions and anti-Communist fears in London, Paris and Warsaw, and in other divergent influences upon national policy. At the same time, historians of the Pacific War have broadened research to include not only Japan and the United States, but also powers such as Britain, Germany, France, the Soviet Union and China. One historian of the war has recently speculated that broadening the scope of analysis renders a new synthesis impossible.[6] None the less, it highlights the inadequacies of the old approach, which made Pearl Harbor both the symbol and a key explanation of the war. The contributions in the present volume by John Garver on China and Antony Best on Japan point the way.

The diversity and complexity of the historiography persuaded the editors to opt for a multi-authored volume. A work of synthesis tends to obscure the continuing academic controversy and drain the debate of its lifeblood: the differences of perspective and approach of individual scholars, which make history such an absorbing and challenging intellectual pursuit. An historiographical approach, while capable of highlighting differences within the specialist literature, inevitably omits much of the evidence on which the different interpretations rest and thus limits the readers' ability to judge for themselves. Each of the contributors to the present volume is a recognised expert in the field; each has been invited to highlight the importance of his or her corner of the canvas. While each chapter stands alone, the book provides a wide-ranging picture of the subject as a whole. By compiling a multi-authored book, the editors hope above all to enable readers to appreciate the open-endedness of historical enquiry. Despite occasional resort to words such as comprehensive or definitive, professional historians rarely expect to have the final word or secure general agreement on a subject as complex as the origins of the Second World War. The present book, if it succeeds in answering certain questions or laying certain ghosts, is ultimately intended to stimulate the debate rather than to close it down. Thus, we may confidently say, the debate continues.

Robert Boyce and Joe Maiolo

Notes

1. The events also brought the Second World War formally to an end, when the German problem was resolved through reunification and the signing of treaties between Germany and its former victims in Eastern Europe.
2. E. H. Carr, *What is History?* 2nd edn (London, 1987).
3. A number of these issues are discussed in the round table, 'The Future of World War Two Studies', in *Diplomatic History* 25 (2001), 347–499.
4. The President's State of the Union Address, 29 January 2002, http://www.whitehouse.gov/news/releases/ 2002/01/20020129–11.html. 'States like these', Bush said, 'and their terrorist allies, constitute an axis of evil, arming to threaten the peace of the world.' Our emphasis.
5. G. Weinberg, 'World War II: Comments', *Diplomatic History* 25 (2001), 495–7.
6. M. Barnhart, 'The Origins of the Second World War in Asia and the Pacific: Synthesis Impossible?', *Diplomatic History* 20 (1996), 241–60.

PART ONE:
THE RESPONSIBILITY
OF THE POWERS

1 Nazi Germany

Christian Leitz

In January 1933, Adolf Hitler came to power with the firm belief that radical changes both at home and internationally were urgently needed in order to enable him to pursue his supreme goal of mastery of Europe through a war of conquest and expansion. Yet, neither politically nor militarily, economically or socially, did Germany offer the necessary preconditions to fulfil Hitler's goal and fight a successful war. Thus, Hitler set out to undertake a radical transformation of Germany. In this endeavour he was willingly assisted by the conservatives who had brought him to power and were now participating in government. With regard to foreign policy, leading non-Nazi members of the regime willingly deceived themselves into believing that the radical changes they assisted and, at times, actively encouraged Hitler to implement were intended simply to regain great power status for Germany and to undo the humiliation of the Treaty of Versailles. They preferred not to confront the possibility that Hitler firmly intended to achieve a much more fundamental transformation of Europe.

The grounds for this delusion were always rather thin. It was, of course, extremely unlikely that other states would voluntarily return territories to the Reich. Thus any attempt to overturn the Versailles Treaty would probably require military force. Yet Hitler's vision of Germany's future place in the world meant that his sights were set well beyond reversing the Treaty. Gaining hegemony over Europe, acquiring *Lebensraum* in the East and possibly even making Germany the leading global power required wars of a different magnitude to those likely to erupt were Germany merely to reverse the terms of the Treaty of Versailles.

In 1933, however, Germany was not even in a position to win a war against its despised eastern neighbour, Poland, let alone against its arch-enemy, France. Hitler's active pursuit of a non-aggression treaty with Poland, against the wishes of his conservative allies in the regime and the *Reichswehr*, was an acknowledgement of Germany's inability to fight Poland – yet. By disrupting the Franco-Polish alliance, however, the treaty signed in January 1934 was also evidence of Hitler's tactic of weakening the ties between Germany's potential enemies. More broadly, the treaty provided early evidence that foreign policy was the area in which the regime would prove to be most successful in preparing Germany for war. Through the skilful use of foreign policy, the Nazi regime between January 1933 and August 1939 manoeuvred Germany into a powerful starting position for war without having to resort to military conflict.

As is shown by other contributors to this collection of essays, Nazi Germany's diplomatic good fortune would have been impossible had other European governments not played into its hand. Hitler's preparations for war were to benefit both from his own shrewd and daring foreign policy, and the foreign policy errors committed by his potential enemies. On its own, however, foreign policy successes would not have sufficed to place Germany in the most advantageous position for war. The regime's domestic preparations were also crucial to Germany's early and surprisingly rapid successes in the war.

From 1933, the Nazi regime made significant strides towards a radical transformation of Germany's military, economy, politics and society. To the outside world, the image of this transformation was greatly enhanced by the regime's extensive use of propaganda.[1] Thus, in April 1939, on the occasion of Hitler's fiftieth birthday, domestic and foreign observers were offered the spectacle of a grandiose four-hour military parade. Yet measured against its own goals and against the potential strength of its likely enemies, Germany's actual transformation and preparedness fell short of the regime's own propaganda image. Some of the problems and shortcomings the Nazi regime faced in 1939 will be surveyed in the following section.

Despite the image of invincible strength, Germany's military still suffered from not insignificant equipment shortfalls when it commenced its invasion of Poland.[2] The problems worried the *Wehrmacht* leaders during the war in Poland, but became even more evident directly afterwards. Albeit brief, the war had sapped the *Wehrmacht* of substantial reserves of war material. Above all, a munitions crisis loomed, which reminded Germany's military of the predicament it had faced during the First World War. With Germany's troops and war material reserves exhausted, the impatient Hitler repeatedly had to postpone the planned attack in the West.

Germany's economy also faced various problems on account of the incomplete nature of its preparations for war. At the outbreak of war, the mobilisation plans for the economy had been implemented only in about 60 per cent of German firms.[3] This meant in particular that, despite taking precedence, firms had not engaged solely in war production, the production of non-essential goods had been only partly reduced, and the corresponding transfer of labour was not completed. Insufficient coordination, indeed continued strong competition among the various German arms producers, also hampered the *Wehrmacht's* preparations. A bewildering array of types of arms and other equipment continued to cause major problems during the war, with rationalisation efforts only belatedly implemented.[4]

Germany's economy continued to be heavily dependent on imported raw materials, with the supply situation a source of constant concern to the *Wehrmacht*. Despite the vehement promises made by Field Marshall Hermann Göring and other officials in his Four-Year Plan Office, the production of synthetic goods had not reached anywhere near the level anticipated in the Plan.[5] At a time when the *Wehrmacht* sought to increase its arms equipment level, the regime was forced to increase the export of high-quality arms to countries not allied with Germany in order to secure supplies of urgently required raw materials.[6]

In 1939, Germany's food supply situation was also far from satisfactory. Despite highly propagandised efforts to increase the country's agricultural production, its self-sufficiency in food supplies grew only slightly between 1933 and 1938–39, from 80 to 83 per cent. Moreover, with the booming rearmament sector increasingly sapping farmers of precious agricultural labour and with shortfalls in both machinery and fertiliser production, the possibility of any radical improvement markedly decreased.[7] As a result, the provisioning of Germany's population and armed forces during the war came to depend heavily on the exploitation of resources of countries occupied by or even allied to the Third Reich.

Even in political terms, the regime was beset with problems. Of greatest concern was the 'polycratic jungle', the 'institutional confusion', which had developed below Hitler during the previous six years. To the German populace and to the outside world, the regime projected the image of a strictly organised, highly coordinated force. The reality was quite different. Due to competing agencies in all areas of the administration, preparations for and the eventual running of the war proceeded far less smoothly than might have been expected from a dictatorial system so set on war. An obvious example for this struggle for power was in the management of Germany's economy where, from 1936, the Reich Economics Ministry was increasingly displaced by the Four-Year Plan Office and to a lesser extent the *Wehrmacht*'s own economic experts.

Germany's armed forces were themselves under attack in their most traditional function as sole bearer of arms. Although Hitler removed the threat posed by the army's first major rival, the *Sturm Abteilung* (SA), in June 1934, he made no effort to halt Himmler's attempts to strengthen his *Schutz Staffel* (SS) to the detriment of the *Wehrmacht*. Although the military wing of the SS was still numerically small (just under 23,000 men in late 1938), Himmler's success in gaining a military role for his organisation foreshadowed its rapid expansion during the war.[8]

That the history of the regime consisted of constant competition, rivalry and infighting among its hierarchy was also evident in areas other than the economic and military. The Reich foreign minister, Konstantin von Neurath, had to contend with the ambitions of his eventual successor,

Joachim von Ribbentrop, and other Nazi *Bonzen*, such as Alfred Rosenberg, Hermann Göring and even the Reich propaganda minister, Joseph Goebbels.[9] The position of Wilhelm Frick, Reich minister of the interior, was undermined from all directions, including by Hitler's deputy, Rudolf Hess, and Himmler, while Franz Seldte's responsibilities as minister of labour were challenged by Robert Ley and his German Labour Front (DAF). Regular rivalries also erupted among the various regional Nazi leaders, the *Gauleiter* and Reich commissioners. In fact, only Hitler's position was never challenged or affected by his subordinates' greed for power – at least not until the final days of the war.

In keeping himself above the petty rivalries of his underlings, Hitler undoubtedly enhanced his popularity among the wider population. His detachment also helped to establish the distinction ordinary Germans increasingly drew between the Führer and the regime. Hitler's popularity after 1933 grew at a much greater rate than that of the regime at large. His immense popularity did not, however, automatically translate into a fervent enthusiasm for all his views and objectives. The central pillars of his ideology, virulent antisemitism and territorial expansion through war, were in fact shared by only a minority of Germans.

German society, despite a small, propagandistically exaggerated pro-war minority, patently lacked the eagerness for military conflict that Hitler had hoped for. This became particularly evident in 1938 during the Sudeten crisis, and more specifically during and directly after the Munich conference. Once war was averted by the transfer of the Sudetenland into German hands, Chamberlain's message of peace was welcomed not only by a large majority in Britain, but also in Germany. As the German diplomat Johann von Herwarth noted in his memoirs, 'the man in the street in Germany considered Chamberlain a hero, for he did not want war.' Yet, Herwarth also added: 'That same man in the street believed Hitler's affirmation that there would be no World War II.'[10] A majority of Germans clearly appreciated Hitler's foreign policy successes, not least because they had been achieved not by military means but peacefully. Intent on having war already in late 1938, Hitler, however, did not hide his anger about the lack of enthusiasm for war among 'his' people.

While the bulk of the population only passively showed their preference for peace, others developed more active plans to prevent a European war. Chamberlain and Daladier's decision to give in to Hitler at Munich came as a major blow to those *Wehrmacht* officers who had intended to use the outbreak of military conflict with Britain and France to overthrow the regime. Although it appears that most of the plotters of 1938 were more worried about the strong possibility of a German defeat than about war *per se*, these first seeds of resistance from members of Germany's conservative élites indicated the potential for future problems for Hitler.[11] Within German society at large, the occurrence of strikes, albeit limited, and other disruptive activities also indicated the continued existence of groups and individuals opposed to the policies of the regime.[12]

It is thus possible to provide a gloomy picture of Germany's state of preparedness for war in 1939. Some historians, in fact, have pointed to the unsatisfactory economic situation and the social frictions as evidence that the Nazi regime confronted a major domestic crisis in 1938–39. Tim Mason, in particular, argues that this crisis forced Hitler to go to war. There is, however, insufficient evidence to substantiate his thesis. In September 1939, Hitler did not take Germany into war to escape growing domestic pressures, but because it seemed to be the right moment to attack Poland.[13]

The problems and shortcomings as presented in this cursory summary obviously contrast with the *Wehrmacht's* rapid military victories in September 1939 and even more so with those achieved between April and June 1940. It is true that the Nazi regime had been fairly successful in preparing Germany's economy and society for war. Nevertheless, the war arrived before all military and economic preparations were completed for rearmament in depth, as Hitler intended. The *Blitzkrieg* strategy was not, as some have argued, intended to compensate for the shortcomings in preparation for war, although it seemed to be the case after the victories were rapidly secured.[14] The problems and shortcomings were mitigated both by the regime's largely successful foreign policy and by the mistakes and at times outright incompetence of other governments. In the following section, the regime's preparations for war as well as the impact of its foreign policy will be examined in more detail.

Political Changes

It has become a commonplace in studies of the Third Reich to highlight the polycratic chaos which rapidly enveloped the various levels of Reich government and administration after 1933. Despite the indisputable turmoil and friction, however, it is important not to lose sight of the fact that the regime was able to carry through major 'achievements'. Although its leaders entangled themselves in personal rivalries and competition for power, the stability of the regime was never threatened by these seemingly injurious processes. It helped, of course, that those opposed to the Nazi dictatorship were unable to exploit its internal predicaments once the regime's early policies of repression had almost completely removed all potential threats to its continued existence.[15]

It appears that the rapid transformation of Germany's political life exceeded even Hitler's own expectations. Barely a year after Hitler became chancellor, Germany had ceased to be a democratic republic. Although his powers were still limited by the president's authority, Hindenburg was becoming increasingly feeble, and the regime had gone far to establish complete control over all spheres of political life. By July 1933, just one party, the NSDAP, still functioned, while the Reichstag had become merely another facet of Goebbels's propaganda machinery: an automated applause chamber for decisions already taken by the regime.

Alongside the elimination of the political system of the Weimar Republic went the oppression of political opponents of the Nazi party. Communists and Social Democrats were the first victims. Most of the initial concentration-camp prisoners were members of the two left-wing parties or organisations associated with them. Yet even Hitler's conservative allies were not immune to persecution. Among those brutally killed on, or directly after, 30 June 1934, the so-called Night of the Long Knives, were Herbert von Bose and Edgar Jung, both close associates of Hitler's vice-chancellor, Franz von Papen. Hitler, in the relentless pursuit of his objectives, did not shy away from eliminating some of his own supporters.

In June 1934, Hitler had acted in order to quell the growing discontent among the army leadership about the ambitious plans of the SA leader, Ernst Röhm.[16] To proceed with preparations for war, a military build-up based on the traditional armed forces was of greater importance than turning the unruly SA hordes into a new military force. Moreover, Hitler accepted the need to sacrifice 'his old friend' Röhm in order to ensure that he, Hitler, rather than one of his conservative allies, would succeed the doddering Hindenburg. After the events of 30 June 1934 and the death of Hindenburg on 2 August, his powers as Führer and Reich chancellor were almost limitless, although he continued to be partly dependent upon the support of non-Nazis in his regime and the military for the rebuilding and rearming of Germany.

Four years later, this dependence upon members of the traditional élites had vanished almost completely. In decisive moves in late 1937 and early 1938, he removed the remaining remnants of the Hindenburg presidency, dismissing Werner von Blomberg and taking personal control of the War Ministry, and replacing the foreign minister, Neurath, with his loyal vassal, Ribbentrop. In a further nazification of the regime, the economics minister, Hjalmar Schacht, had already been forced out, replaced temporarily by Hermann Göring, then in early 1938 by a less prominent Nazi, Walther Funk.

Although these changes did little to reduce the territorial infighting among leaders of the regime, at the highest level of political and military decision-making they undoubtedly strengthened the Führer's position further. Nobody among the Nazi leadership had any doubts that it was Hitler who ultimately determined the policy of the regime. The nearly unlimited loyalty of leading Nazis such as Göring, Himmler and Goebbels to Hitler and his objectives ensured the stability of the regime. Contrasting Hitler's position to that of Stalin, Ian Kershaw has concluded that, while

'Stalin could not believe in genuine loyalty even among his closest supporters, Hitler built his mastery on a cultivated principle of personal loyalty
to which he could always successfully appeal at moments of crisis.'[17] Hitler
was both the regime's sheet-anchor and its compass – no more so than in the
area of foreign policy. By 1939, he was able to chart his course towards war
without unwanted disruptions by political opponents. Even those within the
regime with concerns about Hitler's objectives were of little consequence.
At least in political terms, Germany was now prepared for war.

Social Changes

'We want to educate the Volk so that it moves away from the insanity of
class superiority, of arrogance of rank, and of the delusion that only mental
work is of any value.'[18] Hitler frequently referred to the aim of transforming
German society into a true Volksgemeinschaft (national community), a
harmonious society based on race not class, a society in which all 'racially
sound' Germans enjoyed equal opportunities for advancement. What is not
clear, however, is to what extent Hitler actually regarded this transformation as an important ideological objective or whether it was only a means to
a different end, a ploy to make German society follow him willingly into war
and to avoid the social disruptions experienced in the Great War. In other
words, were policies of Volksgemeinschaft ultimately only a tool for ensuring a community fully committed to the war effort?

Recently, a number of German historians, most notably Rainer Zitelmann, have attempted to demonstrate Hitler's true commitment to the goal
of Volksgemeinschaft. According to Zitelmann, Hitler was serious about
shaking up and reordering German society.[19] There can be no doubt that he
constantly emphasised the notion of social mobility, of widening access to
secondary and higher education, and of breaking the link between social
background and certain professional careers. But the question remains
whether this was not largely an acknowledgement of the need to mollify
Germany's workers in order to ensure their cooperation and compliance
during wartime. Hitler could not risk taking Germany into war with a
substantial section of the population dissatisfied about their social position.

In view of the situation it faced in 1933, the regime had undoubtedly set
itself a nearly impossible task. Despite efforts to achieve greater mobility
within the existing social structure, the Weimar Republic had not succeeded
in overcoming traditional divisions. With the exception of the NSDAP and,
to an extent, the Centre Party, political organisations continued to reflect the
class structure of Germany's society. Both the economic crisis that culminated in the hyperinflation of 1923 and the economic depression of the
late 1920s and early 1930s helped to deepen these divisions.

Despite the success of the NSDAP in attracting support from the working-class,[20] many workers continued to view the Nazis with either outright hostility or at least a strong dose of scepticism. It did not help, of course, that in 1933 the regime deprived a substantial section of workers of their political homes and the various rights they had enjoyed during the Weimar Republic. The trade unions were dissolved and the right to strike removed. The pseudo-socialist rhetoric of many Nazi leaders, not least the DAF leader, Robert Ley, did not square with what must have appeared very much like a pro-employer agenda. Hence, the regime employed a carrot-and-stick approach by, on the one hand, convincing workers to accept or even better support the regime and, on the other hand, eradicating all potential or real opposition by 'incorrigible elements'. The Gestapo, acting as the stick, removed the most oppositional elements to be 're-educated' in concentration camps and prisons, Goebbels's propaganda apparatus and Ley's DAF supplied the various carrots.

The most obvious way of making workers more amenable towards the regime was the eradication of the huge unemployment problem Germany faced in 1933.[21] Beyond threatening the stability and permanence of the regime, the country's horrendous levels of unemployment also posed a huge barrier to any attempt at preparing German society for war. Before Hitler could even begin to ready Germany for war, he needed to restore healthy levels of employment by reviving the economy. He therefore took immediate steps to meet his promise to restore employment by instituting the first Four-Year Plan.

This is not the place to explain the 'multitude of interrelated measures'[22] which the regime employed to resolve the unemployment problem within a very short period of time. Suffice to say that from over six million registered unemployed in January 1933, unemployment fell to just over one million by the summer of 1936. Instead of experiencing a massive over-supply of labour, Germany's economy now faced labour shortages, in particular in those sectors engaged in rearmament or related production.

Although resolving the unemployment problem did not by itself create total social harmony, it undoubtedly enhanced Hitler's popularity even among workers who had traditionally favoured the parties of the Left. In their secret reports, Social Democratic agents had to admit this frustrating development. The conclusion of a report in September 1938 from central Germany can be applied to Germany as a whole. According to the SPD agent, workers 'often complain about the fact that they earn much less now than in say 1929 but, at the end of the day, they always say: "It's all the same to us; at least we have work." ... [T]hey are all scared of losing their jobs. The years of unemployment have not been forgotten.'[23]

Through policies of terror and enticement, the regime undoubtedly reduced the social tensions it had inherited. In 1933, Hitler took the helm of a deeply disunited people. Immediately, his regime set about overcoming this disunity and replacing it with a 'harmonious' racial community. Although ultimately the ambitious project of turning German society into a true *Volksgemeinschaft* did not extend beyond its initial stages,[24] clearly much changed in a very short period of time. However, by 1939 the process of marginalisation, and indeed elimination, of various groups in German society had also been accelerated. Even before the coordinated annihilation of the Jews during the war, the 'racial purification' of German society had been initiated with such atrocious actions as the persecution of 'social deviants', the killing of the disabled and the forced sterilisation of women 'unfit for motherhood'.[25]

Ultimately, Hitler achieved his main goal. As he had intended, Germany's military effort in the Second World War was not disrupted by the kind of social tensions and upheavals experienced in the previous war. As Wolfram Wette writes: 'At the beginning of the Second World War the Germans did not shout "Hurrah!" as in 1914, yet they complied. Most of them did not want a war, least of all a world war, but they nonetheless behaved in precisely the manner the Nazi regime had wished.'[26] To the end, the vast majority of Germans continued to 'do their duty' either at home or at the front.

Economic Changes

After the Second World War, many Germans long remembered the Third Reich's 'economic miracle' of the 1930s. When searching for something positive from a period of their lives that was universally accursed, the fact that many had been lifted out of the abysmal depths of the depression remained an enduring image. Hitler did not, of course, possess any special gifts that enabled him single-handedly to pull Germany out of the depression. He was, however, willing to make use of economic experts as well as unorthodox measures to combat the economic crisis.

While it is true that Hitler 'knew precious little economics', it would be wrong to underestimate his interest in economic policy.[27] He was fully aware that the fulfilment of his military plans hinged upon the state of Germany's economy. In the first instance, the economy needed to be revived and released from the firm (though already diminishing) grip of the depression, since only then would it be possible to create the material basis for rearmament and war. From 1933, these two broad objectives, recovery and rearmament, were not treated as separate stages but remained inextricably bound up together. Rearmament provided the essential component of the state-led economic revival of the 1930s. As Dan Silverman writes: 'in the absence of the transition to a "rearmament economy" during 1935 and preparation for war under the 1936 Four Year Plan, there would have been no talk of Hitler's "economic miracle".[28]

The figures speak for themselves. While the Nazi regime faced a massive unemployment problem in 1933, by 1938 it was confronted with labour shortages, particularly in key industries. 'In June 1938 there were only 292,000 registered German unemployed, of which 43 per cent were classified as unemployable through disability, illness, or psychological disorder.'[29] The radical transformation of Germany's employment situation went hand-in-hand with a change in the nature of government–business relations. Although Hitler accepted the principle of private ownership of Germany's businesses, the effect of the regime's policies was substantially to increase the involvement of the state in the German economy. As Hitler argued in his memorandum on the Four-Year Programme in September 1936, 'the job of the Ministry of Economics is simply to set the national economic tasks; private industry has to fulfil them. But if private industry thinks itself incapable of doing this, then the National Socialist State will know how to resolve the problem on its own.'[30]

Although Hitler's comment was directed at the specific problem of shortages of steel, it applied generally to the approach of the Nazi regime. German businesses, particularly those engaged in rearmament or related production, were given considerable opportunity to profit from the regime's policies, including its antisemitic measures ('Aryanisation' of Jewish businesses).[31] Yet, the primacy of politics was never in any doubt. Under the Nazi regime, the ultimate purpose of the German economy was to serve Hitler's preparations for war.

Decisive contributions to this process were made not by Nazi economic 'experts' such as Gottfried Feder or Otto Wagener, but by conservative officials who had already held leading state or private commercial positions during the Weimar Republic. The outstanding example was Hjalmar Schacht, Reichsbank president in the 1920s and again from 1933 to early 1939 and Reich economics minister from 1934 to late 1937. Schacht's policies were crucial in providing the means for the rapid rearmament of Germany.

His own contribution to Germany's preparations for war notwithstanding, Schacht would become a fierce critic of the pace of rearmament. Increasingly worried by inflationary pressures, labour and raw material shortages and the neglect suffered by Germany's consumer industries, Schacht eventually demanded a slowing down of military production and a reorientation of Germany's industrial output towards world trade. But Hitler was not prepared to close the Pandora's box that Schacht himself had helped to open.

In 1937 Schacht's star was rapidly waning. After his resignation as minister of economics in November 1937, he was also dismissed from the Reichsbank presidency in 1939 when he submitted a memorandum to

Hitler, criticising the effects of rearmament. Yet his successor, Funk, did not possess the power and influence he had previously enjoyed. The real controller of the German economy was now Hermann Göring who, as the official in charge of the Four-Year Plan Office, had successfully undermined Schacht's position in 1936 and 1937.

When Göring aggressively pushed his way to the top of the regime's economic policy-making, one of the last bastions of the conservatives in the government fell. In contrast to Schacht, Göring's first priority was rearmament. Despite his lack of economic expertise, Hitler switched his support to him precisely because, as Kurt Pätzold writes, he 'could be sure that Göring, like he, would reject any suggestion to limit the speed and level of rearmament out of consideration for international trade and inflationary dangers'.[32]

Göring did not disappoint Hitler: rearmament was not slowed down. In 1939, Germany's military expenditure as a proportion of GNP reached 23 per cent, a level far above that of other powers.[33] The inflationary threat that Schacht had warned about was kept under control, though other problems including labour and raw material shortages persisted. Admittedly, the economy had not reached the intended state of preparation when Germany attacked Poland. Yet there is no evidence that Hitler was dissatisfied with Göring's economic efforts. On the contrary, two days before the attack on Poland Hitler added a further office to Göring's ample accumulation of posts when he made him chair of the newly formed Council of Ministers for the Defence of the Reich (and subsequently declared him his successor). Only during the war, when Göring's economic (and military) incompetence was starkly revealed, did Hitler finally take steps to shift responsibilities away from his 'first paladin'.

Military Changes

Due to the severe restrictions imposed at Versailles, Germany was still a military minnow at the beginning of 1933. Although the *Reichswehr* leadership, in collusion with successive Weimar governments, had secretly evaded the limitations set at Versailles,[34] the armed forces remained limited to 100,000 lightly equipped troops with no aerial support and a feeble navy. *Reichswehr* leaders themselves estimated that they stood little chance of withholding an assault by the Polish army, let alone by Poland's ally, France.

For the *Reichswehr* leadership, the goal was clear. As the chief of the Armed Forces Office (subsequently chief of the general staff), Ludwig Beck, succinctly noted in December 1933, 'our military-political position demands a *rapid* elimination of the state of total defensive incapability. To attack [us] must become a risk for our neighbours.'[35] Predictably, the military leaders were pleased when Hitler, on becoming chancellor, immediately proposed a large-scale expansion of the armed forces.

Blomberg and other senior officers strongly endorsed Hitler's commitment to the rapid build-up of a national army based on conscription. In October 1933, they fully supported his decision to take Germany out of the League of Nations, particularly as this meant an end to Germany's participation at the international disarmament negotiations at Geneva. Germany's withdrawal was immediately followed by Hitler's order to create a 21-division army (300,000 men) by 1938. In April 1934, the target date for the creation of this so-called *Risiko-Heer* was revised to the spring of 1935.

Although the plans for the expansion of Germany's armed forces had been drawn up by *Reichswehr* officers before 1933, Hitler's commitment to unilateral rearmament turned into reality what had previously been merely an aspiration. In mid-1933, the financial parameters for Germany's rearmament also radically changed when Schacht, recently reappointed Reichsbank president, made available an extraordinary credit of RM35 billion (over eight years) for the expansion of the Reichswehr.[36] In view of the very limited equipment level of the armed forces – at the end of 1933 a 21-division army would have been able to fight for only six weeks on the existing stocks of arms and ammunition[37] – the credit was absolutely essential. Schacht's contribution marked the beginning of the Reich's rapid military budget expansion.

Between 1933 and the end of August 1939, nearly RM62 billion or 51.9 per cent of the total expenditure of the Reich was spent on the *Wehrmacht*.[38] The regime's major policy ventures of 1935–36 (conscription, unveiling of the *Luftwaffe*, remilitarisation of the Rhineland) were achieved without hostile reaction from abroad – indeed, in the case of the Anglo-German Naval Agreement, with the explicit agreement of a major foreign power. Just over two years after Hitler's promises to the *Reichswehr* leadership in February 1933, Germany not only possessed a fledgling air force, but most importantly, on account of the newly introduced compulsory military service, the capacity rapidly to expand the army.

In 1938–39, the Nazi regime spent RM17,247 million on the military mobilisation of Germany compared to RM5492 million in 1935–36.[39] The army's transformation from a defensive force to a potential tool of aggression had been completed. By 1939 the total strength of the *Wehrmacht* stood at just over 3 million men, the *Luftwaffe* at over 370,000 and even the *Kriegsmarine*, which received less attention from the regime than the other two services, had managed to achieve a fivefold expansion to nearly 74,000 officers and men.[40]

From the beginning, the army leadership had strongly supported Hitler's policy of rearmament. At times, the ambitious demands of the military leaders actually preceded or directly influenced the Führer's decisions.

Occasionally, individuals in the officer corps voiced their concern about the feasibility of a continued expansion of Germany's military capability and consequentially about the eventual application of this massive military force that they so actively helped to create. Largely, however, *Wehrmacht* leaders, enamoured by the regime's commitment to rearmament, either ignored the potentially serious implications of Germany's relentless rearmament or agreed with Hitler on the necessity of war.

In February 1938, Hitler rid himself of Blomberg and the chief of the army, Werner von Fritsch, abolished the War Ministry and took supreme control of the armed forces. In the previous November, at the so-called Hoßbach conference, both generals had reacted with scepticism and concern when Hitler informed them about his immediate expansionist intentions (directed in the first place against Austria and Czechoslovakia). Blomberg and Fritsch were not opposed to the idea of war. But in contrast to Hitler, they feared that Germany would not be able to withstand military action by Britain and France. Hitler's policies had finally overtaken those of his conservative allies. In 1938 the largely harmonious cooperation between the Nazi dictator and his military leadership was briefly disrupted. Yet Hitler could count on plenty of officers more unscrupulous and sycophantic than the ones he sidelined in 1938.[41] Since 1933 the armed forces had obtained almost everything they wanted. As Wilhelm Deist writes: 'In 1939, the *Wehrmacht* clearly did not yet resemble the army envisaged by the military planners. Nevertheless, although particular shortcomings and gaps in armament were evident, these were concealed by the early successes of the war which astonished even the *Wehrmacht*'s own experts.'[42]

Foreign Policy

An obvious question arises from a survey of the rapid military recovery the Nazi regime staged from 1933. As Germany's military build-up was so obviously a contravention of the Treaty of Versailles, why did the signatory powers, most notably Britain and France, not take decisive countermeasures? The answer, of course, highlights the serious failure of their foreign policies *vis-à-vis* Nazi Germany. At various points between 1933 and 1939 the British and French governments were presented with the opportunity to intervene more decisively, but reacted meekly to Hitler's increasingly worrying policies.

This is not the place to discuss British and French policies in the 1930s in detail. It is, however, important to highlight that while Nazi Germany's road to war was made possible by the audacity of Hitler and other members of his regime, it was also helped along by decisions taken by foreign governments. Repeatedly, the Nazis were both surprised and relieved to find British and French politicians so willing to condone Treaty violations and thus facilitate Germany's preparations for war. This was true in March 1935 when the regime's introduction of conscription and the official unveiling of the *Luftwaffe* were accepted without much ado. By signing a naval agreement with Germany only a few months later, the British government, in fact, went even further and actively encouraged the invalidation of the restrictions on the third arm of Germany's armed forces.

Britain's concession did not turn out to be a stepping-stone towards the fulfilment of Hitler's dream of an Anglo-German alliance. Although he did not altogether abandon his hope that the British government might eventually 'see the light' and ally its people with their 'racial cousins', he increasingly based his foreign policy on the assumption that he must act 'without Britain' and eventually 'against Britain'.[43] At the same time, he also became increasingly convinced that neither Britain nor France would resist more daring attacks on the international system erected at Versailles in the 1920s.

A crucial litmus test of British and French reactions proved to be the remilitarisation of the Rhineland in March 1936.[44] In view of the continued military inferiority of the *Wehrmacht* even against the French forces alone, the move could easily have backfired for Hitler. While it was not (as he was later to argue) the first risk he took, it was certainly his greatest up to that time. When it succeeded, only a hollow shell remained of the international framework set up at Versailles and confirmed at Locarno. More importantly, British and French passivity encouraged him to attempt even more daring policies. As he commented with relief, 'the brave man conquers the world. God stands by him.'[45]

In 1936, the Nazi regime organised the Olympic Games on a scale never previously witnessed. The so-called 'Peace Olympics' are an outstanding example of the peace appeals Hitler repeatedly made in the 1930s. While despising the notion of permanent peace, he accepted that such appeals were tactically necessary. As he candidly explained in a secret speech to 400 newspaper editors and journalists on 10 November 1938: 'For years circumstances have compelled me to talk about almost nothing but peace. Only by continually stressing Germany's desire for peace and her peaceful intentions could I achieve freedom for the German people bit by bit and provide the armaments which were always necessary before the next step could be taken.'[46] Frequently, his peace speeches and other conciliatory moves either preceded or followed actions of a rather different nature. The Olympics were no exception. Just as Hitler was taking centre-stage at the largest and most publicised sports event ever, he was pondering the question of how to propel Germany's economic preparations unequivocally in the direction of war. On 1 August 1936 he opened the Eleventh Olympic Games. Just over a month later he announced the new Four-Year Programme to party stalwarts at Nuremberg. Meanwhile, the policies of Britain and France were playing directly into his hands. Apart from hollow commitments to peace, Hitler offered nothing in return. Until September 1939, the balance of military power between the western democracies and Nazi Germany favoured the latter.

More surprisingly, a similar verdict must also be applied to Nazi Germany's relationship to Fascist Italy. Looking over the period 1933 to 1940, it is extremely difficult to detect any benefits Mussolini gained by aligning his country with Germany. In fact, the foreign policies of the Nazi regime were very rarely of advantage to Italy, indeed at times they were manifestly detrimental. Again, without offering any concessions of his own, Hitler was able to prepare Germany for war on the back of concessions made by another government. In July 1934, Austrian Nazis, with Hitler's apparent encouragement, attempted to overthrow their national government. In supporting the plotters, Hitler clearly ignored the express objections of his fellow dictator in Italy. Mussolini, concerned about the potential loss of Austria as a buffer state against revisionist Germany and about Italy's influence in southeast Europe, was forced to intervene. Yet his intervention and his furious outbursts against the Nazis had no lasting effect on German–Italian relations.

After the Austrian débâcle, Hitler attached little tangible substance to attempts at ingratiating himself with Mussolini. Nazi Germany refrained from adopting the economic sanctions imposed by the League of Nations (of which it was in any case no longer a member) against Italy after its forces invaded Ethiopia in October 1935. At the same time, however, Hitler had no qualms in sanctioning secret supplies of arms to the Ethiopian government. Yet again he was spared any serious repercussions for his actions. In fact, the following year, Mussolini aligned his country closer to Hitler's Germany than at any previous time. Yet precisely when the *Duce* made his grand pronouncement about the creation of the Italo–German Axis, Nazi Germany was again taking advantage of Mussolini's misguided decisions.

In the Spanish Civil War, which had erupted after the failed military rising of 17–18 July 1936, Hitler and Mussolini had decided independently of each other to intervene on behalf of General Francisco Franco's Nationalists and against the elected government of Spain. From late July 1936, both Germany and Italy dispatched war material to Spain. But while the defenders of the Spanish Republic were pushed back, the desired victory for the Nationalists did not materialise. To ensure victory, Mussolini, in contrast to Hitler, eventually decided to send a substantial number of troops to Spain. The almost uninterrupted flow of German war material and Italian troops and armaments finally ensured Franco's victory in March 1939.

In view of the additional pressure it put on France's strategic position, the transformation of Spain from a democratic republic to a right-wing dictatorship benefited Germany more than Italy. Economically, Italy's initial attempts to obtain economic advantages from Franco in return for its support were ruthlessly pushed aside by Göring and his representatives in

Spain.[47] Yet it was the Italian regime that bore a much greater burden both in financial expenditure, troop losses and valuable military resources. Although Franco accumulated a heavy financial debt to Germany, it can be argued that the Nazi regime reaped substantially more benefits from the *Caudillo*'s victory.

During the final year of the Spanish Civil War, the attention of the European powers was diverted to events elsewhere on the continent, first in Austria and soon after in Czechoslovakia. Four years after he had shown his determined opposition to the nazification of Austria, Mussolini permitted Hitler to annex it. In return for Mussolini's acquiescence to the *Anschluß* in March 1938, Hitler offered nothing more than gushing expressions of gratitude, the assurance that South Tyrol would remain Italian, and the prospect of a grand future for the two Fascist states. Again, this was scant recompense for allowing a large increase in Germany's power through the incorporation of Austria into the Reich.

In contrast, Hitler showed Mussolini no gratitude during the Munich conference. On 30 September 1938, Britain, France and Italy signed away the Sudetenland into German hands. Czechoslovakia was decisively weakened, and its government yielded without resistance when the *Wehrmacht* marched into Prague in mid-March 1939. Although Hitler blamed Chamberlain for having spoilt his march on Prague in 1938, Mussolini's diplomatic intervention also contributed to robbing the Führer of the war he had so desired.

The annexation of the Sudetenland in October 1938 further boosted Germany's influence in southeast Europe, a process that had been accelerated by the *Anschluß*. Despite his constant buttering up of Mussolini, Hitler had no misgivings about Göring's blatant efforts to undermine Italy's position in southeast Europe. Both Axis and Anti-Comintern Pact certainly made great propaganda material, but they did nothing to stop the Nazi regime from increasing Germany's sphere of influence at Italy's expense.

In May 1939, the hitherto loose relationship between Nazi Germany and Fascist Italy was given a much firmer footing when Hitler and Mussolini signed the grandly named Pact of Steel. After six years Hitler had managed to achieve his objective of an alliance with Italy – despite a foreign policy approach that rarely served the latter's interests. A marked shift had taken place in the relationship between the two dictators. Having occupied a clearly inferior position to Mussolini at the outset, Hitler had gradually propelled himself into a position of dominance. Even though he did not manage to convince his fellow dictator to enter the war in September 1939, Mussolini's hesitation was only temporary. When Italy eventually went to war in June 1940, Mussolini unwittingly set his country on a course towards full absorption into the German orbit.

Ironically, the only occasion when the Nazi regime deliberately set out to win an important concession from another European power, it turned out to be from Nazi Germany's ideological arch-enemy, the Soviet Union.

As Geoffrey Roberts concludes on the crucial period May–August 1939: 'the story of Soviet-German relations ... is one of persistent wooing by Berlin. Not until the end of July 1939 did the Soviets even begin to respond to these German overtures.'[48] Once the Soviets did respond, an agreement was soon reached. The Nazi-Soviet Non-Aggression Pact of 23 August was an immense boon to Hitler's plans for war. It prevented a repeat of the situation Germany had faced in 1914, although with Polish troops in the East and the British and French armed forces in the West, Germany was still threatened by a two-front war.

For more than six years the propaganda machinery of the Nazi regime had produced a relentless stream of anti-Soviet proclamations. From the early 1920s Hitler had constantly expressed his hatred of the 'judeo-bolshevik regime' in Russia. Even more important than the ideological antagonism to Communism was Hitler's obsession with the conquest of *Lebensraum* in the East. If one country was destined to become a major military target of his armed forces, it was without any doubt the Soviet Union.

Yet Hitler was not totally blinded by his ideological fervour. Throughout the 1930s he repeatedly demonstrated an ability to act opportunistically, react quickly to unforeseen developments, allow others in the regime a share in foreign policy-making, and generally retain a certain flexibility in his actions. While Blomberg advocated the decision to leave the League of Nations and pushed ahead with the rearmament of Germany, Neurath played an active role in the process leading to the remilitarisation of the Rhineland. Göring was permitted to play out his foreign policy ambitions in Austria, south-east Europe and Spain while Ribbentrop was able to brag about the Anti-Comintern Pact with Japan and Italy, and to a certain extent the Nazi-Soviet Pact of August 1939 (though of course he failed dismally in the main task Hitler had set him – to return from London with Britain as an ally).

On occasion, Hitler thus kept in the background when a particular foreign policy decision or initiative was undertaken. As Philipp Bouhler, head of the Führer's chancery concluded in 1936: '[t]he *Führer* gives the main priorities, he shows the direction, yet he grants the individual the utmost room to move.'[49] Very rarely did initiatives by others in the regime clash with his own stated objectives and the broader ideological framework he had set. This is even true of the most obvious contradiction, the pact with the Soviet Union. Ultimately, the contradiction was only temporary: 'it did not alter [Hitler's] basic anti-Bolshevik policy; one had to cast out the Devil with the Beelzebub, he would use any means available against the Soviets, even including such a pact.'[50]

By October 1939, Hitler had achieved many of his earlier objectives. Austria and Germany had been united into one Greater Germany. Czechoslovakia had been destroyed, its Czech parts now under German control, and Slovakia a satellite state of Germany. The Treaties of Versailles and

Locarno had been almost completely annihilated. Less than a year later even the territorial changes imposed upon Germany after the First World War were fully reversed with the return of the lands lost to France, Belgium and Denmark. Only Britain continued to resist the Nazi war machine. In 1941, Hitler was finally able to turn to his ultimate and most far-reaching objective, the conquest of *Lebensraum* in the East. It was in the East, however, that his distorted racial view of the world eventually led to the total destruction of the Nazi empire. Instead of defeating the 'inferior Slavs' and their 'Jewish subhuman masters' in the only *Blitzkrieg* that Hitler (and most of his military leaders) truly anticipated as a lightning war, the war against the Soviet Union ultimately reduced Germany to a lesser status than the position Hitler had inherited and vowed to overcome in 1933.

Notes

1. D. Welch, *The Third Reich: Politics and Propaganda* (London, 1993).
2. C. Dirks and K. H. Janßen, *Der Krieg der Generäle: Hitler als Werkzeug der Wehrmacht* (Berlin, 1999), pp. 71–2.
3. D. Eichholtz, 'Ökonomie, Politik und Kriegsführung. Wirtschaftliche Kriegsplanungen und Rüstungsorganisationen bis zum Ende der 'Blitzkriegs'phase', in Eichholtz, ed., *Krieg und Wirtschaft; Studien zur deutschen Wirtschaftsgeschichte 1939–1945* (Berlin, 1999), p. 25.
4. T. Siegel and T. von Freyberg, *Industrielle Rationalisierung unter dem Nationalsozialismus* (Frankfurt/Main and New York, 1991); R. J. Overy, 'Rationalization and the "Production Miracle" in Germany during the Second World War', in Overy, *War and Economy in the Third Reich* (Oxford, 1995), pp. 343–75.
5. On the production of synthetic materials and the companies involved see, *inter alia*, P. Hayes, *Industry and Ideology: IG Farben in the Nazi Era* (Cambridge, 1987); R. G. Stokes, 'The Oil Industry in Nazi Germany, 1936–1945', *Business History Review* 59 (1985), 254–77.
6. C. Leitz, 'Arms as Levers: *Matériel* and Raw Materials in Germany's Trade with Romania in the 1930s', *International History Review* 19 (1997), 312–32; Leitz, 'Arms Exports from the Third Reich, 1933–1939: The Example of Krupp', *Economic History Review* 51 (1998), 133–54.
7. On the experience of German farmers in the Third Reich see G. Corni, *Hitler and the Peasants: Agrarian Policy of the Third Reich* (New York, 1990).
8. On the development and expansion of the SS see B. Wegner, *The Waffen-SS: Organization, Ideology and Function* (Oxford, 1990).
9. An excellent analysis of foreign policy making in the Third Reich and the various individuals and institutions engaged in it is provided by H. A. Jacobsen, 'The Structure of Nazi Foreign Policy 1933–1945', in C. Leitz, ed., *The Third Reich* (Oxford and Malden, MA, 1999), pp. 51–93.
10. Cited in R. J. Overy, with Andrew Wheatcroft, *The Road to War* (London, 1989), p. 51.

11. See G. R. Ueberschär, 'General Halder and the Resistance to Hitler in the German High Command 1938–40', *European History Quarterly* 18 (1988), 321–48.
12. G. Mosch, 'Streik im "Dritten Reich"', *Vierteljahreshefte für Zeitgeschichte* 36 (1988), 649–89.
13. On the debate about internal crisis and war see T. Mason, 'Internal Crisis and War of Aggression, 1938–1939', in Mason (J. Caplan, ed.), *Nazism, Fascism and the Working Class* (Cambridge, 1995), pp. 104–30; R. J. Overy, 'Germany, "Domestic Crisis" and War in 1939', in Leitz, ed., *The Third Reich*, pp. 97–128; G. Niedhart, 'The Problem of War in German Politics in 1938', *War and Society* 1–2 (1983–84), 55–61.
14. K.-H. Frieser, *Blitzkrieg-Legende: der Westfeldzug 1940* (Munich, 1996); R. J. Overy, 'Hitler's War and the German Economy: A Reinterpretation', in Overy, *War and Economy*, pp. 233–56, and ' "Blitzkriegswirtschaft?" Finanzpolitik, Lebensstandard und Arbeitseinsatz in Deutschland 1939–1942', *Vierteljahreshefte für Zeitgeschichte* 36 (1988), 379–436; J. P. Harris, 'The Myth of Blitzkrieg', *War in History* 2 (1995), 335–52; T. Jersak, '*Blitzkrieg* Revisited: A New Look at Nazi War and Extermination Planning', *Historical Journal* 43 (2000), 565–82.
15. On the repression of oppositional activities in the first years of the regime see, *inter alia*, A. Merson, *Communist Resistance in Nazi Gemany* (London, 1986); T. Mason, 'The Third Reich and the German Left: Persecution and Resistance', in H. Bull, ed., *The Challenge of the Third Reich: The Adam von Trott Memorial Lectures* (Oxford, 1986), pp. 95–116.
16. D. Jablonsky, 'Röhm and Hitler: The Continuity of Political-Military Discord', *Journal of Contemporary History* 23 (1988), 367–86.
17. I. Kershaw, ' "Working towards the Führer". Reflections on the Nature of the Hitler Dictatorship', in Leitz, ed., *The Third Reich*, pp. 238–9.
18. Cited in M. Burleigh, *The Third Reich: A New History* (London, 2000), p. 240.
19. R. Zitelmann, *Hitler: Selbstverständnis eines Revolutionärs* (Hamburg, 1987), pp. 173–94.
20. D. Mühlberger, *Hitler's Followers: Studies in the Sociology of the Nazi Movement* (London, 1991); P. D. Stachura, 'National Socialism and the German Proletariat 1925–1933: Old Myths and New Perspectives', *Historical Journal* 36 (1993), 701–18.
21. According to one calculation, a total of 21 million Germans (7.5 million unemployed plus their family members) were directly affected by unemployment; H. Höhne, '*Gebt mir vier Jahre Zeit.*' *Hitler und die Anfänge des Dritten Reiches*, 2nd edn (Berlin, 1999), p. 19.
22. Comment in German Labour Ministry memorandum, 5 Dec. 1934, cited in Overy, *War and Economy*, p. 5.
23. J. Noakes and G. Pridham, eds, *Nazism 1919–1945: A Documentary Reader*, Vol. II, *State, Economy and Society, 1933–1939* (Exeter, 1984), doc. 263, pp. 373–4.
24. J. Dülffer, 'Vom Bündnispartner zum Erfüllungsgehilfen im totalen Krieg. Militär und Gesellschaft in Deutschland 1933–1945', in W. Michalka, ed., *Der Zweite Weltkrieg; Analysen, Grundzüge, Forschungsbilanz*, 2nd edn (Munich, 1990), p. 298.

25. See, *inter alia*, M. Burleigh, *Death and Deliverance; 'Euthanasia' in Germany c.1900–1945* (Cambridge and New York, 1994); D. Kenrick and G. Puxon, *Gypsies under the Swastika* (Hatfield, 1995); G. J. Giles, '"The Most Unkindest Cut of All"': Castration, Homosexuality and Nazi Justice', *Journal of Contemporary History* 27 (1992), 41–61.

26. W. Wette, 'Zur psychologischen Mobilmachung der deutschen Bevölkerung 1933–1939', in Michalka, *Der Zweite Weltkrieg*, pp. 220–1.

27. G. Knopp, *Hitler: Eine Bilanz* (Munich, 1997), p. 198.

28. D. P. Silverman, *Hitler's Economy; Nazi Work Creation Programs, 1933–1936* (Cambridge, MA, 1998), p. 245.

29. R. J. Overy, 'Unemployment in the Third Reich', in Overy, *War and Economy*, pp. 50–1.

30. Noakes and Pridham, eds, *Nazism 1919–1945*, Vol. II, doc. 185, p. 286.

31. See M. Spoerer, *Von Scheingewinn zum Rüstungsboom: Die Eigenkapitalrentabilität der deutschen Industrieaktiengesellschaften 1925–1941* (Stuttgart, 1996).

32. K. Pätzold, 'Der "Führer" und die Kriegswirtschaft', in Eichholtz, ed., *Krieg und Wirtschaft*, p. 50.

33. R. J. Overy, *Goering: The 'Iron Man'* (London, 1984), p. 84.

34. On the military collaboration with the Soviet Union see R.-D. Müller, *Das Tor zur Weltmacht: die Bedeutung der Sowjetunion für die deutsche Wirtschafts- und Rüstungspolitik zwischen den Weltkriegen* (Boppard, 1984).

35. M. Geyer, *Aufrüstung oder Sicherheit: Die Reichswehr in der Krise der Machtpolitik 1924–1936* (Wiesbaden, 1980), p. 352.

36. Ibid., pp. 348–9.

37. M. Geyer, 'Militär, Rüstung und Außenpolitik – Aspekte militärischer Revisionspolitik in der Zwischenkriegszeit', in Manfred Funke, ed., *Hitler, Deutschland und die Mächte: Materialien zur Außenpolitik des Dritten Reiches* (Düsseldorf, 1976), p. 250.

38. W. A. Boelcke, *Die deutsche Wirtschaft 1930–1945: Interna des Reichswehrministeriums* (Düsseldorf, 1983), p. 219.

39. Overy, *War and Economy*, p. 203.

40. Dülffer, 'Vom Bündnispartner', pp. 286–7.

41. Although the ideological proximity of officers to the Nazis, shared military objectives, and, of course, the rapid early victories are major explanatory factors, more 'mundane' motives such as bribery and corruption have also recently been highlighted in more detail. See G. R. Ueberschär and W. Vogel, *Dienen und Verdienen: Hitlers Geschenke an seine Eliten* (Frankfurt/Main, 1999), and N. J. W. Goda, 'Black Marks: Hitler's Bribery of His Senior Officers during World War II', *Journal of Modern History* 72 (2000), 413–52.

42. W. Deist, *The Wehrmacht and German Rearmament* (Basingstoke, 1986), p. 91.

43. On Hitler's attitude towards Britain and the course of Germany's relations with Britain see W. Michalka, *Ribbentrop und die deutsche Weltpolitik 1933–1940: Außenpolitische Konzeptionen und Entscheidungsprozesse im Dritten Reich* (Munich, 1980); G. T. Waddington, 'Hassgegner: German Views of Great Britain in the Later 1930s', *History* 81 (1996), 22–39.

44. See Z. Shore, 'Hitler, Intelligence and the Decision to Remilitarize the Rhine', *Journal of Contemporary History* 34 (1999), 5–18.

45. Höhne, *'Gebt mir vier Jahre Zeit'*, p. 423.
46. J. Noakes and G. Pridham, eds, *Nazism 1919–1945*, Vol. III, *Foreign Policy, War and Racial Extermination* (Exeter, 1988), doc. 529, p. 721.
47. C. Leitz, 'Hermann Göring and Nazi Germany's Economic Exploitation of Nationalist Spain, 1936–1939', *German History* 14 (1996), 21–37.
48. G. Roberts, *The Soviet Union and the Origins of the Second World War: Russo-German Relations and the Road to War, 1933–1941* (Basingstoke, 1995), p. 73.
49. Cited in Knopp, *Hitler*, p. 207.
50. From a note taken by Ulrich von Hassell upon listening to a speech by Hitler in late August 1939; cited in G. R. Ueberschär, 'Hitlers Entschluß zum "Lebensraum"-Krieg im Osten; Programmatisches Ziel oder militärstrategisches Kalkül?', in Ueberschär and Wolfram Wette, eds, *Der deutsche Überfall auf die Sowjetunion: 'Unternehmen Barbarossa' 1941* (Frankfurt, 1999), p. 22.

2 Fascist Italy

John Gooch

Rival Interpretations

Among English-speaking historians, the interpretation of Mussolini's foreign policy first developed three-quarters of a century ago by the distinguished anti-Fascist historian Gaetano Salvemini has exercised a powerful influence. His depiction of a Mussolini operating without plan or principle was taken up and expanded by the doyen of English historians of Liberal and Fascist Italy, Denis Mack Smith. For Mack Smith, Mussolini's distinguishing features were an urge to power, lust for conquest and a quest for prestige. The key element – and instrument – in this policy was propaganda, and its key deficiency was a military machine whose strengths the *Duce* repeatedly exaggerated and whose weaknesses he continually ignored, despite carrying personal responsibility for all three service ministries from 1933. The whole Fascist edifice was a dream built on bluff, and the bluff was called in September 1939 when Mussolini was 'shocked to find that the Germans expected him to fight'.[1] The notion that Fascism – both at home and abroad – was nothing more than a hollow *politica del bluff* is one which has attracted numerous other scholars, Italian as well as English.

By far the most notable recent contribution to the debate over Mussolini's regime has been made by the late Renzo De Felice in his multi-volume biography of Mussolini.[2] For De Felice, the 1920s were a decade in which Mussolini, with nothing more in mind than to maintain and consolidate his domestic position, built the structure of a fascist state on a consensus which rested on the combination of an established theme in the shape of calls to complete the *Risorgimento* of the nineteenth century and a revolutionary one in the form of calls for a new society. Unable to complete this revolution, he turned in the 1930s to a policy that entwined imperialism and war.

In this view, Mussolini's domestic and foreign policies were not two sides of the same coin, but were unconnected. Possessing no clear foreign policy programme in 1922, the *Duce* was a cautious revisionist until 1930, and thereafter sought a general agreement with France and a position equidistant between Paris and Berlin. In the second half of the 1930s he simultaneously turned towards Britain, seeking to set up a second axis and secretly fearing an alliance with Germany towards which his increasingly close alignment with Hitler was propelling him. The general lines of De Felice's interpretation of Mussolini, which is much more sympathetic than that to be found in any of the Anglo-Saxon historiography but which is still largely unknown to English-speaking readers since little of his work has been translated, generated storms of controversy in the two decades since the first volume appeared, but these have started to die down latterly.[3]

For De Felice, and for his pupil Rosaria Quartararo, Mussolini sought until only weeks before the start of the Second World War to stand between Nazi Germany on the one hand and Britain and France on the other, aiming at an acceptance by the democratic powers of his imperial ambitions in the Mediterranean which would free him from Hitler's dangerous clutches. This design has been labelled 'imperialism–realism' by its proponents and contrives to consolidate contradictory elements under the claim that Fascist foreign policy

> while pursuing an imperialist programme and even looking to attain a level of prestige equal to that of Great Britain in the Mediterranean, the Middle East and Africa, pursued this aim with great realism, taking advantage of all the favourable situations offered by the [state of] international competition and, after the accession of Nazism to power in Germany, manipulating [*agitando*] the spectre of an agreement with Germany to exercise pressure on London and [thus] obtain a *general accord* in Europe and in the Mediterranean ... .[4]

This perspective on Fascist foreign policy rests in part on forced interpretations of episodes such as the 'Gentlemen's Agreements' and Mussolini's mediation during the Munich crisis of September 1938. Even Chamberlain's visit to Rome in January 1939 is interpreted in this version of events as an open overture to Britain, which, if sympathetically handled by his visitors, would not have forced the *Duce* into Hitler's arms. Once the war came in 1940, it was a 'parallel war' in which Mussolini sought to maintain some form of partnership with Germany – a pretence that collapsed in the autumn of 1940 with the disastrous performances of his military forces in Greece and in Egypt.

For those who have chosen to occupy intermediate positions between Mack Smith and De Felice, many themes can be, and have been, pursued across the boundary of 1922 and into the Fascist era. Strong elements of continuity can be found between Liberal Italy's search for status and weight among the powers and Fascism's pursuit of aggrandisement. Methods differed: pre-1914 politicians and diplomats used their wiles to try to manipulate Italy into a more advantageous position, whereas Mussolini first used diplomacy in the 1920s and then turned to force in the 1930s. Grounds for the belief that Fascist policy 'turned' in a decisive way in the

early 1930s can be seen in the failure of the attempt at a second wave
of 'Fascistisation', and evidence that Mussolini lost patience with the
chosen policy of the later 1920s – which he defined in 1929 as '*Cloro-
formizzare. Lubrificare*' – in his sacking in 1932 of Dino Grandi, the self-
congratulatory foreign minister whom he had appointed in 1929.[5] In the
1930s, according to this view, the elements of militarism and imperialism which had been staples of the Fascist programme from the beginning
took on new force and new forms as Mussolini changed direction as well
as changing gear, and began to drive Italy towards the goal of a new
Roman empire.

The dismissive attitude taken by earlier Anglo-Saxon historians to
Mussolini, which was underpinned to some degree by their estimations of
his character and personality and also perhaps by unspoken cultural assumptions, has been overtaken by more sophisticated and more penetrating
analyses resting on much deeper probing of the voluminous archival sources
that are now available to historians. As a result, the view that there was no
connection between the *Duce*'s words and his deeds no longer looks as
convincing as it did, and a new generation of historians has identified in
Mussolini a leader who, like Hitler, possessed a coherent ideology from the
outset, and professed it continuously thereafter both in public and in private.
As Stephen Corrado Azzi shrewdly pointed out: 'To call Mussolini an
opportunist with a flighty temperament did not prove that he lacked long-
term goals.'[6]

For historians of this persuasion, Mussolini's world was one in which conflict was omnipresent, revolution was the avenue to advance, and the nation
was both the repository and the beneficiary of the values and aspirations he
held. Fascist Italy's objective was clear. Imperialism, Mussolini told his
followers in January 1919, was 'an eternal and immutable law of life'.
In antiquity, Rome had developed and imposed a 'universal idea', and on
the eve of his accession to power in 1922 he argued that she must do so
once more. Mussolini's goals chimed with those of the nationalists and the
navy in focusing on the need to break the chains that imprisoned Italy in
the Mediterranean: in 1926 he told a group of senior officers: 'A nation that
has no free access to the sea cannot be considered a free nation; a nation
that has no free access to the oceans cannot be considered a great power;
Italy must become a great power.'[7]

Thus, by 1925–26, MacGregor Knox has concluded, 'Mussolini's
programme was set in all essential details.' First came Fascistisation, a
task for internal organisational and educational labour, and then external
action to impose the 'new idea' by force and complete the recreation of a
new Roman empire. The broad targets for this expansion were set by the
mid-1920s: control of the Mediterranean and access to the world's oceans –
the requirements of an imperial power.[8] The path to their achievement

would necessarily involve the flattening of any obstacles in the way, and under the firm hand of its leader the regime would not flinch at using force as the means to do this.

Fascist Foreign Policy in the 1920s

The themes and goals of foreign policy that Mussolini would weave together were present in Italy before he came to power. As well as conducting military adventures in Eritrea and Libya, pre-1914 Liberal Italy had had its eyes on the Austro-Hungarian empire in the shape of the 'unredeemed' lands of the north-east frontier and on Albania as a foothold in the Balkans. In the years between 1918 and 1922, new contours were added to this foreign policy landscape in the shape of nationalist ideas for an alliance with Hungary, Bulgaria, Turkey and Yugoslavia which could further Balkan ambitions, the army's interest in a new war of conquest in Abyssinia, and the navy's concern with the Adriatic and with the threat posed by British bases at Gibraltar and at Suez. In 1922, shortly before Mussolini came to power, the Facta government was postulating ideas of *mare nostrum* which would rapidly become part of the *Duce*'s foreign policy conspectus. The idea voiced by foreign minister Dino Grandi in October 1930 that the Italian nation 'is strong enough to constitute with its military contribution the *decisive* weight in the victory of one or other of the leading players in the European drama' – which Mussolini repeated with evident enthusiasm in April 1932, following Hitler's dramatic electoral successes – seemed to have elements of continuity with Liberal policy.[9] There were, however, important differences between the Fascist era and its Liberal predecessor: Italian arms would now be thrown more aggressively and more prodigally into play, and the international situation which Mussolini sought to use to his advantage was no longer one in which manoeuvres were shaped by the relations of two clearly defined power blocs, but one where opportunities were to be sought in the rather less predictable twists and turns of a more fluid and unstable international political environment.

In 1922, France welcomed the advent of the *Duce* to power because Italy was important to it to redress the balance against Germany. Thus, it remained studiedly neutral when D'Annunzio seized Fiume in spring 1922. France's need for support over the occupation of the Ruhr meant that it did not join in the international chorus condemning the seizure of Corfu in the summer of 1923. Mussolini's early attempt to enhance Italy's position, by the bombardment and seizure of Corfu in September 1923 and the settling of the Albanian frontier dispute, have generally been seen as examples of his 'penchant for minor escapades where some glory could be collected on the cheap'.[10] There was not much glory gained from this episode, as the Italians had to withdraw from Corfu under a face-saving agreement cobbled together by the diplomats of Palazzo Chigi. However, Mussolini was able to turn the international situation to his advantage, making it clear that if he did not get French support he would withdraw Italian endorsement of the Ruhr expedition at the start of September. He may have intended to occupy Corfu permanently, but was persuaded to withdraw with the payment of a sizeable cash settlement.[11]

Mussolini's ability – and willingness – to manipulate the tensions and opportunities present in the international system in the mid-1920s is shown by his first dangling a three-way pact between Italy, Yugoslavia and France before Paris, but then withdrawing it once a bilateral pact had been agreed and French support was no longer necessary. The Italo-Yugoslav accord of 27 January 1924, which gave Mussolini the port of Fiume, was thus an undeniable success for him, but also pointed towards his Balkan ambitions. His offer to support the *status quo* in the Adriatic in return for a French pledge on Italian rights in Tunisia was a particularly Mussolinian form of linkage which France rejected.

At this moment there was, in truth, too much to worry about at home for the *Duce* to go venturing too aggressively abroad. The murder of Giacomo Matteotti in June 1924 was succeeded by a year and more in which Mussolini overcame the crisis and exerted his own authority on the party. Equally importantly, Italy was heavily in debt as a result of the First World War, and did not manage to restore the lira to some sort of stability until he negotiated loans and financing deals with Britain and the United States in 1925–26.

France still needed an Italy that, to some of its diplomats at least, was not merely less germanophile but less aggressively irredentist than it appeared, to guarantee its frontiers against Germany. The invitation to Italy to participate in the Locarno agreement was greeted in Rome with enthusiasm combined with anxiety: enthusiasm at being invited to join in the arrangements rather than being left out of a possible Anglo-French-Belgian alliance, and anxiety lest the guaranteeing of France's Rhineland frontier might turn Germany's attention south towards Austria and encourage *Anschluß*. Mussolini's concern to secure a guarantee of the Brenner frontier spoke of concern at a future German threat – one that became very much alive in the early 1930s. No such guarantees were forthcoming, but the *Duce* was persuaded by his professional advisers that Italy must participate – 'the last success of the professional Italian diplomatists before they were supplanted in 1926 by full-fledged Fascists.'[12] Mussolini belatedly turned up at Locarno and joined in guaranteeing the Franco-German and Belgo-German frontiers chiefly, it has been claimed, in order not to be left out. That he was already looking to other means than diplomacy to advance Italy's international position is borne out by the fact that within three weeks of the signing of the agreement, he announced the need for greater rearmament.

In 1925, during the preliminary negotiations to the Locarno Pact, Briand had spoken of the need for collaboration between sister Latin powers to counterbalance the Anglo-Saxons. However, Ahmed bey Zogu's coup in Albania in 1925 and subsequent Italian support for him led to the conclusion of the Franco-Yugoslav treaty on 11 November 1927. Italy and France were now at odds and would remain so for the next eight years.[13] When the breach was temporarily healed, it was France and not Italy who played the supplicant.

So far, Mussolini's actions on the international stage could be seen as being no great departure from earlier Italian diplomatic practice – albeit in some cases perhaps a little more gauche and ham-fisted. However, there was another dimension to Italian policy in the Fascist era which was already beginning to operate and which was to become ever more prominent as the years went by. Mussolini's interest in taking advantage of – or actively furthering – possible tensions within Europe in order to advance Italy's position, and his willingness at least to explore the value of military links and therefore to hold open the possibility of using force to turn things in his favour, dates back to his earliest years in office. In September 1923, at the height of the crisis over the French reoccupation of the Ruhr and the issue of German reparations, he summoned the Italian ambassador to Berlin, Conte Alessandro De Bosdari, to explore the possibility of aiding Germany against France. Despite being told that Germany's difficulties included not merely the limited state of its armaments but more importantly the moral and political state of the country, which was so divided as to leave the government with no choice but 'shameful capitulation', Mussolini was sufficiently encouraged by very direct approaches from the Reichswehr to look further into the possibilities.

In the spring of 1924, General Luigi Capello was despatched to Berlin, where he had conversations with leading military figures including Field Marshal von Mackenson, General von Seeckt and General von Cramon. Capello learned of a strong German wish for a war of revenge against France and of the enthusiasm of the nationalists for supporting von Seeckt, but warned Mussolini that the Germans were still what they had been before the war, excessive and self-deceiving. 'It would be a good idea to remain aware of this fact if we have to deal with them,' he noted. Word of these discussions reached Stresemann's ears. On being tackled diplomatically but directly about them by the German foreign minister, De Bosdari denied all knowledge of them but, in reporting the conversation to Mussolini, raised the question as to whether it was either advisable or prudent to continue to send such emissaries so long as the government in office was so openly opposed to the nationalist parties. On this occasion the Duce backed off, scrawling on the despatch, 'Si – non ne andranno piu.' ('Yes – no more of them will go.') The episode had come about because of Mussolini's aggressively anti-Yugoslav orientation, but would very likely have expanded into something more than merely securing a bulwark against France had the political complexion in Germany been different.[14]

Military aggressiveness was always a stated core – perhaps it is better to say *the* stated core – of Fascism: Mussolini's co-authored essay on the 'Doctrine of Fascism', published in 1932, declared that war was the true test of nationhood as well as of manhood. And war was something he looked forward to: on Ascension Day 1927, he predicted that a European war would break out at some time between 1935 and 1940; in January 1929 he told Marshal Caviglia the same thing, leading Caviglia to comment in his diary, 'I hope that he's acting like this solely to make an impression'; and a year later, in March 1930, he told Fascist party secretary Augusto Turati that a second European war would break out some time between 1936 and 1940. These were something more than idle verbosities: on 18 July 1927 he called the chiefs of staff of the three armed forces together to begin systematic preparation for war. Domestic politics had readied the country, he told them, so that it was now in a condition in which it would be able to stand a war. So far as international politics went, both obvious and less obvious wheels had been

> set in motion in order to allow us to play our game. From a military point of view the matter is to prepare and co-ordinate the action of all the armed forces in the event of war.[15]

The less obvious wheels were diplomatic ones. From 1927 Mussolini began to encircle Yugoslavia, making agreements with Hungary, aiming to enlist both Greece and Turkey, and plying Austria with aid in the shape of support to the right-wing *Heimwehr*. In October 1929 he began to supply Croat terrorists with arms and money, and the following year made bellicose speeches which deeply alarmed Italian financial circles as the depression began to bite.

Berlin had figured large in Mussolini's view of Europe at least since 1922, and it remained a central but, for the time being, a largely dormant force. In June 1929 he remarked that there was no hope currently of reviving the Capello negotiations as Germany was disarmed, but 12 months later he noted in confidence to his war minister, General Pietro Gazzera, that 'we have completed two stages, Budapest and Vienna, towards Berlin.' In January 1931, with Hitler now holding 107 seats in the German parliament, he predicted that the Right would come to power there in 1934–36, after which time there would be the prospect of German support in a war with France. The likelihood of such support increased when Marshal Italo Balbo reported on conversations with Generals Schleicher and von Hammerstein at the start of 1932, in which he learned that Germany wanted revenge and would go to war for the Polish corridor, for *Anschluß* with Austria and for Alsace Lorraine. 'We must keep an eye on the Alto Adige,' Musssolini added.[16]

With the Nazis on the verge of power in January 1933, the moment seemed to have arrived to settle Yugoslavia's hash. Would they attack, the *Duce* asked General Gazzera? No, was the reply, they were not ready.

> Mussolini: So why do we wait?
> Gazzera: Because we shall gain more than they will. But chiefly for fear of French intervention either at once or when we're deeply involved. France could give us a lesson that would affect us for fifty years.[17]

Faced with determined resistance of a kind that the generals of the succeeding years (whom he chose for their subservience) would not offer, and with hostility from the king, Mussolini abandoned the notion of a war in the Balkans and put up a diplomatic smokescreen in the shape of proposals for a four-power pact which, though it might seem on all fours with Locarno, sat ill with his private goals and ambitions.[18]

The Years of Aggression

The years 1934 and 1935 were aberrations in Fascist foreign policy in two respects: relations with Germany, long seen as likely to give comfort and support to Fascist expansionism once the right was in power, cooled while those with France temporarily warmed up. In April 1933, Mussolini learned from Hermann Göring that the Nazis intended to seize power in Vienna, and in July 1934 a Nazi *putsch* there led to the murder of Chancellor Dollfuss. The Austrian had been a client of Mussolini's, and his wife and children were staying in Italy as his guests at the time of the murder (Mussolini had to inform them of it). More importantly, any threat to the Brenner frontier could endanger Mussolini's support among the conservative nationalists who went along with Fascism, but were not among its true adherents. Italian troops were deployed along the frontier. The murder in October 1934 of King Alexander of Yugoslavia, planned by Italian military intelligence (SIM), together with that of the French foreign minister Louis Barthou, which was unintended, produced a change of attitude and an unexpected opening for Mussolini. Pierre Laval, the new foreign minister, came to Rome in January 1935 and negotiated a deal in which, in return for agreeing to oppose both the *Anschluß* and the remilitarisation of the Rhineland, and giving up treaty rights for Italians in Tunisia, Mussolini got a 'free hand' in Ethiopia.[19] The decks were thus cleared for the first of the Fascist wars towards which Mussolini had looked so eagerly since his advent to power.

Ethiopia

The long-term goal of conquering the Ethiopian empire had been set by Mussolini in July 1925, and the army had begun general planning for such a war in March 1926. Detailed planning began in 1932, against a background of border skirmishes in the Ogaden fomented by the Italians, which had begun in 1928 and steadily increased in frequency. Trying to align himself with the *status quo* powers, Mussolini was looking to take advantage of a period of quiet in order to pull off the conquest of Abyssinia. No complications in Europe need be expected before 1936, he believed, because Yugoslavia was too divided internally to be a threat and Germany still had much to do before she was in any position to challenge for expansion. All that was then necessary, in this way of thinking, was to square Britain and France.

Mussolini's general designs were laid out a week before Laval's arrival. The meeting gave him what he wanted, and while preparations went ahead he went to Stresa in April 1935 to join in the 'Front' with Britain and France that was avowedly designed to preserve the peace of Europe in the face of a hostile Germany. The move was purely a tactical one: the previous month, Mussolini had announced privately that, after taking Ethiopia, 'we shall conquer Egypt and the Sudan!' At the conference, he seems to have believed the British had agreed to his conquest of Ethiopia, but in June Foreign Secretary Anthony Eden arrived for talks in Rome and made it clear that Britain would not consent to the eradication of a member state of the League of Nations. His preparations for war in Africa produced a piece of naval posturing by Britain, who reinforced its Mediterranean fleet in late August, behind which – as Mussolini knew from purloined British documents – lay an acknowledgement that Britain's interests in the area were not such as to justify fighting to maintain the independence of Haile Selassie's kingdom when German rearmament in the West and Japanese expansionism in the East presented a global challenge.[20]

Knowing that the odds were in his favour, and knowing also that the realignment of Italy with Germany, which was developing as a result of Anglo-French hostility towards his Abyssinian venture, was something that Berlin viewed in a positive and sympathetic light, Mussolini gambled and won.[21] The attack on Ethiopia went ahead on 3 October 1935, and although sanctions were subsequently imposed on Italy, they excluded the one commodity whose absence could bring it to its knees – oil. The farcical events of December 1935, when Laval and Sir Samuel Hoare tried to bribe Mussolini with bits of Ethiopia his forces had already taken, only for the plan to leak to the public and force Hoare to resign, simply strengthened his standing in Italy. Germany now came to his aid, providing substitute coal imports amounting to about two-thirds of Italy's needs for a year from the end of 1935.

After some near setbacks from which they were rescued at a crucial moment by the use of gas, Italian forces comprehensively routed their enemy and on 8 May 1936, Mussolini declared the Italian annexation of Ethiopia. The war had cost Italy 10,000–12,000 dead and over 200,000 seriously ill, wounded or injured, as well as 3000 native dead; the Ethiopians lost some 250,000 soldiers and civilians dead from all causes. It also cost Italy almost 39 billion lire, approximately eight times the expenditure Mussolini had anticipated. The war had gobbled up 29,000 motor vehicles, 4.2 million artillery shells and 1600 guns, and had engaged the direct efforts of 569,000 military personnel and 68,000 labourers. Partially supported by the French, the guerilla war in Ethiopia would continue until September 1939 and beyond, draining away more resources that Italy could not afford as further wars, both actual and prospective, loomed. Thus weakened, Italy stood more than ever in need of the German support it had so long been seeking.[22]

After briefly having allowed it to run along a branch line, Mussolini now switched the points and swung Fascist foreign policy back on to the track it had been travelling down from the outset. The fact that the Germans had supplied Haile Selassie with 10,000 Mauser rifles was overlooked as a mere trifle. In January 1936, the *Duce* signalled his switch to Hitler's Germany by telling the German ambassador that if Austria 'as a formerly quite independent state, were ... to become a German satellite, he would have no objection'.[23] On 22 February he told the German ambassador that Stresa was a dead letter; in March he urged Schuschnigg to come to terms quickly with Hitler; and on 21 April he declared solidarity with Hitler by refusing to join in League of Nations sanctions against him because of Germany's reoccupation of the Rhineland while Italy was itself the victim of sanctions. On 11 July, he gave his backing to the Austro-German treaty which brought Vienna to the brink of *Anschluß*. The fact that he had now thrown his lot in with Europe's most ideologically and politically aggressive state was signified and sealed when, on 1 November 1936, he announced the formation of the 'Axis' between Rome and Berlin.

To clear the domestic decks and underscore the importance of the new relationship, a wholesale clear-out of personnel took place. The anti-Nazi ambassador to Berlin Vittorio Cerruti, whose Jewish wife leading Nazis had nevertheless found ravishing company, and who had sent Mussolini a long and damning report on the antisemitic policy unleashed by Hitler on 1 April 1933, which he had described as 'a spectacle at once uncivilized and tasteless ... initiated and pursued with so little moral and psychological sensibility', was shifted to Paris in June 1935.[24] Twelve months later Fulvio Suvich and Pompeo Aloisi, leading members of the Foreign Ministry staff in Rome and anti-Germans both, were sacked and Mussolini appointed his son-in-law Galeazzo Ciano to succeed to the post of foreign minister vacated by Grandi in 1932. Finally, in October 1936, General Federico Baistrocchi was replaced as under-secretary for war by General Alberto Pariani, another pro-German.

'It is difficult to say exactly what Mussolini wanted in Spain, for he did not know himself,' a distinguished Italian diplomat observed at the end of the Second World War.

> He had vague plans for an alliance, or at least a close understanding with Spain, which would change the balance of power in the Mediterranean, menace Gibraltar, and create a third front for the French general staff. He had no clear idea, however, of how this alliance was to work.[25]

Once upon a time Italian intervention in the Spanish Civil war was seen as being activated primarily by a sense of ideological affinity, but latterly it has commonly been seen as motivated more by political and strategic consider-ations.[26] In fact, Mussolini's interest in this potential theatre of disruption antedated Franco's requests for assistance in the summer of 1936: Rome had twice been involved in failed plots against the Republic by dissatisfied army officers in 1932 and again in 1934. Mussolini's incremental build-up of Italian involvement between August and December 1936, beginning with the provision of 12 bombers and five tanks and ending with the decision to allow Italian troops to participate either as 'volunteers' or in a specially prepared division, has been seen as a response to the build-up of Soviet aid and Hitler's decision in November to send the Condor Legion. That is to see Mussolini's policy as primarily reactive, when it was at least to a significant degree proactive. With reports arriving in the late summer from Ambassador Berardis in Moscow stressing Russia's wish not to turn Italy into an enemy, the Duce hesitated. Plans for an expedition were put on hold between September and December. The final decision, made on 6 December, appears to fit with Mediterranean expansionism: in the autumn the newly created foreign minister, Galeazzo Ciano, identified Italy's strategic objectives in the western Mediterranean as Ceuta and the Balearics, and referred to Spain as an 'extension of the Axis toward the Atlantic Ocean'.[27]

By mid-February 1937 there were 49,000 Italian troops in Spain. Had the Nationalists captured Madrid that spring, Mussolini might have achieved a cheap triumph. However, the disaster at Guadalajara in March 1937, which cost the Italians over 400 dead, 1800 wounded and nearly 500 taken prisoner or missing, dashed hopes for a swift end to the war and committed Mussolini to two more years' effort. The war, which ended for the Italians with their seizure of the port of Alicante on 30 March 1939, consumed large amounts of arms and equipment, and much more was donated to the Nationalists. Together, these inroads into Italy's limited resources had drastic effects, leaving its military seriously weakened: the war cost Italy equipment for 15 or 20 infantry divisions and artillery, tanks and trucks for four or five motorized divisions, which would have more than doubled its effective strength in 1940–41 – an increment which would certainly have had some effect on the course of the war in North Africa.

Mussolini's options for trouble-making were much increased by the attempts made by Prime Minister Neville Chamberlain, from the moment that he came into office in May 1937, to appease him because of Italy's strategic threat in the Mediterranean and to woo him as a way to reach Hitler. Mussolini's aims at this time, as stated by Grandi to Chamberlain, were to do nothing that would endanger a Nationalist victory in the Spanish Civil War and to get British recognition of Italy's conquest of Abyssinia. Secretly, they were rather more than this, for Mussolini sought to split Britain from France and thereby gain further room for manoeuvre in the Mediterranean. The British prime minister's evident appetite for improved relations with Italy was whetted during July and August 1937 by allusions to the Rome–Berlin Axis as not the be-all and end-all of Fascist policy and by Italy's apparent willingness to try to abet an Anglo-German agreement. Thus when, after Italian submarines began attacking Soviet merchant shipping in the Mediterranean at Franco's behest in August 1937 and after they unsuccessfully attempted to torpedo the British destroyer *Havock* on 1 September, the Nyon Conference was convened on 10 September 1937, overt criticism of Italy was avoided. Italy, who did not attend and who had called off the actions of its submarines six days earlier, was neither criticised nor punished. In fact, it gained from the episode despite the miserable record of its submarines (Italian submarines had fired 43 torpedoes at 24 ships between 6 August and 11 September 1937, sinking four merchantmen and damaging a Republican destroyer); the USSR stopped using the Mediterranean to ship supplies to the Republic and turned instead to the much less effective route from the Baltic to France and then overland into Spain. Warlike action and aggression had cost Italy little: if Britain still withheld *de jure* recognition of its conquest of Abyssinia, that was, as Chamberlain acknowledged, a concession which 'could not be withheld indefinitely, as it had a declining "marketable value"'.[28]

The German *Anschluß* with Austria in March 1938 came as no surprise to Mussolini: he had discussed it with Ribbentrop the previous November and had indicated that he was prepared to accept Austria as a German state. London's sensitivity to the need to improve relations with a potential enemy in the Mediterranean was Rome's opportunity: the so-called Easter Accords signed on 16 April 1938 promised Britain's *de jure* recognition of Italy's conquest of Abyssinia and parity in the Red Sea in return for a 'settlement' of the Spanish question, a reduction in the Libyan garrison, and the opening of talks with the French. For Mussolini, who certainly never took the latter element of the accord seriously, it was a cheap success and a further step in the plan to separate London and Paris.

In the May prelude to the Munich crisis, when rumours of war abounded, Mussolini was willing to offer open support to Hitler, regardless of whether he intended merely to gain the Sudeten Germans their independence or to destroy Czechoslovakia as an independent power. Speaking in Genoa, he declared the 'lasting friendship' of the German and Roman worlds and warned the democracies that in the event of a war 'based on ideologies ... the Totalitarian States will immediately ally and march together all the way to the end'.[29] The promise of support was renewed at the end of July to the point of war: if France mobilised and if it then attacked Germany, Italy would mobilise and would attack France in turn. By this time, Italy was engaged in military conversations with the Hungarians about likely collaboration if things came to war. Warnings that in the event of a war Britain would join in, and that in those circumstances the puny opposition that Hitler's navy could put up would mean that the weight of the Royal Navy would fall on Italy, were ignored by the *Duce*. On 10 September, Mussolini told the Hungarian military attaché, Colonel Laszlo Szabo, that although he would prefer not to have to fight a war, he thought that it could not be avoided, and that 'He [Mussolini] will help them if the Germans ask for help, because after Germany's fall Italy would be left alone.'[30]

Mussolini had told Szabo on 10 September that if Hitler were willing to compromise, Czechoslovakia would fall into his hands just as Austria had done. On 27 September, he received a memorandum from General Pariani pointing out that if war occurred, the only theatre where Italy could take the offensive would be Libya, where it lacked both the troops and the means (*mezzi*) necessary to take immediate action.[31] Aware of the serious military limitations affecting both his army, which could only mobilise ten divisions to defend the north-western frontier, and his fleet, facing a much more powerful enemy coalition with only two modern battleships, Mussolini now took up the requests from Britain and the United States on 28 September and interceded to prevent the war he had been ready to engage in. A premature war, he realised, could give France a freer hand in Spain, jeopardising Franco's victory and thereby casting away all Italy's previous investment in his forces. The news, in late September, that Japan was at last willing to sign a tripartite pact with Italy and Germany offered a peaceful option for stirring up trouble for the British Empire. Finally, a war in which German forces were concentrated in eastern Europe while Britain and France were drawing closer together did not look so promising a prospect after all.[32]

Evidence that Mussolini's long-term aim to secure Italian domination of the Mediterranean was now increasing in both immediacy and intensity was soon apparent. Italy's colonial claims on France were chanted by the Chamber of Deputies on 30 November 1938 with shouts for Nice, Corsica, Djibuti and Tunis. Mussolini assumed wrongly that Chamberlain would pressure France into some sort of accommodation: when Chamberlain visited Rome in January 1939, his goal was to improve relations with the dictators. The initiative was his, not Mussolini's. Chamberlain's visit came in the aftermath of an agreement signed in Rome on 16 November by which, in return for withdrawing 10,000 soldiers from Spain, Mussolini at last won British recognition of Italian sovereignty over Abyssinia.

In reaching the agreement, the British Foreign Office sought, as Halifax put it, to offer Mussolini 'increas[ed] power of manoeuvre and so make him less dependent on Hitler, and freer to resume the classic Italian role of balancing between Germany and the Western Powers'.[33] In pressing for the meeting, Chamberlain had in mind the strengthening of bonds with France which occurred in the latter part of 1938; he was also aware of the increasing hostility shown by Italy towards France, which had reached a climax with the demonstration in the Italian Chamber of Deputies on 30 November. He also nursed a greatly exaggerated faith in his own ability to influence the *Duce*:

> I feel that Rome at the moment is the end of the Axis on which it is easiest to make an impression ... An hour or two *tête-à-tête* with Musso might be extraordinarily valuable in making plans for talks with Germany ... .[34]

If Mussolini showed a willingness to moderate Hitler's ambitions and also to secure peace in Spain, Chamberlain was willing to open up the possibility of discussions on issues in contention such as Suez Canal tariffs or the Djibouti railway; he would not in any way encourage Italy to think of asking for territorial concessions from France. In the face of growing French anxiety, internal discussion oscillated between the Foreign Office's view that a stiff warning should be issued about Italy's conduct and Chamberlain's preference for a more disinterested attitude. At their first meeting on 11 January, Mussolini told Chamberlain that the Axis remained the cornerstone of Italian policy, but seemed to hint that talks leading to some kind of accommodation might be possible.

The Mussolini-Chamberlain meeting has been taken by De Felicean historians to be an example of Mussolini's policy of genuine openness to an Anglo-Italian agreement as part of his policy of trying to navigate between the democracies and Nazi Germany.[35] Every utterance from Mussolini and Ciano before and after the meeting argues against this. On 2 January, 11 days before Chamberlain and Halifax arrived in Rome, Mussolini declared that he had already decided to adhere to the Tripartite Pact. After their second meeting on 12 January, Ciano noted in his diary that he was more convinced than ever of the value of a military alliance with Germany and Japan: 'having such an instrument in our hands, we shall be able to get whatever we want [because] the English don't want to fight.' And two weeks after the British premier left Rome, Mussolini promised General Vittorio Ambrosio, commanding the 2nd Army facing Yugoslavia, that Italy would soon 'fight France', a comment that came in the context of the imminent fall of Barcelona and pressure from the French Chamber to assist the Republic.[36] The overall consequences of the visit were, as one scholar has noted, that it 'increased that propensity to brinkmanship in Mussolini's foreign policy that sought to use all means short of war to acquire territory and influence at the expense of other states.'[37] What should be added is that by now Mussolini was ready to contemplate stepping across the boundary between peace and war, as he had long itched to do.

The Italo-German military alliance of 22 May 1939 was something Mussolini had supported ever since Hitler had raised the issue in May 1938. His reason was simple: given the direction in which he was steering Italian policy, a clash with Britain and France was growing ever more likely. On 30 November 1938, in the aftermath of the Munich settlement, Mussolini listed for the Fascist Grand Council his next objectives: Albania, Tunisia, Corsica, Djibuti and, in due course, the Gotthard as Italy's frontier with Switzerland. Time limits could not be attached to this programme (the term used in Ciano's account of the speech), he declared; he could only indicate the directions of advance. During the night of 4/5 February 1939, in a formal address to the Grand Council, the themes were set out at greater length and in greater detail. It was both a resumé of his thoughts over some 20 and more years and a clear pointer to his actions in the years immediately to come. States such as Italy which had limited access to the world's oceans were only 'semi-independent', he declared.

> Italy is ... truly a prisoner in the Mediterranean, and the more populous and powerful she becomes the more she will suffer from her imprisonment. The bars of this prison are Corsica, Tunisia, Malta, Cyprus; the guardians of this prison are Gibraltar and Suez.

Having broken the bars of this prison, Italy must advance to the Indian Ocean via the Sudan and to the Atlantic Ocean via French North Africa. To do this, Italy must be sure that its back was secure on the European continent. 'Thus the policy of the Rome–Berlin Axis responds to an historical necessity of the most fundamental kind.' A test of war between Italy and France must come one day, Mussolini forecast, 'if only because France only respects people who have defeated her'. A war would be best timed to occur after 1942 when, among other things, the artillery would have been renewed and eight battleships would be ready. In the meantime diplomacy would work to obtain the best solution, and at the same time the armed forces would hasten their preparation so as to be ready for any eventuality.[38]

The Pact of Steel included a verbal understanding that there would be no war until 1943, and within a week of putting his name to it Mussolini despatched General Ugo Cavallero to Berlin to explain how, because of the military consequences of its Abyssinian and Spanish ventures, Italy would be in no state to wage a general war until then. However, the increasing instability of the European situation was sharpening Italy's appetite. Aware from early May that Berlin was negotiating with Moscow and that Hitler intended to destroy Poland, Rome began to hone its plans for the dismemberment of Yugoslavia and for a simultaneous attack on Greece and Romania, for which enterprises they secretly sought Hungarian assistance. This scheme collapsed in early August, when Italian army manoeuvres revealed that the new mechanised force Pariani was supposedly preparing for combat was hopelessly weak and disorganised.[39]

Aware by now of the West's determination to honour its guarantees to Poland if Hitler used force, and of the Führer's willingness to do just that, Mussolini insisted that Ciano and Ribbentrop meet. When, at the meeting at Berchtesgaden between 11 and 13 August 1939, Count Ciano said that premature war would result from the German ultimatum to Poland, Hitler confidently forecast that his victim would back down. He also suggested that Italy should dismember Yugoslavia after Poland had fallen. By 15 August, Mussolini thought general war was imminent and warned the chief of the armed forces' general staff, Marshal Badoglio, that if forced to it he would attack Greece and Yugoslavia. Ten days later, having just been presented with a demand by King Vittorio Emmanuele III for Italian neutrality because of the 'pitiful' state of the army, Mussolini disengaged himself from the Pact of Steel by sending Hitler a long shopping list of needs which must be met before he could contemplate belligerency.

By autumn 1939, Mussolini was armed with reports describing Germany's belligerent intentions towards the West and the debates which were going on as to whether to repeat the attack of 1914, to focus on the Maginot Line in Luxembourg and then race across Belgium to the sea, or to attack the Maginot Line in the Saar.[40] Over the winter, his attitude towards intervention seems to have been determined chiefly by the state of his military forces: informed that the air force would be ready for war in mid-1941, but the army and navy not until 1943–44, he indicated on 11 January 1940 that he proposed to intervene in the war in the second half of the following year. In early February, he was presented with a battery of statistics at the annual meeting of the State Council of Defence to demonstrate that Italy was in no condition to contemplate a major war. The finance minister pointed out that the country was short of the gold reserves needed to purchase raw materials; the under-secretary of state for war and the chief of the armed forces general staff detailed shortages of reserves of primary products which, if not made good, meant that Italy could not make war for at least a year; and the head of the air force said that he had nothing with which to build aeroplanes and needed 130,000 tons of metal to complete work currently in progress. By now, the *Duce* was pursuing a policy of entryism grounded in speculative assumptions about what a war would be like and not on calculations as to what was within Italy's power, and therefore its interests. A direct collision between the French and German armies was unlikely, he opined, so that the coming conflict would be an 'aero-naval war'. Italy must make the maximum effort to build up stockpiles of coal in March and April; the way out of the raw materials

problems was to requisition copper and scrap iron – of which Mussolini
said, apparently on the basis of no evidence whatsoever, that there must be
500 million tons in the country. His closing advice was that the military
must take the economic situation into account and try to adapt their
programmes to it.[41]

'His will is fixed and decided on war,' Ciano recorded of his father-in-law
on 1 February 1940. This was indeed so. On 11 March, having just learned
that Hitler planned to attack the West in June or July, Mussolini told
Ribbentrop that Italy would intervene at the decisive moment, and a week
later, at his meeting with Hitler on the Brenner Pass, he told the Führer that
he would act 'as soon as Germany thrust forward victoriously'.[42] Shortly
after the German attack on Denmark and Norway, Mussolini told the
Hungarian military attaché, Colonel Laszlo Szabo, 'Italy will enter the war
on the German side – I don't know when; maybe in a week, in a month or in
a year.' When it did, he added, its theatres of operations would be the
Mediterranean and the Balkans.[43] The sweeping successes enjoyed by the
Wehrmacht from the moment it launched its attack on France on 10 May
1940 did not force a reluctant *Duce* out of his preferred neutrality, but
rather provided the final impetus for him to act as he wanted. When Fascist
Italy entered the Second World War on 10 June, Mussolini announced that
this was 'an hour signalled by destiny'.[44] That destiny was his choice, and
the culmination of a process that had begun when he came into office in
October 1922.

Notes

The research on which this chapter is based was carried out with the aid of a grant
from the Leverhulme Trust.

1. D. Mack Smith, *Mussolini as a Military Leader* (Reading, 1974), p. 12. See
    also Mack Smith, *Mussolini's Roman Empire* (Harmondsworth, 1977); and
    Mussolini (London, 1981).
2. R. De Felice, *Mussolini: Il rivoluzionario 1883–1920* (Turin, 1965), *Il Fascista
    I: La conquista del potere 1921–1925* (Turin, 1966), *Il Fascista II:
    l'organizzazzione dello stato Fascista 1925–1929* (Turin, 1968), *Il duce I:
    Gli anni del consenso 1929–1936* (Turin, 1974), *Il Duce II: Lo stato
    totalitario 1936–1940* (Turin, 1981).
3. B. W. Painter, jr., 'Renzo De Felice and the Historiography of Italian Fascism',
    American Historical Review 95 (1990), 391–405; M. Knox, 'The Fascist
    Regime, its Foreign Policy and its Wars: An "Anti-Anti-Fascist Orthodoxy"',
    Contemporary European History 4 (1995), 347–65; D. Mack Smith, 'Musso-
    lini: Reservations about Renzo De Felice's Biography', *Modern Italy* 5 (2000),
    193–210. The only substantive version of De Felice's views in English is M. A.

Ledeen, ed., *Fascism: An Informal Introduction to its Theory and Practice* (New Brunswick, 1976).

4. R. Quartararo, 'Mussolini e la tradizione diplomatica precedente', *Affari Esteri* anno 23 (1991), 6–7.

5. A. Cassels, 'Was there a Fascist Foreign Policy? Tradition and Novelty', *International History Review* 5 (1983), 259.

6. S. C. Azzi, 'The Historiography of Fascist Foreign Policy', *Historical Journal* 36 (1993), 194.

7. M. Knox, 'Fascism: Ideology, Foreign Policy, and War', in A. Lyttelton, ed., *Liberal and Fascist Italy* (Oxford, 2002), pp. 105–38.

8. M. Knox, 'Conquest, Foreign and Domestic, in Fascist Italy and Nazi Germany', *Journal of Modern History* 56 (1984), 1–57.

9. B. R. Sullivan, 'The Strategy of the Decisive Weight: Italy 1882–1922', in W. Murray, M. Knox and A. Bernstein, eds, *The Making of Strategy: Rulers, States, and War* (Cambridge, 1994), pp. 345–9.

10. S. Marks, 'Mussolini and Locarno: Fascist Foreign Policy in Microcosm', *Journal of Contemporary History* 14 (1979), 423.

11. A. Cassels, *Mussolini's Early Diplomacy* (Princeton, 1970), pp. 95–101.

12. Ibid., p. 428.

13. W. I. Shorrock, 'France, Italy, and the Eastern Mediterranean in the 1920s', *International History Review* 8 (1986), 70–82.

14. R. De Felice, *Mussolini e Hitler. I rapporti segreti* (Florence, 1977), p. 115; Ministero degli Affari Esteri, Gabinetto del Ministro b. GM 156, De Bosdari to Mussolini, 19 September 1923, 4248; De Bosdari to Mussolini, 28 November 1923, 5941; De Bosdari to Mussolini, 18 March 1924, 4869; De Bosdari to Mussolini, 18 March 1924, 4870. For a brief allusion to this episode, see Lucio Ceva, 'Pianificazione militare e politica estera dell'Italia Fascista 1923–1940', *Italian contemporanea* 219 (2000), p. 283.

15. Quoted in A. Curami and G. Apostolo, 'The Italian Aviation from 1923 to 1933', in *Adaptation de l'arme aerienne aux conflits contemporains et processus d'indépendence des armées de l'Air des origines à la fin de la Seconde Guerre mondiale* (Paris, 1985), p. 279. See also Enrico Caviglia, *Diario (aprile 1925-marzo 1945)* (Rome, 1952), p. 60 (24 January 1929).

16. Carte Gazzera, Udienze con S. E. il Capo di Stato, 11 June 1929, 30 June 1930, 27 January 1931, 15 February 1932.

17. Carte Gazzera, Udienza con S. E. il Capo di Stato, 8 January 1933.

18. M. Knox, *Common Destiny: Dictatorship, Foreign Policy, and War in Fascist Italy and Nazi Germany* (Cambridge, 2000), pp. 131–2, 135–6.

19. G. Bruce Strang, 'Imperial Dreams: The Mussolini-Laval Accords of January 1935', *Historical Journal* 44 (2001), 799–809.

20. Knox, 'The Fascist Regime', p. 362; Meir Michaelis, 'Italy's Mediterranean Strategy, 1935–39', in M. J. Cohen and M. Kolinsky, eds, *Britain and the Middle East in the 1930s: Security Problems 1935–1939* (London, 1992), pp. 43–50; Arthur J. Marder, 'The Royal Navy and the Ethiopian Crisis of 1935–1936', in Marder, *From the Dardanelles to Oran: Studies of the Royal Navy in War and Peace 1915–1940* (Oxford, 1974), pp. 64–104; R. Mallett, 'The Italian Naval High Command and the Mediterranean Crisis January–October 1935', *Journal of Strategic Studies* 22 (1999), 77–102.

21. Ministero degli Affari Esteri, Affari Politici: Germania, b. 28 fasc.2, 'Circolare riservatissima ai gerarchi socialnazionali sui rapporti italo-germanici', 5 June 1935.
22. B. R. Sullivan, 'The Italian-Ethiopian War, October 1935–November 1941: Causes, Conduct and Consequences', in A. Hamish Ion and E. J. Errington, eds, *Great Powers and Little Wars: The Limits of Power* (Westport, CT, 1993), pp. 167–201.
23. *Documents on German Foreign Policy* Series, C, Vol. 4, no. 485, p. 974–7, Von Hassell to Foreign Ministry, 7 January 1936.
24. Ministero degli Affari Esteri, Affari Politici: Germania b.12 fasc. 2, Cerruti to Mussolini, 5 May 1933. This despatch, in which Cerruti said that the Nazis had 'incited the basest passions of a people who are often brutal and lacking in good sense', was read by Mussolini.
25. M. Donosti (Luciolli), *Mussolini e l'Europa* (Rome, 1945), pp. 49–50; quoted in Michaelis, 'Italy's Mediterranean Strategy', p. 54.
26. J. F. Coverdale, *Italian Intervention in the Spanish Civil War* (Princeton, 1975); De Felice, *Lo stato totalitario*, pp. 331–466; R. M. Salerno, *The Mediterranean Triangle: Britain, France, Italy and the Origins of the Second World War, 1935–40*, Ph.D. thesis, Yale University 1997, p. 96.
27. M. Heiberg, 'Mussolini, Franco and the Spanish Civil War: An Afterthought', *Totalitarian Movements and Political Religions* 2 (2001), p. 61.
28. W. C. Mills, 'The Nyon Conference: Neville Chamberlain, Anthony Eden, and the Appeasement of Italy in 1937', *International History Review* 15 (1993), p. 7. See also Mills, 'The Chamberlain-Grandi Conversations of July–August 1937 and the Appeasement of Italy', *International History Review* 19 (1997), 594–619.
29. B. R. Sullivan, ' "Where One Man, and One Man Only, Led." Italy's path from non-alignment to non-belligerence to war, 1937–1940', in N. Wyllie, ed., *European Neutrals and Non-Belligerents during the Second World War* (Cambridge, 2002), p. 125.
30. Hungarian National Archives, K.100, Foreign Ministry Archives, 671/443, Conversation with the *Duce* on 10 September 1938.
31. Civiche Raccolte Storiche di Milano, Pariani to Mussolini, 27 September 1938, Quaderni Pariani 29.
32. G. Bruce Strang, 'War and Peace: Mussolini's Road to Munich', *Diplomacy & Statecraft* 10 (1999), 160–90.
33. Quoted in P. Stafford, 'The Chamberlain-Halifax visit to Rome: A Reappraisal', *English Historical Review* 98 (1983), 66.
34. Chamberlain to Hilda Chamberlain, 6 November 1938. Quoted in Salerno, *The Mediterranean Triangle*, p. 262.
35. R. Quartararo, *Roma tra Londra e Berlino: La politica estera Fascista dal 1930 al 1940* (Rome, 1980), pp. 404–23.
36. Galeazzo Ciano, *Diario 1937–1943* (Milan, 1980), 2 and 12 January, pp. 233, 238–9; Salerno, *The Mediterranean Triangle*, p. 276.
37. Stafford, *op. cit.*, p. 100.
38. R. De Felice, *Mussolini: il Duce*, Vol. II, pp. 320–5.
39. Sullivan, 'Italy's path from non-alignment', pp. 133–41.

40. Ministero degli Affari Esteri, Affari Politici: Germania, b. 58, Esteri to Ministero della Guerra-SIM, etc., 22 November 1939.
41. Ufficio Storico dello Stato Maggiore dell'Esercito, Rep. F 9, racc. 50 fasc. 2, Consiglio Superiore di Difesa: Verbali della XVII sessione (8–14 February 1940), pp. 62–3, 68, 70, 79.
42. Quoted in M. Knox, *Mussolini Unleashed, 1939–1941: Politics and Strategy in Fascist Italy's Last War* (Cambridge, 1982), p. 87.
43. Hungarian National Archives, K. 100, Foreign Ministry Archives, Szabo to Hungarian Chief of General Staff, 19 April 1940.
44. Quoted in A. Cassels, 'Reluctant Neutral: Italy and the Strategic Balance in 1939', in B. J. C. McKercher and R. Legault, eds, *Military Planning and the Origins of the Second World War in Europe* (Westport, CT, 2000), p. 42.

3 Imperial Japan

Antony Best

In November 1948 the conclusion of the International War Crimes Tribunal in Tokyo handed down to future generations a clear and unequivocal judgement on Japan's responsibility for the Asian half of the Second World War. The Tribunal declared that the evidence it had heard proved that the 25 defendants at the trial, who were referred to as a 'criminal and militaristic clique', had conspired from 1928 to 1945 to wage 'aggressive war' against Japan's neighbours. They were therefore guilty of crimes against peace, as well as, in a number of cases, crimes against humanity.[1] As a result of this judgement seven of the defendants, including the former prime minister, General Hideki Tōjō, and the former prime minister and foreign minister, Kōki Hirota, were executed. The other defendants were sentenced to prison terms ranging from life imprisonment to seven years.

For two decades the Tribunal's judgement remained the orthodox interpretation of war origins and responsibility. If one wanted to know who had begun the war and why, the answer was simple: Japan had initiated the conflict and had done so because the country from the late 1920s had come under the sway of the armed forces and their civilian collaborators who unleashed an unprovoked series of wars of aggrandisement, which culminated in the attack on Pearl Harbor in 1941. Since the 1960s, however, this view of the origins of the Pacific War has been steadily modified, for, as the archives of the various interested powers have been opened up and the writing of history moved into previously uncharted sub-disciplines and methodologies, the roots of the conflict have come to be seen as increasingly complex. For example, the early preoccupation with Japanese-American ties as the key bilateral axis for the region has been reduced and more attention paid to Japan's relations with continental Asia. Important in this has been the realisation that the other regional powers, such as China, the Soviet Union and the leading imperial presence, the British Empire, were not merely passive spectators, but had their own policy agendas which often conflicted with that of Japan. In addition, analysis of the internal dynamics of the Japanese regime has led to a debate about whether it is appropriate to put the responsibility for expansion overwhelmingly on the Imperial Japanese Army (IJA). Recent literature has suggested that instead Japan

should be seen as a country wrestling with the effects of late industrialisation and the tensions created by the modernisation process. The simple and
starkly moral judgement reached at Tokyo has thus largely been discarded,
but that does not mean that it has been replaced by another equally simpli-
fied interpretation. Rather, as the American historian Michael Barnhart
recently observed, it has not proved to be possible to construct a new
synthesis in this rapidly changing field.[2]

In order to make sense of the changes that have taken place in the field
and to come to some understanding of the current state of play, this chapter
is divided into two parts. The first half examines the way in which analysis
of the forces operating within Japan has changed over time, and how
groups other than the army and its most obvious civilian associates have
been implicated in the drive for expansion. The second half deals with the
changing interpretations of the international environment, paying particular attention to the importance of events in north-east Asia and the link
with the simultaneous crisis in Europe.

The Internal Determinants of Japanese Expansion

The judgement laid down by the Tokyo War Crimes Tribunal presented
Japan in the 1930s as a state dominated by a narrow coalition of generals,
admirals and bureaucrats, who were able to dictate policy to other
members of the Japanese political establishment and to the people at large.
This group, it was contended, took over the reins of state power in 1931–32
by usurping the position of the party politicians who had dominated in the
1920s. Thereafter, they maintained their influence by using the existing
power of the state to stultify dissent and indoctrinate the people. More
moderate elements continued to exist, but they were quiescent due to their
increasing powerlessness and the ever-present danger of assassination by
ultra-nationalist elements. Thus, figures such as the post-war prime
ministers, Kijūrō Shidehara and Shigeru Yoshida, who were both diplomats
by training, largely kept their opinions to themselves or at best worked
behind the scenes in an effort to bring about a return to sanity. The
militarist clique was therefore safely ensconced in power and set to work to
build up Japan's war potential and to expand the empire, launching it on
the road that would lead to disaster. The Tribunal's concentration on this
small élite group did, of course, make some sense, for the men brought to
trial were clearly important figures, who had played a major role in
overseeing and directing Japan's shift towards territorial aggrandisement.
However, from the very start questions were raised about whether they
bore the sole responsibility for expansion or were merely agents of a larger
malaise in the Japanese body politic.

One major reason for dissatisfaction with the trial's attempt to stamp its authority on history was that one of the key political figures in Japan was not indicted, for the United States decided that Emperor Hirohito should not stand trial. This decision was chiefly due to General MacArthur, head of the American post-war occupation, who convinced Washington that the emperor could be used to legitimate the reforms that were necessary to remove militarism and feudalism from Japan. Both at the time and ever since, this decision has been controversial. Some historians have argued that the American decision was justified on historical as well as political grounds, for they view Hirohito as a marginal actor in the 1930s. The argument is that the emperor, as a constitutional monarch, had very limited powers and could only really intervene in the political process when his advisers were divided, but that as a consensus existed over such decisions as Japan's entry into the Pacific War, he remained on the sidelines.[3] Other historians, however, have been much more critical, and have attempted to demonstrate that Hirohito encouraged the IJA in its ambitions and more importantly that the emperor should have gone on trial, because this would have brought home to the Japanese people the enormity of the country's war responsibility in a way that the trial of a few senior 'scapegoats' could not.[4] There may be some truth to the latter assertion, but the concentration on the emperor's war responsibility is to some degree a red herring, which tells one more about the political stance of historians than it sheds light on history. For, even if Hirohito had some sympathy with expansion, he was no Hitler.

A far more substantial challenge to the orthodoxy laid by the Tribunal came from those Marxist historians in Japan who in the early post-war period sought to categorise the political structure in the 1930s as essentially fascist. These historians did not accept that the military had somehow hijacked the state, but argued that what they defined as 'emperor-system fascism' had its roots in the Meiji restoration of 1868. In their view, from the outset Meiji Japan was constructed around an 'emperor-system' in which the élite and the bureaucracy used the emperor to legitimise a state that relied upon political absolutism and virulent nationalism. Disagreements existed between Marxist scholars over whether this state was essentially feudal or bourgeois, but they were united in believing that in the 1930s the emperor-system increasingly took on fascist attributes in an effort to protect the interests of monopoly capitalism. This interpretation was subsequently revised by the political scientist Masao Maruyama, who argued that a more correct understanding of the 1930s was to see the introduction of Fascism by the élite, what he termed 'Fascism from above', as a reaction to Japan's crisis of modernisation and the rise of the ultra-nationalists. For Maruyama, the early 1930s witnessed an attempt by a *petit bourgeois*, ultra-nationalist element outside government, who were radicalised by factors such as the grinding poverty in rural areas caused by the depression, to introduce Fascism as an answer to Japan's problems. This eventually culminated in the abortive *coup* by the Imperial Way faction in February 1936. In response to this challenge, the political élite itself co-opted fascist ideas in order to chart Japan through its national crisis, thus taming the ultra-nationalists and acquiring the government apparatus that would support a policy of overseas aggrandisement.[5]

The argument that Japan was a fascist state in the 1930s has met with strong resistance. In particular, western historians, well versed in the history of the major Fascist movements in Europe, have argued that Japan never possessed some of the main attributes of Fascism, including a charismatic political leader and a one-party state based on a mass movement.[6] Certainly, if one has a political scientist's checklist of what constitutes Fascism, then Japan does not fit the bill, but this does not mean that fascist ideas were entirely absent. For example, the ultra-nationalists in the lower ranks of the army and navy, who engaged in political assassinations in the early 1930s and thus helped to end government by the political parties, displayed an intense hatred both of Communism and capitalism which they saw as corrupting forces. Accordingly, they were prepared to use political violence to stimulate a mood of national crisis, which in turn would pave the way for the creation of a new unifying, militaristic state structure that could overcome class struggle and tame the selfish individualism and profiteering associated with capitalism.[7] There is much in common here with the dynamics that operated in Europe. Moreover, elements within Japan's élite were clearly aware and appreciative of the rise of Fascism in Europe and consciously argued for fascist solutions to be implemented. In particular, this was the case in the economic sphere in which both the IJA and the Ministry of Commerce and Industry argued that a move towards corporatism was necessary if Japan was to construct an autarkic war economy. This desire to shift towards a more overtly fascist form of governance was highly significant because it unleashed damaging battles within the Japanese élite about the future direction of the country, which in turn fuelled the drive for foreign expansion.[8]

The work on Fascism in Japan has been reinforced by various studies of the state's involvement in controlling the general population through the expansion of the police, censorship of the press, sponsorship of reservist associations and military training in schools.[9] It is clear from these studies that Japan possessed a highly militaristic and regimented society, but there is a danger in perpetuating the image of a mindless Japanese mass blindly following its political and military leadership. In contradistinction to this approach, a number of recent studies have built on the lead given by Maruyama by looking more broadly at Japan's crisis of modernisation and the reaction of the people to that phenomenon.[10] Far from the people being led, these works stress that the highly literate Japanese were genuinely enthusiastic about the creation of the state of Manchukuo under Japanese auspices in 1932. Many groups in Japan, including businessmen, intellectuals and the rural population, felt that the acquisition of Manchuria would provide a 'lifeline' for Japan that would lead it out of the depression. This enthusiasm was stimulated by the mass media, including radio, film newsreels, newspapers and journals, which took advantage of a large and appreciative mass market for stories that glorified militarism and outlined the opportunities offered by Japan's 'new frontier'. Thus, the Japanese people were not simply manipulated and used as cannon fodder by the regime, but were themselves deeply involved and complicit in Japan's imperialism. This approach is important not merely for what it says about Manchuria, for the obvious implication is that if the history of the early 1930s can be rewritten in such a radical way, then this might also apply to the immediate origins of the Sino-Japanese and Pacific wars as well.

The work carried out in recent years on Japan in the 1930s therefore, instead of portraying a narrow militaristic clique edging its way into power, presents a much broader analysis of the internal dynamics of the Japanese regime. This in turn allows for a much more searching study into the motivations behind Japanese expansionism. One of the problems with the interpretation provided by the War Crimes Tribunal was that its analysis of Japan's drive for expansion boiled down to the assertion that the 'criminal and militaristic clique' sought power for power's sake. Considering the troubled domestic environment in Japan in the midst of the depression, this was never a wholly convincing explanation. The work on the rise of militarism, ultra-nationalism and Fascism in Japan, however, takes account of the atmosphere of crisis, and makes it clear that the re-emergence of Japanese imperialism in the 1930s had deep roots. However, to state that Japanese imperialism was chiefly due to the difficulties that arose from Japan's attempt to adapt to its rapid modernisation is still to provide a rather abstract and insular interpretation. This factor was clearly important, but it is also vital to see that Japan's desire for greater empire was not just the result of its internal problems, for it was also subject to many external influences as it sought to make sense of a rapidly changing outside world.

Japan and the United States

The study of Japan's external policy in the 1930s has changed as drastically as analysis of its domestic politics. The orthodox interpretation laid down by the Tribunal was that Japan actively sought war in Asia and the Pacific and that its territorial expansion was driven by design rather than opportunity or necessity. With the Americans dominating the war crimes process, moreover, the view was established that the Japanese onslaught against the

United States was the logical culmination of its blueprint for expansion. Thus, the defining event in the history of Japanese aggression was the attack on Pearl Harbor when a cruel and duplicitous Japan attacked the United States without provocation or even the decency to declare war beforehand. In the aftermath of the Tribunal, most historical studies of the origins of the Pacific War therefore concentrated on American–Japanese relations in 1941. This trend was facilitated by the fact that, using the translated Japanese documents gathered for the war crimes trial and the published State Department records, it was possible to construct a history of the ill-fated talks that took place in 1941 between the American secretary of state, Cordell Hull, and the Japanese ambassador in Washington, Kichisaburō Nomura.

The first substantial challenge to the orthodox interpretation came in the late 1950s from Paul Schroeder who suggested that the United States had been too intransigent in the talks with Japan.[11] Schroeder contended that America had allowed an overdeveloped sense of morality to cloud its judgement and failed to appreciate that Japan by mid-1941 was edging away from its commitment to its Tripartite Pact partners, Germany and Italy. Thus, by unnecessarily pressing Japan to choose between withdrawing completely from China or continued economic sanctions, Washington drove Japan into war. The reverberations of this controversial theory have been felt ever since, for by making clear that Japan was forced to choose between peace and war in 1941 it undermined the idea that desire for aggrandisement alone explains its actions.

Building on this basis English-language accounts continued over the next decade or more to concentrate on the foreign policy of these two main protagonists. In particular, influenced by the growing methodological interest in the functioning of institutions, the new histories tended to dwell on the way in which institutional perceptions and rivalries contributed to confused policy-making in both Washington and Tokyo. Again the emphasis was not on Japan forcing war on America, but on the two sides blundering their way towards a cataclysm.[12] Various failings were emphasised, but one common theme was that too many actors outside of the foreign ministries, including amateur diplomats, became involved in the delicate task of negotiating a settlement.[13] For example, one argument was that the State Department had no delusions about Japan, which it sought to restrain through the talks with Nomura and by the measured use of sanctions, and thus when the decision to freeze all Japanese assets in the United States was taken in July 1941, it intended to take a flexible approach that would reward Japan for good behaviour. But this policy was compromised in August 1941 when the Treasury Department adopted an exceptionally tough interpretation of the freeze, which virtually brought trade to an end and led to a *de facto* oil embargo of Japan. The United States thus inadvertently raised the stakes in the Pacific, forcing Japan towards war.[14]

The work on the bilateral relationship between the United States and Japan has therefore become more complex and nuanced over time. However, it can be argued that this concentration upon the American–Japanese relationship was not an altogether healthy development. One problem was that such work ignored the fact that the US–Japan confrontation was only one part of the wider global crisis that Roosevelt had to contend with in 1941. Indeed, as Waldo Heinrichs has argued, the events in the Pacific in 1941 must be placed squarely in the context of a crisis for the United States, in which concern for the future of Europe was the main American interest.[15] American actions in the Pacific were always taken with an eye upon their potentially wider consequences for the European war and in the knowledge that Japan had allied itself to Germany and Italy. The Roosevelt administration's policy therefore must be seen in the light of its desire to prevent Japan from opening a new front in the Tripartite Pact's anti-British war, and that in order to achieve this goal it attempted to use both military deterrence and diplomacy to prevent further Japanese aggression. From this perspective it is possible to argue that President Roosevelt deliberately introduced the oil sanctions in July 1941 in order to deny Japan not merely the ability to advance south, but also to expand northwards. The president was concerned that a Japanese attack on the Soviet Union, when it was already reeling from the German offensive that had begun in June, could cause it to collapse, leaving Britain to face Germany alone. Concern for Russia also explains why Roosevelt was prepared to dismiss any chance of a short-term compromise deal with Japan over Indo-China in November 1941.

A second even more serious problem is that concentration on the Washington–Tokyo axis tells us little about the long-term origins of Japan's path to war, for prior to 1939 the United States arguably did not play a central role in Japanese foreign policy. While it was largely responsible for the decisions reached at the Washington conference of 1921–22, American rhetoric in the 1930s indicated that it was ready to complain about the immorality of Japanese foreign policy, but not to act to defend the Washington system. As a result of its isolationism and policy of disarmament, it did not pose more than a potential threat to Japan until the late 1930s.

Japan and East Asia

In order to understand why Japan trod the path of aggrandisement it is therefore necessary to look elsewhere, namely continental East Asia. As John Garver argues elsewhere in this volume (see Chapter 11), one of the key determinants of Japanese aggression was uncertainty about the future of its closest and most important neighbour, China. From the late nineteenth century China had been so weak as to be little more than the backdrop to international competition in the region, and in the grab for the spoils Japan acquired an empire that encompassed Taiwan, Korea and the Kwantung lease in south Manchuria. However, by the 1920s the rise of Chinese nationalism changed the international system in East Asia by threatening the continued existence of imperial privileges.[16] Britain and the United States reacted to the challenge posed by Chinese nationalism to their interests by deciding that they should work with, rather than resist, the new Nationalist government of Chiang Kai-shek. Japan, however, was not prepared to follow suit, for its vast economic, political and strategic interests in southern Manchuria were not a matter for negotiation. This placed Japan in an isolated and precarious position.

Moreover, another potential threat existed in the region. The success of the Guomindang (GMD) party's nationalist crusade in China in 1926–27, which catapulted Chiang into power, was due in no small part to the role of its Comintern advisers who had provided military, financial and political assistance. In 1927 the GMD broke with the Comintern and the Chinese Communist Party (CCP), but this did little to reduce the impression that the Soviet Union intended to do all in its power to undermine the imperialist powers in East Asia. This impression was strengthened by the end of the 1920s when it appeared that Russia, which until that point had been primarily an ideological threat, was increasing its military strength in Siberia and had an interest in bringing both north Manchuria and Inner Mongolia into its sphere of influence. Thus, by 1931 the Japanese position in Manchuria was threatened by two forces, Chinese nationalism and Soviet expansionism.

It is by combining these external concerns with the social and political tensions that existed within Japan during the depression that one can begin to understand the first Japanese move towards expansion – the Manchurian crisis of 1931–33. For Japan, the seizure of Manchuria not only guaranteed the security of its interests there from external threat, but also opened up a 'new frontier' that it could exploit in order to overcome its economic and social problems. Manchuria was therefore the logical solution to both Japan's imperial and domestic dilemmas.[17] Also implicit in its recourse to aggression was the assumption that Japan alone could provide solutions to its problems and that it now rejected the trend towards internationalism that had influenced its diplomacy in the 1920s. This process quickly became more explicit when China eschewed active resistance to Japanese aggression and turned instead to the League of Nations in the hope that international pressure could curb Japan. Japan's reaction was to dismiss the League's condemnations of its seizure of Manchuria and to withdraw from the organisation in 1933 in a spirit of contempt.[18]

Japan's expansion did not, however, end with its transformation of Manchuria into the puppet state of Manchukuo, for the internal problems created by the depression and the lack of active resistance to its designs encouraged it to contemplate a more radical restructuring of the international politics of East Asia. The difficulty, however, was that Japan was by no means united on what it should try to construct in place of the Washington system, for the IJA and the Foreign Ministry had very different ideas about the future of the region.

In order to understand the IJA's activities it is important to see that its local force in Manchuria, the Kwantung Army, precipitated the crisis in September 1931 in order to turn this area into an economic and military fortress that would pave the way for further expansion.[19] Inherent in its thinking was the view held by many up-and-coming officers in the IJA that the Great War had demonstrated that economic autarky was necessary in order to guarantee victory in any future conflict. For Japan, which was resource poor, this meant that if the country was to survive a future clash with a Great Power or Powers, it required a larger empire that would provide it with a much greater measure of self-sufficiency. This desire for autarky was not just an abstract response to a world where conflict rather than conciliation appeared to be the normal mode of international behaviour, but was in fact squarely aimed at the Soviet Union. As the highly regarded *Taiheiyō sensō e no michi* (The Road to the Pacific War) series produced by Japanese historians in the 1960s has demonstrated, anti-Soviet sentiment was a key driving force in IJA thought.[20] This desire to contain Soviet expansion not only inspired the original aggression in Manchuria, but also in turn led the IJA from 1933 to intervene in north China and Inner Mongolia and most notably from 1935 onwards to sponsor autonomy movements in both these regions. These activities in turn led to heightened tensions with Chiang's government, but the IJA showed little concern for Chinese sensibilities for it believed that the GMD government in Nanjing was weak and untrustworthy.

The IJA's policy had the effect not only of worsening relations with Nanjing even further, but also of destroying the second strand in Japanese thinking, the effort made by the Foreign Ministry under Hirota to construct a new relationship with China. The Foreign Ministry's view in the mid-1930s was that China needed to be weaned away from its reliance on the West and brought into a mutually beneficial relationship with Japan. This would allow for the development of a symbiotic economic relationship between the two countries, in which China would provide Japan with raw materials while the latter sold finished goods to Chinese consumers. In addition, a close relationship would aid in the defence of the region against the expansion of Communism. This policy was symbolised by the Foreign Ministry's announcement of what was tantamount to a Japanese Monroe Doctrine for East Asia in the Amō statement of April 1934. Some

Japanese scholars have recently argued controversially that Hirota's China policy was a positive alternative to the coercive path adopted by the IJA and could have delivered satisfactory results (unfortunately none of this work has been translated into English).[21] It is, however, possible to go too far with such an interpretation, since Hirota was not just outflanked by the IJA over China but proved time and again to be too subservient to its demands.

Japanese policy towards East Asia was thus influenced by a number of considerations, such as the drive for autarky, fear of Communism and the desire to construct a new relationship with China, and became a battleground between the IJA and the Foreign Ministry in which the former predominated. However, to understand how the Sino-Japanese War came about in July 1937, it is necessary to look beyond Japan and study the foreign policies of China and the Soviet Union. In recent years the opening of Chinese records from both Beijing and Taipei and access to the Soviet archives have led to a major historiographical shift, for it is now possible to see how the actions of these two powers helped to bring about the conflict. The material from China has emphasised Nanjing's steady drift away from the policy of non-resistance towards Japan that Chiang had introduced in 1931.[22] Interpretations differ on why non-resistance was abandoned. Some argue that it was worn down by domestic criticism and Nanjing's frustration at Japan's inability to build on Hirota's overtures. Others stress that Chiang always saw non-resistance as nothing more than a temporary expedient, which would be dispensed with once China was more unified and certain of foreign support. Scholars agree, however, that by 1937 Chiang had lost all patience with the Japanese and was prepared to resist any future encroachment. Thus, when the Lugouqiao (Marco Polo Bridge) incident took place outside Beijing in July 1937, the Chinese leader was not prepared to back down, and, as the Japanese were equally intransigent, war was inevitable.

The Soviet archives, along with GMD and CCP material on relations with Russia, provide further clarification of this picture, for they demonstrate that the Soviet Union's deliberate decision in 1935 to encourage and even to sponsor Chinese resistance against Japan was a major factor in destabilising the region.[23] Stalin's policy contained two distinct elements: one was to encourage Chinese resistance at a state to state level by holding out the promise of military aid to Chiang, the other was to bring about the end of the civil war between the GMD and the CCP by calling for a 'united front' to resist 'fascist' Japan. This Soviet intervention in Chinese politics arguably had the effect of dramatically reinforcing the trend towards resistance, particularly by removing the one real brake on Chiang and reversing his strategy of destroying the CCP before turning against the Japanese.

The Soviet role remained important once the Sino-Japanese War began. Desperate to see Japan tied down in Asia, while the European situation steadily grew more threatening, Stalin was happy to provide military aid to the Chinese war effort and by 1938 was the most substantial foreign backer of Chiang's regime. This was extremely unfortunate for the Japanese, for the dominant trend in the IJA immediately before the Lugouzhao incident had been to try to reduce Sino-Japanese tensions so that Japan could concentrate on building up its war economy in preparation for conflict with the Soviet Union.[24] The war in China was therefore not one that Japan sought, but one that was forced upon it, in part due to the activities of the very power that it saw as its greatest enemy. In a sense, at least from 1937 to 1940, the conflict in China can therefore be described as a Soviet-Japanese proxy war.

Japan's continental policy of seeking autarky and containing Communism thus backfired and brought about a series of events that was the very opposite of what it had desired or expected. There was no blueprint in Japan that dictated that it should go to war with China. Indeed the Japanese had sought between 1933 to 1937 to reconcile the Chinese to the existence of Manchukuo and the autonomy of north China, believing that the Nationalist regime was too weak to resist their demands. This proved to be a fatal miscalculation, for Japanese arrogance and Soviet scheming helped to unite China in a way that the GMD had never been able to achieve.

Japan and the Global Crisis

The war in China did not, however, necessarily mean that Japan was set on the course that would lead it to the Pacific War. While the fighting did lead to an increase in tensions with Britain and the United States, these powers showed little wish to defend China and it is therefore debatable whether the war by itself would have led to a western confrontation with Japan. Far more significant is how the Sino-Japanese War became part of the global crisis of the late 1930s.

One of the easily overlooked factors in assessing the course of East Asian international history is that the region's destiny was inextricably linked to that of Europe. Four of the Great Powers, Britain, France, the Soviet Union and the United States, had strategic interests in both continents. Thus, once Japan set out on the road to expansion in Asia, it was inevitably buffeted by, and at the same time sought to take advantage of, events in Europe. One way in which the two regions became linked was that from 1935 onwards, the hostility that Japan and Germany felt towards the Soviet Union led these two states to come together. This relationship was formalised in the signing of the Anti-Comintern Pact in November 1936. However, while Japan initially drifted towards Germany's orbit for anti-Soviet reasons, over time this alignment also proved to be significant in its relations with another potential foe, Great Britain.

The significance of Anglo–Japanese relations in the road to the Pacific War was initially overshadowed in the historiography by the preoccupation of American historians with their own country. From the late 1960s onwards, however, this focus has steadily shifted, for with Britain's introduction of the 30-year rule on the release of government records, a number of scholarly studies have revealed that Anglo–Japanese relations played an important role both in the events of the 1930s and in the immediate origins of the Pacific War.[25]

British policy towards East Asia, like American policy in 1941, aimed chiefly at keeping the region quiet to allow for concentration on the far more sinister threat posed in Europe by Nazi Germany. Japan clearly understood Britain's strategic dilemma and hoped that this European preoccupation would persuade the British government to accept that East Asia should be a Japanese sphere of influence. In addition, it had the expectation that British hostility to the Soviet Union was so strong that it would provide a common bond with Japan and encourage Britain to support a Japanese 'free hand' in East Asia.

Some Japanese historians contend that Britain did indeed supinely accept Japanese predominance and engaged in a policy of appeasement that cannot be distinguished from its counterpart in Europe.[26] The evidence for this is, however, far from persuasive, because while some in Whitehall may have been tempted to appease Japan, strong countervailing forces existed. One major influence on British thinking was its concern that a policy of conciliation towards Japan might alienate the United States, which in turn would jeopardise Britain's chances of receiving American support in Europe. Moreover, it was feared that if Britain showed sympathy towards Japan, the latter might attack the Soviet Union, which would reduce Russia's ability to act as a counterweight to Germany. Another important factor was that British intelligence suggested that Japan could not pose a threat unless war broke out in Europe, for it was seen as a backward military power, which was in any case tied down by its strategic competition with Russia for influence over Northeast Asia.[27] Furthermore, appeasement of Japan risked alienating Chinese opinion at a time when British industry and finance were keen to expand their role in the China market. Thus, while the temptation to appease was always present, in the end Britain adopted the line of neither conciliating nor openly resisting Japan. Britain therefore failed to act as Tokyo had predicted and thus exacerbated Japan's sense of isolation.

Anglo–Japanese relations were also important in another way, for arguably the trade competition within the British Empire between the two powers created further insuperable problems that encouraged Japan to pursue territorial expansion. During the early 1930s Japan recovered from the economic depression quicker than any other power. This recovery was based in part on government measures to stimulate demand through rearmament and public works, but also arose from the competitive devaluation of the yen in 1932, which led to a surge of Japanese exports, particularly of cotton textile goods, into world markets. In particular, Japanese textiles flooded into South and Southeast Asia causing a marked downturn in the sale of goods produced by the European colonial powers. Accordingly, in 1933–34 Britain sought to protect its colonial markets by quotas aimed specifically at Japan.

The effectiveness of these trade barriers is a matter of debate. Some Japanese economic historians interested in the development of intra-Asian trade claim that from a statistical point of view they had little substantial effect, and that in fact Britain was keen to encourage imperial trade with Japan, as this helped to finance colonial administration and debt-servicing.[28] However, from the perspective of how Japan perceived these trade barriers, it is apparent that Tokyo felt aggrieved by the British quotas, which it regarded as an act of discrimination similar to the racist immigration policies that existed within the British Empire and the United States.[29] Moreover, the trade rivalry underlined just how dependent Japan was on imports of raw materials, and thus must have reinforced its desire to achieve economic autarky.

In the 1930s therefore the unsatisfactory nature of Anglo–Japanese relations further exacerbated regional tensions. Indeed, it could also be said that Britain indirectly contributed to the outbreak of the Sino-Japanese War, for its interest from 1935 in sparking a Chinese economic recovery threatened to strengthen the Nanjing government thus undermining Hirota's efforts to force a rapprochement on China.

As noted above, however, the Sino-Japanese War did not necessarily contain the kernel of hostilities between Japan and Britain. What made the difference here was that increasing American assertiveness in 1939 and the disruption of normal trade patterns caused by the start of the war in Europe led Japan to become increasingly concerned about its access to raw materials. An answer to its dilemma came in the summer of 1940 when Britain's apparent weakness following the fall of France provoked Japan into its fateful decision to expand its influence in Southeast Asia. Japan had two motives for this, first to stop the West providing military assistance to China via Burma and Indo-China, and second to achieve autarky by taking control of a region rich in oil, rubber and tin. Japan imagined that the mere threat of force would be enough to bring Britain and the other European colonial powers to heel, and that the Tripartite Pact with Germany and Italy would deter the United States from intervention. Japan thus sought to take advantage of the global crisis to free itself once and for all from its economic insecurity.

Unfortunately this proved to be another of Japan's miscalculations, for Britain refused to be coerced. Instead, believing that the signing of the Tripartite Pact meant that a state of undeclared war already existed with Japan, the Churchill government decided to contain the Japanese menace through the use of trade sanctions and by closer ties with Washington. Indeed, the works on British policy reveal that Whitehall in the autumn and winter of 1940/41 initially took a tougher stance than Washington against Japan and then worked hard to bring Roosevelt into line. Moreover, analysis of British thinking makes it clear that Whitehall had little faith in the American negotiations with Japan and that the primary intention, as far as Britain was concerned, was to neutralise the Japanese threat through the use of sanctions. Underpinning this policy was the belief that Japan, based on its apparently indifferent performance in the China conflict, was still a weak power, which did not possess the strength to take on Britain and the United States. In addition, comments made by American policy-makers to their British counterparts hinted that American thinking was moving along similar lines and that the negotiations existed merely to gain time. This work therefore once again casts doubt on the idea that an understanding was possible in 1941 and that only amateurish diplomacy defeated that objective, instead it stresses the incompatibility of Western and Japanese interests and the inevitability of war.[30]

The work done on the international history of the origins of the Sino-Japanese and Pacific Wars thus presents a far more complex picture than that reached by the Tokyo Tribunal. It is now clear that both of these wars were the result of an extraordinarily complex interplay of relations between the various protagonists, and the claim that Japan engaged in a long-term conspiracy to wage aggressive war no longer holds water. Moreover, the concentration on American–Japanese relations to the virtual exclusion of all else now appears parochial and unconvincing. However, it is worth noting that gaping holes remain in our knowledge of this period. In particular, the influence of pan-Asianism on Japanese expansionism remains unclear. This is a difficult area, for it requires the historian to judge whether the Japanese rhetoric in the 1930s about Asian brotherhood and freeing the continent from European influence was mere propaganda or a sincerely held conviction.[31] Greater clarity is also needed on the links between political and economic developments in the 1930s and in particular how the IJA perceived the trade disputes with the West. Further revisions to the historiography of the origins of the Pacific War can therefore be expected in the future.

Japan and War Responsibility

Japan's path to the Second World War contains both similarities and contrasts with the course followed by its Tripartite Pact partners in Europe.

To a substantial degree it is possible to see Japan as activated by the same political, social and economic concerns as Italy and Germany, for it too was a highly nationalistic and militaristic state that sought redemption through expansion. Indeed, it is possible to argue that although Japan was not fully fascist, it contained strong elements of Fascism in its desire for autarky and corporatism and its ability to engage in mass mobilisation of the population. Moreover, Japan had a vague ideological vision of what it wanted to construct; its goal being to build a 'New Order in East Asia', which would cement its leadership over the region. However, unlike Germany and to a lesser extent Italy, Japan seems to have had little control over its own destiny, for increasingly as the 1930s progressed, it was forced to react to events and did not display the inspired opportunism that one associates with Hitler.

Although the seizure of Manchuria was a deliberate and, so far as the Kwantung Army was concerned, premeditated act, Japan's subsequent advances did not fit into any definite blueprint. Japan's actions clearly helped to provoke the war with China in 1937, but it was not a conflict that it had actively sought, but rather a distraction from the main goal of an attack upon Russia. However, once the Sino-Japanese War began Japan found itself trapped in a conflagration from which it could not escape. Desperate to force a successful conclusion it increasingly drifted into Germany's orbit, hoping that this association would bring about the end of Western assistance to China. Faced with the collapse of the western European colonial powers in 1940, it improvised a policy to become the predominant power in Southeast Asia, but succeeded only in provoking a fateful confrontation with Britain and the United States.

The impression generated by these events is that Japan blundered into its wars due to a mixture of hubris and the misplaced hope that one more victory would confound its enemies and solve all of its problems. Reinforcing this relentless drive forward into uncharted territory was the knowledge that retreat would only exacerbate the internal tensions created by its too rapid modernisation. Rather than a conspiracy to wage aggressive war, therefore, Japanese policy from 1937 constituted a series of disastrous and largely short-term reactions to the waxing and waning of its international position. To state that there was no real design to Japan's aggression, however, is clearly not to exonerate it. The fact that Japan chose to react in the way it did to events in the 1930s was not accidental, for it clearly had a thirst for war and was capable of the most appalling and barbaric acts such as the Nanjing massacre of December 1937. However, in the end the difference between Japan and Germany is that while the former stumbled into the Second World War through its own ineptitude and propensity for favouring military solutions over compromise, the latter willed war on the rest of the world.

Notes

1. For analysis of the tribunal, see R. Minear, *Victor's Justice: The Tokyo War Crimes Trial* (Princeton, 1971); and J. W. Dower, *Embracing Defeat: Japan in the Wake of World War II* (New York, 1999).
2. M. Barnhart, 'The Origins of the Second World War in Asia and the Pacific: Synthesis Impossible?', *Diplomatic History* 20 (1996), 241–60. Another very useful historiographical review is L. Young, 'Japan at War: History-Writing on the Crisis of the 1930s', in G. Martel, ed., *The Origins of the Second World War Reconsidered: A. J. P. Taylor and the Historians* (London, 1999), pp. 155–77.
3. See, for example, S. Large, *Emperor Hirohito and Showa Japan: A Political Biography* (London, 1992).
4. H. Bix, *Hirohito and the Making of Modern Japan* (New York, 2000). See also Dower, *op. cit.*
5. M. Maruyama, *Thought and Behaviour in Modern Japanese Politics* (Oxford, 1963).
6. See, for example, P. Duus and D. Okimoto, 'Fascism and the History of Pre-War Japan: The Failure of a Concept', *Journal of Asian Studies* 39 (1979), 65–76.
7. On the ultra-nationalists see R. Storry, *The Double Patriots: A Study of Japanese Nationalism* (New York, 1957); and B. A. Shillony, *Revolt in Japan: The Young Officers and the February 26, 1936 Incident* (Princeton, 1972).
8. M. Barnhart, *Japan Prepares for Total War: The Search for Economic Security, 1918–1941* (Ithaca, 1987); and W. M. Fletcher, *The Japanese Business Community and National Trade Policy, 1920–1942* (Chapel Hill, 1989).
9. G. Kasza, *The State and the Mass Media in Modern Japan* (Berkeley, 1988); and R. Smethurst, *A Social Basis for Prewar Japanese Militarism: The Army and the Rural Community* (Berkeley, 1974).
10. L. Young, *Japan's Total Empire: Manchuria and the Culture of Wartime Imperialism* (Berkeley, 1998); and S. Wilson, *The Manchurian Crisis and Japanese Society, 1931–33* (London, 2001).
11. P. Schroeder, *The Axis Alliance and Japanese-American Relations, 1941* (Ithaca, 1958).
12. D. Borg and S. Okamoto, eds, *Pearl Harbor as History: Japanese-American Relations, 1931–1941* (New York, 1973).
13. The role of the amateur diplomats the 'John Doe Associates' – is dealt with in R. J. C. Butow, *The John Doe Associates: Backdoor Diplomacy for Peace, 1941* (Stanford, 1974).
14. J. G. Utley, *Going to War with Japan, 1937–1941* (Knoxville, 1985).
15. W. Heinrichs, *Threshold of War: Franklin D. Roosevelt and American Entry into World War II* (New York, 1988).
16. A. Iriye, *After Imperialism: The Search for a New Order in East Asia, 1921–1931* (Cambridge, MA, 1965).
17. See Young, *Japan's Total Empire*.
18. I. H. Nish, *Japan's Struggle with Internationalism: Japan, China and the League of Nations, 1931–33* (London, 1993).

19. S. N. Ogata, *Defiance in Manchuria: The Making of Japanese Foreign Policy, 1931–1932* (Berkeley, 1964); J. B. Crowley, *Japan's Quest for Autonomy: National Security and Foreign Policy, 1930–38* (Princeton, 1966); and M. Peattie, *Ishiwara Kanji and Japan's Confrontation with the West* (Princeton, 1975).

20. The English language volumes, edited by J. W. Morley, are *Japan Erupts: The London Naval Conference and the Manchurian Incident, 1928–1932* (New York, 1984), *The China Quagmire: Japan's Expansion on the Asian Continent, 1933–1941* (New York, 1983), *Deterrent Diplomacy: Japan, Germany and the U.S.S.R., 1935–1941* (New York, 1976), *The Fateful Choice: Japan's Advance into Southeast Asia, 1939–1941* (New York, 1980), and *The Final Confrontation: Japan's Negotiations with the United States, 1941* (New York, 1994).

21. See, for example, T. Inoue, *Kiki no naka no kyocho gaiko: Ni-chu senso ni itaru taigai seisaku no keisei to tenkai*, [Cooperative Diplomacy in a Period of Crisis: The Forming and Development of Foreign Policy in the Period Leading Up to the Sino-Japanese War] (Tokyo, 1994).

22. P. M. Coble, *Facing Japan: Chinese Politics and Japanese Imperialism, 1931–1937* (Cambridge, MA, 1991); and Y.-L. Sun, *China and the Origins of the Pacific War, 1931–1941* (New York, 1993).

23. J. W. Garver, 'The Origins of the Second United Front: The Comintern and the Chinese Communist Party', *China Quarterly* 113 (1988), 29–59; M. Sheng, 'Mao, Stalin and the Formation of the Anti-Japanese United Front, 1935–37', *China Quarterly* 129 (1992), 149–70; and J. Haslam, *The Soviet Union and the Threat from the East, 1933–41* (Basingstoke, 1992).

24. Barnhart, *Japan Prepares for Total War.*

25. The first key texts were C. Thorne, *The Limits of Foreign Policy: The West, the League and the Far Eastern Crisis of 1931–33* (London, 1972); S. Endicott, *Diplomacy and Enterprise: British China Policy 1933–1937* (Manchester, 1975); A. Trotter, *Britain and East Asia, 1933–1937* (Cambridge, 1975); and P. Lowe, *Great Britain and the Origins of the Pacific War: A Study in British Policy in East Asia, 1937–1941* (Oxford, 1977).

26. Two useful reviews of Japanese thinking on Anglo–Japanese relations are S. Akita, 'British Informal Empire in East Asia, 1880s to 1930s: A Japanese Perspective', in R. Dumett, ed., *Gentlemanly Capitalism and British Imperialism: The New Debate on Empire* (London, 1999), pp. 141–56; and Y. Kibata, 'Anglo-Japanese Relations From the Manchurian Incident to Pearl Harbor: Missed Opportunities?', in I. Nish and Y. Kibata, eds, *The History of Anglo-Japanese Relations: The Political and Diplomatic Dimension, Vol. II, 1931–2000* (Basingstoke, 2000), pp. 1–25.

27. A. Best, *British Intelligence and the Japanese Challenge in Asia, 1914–41* (Basingstoke, 2002).

28. K. Sugihara, 'The Economic Motivations Behind Japanese Aggression in the Late 1930s: Perspectives of Freda Utley and Nawa Toichi', *Journal of Contemporary History* 32 (1997), 259–80; and Akita, *op. cit.*

29. A. Best, 'Economic Appeasement or Economic Nationalism?: A Political Perspective on the British Empire, Japan and the Rise of Intra-Asian Trade, 1933–37', *Journal of Imperial and Commonwealth History* 30 (2002), 77–101.

30. A. Best, *Britain, Japan and Pearl Harbor: Avoiding War in East Asia, 1936–41* (London: 1995); and Lowe, *op. cit.*
31. A. Iriye, *Japan and the Wider World: From the Mid-Nineteenth Century to the Present* (London, 1997).

4 Soviet Russia and the Spanish Problem

Jonathan Haslam

Was not the war of 1939–45 avoidable? When historians look at the diplomacy of the 1930s that failed to forestall the outbreak of war in 1939, they tend to ignore core elements of continuity with the 1920s. They deal with the earlier period only for an explanation of Germany's relations with the democracies; Britain, in particular. This makes sense. Hostilities were, after all, started against Poland by Hitler's Germany. And was it not London that declared war on Berlin in September 1939? But when one searches for explanations as to why Hitler was not stopped short of war, it no longer suffices merely to focus on British appeasement of Germany or French weakness, or relations between the powers of western and central Europe, or, indeed, on the causes of American isolationism. Although resolutely and consistently shut out of all serious negotiations by the British government and although militarily incapable of launching an offensive against Germany even before Stalin's terror struck the Red Army, the Soviet Union has also to be taken into account; the nature of its relations with the democracies, as well as with Hitler's Germany. And those relations were forged in the 1920s and their nature was incontestably one of barely suppressed hostility; a peace in name only. Moreover, not only was Moscow still seen on all sides as the citadel of revolution in the 1920s, it was also seen as such well into the 1930s; not least because of the Spanish Civil War. For although the Russians might not have been able alone to counterbalance the might of German arms, the consequences of marginalising them into fearful and hostile isolation cost Europe dearly, as the events that unfolded from August 1939 dramatically attested.

The October Revolution in 1917 brought to power in Russia fanatical revolutionaries bent on the destruction of the entire political and socioeconomic order of the known world. To them capitalism was a system of power harmful to mankind in exploiting the worker through immiseration in the factories and in causing states to expand at one another's expense to the point of war. Already deeply opposed to the First World War, Lenin

and the Bolsheviks had their worst assumptions confirmed when Britain led
a war of intervention to crush them from the summer of 1918. The attempt
failed. But the fledgling Soviet state remained committed through every
means at its disposal – which at that time precluded war, since they could
not afford it – to overthrow the capitalist world order. Communist parties
were established throughout the West and the colonial world, organised
and, where possible, armed from Moscow. (Indeed, Communists from
abroad continued to receive military training in the Soviet Union into the
period of Gorbachev's rule (1985–91).) Tension reached a high point in
July 1926 when the British cabinet briefly weighed the option of declaring
war (they decided the taxpayer would be opposed), the occasion being a
border skirmish that brought the Red Army in hot pursuit over the Oxus
into Afghanistan.[1] None the less in April 1927, as the Russians anticipated,
the Baldwin government broke off diplomatic relations with Moscow and
only the arrival in power of a Labour (minority) government in 1929
restored a semblance of normality. Annoyed at the French Communist
party's (PCF) subversion of the armed forces and Moscow's involvement in
the revolt against French rule in Indochina, France launched a trade
embargo against Russia in 1930. And Britain and France were by no means
alone in their hostility. The United States, then not yet a full participant in
the international system, refused diplomatic recognition to Moscow until
1933, when anxiety about Japanese imperialism at last alerted Washington
to the need for potential allies in the Pacific, however unorthodox.

At the root of continued tension were attempts made by Communist
parties joined at the hip to Moscow to copy the Bolsheviks by seizing power.
In Asia, China was the focal point of unrest: the revolution of 1925–27
jeopardised British trade and investment until London outmanoeuvred the
Communists with timely concessions to the nationalists. In Europe, Germany took centre-stage since it held the balance of power. Indeed, it was the
very strength of the Communist Party of Germany that made Hitler such a
credible figure to the ordinary German from 1929 to 1933. That credibility
had no respect for frontiers. It was bitter memory of Bolshevik behaviour in
the 1920s that encouraged the democratic governments of the West to give
Hitler the benefit of the doubt through the 1930s. The occupation of the
factories by the workers of Paris in June 1936 and the outbreak of the civil
war in Spain the following month served only to encourage such fears.
In London anxiety lest Communists or, indeed, anarchists control the straits
of Gibraltar – the lifeline to empire – overrode any lingering concern for
democratic niceties in a Spain where democracy was threatened by pro-
Fascist generals. Even Winston Churchill, who in the autumn of 1933
astonished the Russian ambassador by declaring that Moscow was no
longer the greatest threat to the British Empire, now supplanted by a
rapacious, Fascist Berlin, instinctively took the side of Generals Mola and
Franco against the Spanish Republic. The most the excitable Russian

ambassador, Ivan Maisky, could do was to persuade a reluctant Churchill into morose silence on the subject in the House of Commons.

If Churchill had changed his mind, there was surely some substance at work. The mere possession of power alters the behaviour of society just as it does the behaviour of the individual. Similarly with loss of power: it is a general law of international relations that the weaker a power, the less its ability to initiate and dominate, therefore the more reactive will be its foreign policy. In this sense a country's foreign policy at a time of relative weakness tells us little about the fundamental identity and values of those who govern it. Only once the state has succeeded in accruing significant economic and therefore also military weight relative to its likely rivals, and has thereby shifted the balance of power decisively to its advantage, is one likely to discover its underlying aims and objectives.

In the case of the Soviet Union under Stalin, for the first period of his rule the country was still painfully building an infrastructure focused almost exclusively on the creation of economic self-sufficiency; a fortress Russia that could withstand any and every threat to its security from the capitalist world. Only in the Far East did the Russians acquire that degree of power sufficiently early – by about 1936 – to deter its most obvious adversary: imperial Japan. Even by 1939 the Soviet Union in Europe still lacked capability enough to seriously deter attack from outside: from Nazi Germany.

The logical result was that, whereas Soviet policy in the Far East very soon bore the obvious hallmarks of intentions and objectives that increasingly reflected the truly expansionist nature of Stalin's power, in Europe from 1932 the configuration of Soviet diplomacy for long took on the characteristics of a much more pragmatic and universalist vision: that of Foreign Commissar Maxim Litvinov. The voice of cool reason and empirical solutions, Litvinov's vision complemented Stalin's desperate need for an effective firebreak against the conflagration threatening from West and East. One firebreak, given Moscow's military weakness, urgently required the cooperation of all hands, which meant other (capitalist) powers. This was the basic ground for Litvinov's preferred policy of collective security against likely German aggression. The problem was that such a policy was predicated on the assumption that other powers would be willing to cooperate and also on the assumption that the rest of the party leadership would be content to let ideological priorities be overridden by claims of national security.

Litvinov worked under Stalin's ultimate control. But Stalin himself, at this stage of the proceedings, with Hitler installed in power (1933), had no direct knowledge of the outside world, no foreign languages and no sustained interest (other than a negative one). Litvinov used to say (at home and not entirely accurately) that Stalin could not be thought of as a great statesman because he 'had never been further than Finland'.[2] Stalin was bent on building up Russia so that he could shift the balance of power in the world to Soviet advantage. But this would take time. As late as July 1940 he could still be heard arguing that 'we must change the old balance of power in Europe, which has acted to the USSR's disadvantage.'[3] He also spent a disproportionate amount of time obsessed with the liquidation of any potential source of domestic opposition to his absolute rule. This also, most certainly from the time of his destruction of the officer corps in June 1937, undermined the country's strength. Stalin, however, delegated a good deal of operational control to others, but simultaneously zealously reserved the right of ultimate decision to himself alone. Since 1918 Litvinov and he had – almost uniquely – shared a deep scepticism about the chances of a Communist revolution working in the West (indeed anywhere other than Russia). This meant that both Stalin and Litvinov consciously accepted a hard-headed realist conduct of international relations which was recognisable to the West. Stalin was therefore willing to allow Litvinov to go in search of any and every improvisation, however unprincipled from a Communist point of view, to assure that Hitler's Germany never became a real menace to the security of his Soviet regime. This held out the promise of rectifying the balance of power through a system of alliances. The crucial assumption behind Litvinov's attempts to build a multilateral system for the containment of Nazi Germany was that the ideological differences of the 1920s could easily be buried because the threat Hitler posed was more immediate and more devastating than anything Communism had previously presented.

The problem was, however, twofold: first, Vyacheslav Molotov, Chairman of the Council of People's Commissars, and others at the summit of the Soviet regime did not share Litvinov's view that revolution was dead or that Hitler posed a threat to the security of Russia. As one old Bolshevik, Mikhailskii, told the American ambassador in 1935: 'You must understand that world revolution is our religion and there is not one of us who would not in the final analysis oppose even Stalin himself if we should feel that he was abandoning the cause of world revolution.'[4] Second, leaders of the democracies similarly did not all share the view that revolution was dead and that Hitler posed a direct threat to their own domains. It was not long before the behaviour of the democracies reinforced the view in Moscow that Litvinov's second assumption, at the very least, was seriously faulty, if not downright naïve as well as deeply heretical.

These differences came to a head with the outbreak of civil war in Spain. Up to that point, Litvinov's attempts at mobilising the democracies had yielded some moderate success. Granted, neighbouring Poland had in January 1934 publicly sided with Germany and against Soviet attempts to build an eastern pact or 'eastern Locarno'[5] with which to contain Nazi expansionism. But dissatisfaction with this diversion towards bourgeois world politics found an oblique while also clear echo in the soothing words of reassurance in the Soviet press:

The Soviet Union backs the Eastern Pact, in so far as it might lead to a strengthening of peace and security, and this is the most important issue for the mass of the people. One can find, and there exist, critics who say: 'How come? The Soviet Union stands for the immutability of frontiers; does this mean it is in favour of the Versailles peace?' ... In signing non-aggression pacts, conventions on the definition of aggression ... with bourgeois states, in fighting alongside bourgeois states for the realization of the Eastern Pact, the Soviet Union entertains no illusions about the class nature of its partners and is perfectly well aware that, should a range of bourgeois states support the USSR's peace initiative, it is not from a love of peace in principle, but from their own class interests, which require the preservation of peace for the time being.[6]

In May 1935 the Russians signed mutual assistance pacts with both France and Czechoslovakia. Although the British had secretly sought to sabotage the Franco-Soviet pact, Hitler's timely occupation of the Rhineland in March 1936 secured immediate ratification in Paris. Yet implementation of the pact still fell at the first hurdle. The French military were utterly unwilling to proceed to staff conversations. Stalin expressed his 'full understanding and approval for the policy of state defence carried out by France with the aim of maintaining its armed forces at a level commensurate with its security needs'.[7] Yet the French Communist party (PCF) leadership continued in obdurate resistance to raising the French defence budget. At the Seventh Congress of the Comintern the wily Palmiro Togliatti defended this apparent dissonance between the position of the Soviet government and that of fraternal parties with the argument that 'identity of purpose does not in fact mean that there must be a coincidence in every action, at every moment and on every question ... .'[8] Indeed, as late as February 1936 the PCF Politburo decided 'to intensify the campaign in favour of disarmament'.[9] And deputy leader Jacques Duclos still argued, even after ratification of the Franco-Soviet pact, that a vote for credits on defence would signify 'the maintenance of imperialist goals'. The PCF would only change its attitude if the government satisfied the conditions demanded.[10] In addition, as in 1892–93 the French resolutely held out against any mutual assistance agreement that encompassed the Far East, even though, or should one rather say because, this was the most likely direction from which the Soviet Union would be attacked (by imperial Japan). Moreover, with mistrust of the Bolsheviks never far from their minds, Czech leaders refused to allow the Russians to aid them against attack unless and until the French came in first. Looked at positively, the pacts with France and Czechoslovakia were a step in the right direction and a means of circumscribing German freedom of manoeuvre. However, these gaping holes in the wall were depressingly symptomatic of the strong continuity between the 1920s and the 1930s, and only confirmed to Hitler that differences thus exposed could be exploited. What civil war in Spain did was to expose the existing abyss between Moscow and the democracies. It did not create it.

The last thing Stalin needed, in attempting to build an international coalition of like-minded states against Germany, was the emergence of revolution in western Europe, particularly one that failed, which would only serve to legitimise Hitler's calls for solidarity against the common Communist menace. It was not that Stalin was against revolution as such, merely untimely revolutions dictated by the interests of the Comintern's member parties jeopardising Russian national interests. The Spanish Communist party (PCE), though small (only 50,348 members in January 1936),[11] still reflected its anarcho-syndicalist origins, and anarcho-syndicalism was still the strongest force on the revolutionary left in Spain. It was, moreover, hopelessly out of its depth. After the general elections in February 1936, a middle-class coalition took power under Azaña which promised little in the way of radical reform for the working class. Moscow acknowledged that it was 'not a government of the popular front but a bourgeois government of the left'. 'However,' the instructions proceeded, 'in spite of the fact that it is not a popular front government we consider that you should support the AZANA Government against attacks and possible *coups d'état* from reactionaries, so that it may carry out the electoral programme of the popular front.'[12] But, responding to conditions on the ground and the ever-demanding need to compete for influence among the working class with the more radical anarcho-syndicalists, the PCE will only have alarmed the Russians with a report in early March to the effect that the 'revolutionary position is developing rapidly. The solution of the land-problem by revolutionary methods will not be long in establishing itself with the development of the struggle, and the problem of power.'[13]

The gloomy state of mind in Moscow contrasted sharply with the rising enthusiasm of the Spanish comrades. Only five days after the wildly optimistic telegram from Madrid, the Russians expressed themselves 'much alarmed because deeds are being perpetrated which are helping the cause of the anti-revolutionists, such as frequent clashes between the masses and the armed forces of the Government ... .' This included action by the left socialists, the Trotskyists and the anarchists. 'Do not on any account let yourselves be provoked,' Moscow warned, 'do not precipitate events, as it would be harmful to the revolution at this moment and would only lead to the triumph of the anti-revolutionaries.' The Russians favoured land redistribution by the Azaña Government, but emphasised that 'the creation of Soviet power is not in the order of the day'.[14] The Russians wanted the party instead to stress their anti-Fascist mission and in a subsequent instruction in mid-June also urged it to convince the women of Spain that the party was not anti-Catholic.[15]

Sure enough, the premature revolutionism of the extreme left prompted a decisive riposte from the extreme right. One of the factors that precipitated the *coup* was the assassination of Calvo Sotelo. Following the assassination, Moscow saw the political situation as 'very critical'. 'At the moment,' the Russians counselled, 'the danger comes from the anarchist leaders who persist in prolonging the strikes with the idea of bringing the workers face to face with the Government.'[16] Moscow's initial response to 'the Fascist conspiracy' was to advise a strategy that corresponded to Lenin's during the Kornilov revolt in August 1917: 'To do now what you have omitted to do before, due to lack of firmness on the part of your allies in the Popular Front, that is to say, taking full and immediate advantage of the present alarming situation, create, in conjunction with the other parties of the Popular Front, alliances of workers and peasants, elected as mass organisations, to fight against the conspirators in defence of the workers' and peasants' militia.'[17] But the Russians had no diplomatic representation in Spain; not even a press office. Two days later they were complaining of being uninformed. Soon they discovered that the PCE on the spot was even more badly informed than themselves. On 20 July the PCE, in a macabre misrepresentation of a cruel reality, grandly announced that the 'military insurrection was crushed. In a few parts of the country the struggle is still developing, but there is nothing definite. The fight was fierce and to the death. It was the workers' militia that decided the victory ....'[18] A few hours later this bizarre message sent by PCE secretary José Díaz was followed by another, sent by the Comintern representative, which completely blew apart the nonsense that preceded it. 'The development of the fight shows that the insurgents have a complete military plan and a majority in the army. The situation continues to be difficult.' The rebels were reported to hold Morocco, the Canaries, Seville, Cordoba, Valladolid, Navarre and the like. The main target was Madrid.[19] Moscow countered with advice to form a committee in defence of the Republic in case the government wobbled.[20] They followed this with the admonition: 'You must listen to us every three hours.'[21] 'We are listening all the time,' the PCE retorted.[22]

Díaz continued in his dream world. On the day following this inordinate traffic, monitored and decrypted in London, he sent another despatch, 'convinced that we shall crush the enemy decisively, and that this will be the first step in the realisation of the revolutionary democratic programme'. And in a sentence that in retrospect reads ominously, he declared that if the anarchists remained problematic, 'revolutionary law will be applied'.[23] The next day he suggested that he would soon be asked to join the government, and the day after he again solemnly reassured Moscow that 'The fascist insurrection is definitely crumbling.'[24] In the circumstances the Russians remained remarkably self-possessed – largely, it would seem, because they remained ignorant of the realities on the ground. The Comintern secretariat advised Díaz: 'You must not allow yourselves to be carried away by the

initial successes. Your adversaries may prolong the civil war.'[25] Frustration
began to show through before long, however. On 24 July Díaz was repri-
manded: 'Your information is insufficient; it is not concrete but sentimental.
Once again we ask you to send us serious and effective news.'[26] He was also
told to stick to the defence of the Republic and not to raise a popular militia.
The only radical measure they could pursue with the government was
to demand confiscation of the lands of the rebels and its distribution to
the peasants.[27]

The dire prospects that awaited the Republic began to occur to the
Russians only on 25 July when it became apparent that the Spanish regime
did not now have an effective general staff.[28] Clearly with little confidence
in the PCE, the Russians immediately made contact with Jacques Duclos in
Paris, second in command of the PCF which had, in an unprecedented
breach of Communist discipline, in September 1934 originated the Popular
Front strategy in its widest form – opening to bourgeois as well as socialist
parties. A telegram from Moscow which sounded the alarm called on
the PCF to help the Spanish combatants materially, 'for the defeat of the
Spanish Republic would mean the defeat of the Popular Front in France'.[29]
It went without saying that the defeat of the French Popular Front would
mean the collapse of the Franco-Soviet alliance and an end to the Soviet
bridgehead in western Europe. Nazi Germany was now aiding the rebels
in Spain, so the PCF heard from Moscow on 31 July.[30] This was disastrous
news because the Popular Front regime in France, under pressure from
London, had declared its neutrality and would therefore not supply
weapons. The PCF had sent a mission to Madrid to assess the state of
affairs. 'Gilbert' reported on 7 August that 'Situation very critical because
of non-availability of armaments. The Spanish ambassador confirms situation difficult due to lack of armaments.'[31] The Soviet solution was to
pressure the French Government to act. In a telegram to Maurice Thorez,
secretary of the PCF, that very day the Russians demanded: 'There must be
no hesitation even for a minute in giving real assistance. We insist on urgent
measures on your part. We immediately await news of what has concretely
been done.'[32] 'Prolongation of the civil war is dangerous for the success of
the popular front,' Moscow judged.[33]

It was only when aid from the PCF proved obviously inadequate that the
Russians were driven to provide it on their own account, which meant
surmounting immense logistical difficulties and defying the British and
French governments simultaneously. The first shipment arrived in Cartagena
on 15 October, and although the Russians, like the Germans and Italians,
officially participated in a non-intervention agreement dreamed up by the
British, the war in Spain came to represent a surrogate war between Moscow
and Berlin. The aid, which included sizeable numbers of Soviet officers as
'advisers', was sufficient to save Madrid from collapse but ultimately
incapable of compensating for the deep divisions that had opened up within

the left and between the left and a more conservative population. As Soviet assistance became, inevitably, more overt, the gap between Moscow on the one hand and Paris and London on the other expanded towards an abyss. As tension grew in Spain, the French nervously reached out to patch up relations with the Germans, and as Soviet isolation became ever more apparent, signs appeared that the Russians, too, might drift in the same direction.[34] Even Litvinov pointed out in public that 'Our security does not depend on bourgeois documents and on foreign policy combinations. The Soviet Union is sufficiently strong on its own.'[35] *Pravda*, quoting an obscure foreign source, raised the question: 'How long can and will the Soviet Union act in isolation in the capacity of defender of international order in the West?'[36] In hindsight it is easy to see where all this would lead.

But much hinged on the quality of statesmanship in the democratic West. The great misfortune was that a man of judgement in international relations like Winston Churchill had proved himself dangerously reckless as a minister of war, hopeless at economics as chancellor of the exchequer and naïvely romantic in defending continued possession of India as a believer in the integrity of empire. Instead, the Conservative party had, at least its inner circle, chosen the inexperienced Neville Chamberlain to lead the country at a time when experience in foreign affairs counted for everything. In stark contrast to Churchill, Chamberlain saw no reason to suppress the bitter memories of Soviet attempts to wreck the British Empire and civil peace in the 1920s. He remained fiercely anti-Bolshevik; everything else came second, including Nazi Germany. When, succeeding in Spain, Hitler turned on Czechoslovakia, Chamberlain's response was to press the Czechs to give way. Beset with the complications of defending an empire threatened on all sides (except from Russia), Chamberlain saw all the weakness of his own position and all the potential of Germany (Churchill tended to the reverse). Characteristically, Chamberlain saw an analogy between Hitler's demands in south-eastern Europe and adjustments in the British imperial position. 'I don't see why we shouldn't say to Germany give us satisfactory assurances that you won't use force to deal with the Austrians and Czecho-Slovakians and we'll give you similar assurances that we won't use force to prevent the changes you want if you can get them by peaceful means ... for the Germans want much the same things for the *Sudetendeutsche* [the German minority in western Czechoslovakia] as we did for the Uitlanders in the Transvaal.'[37]

In these circumstances it is a wonder that Stalin did not ditch Litvinov earlier than he did, but he really had little choice in that Berlin offered no opening to the Russians. Moreover, and not without encouragement from the wily Ambassador Maisky in London, Stalin's longstanding respect for Churchill and his understanding of Churchill's wish for an alliance with the Soviet Union gave him cause to pause and wait for Chamberlain's downfall. 'In evaluating Churchill's political line,' Maisky advised, 'one must bear in mind that his point of departure is defence of the integrity of the British Empire and that now the main danger to the latter he sees as Germany. Churchill is extremely Germanophobe by nature, and he is prepared to subordinate everything to the goal of fighting Germany.'[38] As the American ambassador recalled: 'He stated that in his opinion Chamberlain did not represent the English people and that he would probably fail because the Fascist dictators would drive too hard a bargain.'[39] This did not, of course, happen until it was far too late. The Munich settlement gave Hitler what he demanded and was only possible by cutting the Russians out.[40] British motivations are not in doubt. Lord Home relates: 'One of Neville Chamberlain's motives – and I was with him at the time of Munich – in trying to dissuade Hitler from war and in doing so risk slipping over the edge of reconciliation into the pit of appeasement, was that he felt certain in his mind that if Europe weakened itself in another war, Russia would try to dominate the continent of Europe.'[41] Although Litvinov continued as Commissar, he was on borrowed time, increasingly shut out of Stalin's presence and deprived of intelligence material. He was dismissed within months, and although he formally took charge of international information for the party, he was effectively consigned to the political dustbin. He was permitted to live on in relative peace, though dismissed from the Central Committee in February 1941 after delivering a devastating critique of the direction foreign policy had taken since his removal from office.

After so many years of isolation, the Russians always had particular difficulty seeing themselves from the vantage-point of others. When the British and French reacted negatively to Soviet efforts in Spain and then again to Russian attempts to bolster Czech resistance against Nazi pressures, the Russians were puzzled. At the time of Munich, Chamberlain had remonstrated with the lord privy seal for approaching the Russians, warning of the dangers of allowing the Red Army into central Europe, with all the consequences of opening up the continent to Bolshevism.[42] But the fear of Communist revolution expanding across Europe on the back of an internecine war was not confined to the Great Powers. The Social Democrats ruling Czechoslovakia were also equally worried, as the Czech leader Beneš patiently explained to the bewildered Soviet ambassador:

He [Beneš] expresses surprise when people say that they do not understand the wavering and hesitation of England and France, for example, on the Spanish question, in respect of aid to Czechoslovakia etc. The secret is simple. Europe knows what were the consequences of world war in 1914–18 even for the victors. Another such war would mean arming many millions among the masses. The experience of the Russian revolution, the collapse of Austria-Hungary, the German revolution, social turbulence in victorious countries were already lesson enough. But at that time there did not yet exist such a 'hostile' institution as the Comintern. Not only does it now exist, but it has issued the slogan that imperialist war must be turned into civil war, turning weapons received into their hands against their own bourgeoisie. Who now has any inclination to be drawn into a world war?![43]

When the hapless Spanish refugees washed up on the shores of the Soviet Union in mid-April 1939, they were met by Manuilsky, long a leading light in the Comintern, who briefed them on the international situation. He assured them that 'for the world war that was now inevitable, the USSR needed to gain time and our long resistance had made this easier ....'[44] Litvinov's forward position of the previous five years was dead and buried. This reserve did not, however, preclude renewed openings to Berlin. The now much commented conversation between Soviet ambassador Merekalov and State Secretary Weizsäcker on 17 April typically began with matters of trade and drifted on to meatier, general matters of international relations. It was Weizsäcker who – at least, in the Soviet record – suggested they extend the discussion, which instantly focused on German negotiations with Poland for the reacquisition of the port of Danzig and the creation of a corridor through what was once east Prussia, but was now part of Polish territory. What Weizsäcker had noticed was that Soviet press coverage of recent events was more cautious than that in Britain and the United States. But nothing concrete was on offer except in the field of trade.[45] Meanwhile, in Moscow later that month Maisky witnessed the deterioration in Litvinov's standing at first hand. 'The atmosphere was about as tense as it could get. Although outwardly Stalin appeared at peace, puffing at his pipe, I felt that he was extremely ill disposed towards Litvinov. And Molotov became violent, colliding with Litvinov incessantly, accusing him of every kind of mortal sin.'[46] A decisive shift in attitude was signalled when, a matter of days later, on 3 May 1939 a telegram from Stalin to leading Soviet diplomats announced that 'As a result of a serious conflict between chairman of the Council of People's Commissars comrade Molotov and People's Commissar for Foreign Affairs comrade Litvinov, arising from Litvinov's disloyal attitude to the Council of People's Commissars, comrade Litvinov has turned to the Central Committee [Politburo] with the request that he be freed from the obligations of the Commissariat of Foreign Affairs.' The Politburo had agreed to the request. Molotov was now in charge of the Commissariat.[47]

In place, Molotov took a tougher line in every direction, *inter alia* making Germany's attempts to improve trade dependent on an improvement in political relations, as Weizsäcker noted in conversation with Soviet *Chargé d'Affaires* Astakhov at the end of that month.[48] This prompted no immediate flexibility from Berlin. On 17 June, however, German ambassador Schulenburg visiting Astakhov in Berlin responded with the comment that Germany also recognised the interconnection between the two. The Germans were ready for far-reaching conversations. He had this from Ribbentrop, who fully reflected Hitler's views.[49] And between 17 and 19 June Soviet agent Kleist at the German embassy in Warsaw told the Russians that Hitler was said to have told Ribbentrop that Berlin required a rapprochement with Moscow in order to settle the Polish question and for two years in order to resolve problems in western Europe.[50] When Deputy Commissar Potemkin saw Schulenburg on 1 July, a further carrot was dangled before Soviet eyes – German assistance in improving Moscow's relations with Tokyo (which were at their nadir) to the point of friendly and cooperative relations.[51] Hints from Berlin began to become more pointed, as when the deputy head of the press department at the Ausamt pointed out that the Brest peace between Germany and Russia in 1918 was more favourable than the Versailles Treaty which followed in 1919. The Soviet press attaché Smirnov protested that there was scarcely anything to be said in favour of the Brest peace, to which von Stumm responded: 'but I have only the frontier in mind, and according to Brest the USSR's frontiers ran further to the West than the existing frontiers'.[52] At a crucial conversation that dispensed with all prior pretence, on 2 August Ribbentrop insisted to Astakhov that the two sides could come to terms on all territorial matters from the Baltic to the Black Sea. Bluntly, he asserted that 'Danzig will be ours' and there would be no great delay in resolving this question. 'We do not take Poland's armed forces seriously,' he added. 'For us a military campaign against Poland is a matter of a week, ten days.' Of course, he hoped this would not be necessary. Before going into any details, he had no knowledge whether the Soviet government was prepared to enter into talks.[53]

'We would have preferred an agreement with the so-called democratic countries,' Stalin told Dimitrov early in September, 'and therefore we conducted negotiations. But the English and French wanted to have us as hired hands; besides which they would pay us nothing! We, of course, would not become hired hands, even less so receiving nothing.'[54] Against this needs to be set Stalin's effusive remarks to Ribbentrop to the effect that he had always preferred Germany to Britain.[55] The fact was that Stalin liked neither. The question was who could offer what the Soviet government required. After Ribbentrop's offer of negotiations to Astakhov, the Russians sat on their hands, waiting for the long-delayed Anglo-French delegation. But four days before the delegation turned up in Moscow Stalin received word that the Germans would be in a condition to take military action any day after 25 August. The very day the delegation arrived with insufficient powers to negotiate an alliance, Stalin summoned a Politburo meeting which decided on opening talks with Berlin on the issues Ribbentrop had raised.[56] The ludicrously unserious military mission sent by London under Admiral, the Honourable Sir Reginald Plunkett Ernle-Erle-Drax, which arrived in Moscow after a leisurely six-day journey was scarcely sufficient reassurance to the Soviet leadership that, should the Germans move East, they would not have tacit British acquiescence. Poland might have a unilateral guarantee of security from Britain; the Baltic states did not. But Czechoslovakia had also had a British guarantee which, when broken, led merely to an unseemly washing of hands in London. A member of the American embassy commented: 'Members of the British embassy were appalled by this low-level delegation. It should have been headed by the French and British foreign ministers to demonstrate Paris's and London's seriousness about making a deal. The half-hearted British-French approach had the mark of failure on it right from the beginning.'[57] Despite French anxieties, the British wrote the script. As a consequence they came with no remit to sign a pact. The Russians understood that not only could Paris and London not guarantee Polish cooperation with Moscow against Berlin, but that between Britain and Poland the 'close politico-military alliance, mutual trust and massive financial support of England exist only on newspaper and not even on ministerial paper.'[58] And would not Chamberlain attempt to weasel out of the obligation given in return for a second Munich? In London Chamberlain was conducting secret negotiations with Göring and Hitler 'through a neutral intermediary'.[59] And on 21 August Lord Halifax, the foreign secretary, approved a letter to Hitler to persuade him into a peaceful settlement on Poland. The head of MI6 told Halifax and Chamberlain 'that he has received an approach suggesting that Göring should come over to London if he can be assured that he will be able to see the Prime Minister. It was decided,' Halifax noted, 'to send an affirmative answer to this curious suggestion, and arrangements were accordingly set in hand for Göring to come over secretly on Wednesday, the 23rd. The idea is that he should land at some deserted aerodrome, be picked up in a car and taken direct to Chequers.'[60] Stalin beat Chamberlain to it, and the non-aggression pact with Germany and its secret protocol dividing eastern Europe was signed in the early hours of 24 August, Moscow time.

A member of the Soviet embassy in Berlin explained the reasons to an American counterpart as 'based on the Soviet mistrust lest the present British Government be preparing to arrange a second Munich at Poland's expense, the British concessions to Japan, the Anglo-French refusal to promise more than consultations in the event of war, and the refusal on the part of the military authorities of both England and France to give full information to Russia'.[61] The British, normally so pragmatic but, under Chamberlain, in the grip of their own fatal prejudices, took ideological matters so seriously that it prompted them to rule out entirely any possibility of a Soviet-German rapprochement on the grounds that the deep abyss in *Weltanschauung* between Moscow and Berlin was unbridgeable: a fatal misjudgement of monumental proportions, with disastrous consequences for Britain's security. Chamberlain had resisted to the utmost an alliance with the Soviet Union because he did not wish to facilitate what

Stalin most demanded; a rectification of the balance of power in Europe to
Russian (and therefore Bolshevik) advantage. Even after London and
Moscow became allies – as a result of the invasion of 22 June 1941 – this
underlying problem remained and resurfaced in the diplomacy of war with
incalculable consequences for the peace that followed.

Notes

1. The idea of war was proposed by the secretary of state for India, Lord
   Birkenhead: Public Record Office, Kew, Committee of Imperial Defence
   (hereafter PRO, CID, etc.), 22 July 1926. See also the note in the papers of the
   foreign secretary, Austin Chamberlain, PRO FO800/259.
2. Quoted in J. Carswell, *The Exile: A Life of Ivy Litvinov* (London, 1983),
   footnote, p. 148. Carswell's book was based on extensive conversations with
   Litvinov's assertive and outspoken widow.
3. *Dokumenty Vneshnei Politiki*, Vol. 23, Part 1 (Moscow, 1995), Doc. 240,
   memorandum of a conversation with British ambassador Stafford Cripps,
   1 July 1940.
4. J. Haslam, 'Political Opposition to Stalin and the Origins of the Terror in
   Russia, 1932–36', *Historical Journal* 29 (1986), 412.
5. The model was the Locarno Pact of December 1925, which provided for a
   multilateral system of interrelated security guarantees for Germany, France
   and Belgium underwritten by Britain.
6. *Dokumenty Vneshnei Politiki*, Vol. 23, Part 1 (Moscow, 1995), p. 410.
7. *Pravda*, 16 May 1935.
8. J. Haslam, 'The Comintern and the Origins of the Popular Front, 1934–1935',
   Historical Journal 22 (1979), 690.
9. Politburo PCF, Procès-verbal, 6 February 1936, *Cahiers du Bolchévisme*,
   Nos. 3–4, 15 February 1936, p. 226.
10. J. Duclos, 'Réponses aux questions posées par les journalistes, à la Mutualité',
    Cahiers du Bolchévisme, Nos. 8–9, 15 May 1936, p. 496.
11. If anything, this is probably an overstatement: PRO, HW17/26 (British
    decrypts of intercepted communications between the Comintern and member
    parties), PCE to Moscow, 31 January 1936.
12. Ibid., Moscow to PCE, 26 February 1936. A follow-up telegram then omitted
    the first statement referring to the government as 'a bourgeois government of
    the left'.
13. Ibid., PCE to Moscow, 4 March 1936.
14. Ibid., Moscow to the PCE, 9 April 1936.
15. Ibid., Moscow to the PCE, 15 June 1936.
16. Ibid., HW17/27, Moscow to the PCE, 13 July 1936.
17. Ibid., Moscow to the PCE, 17 July 1936.
18. Ibid., PCE to Moscow, 20 July 1936.
19. Ibid., PCE to Moscow, 20 July 1936.
20. Ibid., Moscow to PCE, 20 July 1936.

21. Ibid., Moscow to PCE, 20 July 1936.
22. Ibid., PCE to Moscow, 20 July 1936.
23. Ibid., PCE to Moscow, 21 July 1936.
24. Ibid., PCE to Moscow, 21 July 1936.
25. Ibid., Moscow to PCE, 23 July 1936.
26. Ibid., Moscow to PCE, 24 July 1936.
27. Ibid., Moscow to PCE, 28 July 1936.
28. Ibid., Moscow to PCE, 25 July 1936.
29. Ibid., HW17/14, Moscow to Paris (in French), 29 July 1936.
30. Ibid., Moscow to Paris, 31 July 1936.
31. Ibid., PCF to Moscow, 7 August 1936.
32. Ibid., Moscow to PCF, 7 August 1936.
33. Ibid., Moscow to PCF, 8 August 1936.
34. For details, see J. Haslam, *The Soviet Union and the Struggle for Collective Security in Europe, 1933–39* (London, 1984), pp. 121–2.
35. Ibid., p. 122.
36. Ibid., p. 125.
37. Ibid., p. 166.
38. Ibid., p. 169.
39. Ibid., p. 168.
40. Ibid., pp. 176–94. I have seen nothing to alter the conclusions I reached on this in 1984. And it is revealing that those who argue in an entirely different direction fail even to refer to this account or deal with the evidence it presents.
41. Lord Home, lecturing at the University of Leeds on the 200th anniversary of the foundation of the Foreign Office, 3 November 1982.
42. Haslam, *The Soviet Union and the Struggle*, p. 188.
43. *Arkhiv vneshnei politiki SSSR* (Moscow), fond 230, delo 3 (173), papka 115, diary of Alexandrovsky during his posting in Bucharest, 26 April 1938.
44. M. Tagueña Lacorte, *Testimonio de dos guerras* (Mexico, 1973), p. 337.
45. *Dokumenty Vneshnei Politiki, 1939 god* (hereafter *DVP*), Vol. I (Moscow, 1992), Doc. 236, Astakhov's record of the conversation, 17 April 1939.
46. Haslam, *The Soviet Union and the Threat from the East, 1933–41* (London, 1992), p. 129.
47. *DVP*, doc. 269.
48. Ibid., doc. 342, Astakhov (Berlin) to Moscow, 30 May 1939.
49. Ibid., doc. 378, Astakhov's record of his conversation, 17 June 1939.
50. From the archives of the former KGB: ibid., Vol. II (Moscow, 1992), p. 559 n. 136.
51. Ibid., Vol. I, doc. 402, Potemkin's record of the conversation, 1 July 1939.
52. Ibid., doc. 442, Smirnov's diary, 31 July 1939.
53. Ibid., doc. 445, Astakhov's record of the conversation, 2 August 1939.
54. Dimitrov's record of the conversation, 7 September 1939: *Pravda*, 24 December 1989.
55. Quoted at length from the private papers of Schulenburg: *DVP*, Vol. II, pp. 609–10.
56. Information unearthed by the Commission on the Soviet-German non-aggression pact: *Pravda*, 24 December 1989.
57. Haslam, *The Soviet Union and the Struggle*, p. 225.

58. Assessment by Sharonov, ambassador to Warsaw: *DVP*, doc. 489, Sharonov (Warsaw) to Molotov (Moscow), 23 August 1939.
59. Chamberlain's words, in Haslam, *The Soviet Union and the Struggle*, p. 227.
60. Ibid.
61. Sumner Welles to Roosevelt, 23 August 1939: *Franklin D. Roosevelt and Foreign Affairs,* 2nd series, January 1937–August 1939, Vol. 16 (New York, no date) p. 2004.

5 France

Peter Jackson

The fall of France in June 1940 brought the end of its status as an undisputed Great Power. The international system that emerged in the aftermath of the Second World War was vastly changed as the great European empires were progressively dismantled and France, Britain and Germany were relegated to the status of middle-ranking powers. These events have cast a long shadow over historical interpretations of French foreign policy between the wars. The traditional view has tended to understand this policy within a larger narrative of decline and fall. According to this approach, the leadership and institutions of the French Third Republic were in the terminal phase of a long decline. Thus France's failure to respond to the German remilitarisation of the Rhineland in 1936, its unwillingness to intervene in the Spanish Civil War, and its refusal to stand up to Hitler during the crises of 1938, were all the short-sighted policies of a 'decadent' nation on the verge of collapse.[1] More recently, a number of historians have challenged this approach. They have placed greater emphasis upon the extraordinarily difficult political, economic and strategic position that confronted France in the 1930s and constrained its freedom of action. In the circumstances, they argue, French national leaders responded with reasonable policies.[2]

The central argument in this chapter develops the revisionist analysis by emphasising the central role of ideas, perceptions and policy-making culture in the shaping of French foreign policy. On another level, French foreign policy was influenced by the character of the international system after 1918. But contested notions of France's national and international identity also conditioned policy choices, as did the specific character of French political and diplomatic culture. Historians have tended either to ignore these non-material or ideational determinants to policy-making or to interpret them within the rigid conceptual framework of 'decadence'. I will argue that policy culture and constructions of French identity conditioned the way material considerations such as the balance of power were interpreted by decision-makers. They should therefore be considered in their own right as important sources of French foreign policy before the Second World War.

The following pages will first outline the key sources of French foreign policy, then analyse their role during the three distinct phases of policy in the pre-war decade. During the first two phases, lasting until 1938, French political responses to the international situation were shaped by the strength of a pacifist identity for France, by debates over its political identity and by the Foreign Ministry's strong cultural tendencies toward legalism and multilateralism. The result was a steady retreat before the Axis challenge. During the third phase France's pacifist identity was displaced by an opposing image of France as a European Great Power and defender of civilisation. This contributed crucially to the emergence of a more confident and resolute mood among policy-makers and the general population. Along with important improvements in the material situation in France, it contributed to the more optimistic assessments of the strategic situation and underpinned the decision to challenge Germany's bid for hegemony in 1939.

Determinants of French Foreign Policy

A familiar analytical model for students of international history is one that distinguishes between the role of internal and external factors in shaping policy-making. Such a distinction remains very useful, but it is also helpful to make further distinctions between material and non-material determinants to foreign policy.[3] Material factors are typically those elements that can be translated into military and economic strength. They include a state's geography, the size of its population, the wealth generated by its economy, and the industrial and technological base vital to waging modern war. The study of the distribution of material strength among states, usually understood as the balance of power, has long occupied a central place in the study of international relations. But material factors are interpreted by decision-makers who operate in specific psychological, ideological and cultural contexts. 'Ideational' factors such as these are more difficult to pin down and to analyse. They cannot be ignored, however, because they constitute the perceptual lens through which policy-makers interpret the world. During the 1930s contending visions of 'the identity of France' combined with French policy-making culture to give foreign policy its distinctive character.

The International System

French foreign policy was influenced by both the structure of the post-1919 international system as well as the character of international politics between the wars. The structure of the European political system was determined by geography and by the distribution of power. Its most important feature from the French perspective was the continued presence of 65 million Germans in a well-organised, modern industrial society at the heart of Europe. After the Treaty of Versailles, Germany largely retained the industrial and demographic strength that had permitted it to sustain a total war for more than four years against the combined might of France, Britain, Russia and eventually the United States. It thus continued to pose a potentially mortal threat to France's continued existence as a Great Power. Also important was the fact that the Imperial Russian and Hapsburg empires had disappeared after the war. In their place a number of successor states had emerged in East-Central Europe from Poland and the Baltic states in the north to Yugoslavia in the south. France acted as a patron to these young states in the hope that they could replace Czarist Russia as an eastern counterweight to German power and a barrier to the spread of Communism over Europe.

As already suggested, French foreign policy was influenced by the character of international relations after 1918. To be viable an international system must be based on shared expectations and understandings among its constituent states. Generally agreed norms of state behaviour provide the necessary common ground for relations between the states. Two such norms shaped international politics after 1919. The first was the expectation that states would not resort to violence in pursuit of their national interests. Second, political leaders were expected to abide by international law and participate in a multinational collective security regime that would serve as the basis of a peaceful international order. These expectations were greatly strengthened by transnational movements for pacifism and disarmament, which held tremendous appeal for a European population that had lived through the unparalleled destruction of the Great War. Another key feature of inter-war international politics was the impact of another transnational political phenomenon: Soviet-sponsored revolutionary Communism. In 1919 the Soviet government established the Communist International as a means of spreading the worker's revolution. Through the 'Comintern', Moscow exercised important influence over Communist parties abroad. The Soviet Union thus acquired political constituencies inside virtually every state in western Europe. Ideology was a more prominent feature in the international system than it had been at any time since the late eighteenth century.

In short, until 1933 the international system was based on a range of rules and norms to which French decision-makers felt compelled to adapt in the interests of preserving the system and thus the *status quo* in Europe. The normative standards of the new international order in any case made it all but impossible for France to obtain solid security guarantees from its erstwhile allies Britain and the United States. Military alliances were anathema in the new international environment. A powerful current of opinion in Britain believed that the country had been dragged into war by secret staff conversations with the French before 1914. Britain steadfastly

refused to enter into any similar arrangements until the very eve of war.
After 1919 the United States adopted a position of political neutrality in
European affairs. International support for disarmament also made it
increasingly difficult to maintain a large standing army or pursue an assertive foreign policy in Europe. Albeit difficult to measure, world opinion
weighed heavily upon French policy.

Even more important was the changed international environment of the
1930s. The economic depression and the advent of the Nazi regime
combined to undermine the bases of European politics. By the mid-1930s
several of the most important European states rejected the international
norms of the post-war decade. The Nazi and Fascist regimes had very
different expectations and understandings of what constituted acceptable
state behaviour. For these states war was a natural, indeed vital, state
activity. In the German case it constituted the organising principle around
which domestic and foreign policy was shaped. With the revisionist powers
playing by different rules, the normative standards of the 1920s were no
longer viable. The problem was that the leaders of western democracies were
slow to come to terms with this fact. Consequently, when the 1920s system
collapsed, the initiative in international politics shifted to the revisionist
powers. Given the belief systems of the Nazi and Fascist regimes, some
kind of war in Europe became virtually inevitable. It took time, however,
before this realisation penetrated French attitudes and perceptions.

Material Determinants

The central material factors that shape the foreign policies of states are
usually geography, demography, and economic and financial strength.
France's geographic position was crucial in determining the structure of its
economy as well as its commercial and political relations with the outside
world. Here the main elements were its frontier with Germany, its long
maritime frontier and its extensive colonial empire. Policy-makers faced
difficult choices. The security of its long coastline and extensive colonial
empire required a world-class navy. But the heavy investment that this
demanded during the 1930s frequently at odds with the financial
commitments required to secure France's land frontier to the east.[4]

Demography was another material determinant of French foreign policy.
In France a large population has always been considered a prerequisite of
Great Power status and population growth a key indicator of French
national vitality. By the 1930s France's birth rate had been in relative
decline for decades. The size of Germany's population had surpassed that of
France by 1861 and had continued to grow at a much faster rate until 1914.
The experience of the Great War only reinforced this obsession with

natalité. Without large human resources the industrial state could neither field the mass-conscript armies of the modern era nor muster the labour necessary to drive its war industry. By 1932 Germany's population out-numbered that of France by 62 million to 36 million. France's demographic inferiority was a central factor in the evolution of strategic planning throughout the 1930s and in particular the pessimistic assessments pro-duced by the French military establishment.[5]

The strength of the French economy was another determinant of foreign policy. The experience of total war in 1914–18 had driven home the impor-tance of industrial and financial power in world politics. French heavy industry had developed more slowly than that of Britain and Germany since the mid-nineteenth century, and until the inter-war years the French economy remained predominantly agrarian. Moreover, France's industrial infrastructure was decrepit. In the mid-1930s industrial machinery was on average 20 years old, as compared to an average age of seven years in Germany and four years in the United States and Japan.[6] This predicament was exacerbated by the debilitating impact of the Great Depression, which arrived later in France than in the rest of Europe, but lingered on long after most other economies had begun to recover. The effects of the crisis slowly paralysed the entire economy. Between 1929 and 1938 France's industrial production declined by more than 27 per cent. Manufacturing in key industries such as metallurgy, textiles and agriculture plummeted even more dramatically. Prices fell, the home and export markets contracted, un-employment increased. The result was that national income fell by nearly 30 per cent and a series of French governments faced ever-larger budgetary deficits. France spent most of the 1930s lurching from one financial crisis to the next, with successive governments falling over their failure to redress the situation. The diplomatic impact was substantial. Foreign investment had always been an important instrument of France's international influence, especially east of the Rhine. The erosion of French financial power over the course of the 1930s undermined French prestige and authority in Europe.[7]

Ideational Determinants

National Identity

The concept of identity is often used with frustrating vagueness in the study of international relations. But it can be helpful in understanding how both élite and public opinion understood France's role in international politics. National identities in this context are best understood as conceptions of collective distinctiveness, although it should be said that there is no such thing as a monolithic and unchanging national identity. There are instead contending identities, which are fluid rather than static.[8]

Any discussion of identity as a determinant of foreign policy must begin by underlining the central importance of the First World War to the French national experience. The unprecedented slaughter on the battlefields of northern France had claimed the lives of nearly one and a half million soldiers, brought wholesale destruction to some of the country's richest industrial regions and left a legacy of collective trauma that dominated all discussions of peace, war and international politics. The Great War also radicalised domestic politics, gave rise to a powerful pacifist movement and thus shaped the identity of France in fundamental ways.

Since the Revolution of 1789 France's political identity has been the subject of intense disagreements. At the risk of over-simplification, the left has tended to represent France in terms of the republican ideals of citizen-ship, the rights of man, and the triad of liberty, equality and fraternity, whereas the right has imagined France in terms of a national (often Catholic) community with clearly ordered social and political hierarchies.[9] The First World War exacerbated this ideological division by, among other things, raising political expectations among women and the working classes. These were largely disappointed after the war, bringing frustration with the political system and increased ideological tensions. These tensions were further intensified by the impact of the Russian Revolution and the rise of the Communist movement in the early 1920s. The French Communist party did not recognise France as a distinct political community. It identified instead with the Soviet Union and preached the doctrine of international class war. Politics were further polarised by the onset of the economic depression. One eminent historian has described the 1930s as 'one long crisis of national identity'.[10] These opposing ideological conceptions were crucial in shaping debates over French foreign policy.

The experience of war made French opinion more receptive than ever to arguments for pacifism and disarmament, which surged through Europe after 1918. A variety of pacifist doctrines, some qualified, others absolute, claimed adherents from all over the political spectrum.[11] Pacifism was particularly strong among the influential veteran's associations and the increasingly important women's movement. In parliament, the Commu-nist and Socialist parties clamoured relentlessly for disarmament (even unilateral disarmament) and revision of the Treaty of Versailles. The strength of pacifist opinion also reflected France's identity as a *status quo* power. For the majority of French opinion in the early 1930s, France stood for peace, disarmament and reconciliation in international politics.[12]

Yet existing alongside the image of France as a peaceable, *status quo* power was the equally pervasive conception of France as a great power and an important player in international politics. For centuries an integral component of French national identity has been the conviction that France has a special role to play in the world as the bearer of a universalist message. There have always been disagreements about the nature of this message. During our period the moderate left saw France as standing for the republican principles of the revolution, whereas the right looked to France to export its superior culture and civilised values to the rest of the world.[13] Yet both views were compatible with quasi-messianic notions of France's inherent greatness, its *mission civilatrice* and its duty to play a prominent role on the international stage. This notion of French *grandeur* was also a determinant of policy. It set limits beyond which foreign policy could not go without sacrificing France's identity as a Great Power.

One final aspect of the role of identity is worth mentioning. In order to reinforce the collective distinctiveness, national identities are often defined in opposition to external phenomena. During the 1930s Germany served as the chief foil for most constructions of French identity. French *civilisation* was compared favourably with German *Kultur*, and the French conception of a national society was represented as preferable to the German model of an integral national community. At the same time, France's declining birth-rate and its slower rate of modernisation contrasted unfavourably with the impressive growth of Germany's population and heavy industry. This contributed to the self-image of France as an ageing nation, exhausted by the Great War, but obliged none the less to confront the youthful dynamism of the Nazi and Fascist regimes. This particular construction of French identity was important because self-perception usually conditions the way threats to national security are perceived. Changes in the prevailing image of France in the minds of French élites played a fundamental role in the evolution of French policy from compromise to retreat to resistance over the course of the 1930s.

Policy-Making Culture

The notorious ministerial instability of the Third Republic has often been cited as evidence of a national malaise and an explanation of France's failure to meet the Nazi challenge before 1940. Between 1917 and 1940 there were 43 different governments in France. Between the rise of Hitler and the fall of France there were 34 separate governments, nine different premiers and seven foreign ministers. Britain during the same period had three premiers while the leaders of Germany, Italy and the USSR did not change. But the impact of parliamentary upheaval on decision-making can be exaggerated. One consequence was to increase the influence of permanent officials whose responsibility was to advise the government and to oversee the day-to-day planning and execution of policy. Newly appointed ministers depended on these officials not only for their expertise, but also to manage the ever-increasing mass of information that flowed into government ministries. This meant that diplomatic staff did much more than advise politicians on policy questions, they determined how these questions were framed. It is thus worth giving some consideration to the cultural environment in which diplomats worked.

The French diplomatic corps was a highly educated social and cultural élite drawn primarily from the upper middle classes and the remnants of the aristocracy. More than 80 per cent had been educated at the *École libre des sciences politiques*. The result was a fairly cohesive cadre that considered itself the nation's repository of expertise on international politics. Moreover, this élite enjoyed a significant measure of independence from political authority. Less than one per cent of all written parliamentary questions concerned issues of foreign policy and public debates on international issues were rare. The Foreign Ministry's approach to international relations between the wars was characterised by a preference for multilateral regimes based on sound legal foundations. This multilateralism evolved as a response to the changed normative standards of the 1920s. After 1925 instead of alliances aimed specifically at containing Germany, French policy pursued security through the construction of international security regimes. Alliances forged with Poland in 1921 and Czechoslovakia in 1924 were re-conceptualised and became components of French projects for a vast European security network.

French political culture also promoted a legalistic approach to international politics. International, public and private law were central components of both the curricula of the École libre and the Foreign Ministry entrance examination. Within the Quai d'Orsay one of the most important departments was the *Section Juridique*, responsible for advising all branches of the ministry on international law, the interpretation of international agreements or their compatibility with the French constitution. The director of this section was a key member of the diplomatic corps, whose influence was often second only to that of the secretary-general (permanent director) himself.[14] The observance of international law had undeniable attractions for a power interested above all in maintaining the *status quo* in Europe – particularly in an era where power politics had been so thoroughly discredited by the experiences of 1914–18.

The model for France's international policy for most of the inter-war years was the Locarno agreement of 1925. The 'spirit of Locarno' became a metaphor for European reconciliation and Franco-German rapprochement. But at the heart of the Locarno accords was a series of clearly defined security commitments by France, Germany, Italy, Belgium and Britain, which provided France with guaranteed military assistance in the event of future German aggression. Locarno served as a template for French ambitions to forge a wider security system that would include France's smaller allies in eastern Europe. The hope was to enmesh Germany in a vast multilateral regime that would limit its freedom to manoeuvre and thus contain its efforts to revise the Treaty of Versailles.[15]

To sum up, until the late 1930s French policy-making culture eschewed force or the threat of force as a central instrument of European policy.

When faced with a foreign policy problem, the reflexes of the Quai d'Orsay were to fashion a multilateral solution based on the letter of international law. This approach, of course, assumed that other European states would observe their commitments under Locarno.[16] Its usefulness declined sharply after the economic depression and the rise of Hitler destroyed the international system of the 1920s.

The Course of French Foreign Policy in the 1930s

Compromise, 1930–36

France entered the 1930s in a relatively strong position, its foreign and security policy resting upon three central pillars. The first was its clear military superiority over Germany, the result of the disarmament clauses of the Treaty of Versailles. The second was a series of bilateral alliances with Poland, Czechoslovakia, Romania and Yugoslavia. The aim was to weld this loose collection of successor states into a more coherent political and military bloc, and then to integrate this bloc into a wider European security regime. The final and most important pillar of French security was Locarno. As long as the Locarno system remained in force, any German aggression against France had little prospect of success. By the summer of 1936, however, this security edifice was in ruins. The Nazi regime in Germany had thrown off the disarmament restrictions of Versailles, embarked on a policy of unlimited rearmament and unilaterally destroyed the Locarno Treaty by sending troops into the Rhineland in March 1936. France's legalistic, multilateralist approach to European politics proved unable to deal with the Nazi challenge to the European *status quo*.

French political and diplomatic reactions to the rise of Hitler were based on a fundamental misreading of Nazi radicalism. The Foreign Ministry as well as most of France's political leadership concluded mistakenly that the constraints imposed by the international system would limit Germany's freedom of action and force Hitler to behave like other European leaders. The French military establishment disagreed and predicted that the Nazis were bent on war. The intelligence services and high command warned that if France wanted to maintain its position as a European Great Power it must begin preparing in earnest for a war with Germany.[17] France's civilian policy-makers were unable to accept this diagnosis because it challenged the very foundations of French external policy, which was formulated according to the normative standards of the mid- to late 1920s. The aim of French diplomatic projects such as the Tardieu Plan of 1931–32 and various 'eastern pacts' was the construction of a security regime in east-central Europe that would ensnare Germany in a web of multilateral commitments and thus restrict Hitler's room for manoeuvre. The project did not rule out the appeasement of German grievances through revision of the 1919 settlement. The hope was instead to ensure that treaty revision would be limited and obtained by peaceful means. The ultimate objective was a durable Franco-German entente.[18]

French diplomacy failed to secure German participation in this scheme. Instead, Nazi policy was able to undermine French attempts to build a comprehensive security system by forging a series of bilateral political and economic arrangements with Poland, Britain, Romania and Yugoslavia. French diplomacy has been criticised as having been dominated by 'illusions of pactomania'. But it is difficult to imagine another approach achieving greater success. In material terms, the need to contain Germany in a broad security network was based on a recognition of its superior war potential and British and American unwillingness to underwrite French security with military alliances. Britain and the United States were both more interested in securing disarmament concessions from France than in taking measures against a future military threat from Germany.[19]

A warlike policy was out of the question. For one thing, France lacked the military means to undertake an invasion of Germany. Since 1927 a series of reforms to the military system and deep cuts to the defence budget had reduced the army to a training cadre and organisational basis for a future nation in arms. Between 1931 and 1935 military spending was further cut by more than 25 per cent. In addition to its long-term affect upon the European balance of power, the course of defence policy also forced a revolution in French strategic planning. The emphasis shifted from a punitive offensive into western Germany to preparing for a long war in which France would stand on the defensive until it was able to mobilise all of its national resources for a strategic offensive. The construction of the Maginot Line was an integral component of this new strategic posture. Thus the armed forces ceased to be an offensive tool at the disposal of French foreign policy.[20]

These diplomatic and defence policies were made within a very specific cultural and psychological context. French pacifism reached its zenith in the early 1930s, with over 200 organisations professing pacifist beliefs and more than 16 million adherents to the *Rassemblement Universal Pour la Paix*. All sections of the left remained committed to disarmament and conciliation. The slow evolution of left-wing opinion from pacifism and disarmament to anti-Fascism and rearmament did not gain real momentum until later in 1935.[21] This set important limits on the kinds of policies France's leadership could imagine adopting. French policy remained committed to legalism and multilateralism rather than rearmament and alliance building. Premier Edouard Herriot's explanation of disarmament policy is illuminating in this regard: 'A country's defence resides not only in its soldiers and its cannons, but also in the excellence of its legal position.' Army chief General Maxime Weygand was left to protest in vain that he was 'responsible to defend the frontier with forces and not with words'.[22] But war was not part of the conceptual framework within which most policy-makers operated. As a Foreign Ministry memorandum on Nazi violations of the Treaty of Versailles observed: 'all military action must be ruled out.'[23] The multilateral designs of the Quai d'Orsay were eminently preferable to direct confrontation with Germany. As the chief patron of an east-west security regime, France would maintain and even enhance its status as a Great Power in Europe. This would both reduce the risk of war and satisfy the aspirations for greatness that co-existed with the self-image of France as a peaceful nation.

French foreign policy appeared to change when a 'government of national union' came to power in 1934. The premier, Gaston Doumergue, included in his cabinet prominent figures of the nationalist right who were advocates of a policy of firmness towards Germany. The government's first important act was to break off disarmament talks aimed at convincing Germany to return to the League of Nations. After the Nazis announced a large increase in German military spending, it responded with the 'April Note' which formally outlined France's intention to 'place at the forefront of its preoccupations the conditions of its own security'. The foreign minister, Louis Barthou, then undertook negotiations that led to a Mutual-Assistance Pact with Soviet Russia and a military agreement with Fascist Italy.[24] The historian Jean-Baptiste Duroselle argues that the summer of 1934 'stands apart' as a 'brief but incontestable recovery in the slide towards decadence'. He juxtaposes Barthou's 'realism' with the complex system building that had characterised foreign policy through 1933. For Duroselle, Barthou's assassination in autumn 1934 marks 'the end of a great policy'.[25]

This interpretation overstates the differences between Barthou's approach and that of his predecessors. It also ignores the obstacles in the way of a return to traditional alliance diplomacy. A closer look at the documentary record reveals that Barthou's approach was heavily influenced by the multilateralist designs of the Foreign Ministry. Barthou opposed ending disarmament talks. The 'April Note' was written by the premier rather than the foreign minister. Barthou, in agreement with his diplomatic advisors, argued that obtaining some kind of formal commitment from Germany might limit its rearmament in the short term. If not, world opinion would be far more likely to support France if it stayed at the bargaining table and avoided a unilateral response to Nazi rearmament. This reasoning reflected the legalist and multilateralist assumptions that prevailed within the Quai d'Orsay.[26] Similarly, Barthou's alliance diplomacy was closer to the multilateral approach of the Foreign Ministry than is commonly appreciated. The foreign minister worked closely with his advisors at the Quai d'Orsay and particularly with the secretary-general, Alexis Léger, when devising his eastern policy. The alliance with the USSR, for example, was conceived primarily as one cornerstone of another 'eastern Locarno' project. The immediate objective was a regional assistance pact that would include the smaller states of east-central Europe as well as Germany and the Soviet Union. The larger design was an east-west security regime underwritten by France and Britain. Such a system would contain both Germany and the USSR and thus guarantee the *status quo*.[27] Significantly, in negotiations with the Soviets, the French negotiators resisted all talk of an 'alliance' and especially a 'military alliance. They insisted instead on a mutual assistance pact as part of a broader eastern system. The Franco-Soviet agreement that was eventually signed on 2 May 1935 was full of legal qualifications and was linked formally to the League of Nations Covenant.[28] It was not a classic alliance of the pre-1914 variety and not a resurrection of the Franco-Russian relationship before the First World War. It was instead a product of inter-war French diplomatic culture and the international norms of the post-war era.

Barthou was assassinated by Croatian terrorists in October 1934. Under his successor, Pierre Laval, French policy became more committed than ever to forging a peaceful European order. Laval was a legendary political operator who set little store in the complex schemes of the Quai d'Orsay. But he was also deeply pacifist. His approach to international politics was shaped by a 'peace mystique' in which another European war was 'unthinkable'.[29] Laval's first major initiative was to meet with Mussolini in January 1935. The result was the Rome Accords wherein France and Italy agreed to consult in the event of German threat to peace in Europe. Mussolini later claimed to have obtained tacit consent for his plans to attack Ethiopia, something which Laval denied. Whatever the case, the accords were followed by staff conversations between the French and Italian army and air force staffs which produced detailed plans for a coalition war against Germany. The Quai d'Orsay characteristically tried to broaden the accords with Italy into a multilateral security arrangement that would include the states of central and south-eastern Europe.[30] Laval then travelled to Moscow to sign the Mutual Assistance Pact with the USSR. There he obtained a commitment from Stalin that the French Communist party would not undermine France's defence policy. But for Laval the overriding objective of both the Rome Accords and the Franco-Soviet pact was to strengthen France's hand in the negotiation of a general settlement with Germany. This is why secret assurances were given to Berlin that the pact with Russia posed no threat to Germany. Laval met with Göring in mid-May to reiterate this. He went even further to propose a summit meeting with Hitler where the two could have a 'useful conversation' that would establish the bases for Franco-German rapprochement. But Hitler was not interested and subsequent efforts to initiate talks also failed.[31]

Laval's foreign policy has been contrasted unfavourably with that of Barthou. Yet, while Barthou was undoubtedly more suspicious of Germany,

both aimed at rapprochement with the Reich and used multilateral diplomacy to create conditions favourable for achieving this goal. Both,
moreover, were constrained by material factors. An alternative policy based
on alliances and deterrence would require large-scale rearmament. But
France lacked both the political will and the financial resources to embark
on a massive programme of armaments build-up. Even the relatively
modest rearmament scheme introduced by the Doumergue government in
1934 was eroded by repeated cuts to the defence budget the following year.
By 1936 France would spend 26.5 per cent of state revenues on defence
while the Reich devoted 62.4 per cent of its much larger income to military
expenditure.[32] A gulf began to open up between France's strategic capabilities and its political commitments in Europe.

This was the situation when German troops marched into the Rhineland
in March 1936. French foreign policy had already been dealt a serious blow
by the Italian invasion of Abyssinia and the threat of war between Britain
and Italy. The Laval government was forced to choose between British
goodwill and the newly forged military agreements with Italy. After some
hesitation, it chose Britain and supported the policy of economic sanctions
against Italy. The resulting tensions provided Germany with a golden
opportunity to repudiate Locarno. The remilitarisation of the Rhineland
had long since been predicted by French military intelligence and probably
surprised no one in Paris. But it destroyed the bases of France's multilateral
foreign policy. Significantly, policy-makers never seriously contemplated
war. Aside from a series of public rebukes, there was no coordinated
international response to the destruction of Locarno.

Hitler had exposed once and for all the shaky foundations of French
external policy. There can be little argument that disarmament and
multilateralism were misguided responses to the challenge of Nazi foreign
policy. But the problem was not that France and its leadership were decadent
or defeatist. It was instead that they were incapable of comprehending the
Fascist pursuit of war and its implications for the international politics of
the 1930s.

Retreat, 1936–38

The remilitarisation of the Rhineland demolished the last remnants of the
international politics of the Briand-Stresemann era. Between the spring of
1936 and the autumn of 1938, France's policy-making élites struggled to
fashion a new approach to foreign policy. Their task was all the more
difficult as it was during this period that Germany transformed its greater
war-making potential into actual military superiority. By autumn 1938
Germany possessed a substantial army and a powerful new air force while
France struggled to jump-start its own halting rearmament effort. The Nazi

regime also made substantial progress in establishing the social and psycho-logical foundations for the war it was planning. The contrast with the situation in France during the same period was striking. The arrival to power of the Popular Front in 1936 intensified existing ideological divisions and social tensions. Despite the worsening international situation of 1936–38, French political discourse remained focused primarily on what kind of society France should be. Ideological clashes over the identity of France had a devastating effect on efforts to construct a new external policy.

The collapse of the Locarno agreement demonstrated the need for allies that could help deter future German aggression. But, as European politics became increasingly polarised during the Popular Front era, the process of choosing allies raised internal political difficulties. The French Popular Front was an alliance of political parties of the centre and left, and was part of a larger movement that emerged in 1935 across Europe as a reaction to the rise of Fascism. Its emergence signalled that on the left-wing advocacy of pacifism and disarmament had given way to policies of rearmament and anti-fascist resistance. The Communist party, responding to instructions from Moscow, completely reversed its position and expressed support for rearmament and a policy of firmness towards Germany and Italy. Mean-while, perceptions of the fascist threat had undermined all but the hardest core of pacifists within the Socialist party. The result was that national defence became a central pillar of the first Popular Front when it took office in June 1936 with the Socialist Léon Blum as premier.[33]

The single most important initiative undertaken in either foreign or defence policy by Blum's government was its rearmament programme of 1936. This was by far the most ambitious rearmament scheme undertaken by any government since 1918. Massive sums were devoted to land and air rearmament programmes and an ambitious programme was undertaken to nationalise, decentralise and renovate France's decrepit armaments and aircraft industries. In order to finance this rearmament, the government sacrificed many of its social programmes and took the controversial decision to devalue the French currency. As Robert Frank has conclusively demonstrated, the Popular Front gave priority to defence over domestic policy when it came to power.[34]

But this seismic shift in centre-left attitudes towards rearmament did not generate greater national unity over the question of France's international role. Quite the opposite. Foreign policy questions were more divisive than ever between 1936 and 1938 because internal politics had been radicalised. Blum's government came to power after an especially bitter election campaign. Its election was followed by a wave of paralysing strikes that plunged the country into the most intense period of social unrest since the days of the Paris Commune. The right was seized with fears that France was on the brink of a revolution similar to that which was taking place across the border in Spain. The ideological fissures that had always been a part of French political culture were deepened and conflicts in domestic politics inevitably conditioned foreign policy choices.

There were three potential great power allies for France in 1936. The most attractive of these was Great Britain. With its financial and industrial power, its empire and its powerful fleet, Britain was a factor in the balance of power that no French strategist could afford to underestimate.[35] There were also important non-material factors that made the British the most important of France's potential allies. Britain's was a democracy whose leaders were perceived as sharing many of the same basic assumptions about international politics as French statesmen. 'I speak with Chamberlain,' Daladier once observed, 'we have many disagreements, and he often does not like what I say, but we understand one another. I cannot speak in this manner with Mussolini. We do not understand one another.'[36] There were also memories of the shared experience of the First World War that contributed to the widespread assumption that Britain was a natural and dependable ally for France. Finally, and every bit as important, the prospect of an alliance with Britain did not divide France. The vast majority of French opinion could identify Britain as an ally in Europe.[37] This was not the case with either Soviet Russia or Fascist Italy.

There was an abiding suspicion that the Soviet regime was more interested in using a European war to spread revolution than in joining with France to resist Nazi aggression. These suspicions were strongest on the right and within the army general staff (with a few notable exceptions in both cases), but they were also prevalent within the Foreign Ministry and among many Radicals and Socialists. Both Edouard Daladier (now minister of national defence) and Léger were deeply mistrustful of Soviet motives and counselled against a military agreement with Moscow.[38] The question of an alliance with the USSR was therefore an intensely divisive issue. On the one hand, such an alliance could serve as a traditional 'eastern counterweight' to German power. This was the argument of the Communist party along with a number of 'realists' from elsewhere on the political spectrum. On the other hand, it could also mark the first stage in the feared worker's revolution that would bring an end to France as a distinct political entity. This is the primary reason why French continued to resist Soviet overtures to transform the mutual assistance pact into a full-blown military alliance through to the spring of 1939.

An alliance with Mussolini's Italy raised similar difficulties. A shared interest in containing German expansion in central and eastern Europe provided common ground for Franco-Italian cooperation. But Franco–Italian relations were compromised from the very beginning by Mussolini's ambitions to make the Mediterranean an 'Italian lake', threatening France's material interests in Africa and the Middle East and thus its identity as a great Mediterranean power. Even more important was the ideological gulf between the Socialist-led Popular Front and Italian Fascism. Mussolini's regime enjoyed considerable sympathy on the French right but was loathed by all parties on the left. Franco–Italian relations, already badly strained by the Abyssinian crisis and French support for a policy of sanctions, were allowed to collapse altogether once the Blum government assumed power in the summer of 1936. From the autumn of 1936 until November 1938 there was neither a French ambassador in Rome nor an Italian ambassador in Paris. During this time Italy moved inexorably towards the Rome–Berlin Axis.[39]

In the circumstances, Britain was by far the most desirable great power ally for France. Léger never ceased underlining the importance of Britain to French security. Before every meeting of French and British foreign ministers or heads of government, his officials would prepare strategy papers aimed at drawing Britain into a military relationship with France.[40] Premier Blum agreed completely as did Daladier (who assumed the premiership in April 1938). For Daladier 'complete co-operation with Great Britain' was the 'fundamental principle' of French policy.[41]

But pursuit of this cooperation carried important costs. The desire not to alienate Britain forced Laval to abandon his neutral attitude towards Italian policy in Ethiopia in 1935, to the detriment of newly improved relations with Rome. Similarly, Britain's clear opposition to a Franco-Soviet military pact was a constant factor in French policy towards the USSR. The same was true of British unwillingness to fight over Czechoslovakia. France's strategic dependence on Britain provided London with leverage with which to influence French foreign policy. This has led many historians to conclude that French policy was made in London. This argument is misleading. It is true that France's unwillingness to risk war without British support set limitations on its freedom of manoeuvre. But such limitations affect most states at most times. To better understand the dynamics of French appeasement, it is essential to recognise that there was little internal consensus about France's role in the world. The great ideological divisions between left and right, the continued strength of pacifism, the weakness of the French economy, and the unprepared state of its armed forces were all just as important as France's diplomatic isolation.

These factors are all evident in France's policy of neutrality during the Spanish Civil War. Although tempted to intervene in support of the Republican government, diplomatic isolation, mistrust of Soviet motives and fear that revolution might spread to France all combined to produce a policy of non-intervention. France was the chief architect of this policy, which was violated with impunity by Italy, Germany and the USSR. The most famous episode of French retreat, however, is the Czech crisis of September 1938. French inaction after the German take-over of Austria in March set the stage for the abandonment of France's only remaining European ally at the Munich conference the following autumn. The Munich agreement has been widely condemned as a classic example of short-sighted and even cowardly decision-making. A closer look at the sources of France's Munich policy yields a different perspective.

There were powerful material considerations that augured for a policy of appeasement. Foremost among these were the balance of military power and the poor state of the French economy. During the summer of 1938 French intelligence warned that the German *Wehrmacht* was capable of withstanding a French offensive in the West while simultaneously crushing Czechoslovakia in the East. This assessment exaggerated the state of German military power and the strength of its fortifications along the Franco-German frontier. But the importance of this misreading of German armed strength has been exaggerated by historians. The fact remained that the French army was under-equipped and had no plans for a large-scale invasion of Germany. Even more importantly, the French air force was in a state of collapse and possessed fewer than 50 modern combat aircraft. The realisation that Germany would possess overwhelming superiority over both France and Czechoslovakia was a key factor in all French strategic assessments during the crisis.[42] Serious economic and financial weakness compounded the situation. Although the franc had been devalued three times since 1936, industrial production had failed to recover and national revenue had continued to fall. To make matters worse, an exodus of capital investment had drained the gold reserves of the Bank of France. During the crisis days of September a run on the franc raised the spectre of complete financial collapse and the government was forced to impose tight restrictions on foreign investment in order to prevent the bankruptcy of the treasury. France lacked the military, industrial and financial strength to undertake war with any major power.[43]

And if France stood by its Czech ally, it would be isolated. The French eastern security 'system' had collapsed altogether. Romania and Yugoslavia were neutral and Poland desired to share in the spoils in any dismemberment of Czechoslovakia. Italy also seemed likely to enter the war on the side of Germany. As for France's erstwhile allies, the United States repeatedly affirmed its intention to observe strict neutrality and the British government stated publicly that it would not go to war over Czechoslovakia. The only potential source of aid was the Soviet Union. Soviet policy was and remains the great enigma of the Czech crisis. French élites, however, were unwilling to place their trust in Soviet promises to help defend Czechoslovakia. This judgement was based partly on ideological mistrust but also on the terrible effect of the purges on Russia's armed forces. The operating assumption of the newly appointed Daladier government was that if France marched to the aid of Czechoslovakia it would do so alone.[44]

The prevailing psychological context in France in 1938 ensured that these material factors would be interpreted in the most unfavourable light. France remained a deeply divided society. There were two contending visions of France at stake in debates over French policy in September 1938.

Adam th 4, France
175-199

The first was the image of France as a Great Power and a loyal ally. This France had no choice but to keep its commitments to Czechoslovakia. The second was that of France as a peaceful country that had suffered irreparable harm during the First World War and desired above all to avoid another such bloodletting. This France had no choice but to try every means possible to avert another great war. The point is that there was no consensus, either among decision-makers or within the public at large, over the right policy to follow. Daladier could not hope to lead a united nation into war in 1938. As a result the military and civilian officials exhibited a clear tendency to focus on the negative aspects of the strategic situation, on France's demographic and industrial inferiority, on its financial weakness, and above all on German air superiority. Positive factors such as evidence of Germany's economic vulnerability, its lack of the raw materials necessary to wage a long war or evidence of wavering morale among the German population, tended to be ignored in calculations made in Paris. The fundamental fact that France was neither materially nor psychologically prepared for war functioned as a prism through which strategic considerations were filtered as they were integrated into the decision-making process.[45]

Historians have frequently failed to distinguish between French and British appeasement at this crucial juncture. At the heart of British policy was Prime Minister Neville Chamberlain's conviction that he could negotiate a lasting arrangement with the Nazi regime that would preserve the peace of Europe. The Daladier government was always more sceptical of Nazi intentions but determined not to make war without British support. This support became the precondition of an opposing policy of active resistance to Nazi revisionism. 'More than ever,' warned General Maurice Gamelin, commander-in-chief designate of France's armed forces, 'it is essential that we have Britain with us.' This is why French statesmen tried to parlay every concession made to Hitler, over the Rhineland, Austria or Czechoslovakia, into a British military commitment. Through to the end of 1938 this strategy met with little success.[46]

Recovery and Resistance, 1938–1939

Eleven months after the capitulation at Munich, France went to war with Germany. To understand the reasons why France retreated in 1938 but made war in 1939, it is essential to consider the relationship between the material and ideational forces that influenced decision-making. While the industrial, financial and military situation was considerably improved in France by the summer of 1939, there were equally important developments in the national mood. Pacifist sentiment waned and the outlines of a national consensus over foreign policy emerged in late 1938 and 1939. The result was the decision for war the following August.

The more resolute national mood was greatly reinforced by marked improvements in France's material situation. Using wide-ranging decree powers obtained from parliament, Daladier and the newly appointed finance minister, Paul Reynaud, introduced a series of liberal economic and financial policies that regained the confidence of French investors. Over the next eight months more than 26 billion francs worth of foreign investment was repatriated to the coffers of the Bank of France. This made it possible to borrow huge sums to finance rearmament. Consequently, spending on the military increased dramatically after Munich. Estimates for the defence budget for 1939 rose from 25 billion francs in the autumn of 1938 to 37 billion francs by the following June. Moreover, as war broke out, the army staff was finalising plans for yet another huge armaments programme.[47] Industrial production also began a dramatic recovery in late 1938 and by the following summer national output increased by nearly 25 per cent. The greatest progress was realised in the defence industry. Crucially, the terrible bottlenecks that had constrained rearmament ever since 1936 began to disappear. Production of armour, artillery and especially aircraft rose steadily over the ensuing months. On the eve of war, though its leaders did not know it, French factories were producing more tanks and aircraft than their counterparts in Germany.[48]

The mood of national resolve and improvements in the industrial and financial situation underpinned France's more robust policy after Munich. This was first evident in the government's defiant response to Italian claims on Nice, Corsica and Tunisia in November 1938. Dismissing British pressure to negotiate with Mussolini, Daladier made an ostentatious tour of France's North African possessions. He declared that 'not one inch' of French territory would be ceded to any foreign power. Yet, although this was an important first step away from appeasement, a hard-line stance towards Germany still could not be adopted without British support. The government therefore pursued a military alliance with Britain more aggressively than ever after Munich. These efforts finally bore fruit in late January when, in the midst of ill-founded rumours of an imminent German offensive into western Europe, the British cabinet finally approved staff conversations with France based on the hypothesis of war with the Axis powers. France had gained the continental commitment it had sought since 1919.[49]

The internal and external conditions for a policy of resistance were thus in place even before Germany occupied the Czech principalities of Bohemia and Moravia on 15 March 1939. The French response to the 'Prague coup' reveals the extent to which its international posture had changed since Munich. Historians have often represented France as trailing along behind Britain at this stage. This is misleading. During the final months of peace it was the French government that took the lead in diplomatic attempts to build an anti-German front in Europe. France joined Britain in issuing a political and military guarantee to Poland. Both soldiers and diplomats argued that allowing Germany access to essential raw materials in eastern Europe would be a grave strategic error. Consequently, the Daladier government insisted on an additional guarantee to Romania. Plans for a vast eastern front against further German aggression, begun by the army staff the previous December, were now elaborated. At this stage, significantly, ideological opposition to a Soviet alliance was also overcome. The USSR came to be viewed as a potential arsenal that could provide vital war material to Poland, Romania and Yugoslavia. From the beginning of April until the outbreak of war, the French government assumed the initiative in pressing both the British and the Soviets to negotiate a tripartite alliance against Nazi aggression. Daladier took greater control of foreign policy at this stage. Working closely with Léger, he swept away Bonnet's schemes for Franco-German *rapprochement* and set French policy on a course of resistance and ultimately war.[50]

The evolution of the internal situation shaped the way decision-makers interpreted the German threat. Whereas in 1938 military and civilian officials had focused overwhelmingly on the size of Germany's armed forces and the pace of German rearmament, in 1939 their attention was drawn more towards the weakness of the German position. A perceived decline in German morale as well as Germany's ongoing lack of raw materials and currency reserves called into question its ability to sustain a long war. This gave French leaders hope that the Nazis could be deterred by a policy of firmness. It also suggested that, if war came, the Reich would be vulnerable to Allied plans for a long war and a suffocating economic blockade. Gamelin thus advised Daladier that 'we can envisage with calm the possibility of a conflict pitting France and Britain against the totalitarian states.' Daladier agreed: 'If it comes to a duel between France and one other nation, I would have no mortal concerns for the outcome.'[51] Significantly, there had been little change in the balance of power since the Czech crisis, since both French and German military strength had increased. The key difference was the perspective from which this balance was interpreted. The perceptions of French decision-makers were influenced by the improved material situation inside France. But the ideational context had also evolved. Growing self-confidence and a greater awareness of France's role as a European power also conditioned calculations of the balance of power. The end result was the decision for war.

It would be wrong, however, to depict the national mood as warlike in 1939. Deep misgivings about Soviet intentions persisted and would resurface when negotiations for a grand alliance failed in August. Similarly, one should not over-emphasise the extent of the national recovery of 1938–39. Nor had the ideological fissures in French society been completely repaired. The Daladier government's industrial reforms led to a bitter confrontation with the labour movement. This alienated the left and led to the final collapse of the Popular Front. There would be no revival of the 1914 *union sacrée* in September 1939. Finally, deep-seated anxieties about the terrible consequences of another war remained a constant in both official and popular attitudes. As one Foreign Ministry official put it in his diary in late August: 'One can be firm, resolute and even hard-line and at the same time find all of this horrible.' These fears were reflected in a French war plan that counted on avoiding the slaughter of the previous war by bringing Germany to its knees with an economic blockade. None the less, it is clear that French opinion was at last ready to accept the risk of war in order to preserve France's status in Europe. As tension mounted over Poland in the summer, only 17 per cent of those polled were opposed to war in the event of a German seizure of Danzig. French self-perception had changed.[52]

Constructions of national identity and conceptions of France's international role were important factors in the decision for war taken in late August 1939. Even after the signature of the Nazi-Soviet pact, which ended hopes of building a grand alliance that would deter Germany, army chief Gamelin advised Daladier that 'France has no choice' but to honour its commitments to Poland. In explaining his reasoning afterward, Gamelin observed that 'In the end ... to have given way, to have trusted Germany, would have been to become in our turn the "brilliant second".' In other words, capitulation would have been completely at odds with conceptions of France as a great European power that were so firmly imbedded in the French national psyche. This explains why the declaration of war was approved overwhelmingly by both houses of parliament. Daladier summed up the majority view when he observed that 'France cannot hesitate' but 'must make war and win'.[53]

Conclusions

Two central conclusions emerge from this consideration of French foreign policy. The first is that, while policy-making culture and contending constructions of French identity were not independent causal factors, thinking about their role helps us understand why political leaders found it difficult to conceive of war as a serious option for much of this period. A robust foreign policy based on alliance-building and extensive rearmament was contrary to both the normative standards of the early 1930s and predominant notions of France's proper role in international politics. At the same time such a focus also illustrates the importance of conceptions of French greatness in the emergence of a policy of firmness after Munich. Popular belief in France's role as a bastion of civilisation made it ultimately impossible for policy-makers to abandon France's status as a European Great Power. At different moments, in different political and strategic contexts, notions of the identity of France exercised a crucial influence on foreign policy decisions.

The second major point to be made is that assumptions of decline and decadence are unhelpful in explaining France's role in the coming of the Second World War. 'Decadence' is a morally charged term that ultimately explains very little. Decision-makers did not understand their role in these terms. They could not foresee the future and were not convinced that the Third Republic was in the final stages of terminal decline. Mono-causal theories of decline cannot explain the evolution of French foreign policy from the system building of the early and mid-1930s to appeasement and then eventually to deterrence and war in 1939. Nor can theories of decadence explain the recovery of 1938–39. A focus on the influence of ideas points towards a different approach to the question of moral judgement. It reminds us that Herriot, Blum and Daladier held fundamentally different conceptions about the nature of international politics from those of Hitler, Mussolini or Stalin. The gulf between contending belief systems in the 1930s ultimately made it impossible to construct a viable international system including both revisionist and non-revisionist states. But this does not mean that France and its leadership were morally degenerate. It is time to move the study of international relations between the wars out from under the shadow of the Cold War. Treating French hesitation and indecision as evidence of decline and decay suggests an approach to international politics that is dangerously close to militarism. Should national leaders who shrink before the prospect of world war be dismissed as decadent? If so, what is to be made of their counterparts in Germany and Italy who glorified war and pursued it as a political end in itself? These are questions which historians of twentieth-century Europe cannot afford to ignore.

Notes

1. This view is in keeping with a long tradition of interpreting French history in terms of decline, fall and renewal. Its chief proponent is J.-B. Duroselle, *Politique étrangère de la France 1932–1939: la décadence* (Paris, 1979). But see also A. Adamthwaite, *Grandeur and Misery: France's Bid for Power in Europe, 1914–1940* (London, 1995); P. Wandycz, *The Twilight of French Eastern Alliances, 1926–1936* (Princeton, 1988); N. Jordan, *The Popular Front & Central Europe* (Cambridge, 1992); and the essays by J. Cairns, V. Caron, C. Fink and O. Bartov in J. Blatt ed., *The French Defeat of 1940* (Oxford, 1999).

2. J. Cairns, 'Along the Road Back to France 1940', *American Historical Review* 64 (1959), 583–603; G. Warner, *Pierre Laval and the Eclipse of France* (London, 1968); J. Néré, *The Foreign Policy of France* (London, 1975); R. Young, *France and the Origins of the Second World War* (London, 1996);

R. Frank, *La hantise du déclin* (Paris, 1994); M. Alexander, *The Republic in Danger, 1935–1940* (Cambridge, 1993); M. Thomas, *Britain, France and Appeasement: Anglo-French Relations in the Popular Front Era* (Oxford, 1996).

3. The approach outlined in this paragraph owes a considerable debt to the pioneering work of P. Renouvin and J.-B. Duroselle in *Introduction à l'histoire des relations internationales*, 4th edn (Paris, 1991), and to recent applications of social constructivism to the study of international relations. For good introductions, see P. Katzenstein, ed., *Cultures of National Security* (New York, 1996); A. Wendt, *Social Theory of International Politics* (Cambridge, 1999).

4. J. Keiger, *France and the World Since 1870*, (London, 2001), pp. 7–53; Renouvin and Duroselle, *Introduction à l'histoire des relations internationales*, pp. 6–29.

5. H. Dutailly, *Les problèmes de l'armée de terre français, 1935–1940* (Vincennes, 1984), pp. 66–72; R. Tomlinson, 'The Disappearance of France: French Politics and the Birth Rate, 1896–1940', *Historical Journal* 28 (1985), 405–16; and S. Reynolds, *France between the Wars: Gender and Politics* (London, 1996), pp. 18–37.

6. P. Jackson, *France and the Nazi Menace* (Oxford, 2000), pp. 38–47; S. Berstein, *La France des années 1930* (Paris, 1990), pp. 9–15.

7. On the depression see J. Jackson, *The Politics of Depression in France* (Cambridge, 1985); A. Sauvy, *Histoire économique de la France entre les deux guerres*, Vol. III (Paris, 1967); and K. Mouré, *Managing the Franc Poincaré* (Cambridge, 1991). On financial diplomacy see R. Boyce, 'Business as Usual: The Limits of French Financial Diplomacy', in Boyce, ed., *French Foreign and Defence Policy* (London, 1998), pp. 107–31; and Frank, *Hantise du déclin*, pp. 149–91.

8. Wendt, *Social Theory of International Politics*, pp. 92–138 and 177–226.

9. Good introductions to these complicated issues are P. Weil, *Qu'est-ce qu'un Français? Histoire de la nationalité française depuis la Révolution* (Paris, 2002); P. Birnbaum, *La France imaginée* (Paris, 1998); and S. Hazreesingh, *Political Traditions in Modern France* (Oxford, 1994).

10. P. Laborie, *L'opinion française sous Vichy: les française et la crise d'identité nationale, 1936–1944* (Paris, 1990), p. 20.

11. Young, *France and the Origins*, p. 117.

12. A. Prost, *In the Wake of War: 'Les anciens combattants' and French Society* (Oxford, 1992), esp. pp. 51–78; Reynolds, *France Between The Wars*, pp. 181–203; N. Ingram, *The Politics of Dissent: Pacifism in France, 1919–1939* (Oxford, 1991); M. Vaïsse, ed., *Le Pacifisme en Europe* (Brussels, 1993); J. P. Blondi, *La mêlée des pacifistes* (Paris, 2000); Y. Lacaze, *L'Opinion publique française et la crise de Munich* (Berne, 1991).

13. Birnbaum, *La France imaginée*, pp. 9–19, 273–369.

14. R. Young, *French Foreign Policy, 1918–1945*, 2nd edn (Delaware, 1991), p. 19.

15. E. Keeton, *Briand's Locarno Diplomacy* (New York, 1987); S. Schuker, *The End of French Predominance in Europe* (Chapel Hill, 1977); S. Marks, *The Illusion of Peace* (London, 1976; 2nd edn Basingstoke, 2002); Wandycz, *Twilight*, 3–46; and Poidevin and Bariéty, *Les relations franco-allemandes*, 2nd edn (Paris, 1979), pp. 258–76.

16. J.-B. Duroselle, 'The Spirit of Locarno: Illusions of Pactomania', *Foreign Affairs* 50 (1972), 752–64.
17. Jackson, *Nazi Menace*, pp. 45–82.
18. Wandycz, *Twilight*, esp. pp. 299–422; Duroselle, *La décadence*, pp. 102–11; and Jordan, *Popular Front*, pp. 11–43.
19. Duroselle, 'The Spirit of Locarno'; P. M. H. Bell, *France and Britain, 1900–1940* (London, 1996), ch. 10; and M. Rossi, *Roosevelt and the French* (Westport, 1993), pp. 19–146.
20. R. Young, *In Command of France, 1932–1940* (Cambridge, 1978), pp. 21–68; Alexander, *The Republic in Danger*, pp. 43–99; and M. Vaïsse and J. Doise, *Diplomatie et outil militaire* (Paris, 1993), pp. 345–62.
21. Ingram, *Politics of Dissent*, pp. 2–7; E. Hermon, 'Une ultime de sauvetage de la Société des Nations: la campagne du Rassemblement Universal pour la Paix', in Vaïsse, ed., *Le pacifisme en Europe*, p. 199; and P. Buffotot, *Le Socialism français et la guerre* (Paris, 1998), pp. 106–54.
22. Cited in J. Bariéty, 'Les relations internationales en 1932–1933', *Revue Historique* 238 (1967), p. 352.
23. France, Imprimerie Nationale, *Documents Diplomatiques Français* [hereafter DDF], 1ère série, Vol. IV, no. 448, 4 July 1934.
24. M. Vaïsse, *Sécurité d'abord: la politique française en matière de désarmement* (Paris, 1981), pp. 562–9.
25. *La décadence*, pp. 88, 92 and 112.
26. The best analyses are Vaïsse, *Sécurité d'abord*, 532–85; and R. Young, *Power and Pleasure: Louis Barthou and the Third Republic* (Montreal, 1991), pp. 211–16.
27. *DDF*, 1ère série, Vol. VI, no. 54, 30 March 1934 and ibid., no. 154, 28 April 1934.
28. S. Dullin, *Des Hommes d'influences* (Paris, 2001), pp. 122–35; and Duroselle, *La décadence*, p. 142.
29. Cited in F. Kupferman, *Laval* (Paris, 1988), pp. 125, 127. On Laval's foreign policy in the 1930s see also J. P. Cointet *Pierre Laval* (Paris, 1993), pp. 134–71.
30. *DDF*, 1ère série, Vol. IX, no. 86, Léger to Chambrun, 26 January 1935.
31. *Documents on German Foreign Policy*, Series C, Vol. IV, no. 384, Rintelen to Köster, 29 October 1935; and Cointet, *Laval*, pp. 174–5.
32. Jackson, *Nazi Menace*, pp. 157–9.
33. See above all J. Jackson, *Defending Democracy: The Popular Front in France* (Cambridge, 1988).
34. Frank, *Hantise du déclin*, pp. 36–58; Alexander, *Republic in Danger*, pp. 108–31.
35. Young, *Command of France*, pp. 18–24; Alexander, *Republic in Danger*, pp. 237–74.
36. France, Fondation Nationale des Sciences Politiques, Archives Roger Génébrier, GE 15, conversation with Daladier, 26 January 1939.
37. On these questions see especially Thomas, *Britain, France and Appeasement*, pp. 103–67; and Bell, *France and Britain*, 204–26.
38. On French politics and Franco-Soviet relations see Duroselle, *La décadence*, pp. 104–21, 141–87, 192–7 and 359–68; J. Dreifort, 'The French Popular Front and the Franco-Soviet Pact', *Journal of Contemporary History* 9 (1976),

217–36; and the far from neutral account in M. Carley, *1939: The Alliance that Never Was* (Chicago, 1999).

39. W. Shorrock, *From Ally to Enemy: The Enigma of Italy in French Foreign Policy* (Kent, OH, 1985), pp. 141–212.

40. France, Minstère des Affaires Étrangères [hereafter MAE], PA-AP, 217, *Papiers Massigli*, Vol. X, 'Projet de note pour le gouvernement britannique', 28 August 1936; 'Réarmement en Europe', 3 November 1936; Vol. XVI, 'Elements pour la conversation franco-britannique,' 27 November 1937; and 'Mémento pour la conversation britannique du 25 janvier 1938', 11 January 1938.

41. Both cited in Jackson, *Nazi Menace*, p. 245.

42. E. du Réau, *Edouard Daladier* (Paris, 1993), pp. 234–87; and Jackson, *Nazi Menace*, pp. 269–94.

43. M. Thomas, 'France and the Czechoslovak Crisis', *Diplomacy & Statecraft* 10 (1999), 122–59; R. Frank, 'The Impact of the Economic Situation on the Foreign Policy of France', in W. J. Mommsen and L. Kettenacker, eds, *The Fascist Challenge and the Policy of Appeasement*, (London, 1985), pp. 209–26.

44. A. Adamthwaite, *France and the Coming of the Second World War*, pp. 175–99; and Thomas, 'France and the Czechoslovak Crisis'.

45. Jackson, *Nazi Menace*, pp. 247–97; Lacaze, *Opinion publique française, idem.* 'Daladier, Bonnet and the Decision-Making Process During the Munich Crisis, 1938', in Boyce, ed., *French Foreign Policy*, pp. 215–33; Duroselle, *La décadence*, pp. 338–64; du Réau, *Daladier*; and Young, *France and the Origins*, pp. 79–97 and 113–29.

46. Gamelin quotation in MAE, *Papiers 1940*, Fonds Daladier, 'Note sur la collaboration militaire franco-britannique', 24 April, 1938. Léger cited in Adamthwaite, *France*, pp. 88.

47. M. Margairaz, *L'état, les finances et l'économie*, t.1 (Paris, 1991), pp. 473–85 and Frank[enstein], *Le prix du réarmement français 1935–39* (Paris, 1982), pp. 281–319.

48. R. Frank[enstein], *Le prix du réarmement*, pp. 197–217; du Réau, *Daladier*, pp. 299–324; Young, *France and the Origins*, pp. 121–7.

49. Daladier cited in Jackson, *Nazi Menace*, p. 323; on Franco–British relations see Young, *Command of France*, pp. 220–68; Adamthwaite, *France*, pp. 227–334; Bell, *France and Britain*, pp. 220–34; and especially T. Imlay, *Confronting War: France and Britain, 1938–40* (Oxford, forthcoming).

50. P. Jackson, 'France and the Guarantee to Romania, 1939', *Intelligence and National Security* 10 (1995), 242–72; and Imlay, 'Retreat or Resistance? Strategic Reappraisal and French Power in Eastern Europe', in M. Alexander and K. Mouré, eds, *Crisis and Renewal in France, 1918–1962* (Oxford, 2002), pp. 105–31. On Franco-Soviet negotiations see Duroselle, *La décadence*, pp. 403–39; Imlay, *Confronting War*, ch. 2.

51. Cited in Jackson, *Nazi Menace*, pp. 336 and generally pp. 298–395.

52. Quotation from R. de Sainte-Suzanne, *Une politique étrangère: le Quai d'Orsay novembre 1938–juin 1940* (Paris, 2000), p. 71. The crucial source on the mood in France in 1939 is J.-L. Crémieux-Brilhac, *Les français de l'an 40*, 2 Vols (Paris, 1990).

53. Gamelin cited in Alexander, *Republic in Danger*, p. 313; Daladier in Jackson, *Nazi Menace*, p. 387.

6 Britain

Williamson Murray

On 9 May 1940 three men, Winston Churchill, Neville Chamberlain and
Lord Halifax met to decide who was to become the next prime minister of
Great Britain. At that moment Nazi Germany's *Wehrmacht* was poised to
invade France and the Low Countries and win one of the most spectacular
victories in the twentieth century. Churchill himself, after long years in the
wilderness, had only become a member of the government on the outbreak
of war in September 1939. In the period before the war he had waged a
long and lonely struggle against the government's policy of appeasement of
Nazi Germany. On the other hand Neville Chamberlain had resigned as
prime minister, having just received a stinging rebuke in a vote of no-
confidence in the House of Commons two days earlier.[1] Chamberlain had
clearly believed that Britain could reach an accommodation with Nazi
Germany that would meet Adolf Hitler's goals, while avoiding another
great European conflict. In that effort Halifax had been the prime minister's
steadfast supporter. How these men had reached that room and why Britain
now confronted the most dangerous challenge in its history is the subject of
this essay.

Strategy is inevitably a matter of hard choices. As his plans for the capture
of Quebec unravelled, General Wolfe observed: 'war is an option of
difficulties.'[2] For Britain's political and military leaders, the 1930s brought
one hard choice after another, none providing simple or easy solutions and
many of them threatening disaster. The decade had begun with the Great
Depression, which by 1931 had presented the possibility of a complete
collapse of the British economy and with it the very survival of the empire.
No sooner had Britain begun to restore its economic position, at considerable cost to its social fabric, than the international order began to unravel
at a frightening pace. The combination of three factors, memories of the
Great War, the economic collapse of 1931, and a disintegrating international order all exercised their influence over British policy-makers through
to 1939. Yet, whatever the difficulties confronting British leaders in the
1930s, one should not forget that politicians actively seek positions of
power because they believe they possess qualities that will allow them
to master great challenges. Nor should one ignore the fact that whatever

the complexities of the strategic environment, Britain's leaders remained, for the most part, smugly self-satisfied with the decisions they made throughout the decade – at least until the smash-up of 1940. Thus modern historians should judge decision-makers of the 1930s not only on the complexity of the choices that confronted them, but also on their willingness to deal with the realities of the unfolding situation and on the results of their policies. Any proper judgement on the strategic policy of a regime should rest on the realism and the capacity to adapt that statesmen, politicians and military leaders exhibit in confronting threats to the security of the state.[3] Policy exists in an uncertain and ambiguous environment, so it is the capacity to adapt to the realities of the world that separates the few first-rate statesmen from the great majority, who rely upon their own flawed and ill-informed views and persist in strategic courses that can and at times do lead to disaster.[4]

The Cultural, Institutional, and Economic Framework of British Policy

At the start of a new century, when the Second World War generation is fast disappearing and the comfortable assumptions of post-modernism hold sway, it is hard to visualise the price that Britain and its Allies bore in defeating the Central Powers in the Great War.[5] By the end of that conflict, 744,702 British soldiers, sailors and airmen had died on the war's terrible battlefields, while a further 1,693,262 had been wounded, many of them maimed for life.[6] For the duration of the 1920s and 1930s the shadow of the recent conflict hung over the strategic decision-making processes of the British government. To most politicians as well as military officers, it seemed inconceivable that their nation might again confront another great war.

A less than satisfactory peace ushered in an era of increasing disillusionment with the war. Literary outpourings, many of them of the highest quality, further underlined the horror of the trenches and what appeared to be the meaningless sacrifices that the war had inflicted on a whole generation.[7] By the early 1930s, at almost precisely the moment that the international environment went south, much of Britain's élite had become convinced that no one had won the last war.[8] The corollary to this view was the belief that in future there would be no cause, no issue worth the price of fighting another great war. Few of Germany's élite shared such sentiments.

The growing strength of such attitudes resulted in general agreement across the political spectrum against any sort of serious rearmament. The Labour party went so far as to vote against every single defence budget from the early 1930s through to the outbreak of the war. Kingsley Martin in the *New Statesman* best summed up such attitudes shortly after the

Anschluß (the German seizure of Austria): 'Today if Mr Chamberlain would come forward and tell us that his policy was really one not only of isolationism but also of Little Englandism in which the Empire was to be given up because it could not be defended and in which military defence was to be abandoned because war would totally end civilization, we for our part would totally support him.'[9] Even B. H. Liddell Hart, the noted military theorist and advocate of transforming the British army into an armoured-mechanised force, argued that Britain should never commit ground forces to the defence of the continent.[10] It was this horror of the previous war, so eloquently expressed by Neville Chamberlain in a speech at the height of the Czech crisis in September 1938 that marked the entire decade: 'how horrible, fantastic, incredible it is that we should be digging trenches ... because of a quarrel in a far away country between people of whom we know nothing'; and that determined so much of the Britain's strategic response to the rise of Nazi Germany.[11]

Combined with this fear was a belief that somehow military force and strategic factors no longer counted in the modern world. As the British ambassador to Berlin, Sir Nevile Henderson, noted in summer 1938 about Lord Runciman's mediation efforts in the Czech-German confrontation: 'Personally I just sit and pray for one thing, namely that Lord Runciman will live up to the rule of the impartial British statesman. I cannot believe that he will allow himself to be influenced by ancient history or even arguments about strategic frontiers and economies in preference to high moral principles.'[12] Admittedly, appeasement had as its goal the preservation of Europe's peace, but it rested on a rejection of history and a belief that in the end the dictators, whatever their peculiarities, also rejected the idea of war. As Chamberlain noted to the Soviet ambassador in 1937: 'If we could only sit down at a table with the Germans and run through all their complaints and claims with a pencil, this would greatly relieve tensions.'[13] In certain circumstances appeasement could achieve worthwhile strategic goals: it managed to assuage Japanese sensibilities sufficiently to keep them out of the war until December 1941. However, even with powers who posed no threat, appeasement could have the most appalling consequences, as when Britain surrendered the Treaty Ports to the Irish Republic in April 1938. The denial of those ports to the Royal Navy in the Second World War led to the deaths of thousands of Allied sailors in the Battle of the Atlantic.

Equally important to an understanding of Britain's response to the challenges of the 1930s was the structure of its decision-making machinery. Political governance rested upon a highly organised bureaucratic framework in which a series of committees guided and determined the course of rearmament and strategic policy. The system largely resulted from the efforts of one man, Sir Maurice Hankey. Hankey helped in the creation of a host of committees and sub-committees in the 1920s that regularised and coordinated the making of strategic policy among the government's various departments.[14] However, the bureaucracy generated innumerable studies, strategic appreciations and interdepartmental memoranda, none of which were conducive to rapid decision-making.[15] The blizzard of papers led a senior Foreign Office official, Sir Robert Vansittart, to exclaim: 'it seems clear that all the machinery here contemplated will involve the maximum delay and accumulation of papers. We do not want any more written "European Appreciations". We have been snowed under with papers from the Committee of Imperial Defence for years. Moreover, the procedure by stages implies a certain leisureliness which is not what we want at this present moment.'[16] In the Second World War, under Churchill's driving leadership typified by his notes demanding 'action this day' on important documents the system of government played a major role in Britain's survival. However, until the outbreak of war the system, under less gifted leadership, proved at times a significant impediment to making timely and effective decisions. The extensive bureaucratic search for consensus more often than not led politicians and generals to decide in favour of the least risky rather than the most effective course of action, while at times it allowed policy-makers and bureaucrats to derail courses of action with which they disagreed.

As Britain confronted growing threats in the 1930s, its leaders also worried about the deterioration of the country's economic position. Unlike Nazi Germany, Britain and the Commonwealth had access to considerable financial and natural resources.[17] Nevertheless, throughout the 1930s the British economy balanced precariously on the need to pay for much of the nation's imports by the export of finished goods, and only for one year during the decade did Britain have a favourable balance of trade.[18] Not surprisingly, given memories of 1931, arguments about rearmament were dominated by worries over the state of the British economy and the possibility that over-expenditure on armaments would lead to further economic troubles. As Chamberlain put it in December 1937, 'the maintenance of Britain's economic stability represented an essential element in the maintenance of her defensive strength.'[19] As a result, governments in the 1930s consistently minimised defence expenditures because of worries about their impact upon the nation's economic stability. Shortly before he became prime minister in the spring of 1937, Chamberlain warned the Cabinet that rearmament was 'placing a heavy strain on our resources. Any additional strain might put our present [economic] programmes in jeopardy.'

In his last months as the chancellor of the exchequer, Chamberlain had initiated a comprehensive Treasury review of how large a defence budget Britain could sustain without suffering economic damage or without introducing economic and financial controls. As the result of its initial assumptions, the review suggested that there were severe limits on what Britain could support in face of the gathering threats.[20] Chamberlain warned the Cabinet in May 1937:

He could not accept the question at issue as being a purely military matter. Other considerations entered into it. He himself definitely did challenge the policy of [the government's] military advisers. The country was being asked to maintain a larger navy than had been the case for many years; a great air force, which was a new arm altogether; and, in addition, an army for use on the Continent, as well as the facilities for producing munitions ... .[21]

Not until the end of March 1939 would the prime minister have occasion to change those views, and then only under pressure from a public that had awoken to the dangers confronting the nation.

Strategic and Military Planning

Throughout the 1920s the British military confronted a relatively benign environment. As late as 1932, there appeared to be no direct threat to Britain's security. Defeat, the Treaty of Versailles and the economic depression had seemingly removed Germany as an immediate threat. Russia had collapsed into the turmoil of revolution, and while the Soviet Union proclaimed its hostility to the capitalist world, it was hardly a direct threat in a military sense. Japan appeared unsure of its role in world affairs with the ending of the Anglo-Japanese Alliance in 1922, but its focus was on the Soviet Union and China. The Italians may have been unhappy with their rewards in 1919, but to many in Britain Mussolini's Fascist regime appeared to have brought political stability to the Italian state as well as making the trains run on time. Finally, whatever the difficulties Britain had with France and the United States, neither power represented a threat.

But the 1930s were a decade of extraordinary fluidity and change. As Paul Kennedy observes, '[by the mid-1930s] Japan appeared as a distinct challenge to British interests in the Far East, Germany had fallen under Nazi rule and was assessed [by British strategic planners] as the "greatest long-term danger," and Italy's policies appeared aggressive and hostile, whereas the United States was more unpredictable and isolationist than ever.'[22] Given the multitude of threats confronting Britain in the mid-1930s, it is not surprising that the chiefs of staff would warn during the Munich crisis in September 1938 that 'without overlooking the assistance that we should hope to obtain from France and possibly other allies, we cannot foresee the time when our defence forces will be strong enough to safeguard our territory, trade and vital interests against Germany, Italy and Japan simultaneously.'[23]

In the 1920s the strategic environment had been such that there was no reason for a serious programme of armaments. The Washington Naval

Treaties of 1922 had removed the threat of a naval race between the United Kingdom, the United States and Japan. For the rest of the decade Britain confronted relatively minor challenges in the empire. The most serious of these, the rise of the Congress party in India, represented more of a political than a military challenge. The strategic situation was such that the government developed the Ten-Year Rule. This policy posited that Britain would cast its armaments programmes yearly on the belief that the nation would not confront a major military conflict for ten years. While the rule seemed to make sense in the 1920s, it had a number of unfortunate consequences. First, it allowed the politicians to put off virtually all programmes required to renew or replace ageing military equipment. This not only made the service's equipment increasingly obsolete, but it harmed the industrial base on which future rearmament would depend. Moreover, the paucity of resources made it increasingly difficult for the services to adapt when technological change accelerated. Finally, the Ten-Year Rule made it essential for the government's leaders to recognise potential threats as they emerged and take the steps required to match them. But therein lay the rub, for the very culture of British politics and the attitudes of the nation's élite guaranteed that its response would be late and inadequate.

Thus, by the mid-1930s the services found themselves in a strategic situation that equated to their worst nightmares. Japan represented a clear threat to Britain's colonial empire in Southeast Asia.[24] In the Mediterranean Mussolini threatened Britain's sea lines of communications to India and Southeast Asia through the Suez Canal.[25] Finally, the rise of Nazi Germany was a direct threat to the British Isles themselves, as Stanley Baldwin underlined in a speech that predicted that 'the bomber would always get through.' Confronting this strategic environment, the services were strenuous supporters of rearmament. However, there was little coherence in their demands: the Royal Air Force for a great bomber fleet to attack Nazi Germany; the Royal Navy for battleships for a war in the Far East; and the army for ground forces to support Britain's allies on the continent. On the other hand, the government's response was crystal clear: it would only grudgingly supply the resources for rearmament, regardless of what the experts in the services thought they needed.

The first governmental discussions about rearmament could only have further depressed the military leadership. Beginning in November 1933, Vansittart, Hankey and Sir Warren Fisher, the permanent secretary of the Treasury, formed with the chiefs of staff the Defence Requirements Committee.[26] After innumerable meetings the committee recommended in March 1934 that the government spend £71 million over the next five years to correct military deficiencies.[27] Given the amounts that Hitler was already lavishing on the German military, this was a laughable proposal. Nevertheless, the Cabinet proceeded to ignore the committee's report for a month before referring its recommendations to another committee, the

Committee on the Disarmament Conference, a conference that was already a dead letter. After considerable infighting, which involved not only the services but the Treasury as well, the Cabinet agreed to the amended recommendations on 31 July 1934.[28] The whole process had taken eight months, countless discussions and vast amounts of bureaucratic paperwork to decide on a minimal increase in defence spending, a decision soon overtaken by events.

In the circumstances, the services took a gloomy view of their ability to handle any major military confrontation, and for much of the decade they cast their strategic and operational appreciations in the darkest colours. In part, this represented an effort to awaken Britain's political leaders as to the lamentable state of the nation's defences and the risks they were running. The result was that Britain's strategic policies revolved around two contradictory appreciations. On the one hand the political leadership continued to believe that Hitler and Mussolini would not embark on war and that their demands were reasonable, in retrospect a best-case analysis of the international situation. On the other hand the government's military advisers consistently provided worst-case analyses of the strategic situation, often deliberately misstating the actual correlation of forces in order to make it appear even darker. The advice proved of little value in persuading the government to increase spending, but it certainly provided Chamberlain with ammunition to argue against strong stands against the dictators.

Diplomacy, Strategy and the Evolution of British Policy in the 1930s

With the benefit of hindsight, it is easy to follow the path British governments followed to the catastrophe of 1939. However, at the time the path was not so clear. Of the leading British politicians, only Churchill recognised that Nazi Germany was not only a moral danger, but also an enormous strategic danger to Britain's security. Between January 1933, when he was appointed chancellor, and 1936, Hitler destroyed the main security provisions of the Treaty of Versailles. In 1933 he withdrew Germany from the League of Nations and the Disarmament Conference. At the same time he ordered the German military to embark on a massive programme of rearmament, for which he provided a blank cheque.[29] In 1934, much to the chagrin of Germany's military leaders, he signed a non-aggression pact with the Poles, which undermined the French alliance system. In early 1935 he regained the Saar when it returned to the Reich after an overwhelmingly favourable vote in a plebiscite conducted by the League of Nations. That same year, no longer able to conceal the military build-up, he announced conscription and creation of the Luftwaffe.

In March 1936, he remilitarised the Rhineland by sending a few scratch units across the Rhine to resume full military control over Germany's territories.

These three years represented a revolution in Europe's strategic landscape. To a great extent they reflected the fact that Germany had been the long-term strategic victor of the First World War. Certainly, by 1935 the other major powers recognised that Germany's growing economic and military strength called into question the continent's future stability. Italy, France and Britain formed a front, ostensibly to discourage any active German moves, such as the attempted Nazi *coup* against Austria the previous year. In fact, Mussolini had little interest in containing Hitler, but was very interested in using the Stresa Front and worries about Germany as a smoke-screen to attack Ethiopia and avenge the Italian defeat at Adowa in 1896. The resulting crisis marked the beginning of a period of distraction for British statesmen and strategists away from the growing threat in central Europe.

As the Italian build-up for the invasion of Ethiopia proceeded, Britain's leaders found themselves in a difficult situation. On one hand they had no desire to provoke a break, which would lead to a collapse of the Stresa Front. On the other hand British public opinion was all for supporting the League of Nation's opposition to Italian aggression. Publicly, therefore, the British government took a strong stand against Italian aggression. But at the same time its private efforts to promote a compromise served only to encourage Mussolini. Once Italian military operations commenced, the British joined in the League's branding of Fascist Italy as the aggressor and its imposition of sanctions. Nevertheless, the British refused to support oil sanctions on the Italians, which might have led to war, nor did they close the Suez Canal to the flow of soldiers and *matériel* to the Ethiopian front. As the crisis mounted, the government's military advisers warned about the dangers of a war with Italy and provided a number of gloomy assessments, which in fact did not reflect their real views as to Italian military effectiveness.[30]

British and French political leaders then attempted to broker a deal in which the Italians would gain control of most of Ethiopia. However, this attempt resulted in an enormous public relations disaster for British politicians who had so loudly proclaimed their support for the League. The government found itself in an impossible position. The very public which stood so strongly behind the League was also vociferously opposed to any measures that might lead to war or to a larger programme of rearmament. Meanwhile, as the government dithered, the Italians broke the back of Ethiopian resistance in a relatively short campaign, remarkable for its brutality and the use of mustard gas. By early spring 1936 the war was over. The Stresa Front was now a dead letter, and the Italians drew closer to the Germans – a factor in European relations that would have occurred anyway, given Mussolini's ideology and megalomaniacal goals.[31]

Almost immediately after the end of the Ethiopian conflict, the peace of the Mediterranean collapsed with the outbreak of civil war in Spain. In July 1936 much of the Spanish army, aided and abetted by right-wing parties, revolted against the Marxist-influenced Popular Front government in Madrid. The *coup* was bungled, and considerable territory and resources remained in the hands of the Republic's supporters. A vicious civil war ensued, which had as much to do with the vagaries of Spanish history as the ferocious passions that it raised outside of Spain, especially among the left. The fighting occasioned almost immediate intervention by Italian, German and Soviet 'volunteers'. However, while Mussolini wholeheartedly supported General Francisco Franco, the leader of the rebels, Hitler strictly limited the Nazi commitment in the belief that a prolonged war in Spain would distract the rest of Europe from the growing German threat.[32]

The Spanish Civil War lived up to Hitler's expectations. British and French statesmen attempted to avert the danger of a direct confrontation among the powers involved by establishing a non-intervention committee. All they succeeded in doing was to muddy the water. The left in both countries raised a hue and outcry for massive aid to the Republic – a demand which political leaders, seeing no national interests at stake, refused. But those supporting the Republic possessed little common sense. The British Labour party urged all possible aid for the Republic at the same time as it voted against legislation providing for British rearmament. As one 'critic' commented in the *New Statesman* in 1936: 'I see no intellectual difficulty in at once working for the victory of the Spanish people [that is the Republic] and in being glad of the growing pacifist movement in England.'[33] Hugh Dalton, one of the few Labour MPs to recognise the absolute need for a serious rearmament programme, acidly commented that most of his colleagues regarded collective security as something to which Britain should make little contribution 'except to sponge on the Red Army'.[34]

In November 1937 Hitler conducted the last serious strategic discussions to occur in the history of the Third Reich, when he held forth on the Reich's strategic situation before a group of senior military and civilian leaders.[35] In a rambling monologue he made clear his belief that Germany would soon have to move against its enemies, because of the serious problems the rearmament programme was confronting. Several of the individuals present, including the *Wehrmacht*'s overall commander, Werner von Blomberg, the army's commander-in-chief, Werner von Fritsch, and the foreign minister, Konstantin von Neurath, strongly protested that Germany was not yet ready for a major conflict. Two months later Hitler sacked the three of them, Fritsch on trumped-up charges of homosexuality. The Fritsch affair caused the most serious crisis in civil–military relations in the Third Reich's history.

While facing a major confrontation with his generals, Hitler, ever the gambler, manufactured a crisis with Austria. In March 1938 the Austrian government collapsed under intense German pressure. To the acclaim of enormously enthusiastic crowds, the *Wehrmacht* marched into Austria, while the hard hand of the SS settled on dissidents and Jews alike.[36] There was no response from the British and French governments. In a philosophical sense the Treaty of Versailles had rested on the belief that the self-determination of people was not only a political but a moral right. The huge crowds that greeted the German Army as it marched into Austria underlined the popularity of the *Anschluß* among most Austrians. The French government immediately fell, which ensured that no French politician could be blamed for the strategic consequences that would flow from Germany's incorporation of Austria. British leaders found the matter most distasteful. As Chamberlain admitted to the Cabinet, Hitler's methods had shocked and distressed the world 'as a typical illustration of power politics', which would only make further appeasement more difficult.[37]

Almost immediately the British confronted the knottier problem of Czechoslovakia. Here the danger lay in the fact that the border areas, where the main Czech defences lay, were inhabited by a German-speaking population. But unlike Austria, Czechoslovakia was an ally of France. Moreover, the Czechs were clearly willing to defend their Republic against German aggression. A war between the Czechs and Germans thus had the potential to bring France into the conflict, which would then put considerable pressure on Britain to support its First World War ally.

Chamberlain turned to the chiefs of staff for an appreciation of the overall strategic situation, but the terms of reference he provided clearly indicated the answer he wished to hear. His directions assumed that Britain would only fight with France at her side, that Poland would be neutral, and that the Soviet Union would also be neutral.[38] Predictably, the chiefs of staff came up with a thoroughly gloomy estimate of the strategic situation. They cooked the books by overestimating German strength – including the three *Deutschland*-class commerce raiders as battleships, for example – underestimated French military strength by an order of magnitude, and ended with the dark comment that Britain had no chance of winning a war against Germany, Japan and Italy.[39]

Throughout the summer of 1938, Chamberlain manoeuvred through the shoals of increasingly treacherous waters. In mid-summer he went so far as to send an unofficial negotiator, Lord Runciman, to resolve the situation.[40] But the conflict between the Czechs and Germans was irreconcilable; Hitler, angered by the seemingly tough stance the Czechs and Western Powers had taken over rumours about a German move against the Republic in May 1938, was bent on destroying Czechoslovakia in a war. By early September, German preparations for an invasion were too advanced to hide, while Dr Joseph Goebbels's Propaganda Ministry was grinding out horror stories to justify military action.

The British Cabinet papers, diplomatic correspondence and strategic analyses underline the desperate situation from the British point of view. It was not so much a belief that Britain confronted defeat in a European war as simply horror at the possibility of another war that drove British policy. In mid-September Halifax told the Cabinet that 'he had no doubt that if we were involved in war now we should win it after a long time,' but then added that he 'could not feel we were justified in embarking in an action which would result in such untold suffering.'[41] In fact, one of the more interesting aspects of the 1938 crisis was the generally blasé attitude British leaders displayed toward strategic questions, on which the matter of whether or not to embark on a war with Nazi Germany should have rested. On 8 September Halifax, on reading a telegram from Prague, admitted that up to that moment he had not known that the Czech fortifications lay inside the Sudetenland, the area the Germans were demanding.[42]

In the mad scramble to assess a rapidly evolving situation, the British failed utterly to come to grips with the fundamental question as to how a surrender of Czechoslovakia, its well-armed military, and its military-industrial complex might affect the future strategic balance. Not until 16 September did a minister raise the question in a Cabinet meeting. By that point pressures on the chiefs of staff were such that they never got around to providing an assessment of the crucial question. Their advice that month ranged from recapitulations of the gloomy forecasts they had rendered in March to far more optimistic estimates. On 23 September the Joint Planning Committee, consisting of the chief planners of the individual services, commented in a paper that appeared later in the day under the imprimatur of the chiefs of staff: 'The attempt to take offensive action against Germany until we have time to bring our military, naval, and air forces, and also our passive defence services onto a war footing would be to place ourselves in the position of a man who tries to show how brave he is by twisting the tail of a tiger which is preparing to spring before he has loaded a gun.'[43] Yet that same day the chiefs of staff were issuing their own paper, which gave a far more optimistic picture of the strategic situation. '[T]he latent resources of the Empire and the doubtful morale of our opponents give us confidence of the outcome [of a war].'[44] The more optimistic assessment undoubtedly reflected the fact that the British had finally begun to pick up how gloomily the German military were assessing their own strategic situation. Britain's military chiefs were finally making an assessment of the balance of forces that provided a more realistic view of Britain's prospects.

None of this change of heart had any effect on the course of British policy. In the end it came down to how Britain's leaders assessed Hitler. Early in the month Halifax suggested to the Cabinet that the Führer might be quite mad and that such a 'view ... was supported by a good deal of information from responsible quarters [in Germany]'. Nevertheless, the foreign secretary thought that a firm stand would destroy whatever chance existed to bring Hitler back to sanity.[45] Chamberlain had made up his mind. He would go to almost any length to preserve the peace. On 15 September, undertaking his first flight, the prime minister met Hitler at his mountain retreat of Berchtesgaden. After listening to Hitler's ranting and ravings, Chamberlain managed to elicit a rough picture of Hitler's demands on Czechoslovakia. He then returned to London, where he first persuaded his colleagues, then the French, and finally the Czechs, that Hitler's demands should be met. Returning again to Germany, this time to Godesberg, Chamberlain recounted his success to the Führer in getting the French and the Czechs to surrender. Hitler simply replied that that was not good enough; he had additional demands. There is no doubt that Hitler was still firmly determined on a localised war over Czechoslovakia.

On his return to London, Chamberlain confronted a Cabinet that was split down the middle as to whether to make more concessions to Hitler.[46] The French were desperate, while only the Czechs displayed some resilience. Yet, with German troops moving into their final jump-off positions, Hitler changed course and at Mussolini's instigation agreed to a conference at Munich. There, with Mussolini, he met Chamberlain and the French premier, Edouard Daladier, who yielded to his demands on Czechoslovakia. Daladier was so depressed at the results that he had his aircraft circle the Paris airport, Le Bourget, to make sure the crowds below were not waiting to lynch him – they were not. Chamberlain returned to cheering crowds in London. Only Churchill, before a thoroughly hostile House of Commons, warned that Britain had made a terrible strategic mistake. In effect, the Munich conference had handed Hitler Czechoslovakia on a platter. Stripped of their defences the Czechs could at best only become Germany's satellite.

The Strategic Results of Munich

In every respect Munich was a strategic disaster for the Western Powers. In the autumn of 1938 the military situation was still relatively favourable to them.[47] Whatever the weakness of their air defences, they faced little threat from a *Luftwaffe* which was running 50 per cent in commission rates throughout summer 1938 and which possessed no capability to execute blind bombing attacks against either French or British cities. Moreover, Germany possessed only three *Panzer* divisions, so that the *Wehrmacht* was not in a position to launch a decisive campaign against the French army. While the Czechs would probably not have lasted much longer than the Poles did the following year, given their superior armaments and advantageous terrain, they would have inflicted heavier casualties on the Germans.

Moreover, heavy fighting against the Czechs would have destroyed most of the Czech equipment that was to fall into German hands in undamaged condition the following year and would probably have severely damaged the Czech armaments industry as well. As for their long-range prospects, the Germans confronted an even more serious situation. They were in the midst of a serious economic crisis; the Reich possessed virtually no stocks of raw materials; and Germany's neighbours, with the possible exception of the Hungarians, were almost uniformly hostile.

But the Germans entirely escaped the possibility of war in such unfavourable circumstances, and thus had a full year to continue their massive rearmament programmes. Nevertheless, Hitler almost immediately regretted that he had lost the opportunity of war against the Czechs; on 19 October he ordered General Wilhelm Keitel, his chief military adviser, to begin drawing up plans for the occupation of the remainder of Czechoslovakia. Meanwhile, he bitterly attacked the British for attempting to act like a governess to the Reich, while Goebbels attacked the British rearmament programme as assuming 'a scale which far exceeds the security requirements of the Island kingdom ... '.[48] Thus German actions did nothing to reassure the British, particularly since Nevile Henderson, Britain's slavishly pro-German ambassador, was no longer in Berlin to provide a positive spin on German actions. At the same time two additional factors provided an even darker picture of Europe's future. It appears that the German resistance began to feed reports of a Nazi move against the Netherlands to both the British and the French. British overtures to the French as to a possible united response received the frigid reply that, given the surrender of Czechoslovakia and its 30 plus divisions, the French did not see any action they might take in response, unless Britain were able to commit sizeable ground forces to the continent.[49] This worrying prospect would eventually lead the British Cabinet to force their reluctant prime minister to commit the British army to the defence of France at the end of February. But by that point the Chamberlain government had lost five months during which it might have taken action to repair the glaring deficiencies in Britain's military position.

In arguing for their policy of appeasement over 1938, Chamberlain and his allies had consistently argued that Britain's military weaknesses allowed no other choice. Now, he confronted the fact that any substantial increase in British defence spending could only imply significant distrust of Hitler's intentions. In the immediate aftermath of the Munich conference, he had warned the Cabinet that 'the burden of armaments might break our backs.'[50] The result was a minimal programme of increases: the contract for Spitfires and Hurricanes was extended from its termination date in summer 1940 to 1941 (thus no increase in fighter production); as suggested above, nothing was done for the army until late February 1939; and the navy received an additional 20 escort vessels, 12 minesweepers, the dredging of two harbours, and an airbase at Scapa Flow.[51] Meanwhile, German rearmament was galloping full-speed ahead, while the *Wehrmacht* was about to acquire the Czech arms dumps and industrial complexes.

Henderson's return to Berlin in mid-February 1939 ended realistic reporting to London from the German capital. As he suggested on 22 February in a letter to the king: 'Hitler has for the moment definitely come down on the side of peace.'[52] Three weeks later, on 15 March 1939, the *Wehrmacht* occupied the remainder of Czechoslovakia. Hitler had thus ripped up the Munich agreement less than six months after its signing. With his policy of appeasement in tatters, an unwilling Chamberlain had to abandon it for one of containment. Even then the change came only because of intense pressure from public opinion. The prime minister himself suggested in his first speech after the German occupation of Prague that 'I ... bitterly regret what has occurred. But do not let us on that account be deflected from our course.'[53] The indignation of the House in response to the prime minister's speech matched the anger in the country. Even the *Times,* a notorious supporter of the government's policy of appeasement, gave voice to displeasure at the German seizure of the remainder of Czechoslovakia.

The Run-Up to War

The problem confronting the government was what was to be done in the immediate future. As far as defence expenditure went, the services finally received a substantial portion of their demands. By July 1939 the government had added nearly £1,000,000,000 to defence spending for the next three years, in effect coming close to doubling the defence budget.[54] This did not occur without substantial opposition from the Treasury, but that department was finally on the defensive for the first time in the 1930s.[55] The most dramatic change came with regards to the army. Having finally accepted the need for a relatively small commitment to the continent in February, Chamberlain now agreed to a doubling of the Territorial Army. With the German threat looming just over the border, the French pressed for more. On 19 April the chiefs of staff proposed a field army of 16 divisions with 16 divisions in the Territorial Army. But Chamberlain was moving even beyond those numbers. By the end of April, he had concluded that Britain must introduce conscription and create a great army to support the French on the continent. Nevertheless, he continued to hope that these major efforts at rearmament might in the end prove unnecessary. As a Cabinet paper pointed out, 'it was not proposed either that the scheme for Compulsory Military Training should supersede our traditional methods of military service or that it should become a permanent feature of our system.'[56]

However important these measures of preparation to meet the Nazi threat, the government's decision to support a massive build-up had one unfortunate effect. Before any of these decisions produced a single tank or aircraft, the chiefs of staff clearly altered their pessimistic view of the strategic situation. Whereas in 1938 they had assessed the military balance in terms of their own weaknesses and the minimal defence efforts that the government had thus far allowed, they now tended to judge the balance in terms of their own prospects.[57] The irony in this change of attitude toward the strategic balance lay in the fact that German rearmament programmes were now at last altering the balance in the Reich's favour. With the addition of the Czech arms dumps, raw material reserves and industrial production, the Germans could not only field formidable conventional forces, but revolutionary new armoured mechanised forces, capable of winning stunning victories against the ground forces of their opponents.[58] Moreover, by spring 1939 the *Luftwaffe* was well on the way to re-equipping its front-line squadrons with a new generation of aircraft, which would allow it to conduct the first strategic bombing offensive in history.[59] Nevertheless, the chiefs' strategic appreciations over the course of spring and summer 1939 were increasingly optimistic despite the reality that the increases in British defence spending would have little impact for some considerable time.

But the Chamberlain government really was not thinking in terms of a military confrontation with the Germans. Instead, British diplomatic and strategic policy aimed at deterring the Germans from undertaking any military action that might actually result in war. Moreover, as rumours swirled around central Europe in the aftermath of the German occupation of Prague and with political pressures mounting at home to resist Nazi moves, Chamberlain acted without a thorough analysis of the strategic situation. The mood of desperation was exacerbated by the German occupation of the Lithuanian port of Memel and the surrounding territory at the end of March. Alarmed by unconfirmed rumours of an impending German move against Poland in the near future, the prime minister extended a guarantee to the Polish state, one that the Poles were delighted to accept. In fact, while they were under no immediate threat of a German military move, the Poles had been under increasing pressure from the Germans to make a deal and place themselves under German protection. At the end of March Chamberlain admitted to the Cabinet that because of the Munich agreement there was no longer a Czech army to help the Western Powers, while Czechoslovakia's military and economic resources were now available to the *Wehrmacht*. He then added that it would be a mistake to allow the same thing to happen to Poland.[60]

On 31 March 1939 Chamberlain announced to the House of Commons that 'in the event of any action which clearly threatened Polish independence, and which the Polish government accordingly considered vital to resist with its national forces, His Majesty's Government would feel themselves bound at once to lend the Polish government all support in their power.'[61] Churchill in his memoirs accurately underlined the results of the government's tardy decisions with regard to Nazi Germany:

> When every one of these aids and advantages had been squandered and thrown away, Great Britain advances, leading France by the hand, to guarantee the integrity of Poland .... There was some sense in fighting for Czechoslovakia in 1938 when the German army could scarcely put half a dozen trained divisions on the Western Front .... But this had been judged unreasonable, rash below the level of modern intellectual thought and morality. Yet now at last the two Western Democracies declared themselves ready to stake their lives upon the territorial integrity of Poland. History ... may be scoured and ransacked to find a parallel to this sudden and complete reversal of five or six years' policy of easy-going placatory appeasement, and its transformation almost overnight into a readiness to accept an obviously imminent war on far worse conditions and on the greatest scale.[62]

The Germans certainly understood the British challenge as one that directly implied the use of force. Hitler was furious. He immediately determined on an invasion of Poland, a military operation that his military planners turned to with an eagerness they had not displayed the previous year. The head of German intelligence, Admiral Canaris, heard the Führer remark that he would soon cook the British a stew on which they would choke.[63] Hitler did aim at keeping the British and French out of his war against Poland, but there would be no diverting him from a course aimed at destroying Poland in a sudden and brutal military operation. There would be no new Munich.

Chamberlain, with the support of Halifax, embarked on a policy of distributing guarantees to virtually all the states in eastern Europe. Despite the fact that there was even less the Western Powers could do for countries such as Rumania and Bulgaria than they could do for Poland, France followed in Britain's wake – the French so delighted at finally achieving a commitment from Britain for the defence of the continent that they were willing to overlook details, such as how one might go about the defence of such far-away and strategically isolated countries. Here one has to remember that as recently as September 1938, the British government and its military advisers had hardly been forthcoming about the level of support they might be willing to tender even France in case war broke out. Just before the Munich conference Halifax had actually indicated to the French that while Britain would never allow France's security to be threatened, His Majesty's Government 'were unable to make precise statements on the character of their future action, or the time at which it would be taken in circumstances they cannot at present foresee.'[64]

On the other hand, as they had made clear at the same time, the French had no intention of undertaking any military action against Germany's western frontier, now protected by the _Westwall_.[65] The French army, as de Gaulle commented in 1938 about a future war, was simply unwilling to do anything: 'It's quite simple .... Depending on the actual circumstances, we will recall the reserves. Then looking through the loopholes in our fortifications, we will passively witness the enslavement of Europe.'[66] And this was the heart of the problem in the summer of 1939: neither country's leadership, political and military, had any real stomach for the coming war. Only new leadership, willing to address the murderous Germans on their own terms, would be capable of confronting the strategic and operational questions that war would raise.[67]

For the British, the distribution of guarantees and the announcement of great programmes of rearmament seemed to have worked wonders. By late May Halifax was telling the French that:

> it should be remembered that the position of France and Great Britain is quite different than it was six months ago. They had embarked on a policy which was both decisive and firm and which had had great effect upon the psychology of the whole world .... The general effect of this was to place our partnership in a position of evident strength.[68]

Nothing showed this more clearly than the tangled web of British attitudes towards the Soviet Union over the course of the six months leading up to the outbreak of the war. During Cabinet discussions dealing with the proposed guarantee to Poland, the question of the Soviet Union had come up. Halifax had commented 'that the present [guarantee] was only an interim arrangement and that the inclusion of Russia was a matter which it was intended to deal with in the discussion ... next week.'[69] And so the crucial strategic question of creating a viable Eastern Front was put off by interminable discussions that took place over the coming months, almost right up to the outbreak of the war.

As we now know, there was virtually no chance the Western Powers could have reached an agreement with an avaricious and suspicious Soviet Union. Yet what is astonishing was the dilatory nature with which the British approached the Soviets. By the time the government finally summoned up the willingness to deal with Stalin, he was deep in negotiations with the Germans. Halifax's remarks after Ribbentrop and Stalin had completed negotiations in late August 1939 suggest an astonishing inability to understand strategic factors or the realities of the balance of power. The foreign secretary discounted the importance of the Nazi-Soviet non-aggression pact to the Cabinet as being of little strategic importance, although its moral importance might be enormous.[70]

Desperate to the last to avoid a looming war, some in the British establishment even went so far as to offer the Germans a bribe of an

enormous loan to behave themselves. The British side was represented by
Chamberlain's close adviser Sir Horace Wilson as well as a senior member
of the Conservative party, Sir Joseph Ball.[71] The negotiations foundered on
two rocks: Hitler had no interest in anything that would actually prevent
war, while news of the attempt was soon leaked to the British newspapers – probably by that arch anti-appeaser, Sir Robert Vansittart.

Despite Germany's refusal to respond to British overtures, the leadership
continued to hope for the best. But hemmed in by popular opinion and the
prospect of a general election in the near future, Chamberlain had no choice
but to back Poland. Nevertheless, the British and French put considerable
pressure on the Poles not to mobilise; the result was that in its attack on
1 September the *Wehrmacht* caught the Poles in the midst of mobilisation, thereby exacerbating Poland's desperate strategic situation. In the end,
it would not matter because the Poles were terribly outmatched, and they
would receive precious little help from their allies in the West. The British would finally honour their obligations on 3 September with a feeble
speech from the prime minister. The French followed later in the day,
hardly suggesting by their tardiness that the Western Powers were united in
the decision to stand up to German aggression.

The Allied approach to the war unleashed by the Germans says a great
deal about how they had got themselves into this dismal situation of having to fight another great conflict. Basically, Allied military planners and
strategists envisioned a long war in which the Western Powers would be
able to strangle Nazi Germany economically, while they built up their
own strength and repaired the deficiencies in their own defences.[72] Such a
strategy would have to aim at cutting Germany off from access to the raw
materials that its wartime economy would so desperately need.[73] It also
implied the use of military forces to use up Germany's scarce resources and
to impair the Reich's ability to prosecute a major campaign against western
Europe. And therein lay the problem, because in every case Allied military
and political leaders talked themselves out of taking any action that might
have hurt Germany's ability to prosecute the war.

As mentioned above, the French had already determined not to attack
the Reich's western borders; thus, for the next six months the Saar's
industry continued in full production within sight of the French border.
In June 1939 Chamberlain had seen the possibility of attacking the Italians,
should the Germans invade Poland. But the government's military advisers
talked their civilian masters out of that possibility, despite a most favourable balance of forces in the Mediterranean.[74] Finally, once war began,
convoluted arguments were raised against mining the Norwegian Leeds, a
move that would have halted the significant trade in Swedish iron ore which
moved out of the port of Narvik and which was essential for German steel
production. Almost the only military action the British were willing to
undertake was to drop propaganda leaflets over the German countryside, a

campaign which the future commander of Bomber Command, Arthur Harris, derisively but accurately described as providing the Germans with toilet paper. The failure to put any military pressure on the Germans allowed them to husband their rapidly shrinking stockpiles of raw materials for one great campaign in the spring of 1940.[75] An Allied strategic appreciation noted in April 1940 that 'the Reich appears to have suffered relatively little wear and tear during the first six months of war and that mainly as a result of blockade. Meanwhile, it has profited from the interval to perfect the degree of equipment of its land and air forces, to increase the officer strength and complete the training of its troops, and to add further divisions to those already in the field.'[76] When the war began one month later, events soon proved the accuracy of that strategic assessment.

Notes

1. Chamberlain did not lose the vote, but so many members of the Conservative Party had abstained as to make it impossible for him to remain in office.
2. For the extent of those difficulties, see F. Anderson, *Crucible of War: The War for North America, 1754–1763* (New York, 2000).
3. For the problems involved in the making of strategy through the ages, see W. Murray, MacGregor Knox and Alvin Bernstein, eds, *The Making of Strategy: Rulers, States, and War* (Cambridge, 1994).
4. For the role of competence and incompetence in human affairs, see W. Murray, *The Change in the European Balance of Power, 1938–1939: The Path to Ruin* (Princeton, 1984), ch. 11.
5. For the extent of that difficulty, see N. Ferguson, *The Pity of War* (New York, 1999), and Sir Michael Howard's brilliant reply, 'The Greatest War', *The National Interest*, no. 64, Summer 2001.
6. C. R. M. F. Crutwell, *A History of the Great War* (Oxford, 1934), p. 630.
7. It is impossible to list all such works here, but the reader unfamiliar with such literature might begin with G. Chapman, *A Passionate Prodigality* (London, 1933); F. Manning, *The Middle Parts of Fortune* (London, 1930); and S. Sassoon, *Memoirs of an Infantry Officer* (London, 1930).
8. A view that most in Germany would thoroughly have disagreed with. In fact, it is well worth the effort to compare the British literature of the late 1920s with the work of the German novelist Ernst Jünger.
9. Quoted in N. Thompson, *The Anti-Appeasers* (Oxford, 1971), pp. 156–7.
10. For a brilliant reconstruction of the development of concepts of armoured, mechanized warfare in Britain from the First World War through to 1939, see J. P. Harris, *Men, Ideas, and Tanks* (Manchester, 1998).
11. Quoted in W. L. Shirer, *The Rise and Fall of the Third Reich: A History of Nazi Germany* (New York, 1960), p. 403.
12. *Documents on British Foreign Policy (DGFP)*, 3rd Series, Vol. II, doc. 590, letter from Henderson to Halifax, 6 August 1938.

13. M. Gilbert and R. Gott, *The Appeasers* (New York, 1967), p. 52. On another occasion Chamberlain commented in a letter that the dictators 'were men of moods – catch them in the right mood and they will give you anything you ask for'. Public Records Office, Kew, PREM 1/276, Chamberlain to Halifax (hereafter PRO, PREM 1/276, etc.)

14. For Hankey's contributions, see S. Roskill, *Hankey, Man of Secrets*, Vols I and II (London, 1972, 1974).

15. How interminable the processes of the British government could be is suggested by a request the Belgian government made in May 1936 to purchase arms from the United Kingdom. After receiving no response for two months, the Belgians repeated their request in July. The Foreign Office then passed the request along to the War Office, which suggested that diplomats handle the negotiations. The Foreign Office then passed the request along to the Committee of Imperial Defence. Not until January 1937 did the Belgians receive a favourable reply, but the War Office then stepped in to suggest that the government examine the political implications. There the matter rested until the Cabinet authorised a favourable response in February 1938 – a response the Belgians did not receive until July. D. O. Kieft, *Belgium's Return to Neutrality* (Oxford, 1972), pp. 164–6.

16. PRO FO 371/22922, C1545/281/17, Minute by Sir Robert Vansittart, 10 February 1938.

17. For the formidable economic problems that Nazi Germany's leaders confronted, see Murray, *The Change in the European Balance of Power*, pp. 12–30.

18. R. S. Sayers, *The Bank of England, 1891–1944*, Vol. III (London, 1976), appendix 12, table A, pp. 308–9.

19. PRO CAB 23/90A Cab 43 (17), Meeting of the Cabinet, 22 September 1937.

20. For discussions of the Treasury's role in the pre-war rearmament effort, see G. C. Peden, *British Rearmament and the Treasury, 1932–1939* (Edinburgh, 1979); and R. P. Shay, Jr., *British Rearmament in the Thirties* (Princeton, 1977).

21. PRO CAB 23/88, Cab 20 (37), Meeting of the Cabinet, 5 May 1937.

22. P. M. Kennedy, 'British "Net Assessment" and the Coming of the Second World War', in W. Murray and A. R. Millett, eds, *Calculations, Net Assessment and the Coming of the Second World War* (New York, 1992), p. 35.

23. PRO CAB 53/37, COS 697 (Revise) (see also DP[P] 220, CID), COS Sub-Committee, 'Military Implications of German Aggression Against Czechoslovakia', 28 March 1938.

24. The Japanese invasion of Manchuria in 1931 proved to be the opening shot in what was to be the most catastrophic decade in the world's history. For the inadequate response of the powers to that move, see C. Thorne, *The Limits of Foreign Policy: The West, the League and the Far Eastern Crisis of 1931–1933* (New York, 1972).

25. On the nature of Mussolini's goals see M. Knox, *Mussolini Unleashed, 1939–1941: Politics and Strategy in Fascist Italy's Last War* (Cambridge, 1982).

26. PRO CAB 16/109, 1st Meeting of the Defence Requirements Committee, 14 November 1933.

27. CAB 24/247, CP 64 (34), 5 March 1934.

28. Shay, *British Armament in the Thirties*, p. 44.

29. There was in fact no coordinated rearmament effort in Nazi Germany, nor did Hitler and the military services make any effort to cast the Reich's rearmament programmes within a rational economic framework. By 1937 the result was a serious economic crisis that severely impeded the build-up and which probably led Hitler to speed up the tempo of his aggressive policies. For an analysis of these issues, see Murray, *The Change in the European Balance of Power*, ch. 1.

30. A. Marder, 'The Royal Navy and the Italo-Ethiopian Crisis of 1935–1036', *American Historical Review* 75 (1970), 1327–56.

31. See particularly M. Knox, *Common Destiny: Dictatorship, Foreign Policy, and War in Fascist Italy and Nazi Germany* (Cambridge, 2000), ch. 2.

32. G. Weinberg, *The Foreign Policy of Hitler's Germany*, Vol. I, *1933–1936* (Chicago, 1970), p. 298.

33. *The New Statesman*, 12 August 1936.

34. Harold Macmillan, *Winds of Change* (New York, 1966), pp. 407.

35. The transcript of this meeting, kept by Hitler's army aide, Colonel Friedrich Hoßbach, is in *Akten zur deutschen auswärttigen Politik*, Series D, Vol. I, no. 19, 'Niederschrift über die Besprechung in der Reichskanzlei am 5. November 1937 von 16,15–20,30 Uhr', 10 November 1937.

36. A drastic purge of the Austrian officer corps immediately occurred. Thirty senior officers soon found themselves as guests of the SS in Dachau, while the last Austrian Minister of War, General Wilhelm Zehner was murdered by the Gestapo. T. Taylor, *Munich* (Garden City, NY, 1979), p. 373.

37. PRO CAB 23/92, Cab 12 (38), Meeting of the Cabinet, 12 March 1938.

38. PRO CAB 53/36, COS 697, CID, COS Sub-Committee, 'Situation in the Event of War against Germany', 16 March 1938.

39. PRO CAB 53/37, COS 698 (Revise), COS Sub-Committee, 'Military Implications of German Aggression against Czechoslovakia', 28 March 1939.

40. Since the British government could at any time disassociate itself with any findings that he might make, Runciman characterised his position as being put out 'in a dinghy in mid-Atlantic.' PRO CAB 23/94, Cab 35 (38), Meeting of the Cabinet, 27 July 1938.

41. PRO CAB 23/95, Cab 19 (38), Meeting of the Cabinet, 17 September 1938.

42. PRO FO 371/21770, C9101/4786/18, Newton to Halifax, 2 September 1938, minute by Halifax dated 8 September 1938.

43. PRO CAB 53/13, JP 327, Joint Planning Committee, 'The Czechoslovak Crisis', 24 September 1938.

44. PRO CAB 53/41, COS 773, COS Committee, 'The Czechoslovak Crisis', 24 September 1938.

45. PRO CAB 23/95, Cab 37 (38), Meeting of the Cabinet, 12 September 1938.

46. There is substantial evidence that Chamberlain faced a revolt in the Cabinet as he attempted to force through further concessions to Hitler. See Murray, *The Change in the European Balance of Power*, pp. 206–9.

47. For the military situation at the time of Munich as well as an examination of the strategic and economic factors that would have played in a European war at that time, see Murray, *The Change in the European Balance of Power*, ch. 7.

48. PRO FO371/21658, C12816/42/18. Ogilvie-Forbes to Halifax, 21 October 1938.

49. Murray, *The Change in the European Balance of Power*, p. 274–5.

50. PRO CAB 23/95, Cab 48 (38), Meeting of the Cabinet, 3 October 1938.

51. Murray, *The Change in the European Balance of Power*, p. 273.

52. PRO 800/270, letter from Henderson to the king, 22 February 1939. On the same day Henderson wrote to Halifax that he felt confident of the prospects of peace were it not for that section of the British press inspired by the Jews and intelligentsia who hated Hitler and the Nazis. PRO FO 800/315, Henderson to Halifax, 22 February 1939.

53. Hansard, *Parliamentary Debates*, 5th Series, Vol. 345, House of Commons (London, 1939), col. 440.

54. PRO CAB 24/287, CP 149 (39), 'Note on the Financial Situation', 3 July 1939.

55. Murray, *The Change in the European Balance of Power*, p. 295.

56. PRO CAB 23/99, Cab 22 (39), Meeting of the Cabinet, 24 April 1939.

57. The one exception to this, as we shall see, turned out to be their evaluation of the military and strategic balance in the Mediterranean.

58. For how the Germans came to develop these forces, see Williamson Murray, 'Armored Warfare: The British, French and German Experiences', in W. Murray and A. R. Millett, eds, *Military Innovation in the Interwar Period* (Cambridge, 1996). For how close the German margin of victory was even with their 'new model army', see W. Murray, 'May, 1940: Contingency and Fragility of the German RMA', in M. Knox and W. Murray, eds, *The Dynamics of Military Revolution, 1300–2050* (Cambridge, 2001).

59. Which it was certainly in no position to do in autumn 1938 at the time of the Munich crisis.

60. PRO CAB 23/98, Cab 16(39), Meeting of the Cabinet, 30 March 1939.

61. Text in PRO CAB 23/98, Cab 17(39), Meeting of the Cabinet, 31 March 1939.

62. W. S. Churchill, *The Second World War*, Vol. I, *The Gathering Storm* (London, 1948), p. 347.

63. A. Bullock, *Hitler: A Study in Tyranny* (London, 1964), p. 445. Hitler remarked later in the summer that he had seen his enemies at Munich and they were worms.

64. *Documents on British Foreign Policy*, 3rd Series, Vol. II, doc. 841, Chamberlain to Halifax, 12 September 1938.

65. *Documents Diplomatiques Français*, 2nd Series, Vol. XI, doc 376, 'Compte Rendu des Conversations techniques du Général Gamelin au Cabinet Office 26 septembre 1938'. Gamelin made clear that he had no intention of launching major military operations into Germany or even attacking the Saar: an approach of sitting on his hands which he would replicate in September 1939.

66. P.-M. de la Gorce, *The French Army* (New York, 1963), p. 270.

67. For the extent of the change that would be required, see the discussion of the strategic and operational utility of the Combined Bomber Offensive against Germany in W. Murray and A. R. Millett, *A War to Be Won: Fighting the Second* (Cambridge, MA, 2000), ch. 12.

68. *Documents on British Foreign Policy*, 3rd Series, Vol. V, doc. 570, 'Extract from Record of Conversation between the Secretary of State and MM. Daladier and Bonnet at the Ministry of War, Paris', 20 May 1939.

69. PRO CAB, 23/98, Cab 16 (39), Meeting of the Cabinet, 31 March 1939.

70. PRO CAB 23/100, Cab 41 (39), Meeting of the Cabinet, 22 August 1939. Strategic naïvety was not just a mark of the British government in this period.

Less than a year later the Soviet foreign minister Molotov was to extend to the German ambassador 'the warmest congratulations of the Soviet government on the splendid successes of the German *Wehrmacht*' in its campaign against France and the Low Countries. *Documents on German Foreign Policy*, Series D, Vol. IX, doc. no. 471, 18 June 1940.

71. Murray, *The Change in the European Balance of Power*, p. 307.
72. For a general examination of Allied strategy towards Germany in 1939, see Murray, *The Change in the European Balance of Power*, pp. 310–14.
73. In summer 1938 the Advisory Committee on Trade Questions in Time of War, one of the sub-committees of the Committee on Imperial Defence, pointed out the weaknesses of the German economy and recommended that 'our aim should, therefore, be: 1) The maximum interruption of these goods in all cases where it is practicable, and to create a shortage of them in Germany. 2) Any diminution of Germany's economic resources as a whole.' PRO CAB 47/14, A.T.B. 181, 'Plan for Economic Warfare Against Germany', 12 July 1938.
74. In 1940 British forces alone were able to destroy Italy's position in Libya and sink a substantial portion of the Italian battle fleet. In 1939, British and French forces in the Mediterranean were even more favourably positioned to launch a series of devastating blows against the Italians which, even if they had not knocked the Italians out of the war, would have forced the Germans to provide significant military forces, which would then not have been available for the campaign in the West. For the arguments of Mediterranean strategy among British policy-makers, see the discussion in Murray, *The Change in the European Balance of Power*, pp. 314–21.
75. For the seriousness of the German economic situation, see Murray, *The Change in the European Balance of Power*, pp. 326–32.
76. PRO CAB 85/16, M.R. (J) (40) (s) 2, Allied Military Committee, 'The Main Strategy of the War, Note by the French Delegation', 11 April 1940.

7 The United States

Warren F. Kimball

On April 6, 1917, the United States formally joined a wartime coalition for the first time in its history. America's entry into what later became known as 'World War I' (a christening in which Franklin Roosevelt apparently played a role) demonstrated that it had accepted the challenge thrown out by former President Theodore Roosevelt, to 'play a great part in the world'. Inspired by President Woodrow Wilson's rhetoric about making the world safe for democracy, Americans set out upon their own 'Great Crusade'.

Wilson's proposal for a League of Nations has rightly occupied a prominent place in the history of the post-war period. His concept of collective security, however incompletely developed, represents one of the few attempts by a world statesman to find a workable substitute for power politics – that diplomacy of shifting alliances and coalitions. But Wilson's proposal had two fatal flaws: it depended upon the creation of a single, global economic-political system; and it assumed (a fake) equality among all nation states. His 'collective security' also demanded extensive cooperation and trust among the major world powers, but such trust could develop only when they shared similar political and economic creeds, and that was not to be.

Instead, the peace settlements that followed the First World War created a renewed structure of alliances and ententes by which the victors hoped to preserve the *status quo*. The problem was that there were multiple '*status quos*'. British and French élites had their own similar yet differing versions, with both powers fixated on maintaining colonial empire. The United States, with its powerful and expanding economy, held to a somewhat different vision. Then there were the revolutions – from the Bolshevik Revolution in Russia (aimed at a corrupt ruling clique and capitalism), to anti-imperialism in China (aimed against a corrupt ruling clique and the Europeans) and on to Mexico (aimed at a corrupt ruling clique and the United States). On the fringe was Japan, which had enhanced its empire during the First World War almost without effort. Then there was Germany, defeated but not vanquished, and waiting in the wings. But perhaps most important of all, at least for the next decade, the 'Great Powers' in Europe were not prepared to abdicate their dominant roles and accede to an American century.[1]

The result of these developments, combined with domestic party politics, was United States' rejection of membership in the League of Nations – which seemed a rejection of any formal role in Europe. Somehow, the Atlantic Ocean seemed to widen again, despite memories of German submarines attacking American ships, and it soon became common once more for Americans to speak disdainfully of Europe's power politics. The United States became isolationist in the peculiarly American use of the word, choosing to remain aloof from the political squabbling that beset post-war Europe. Economic issues were, as always, a different matter.

The great power international system in Europe, only superficially similar to what had existed before the war, operated without overt American support, but what developed in Asia sprang principally from the efforts of the United States. The Washington Naval Conference of 1921–22, convened by the American secretary of state, Charles Evans Hughes, resulted in a series of treaties, each of which involved the United States in Asian power politics (or more accurately, in European power politics in East Asia). A Five-Power Naval Disarmament Treaty was aimed directly at ending the arms race between Japan, Britain and the United States. A Four-Power Treaty between Britain, Japan, France and the United States replaced the old Anglo-Japanese Alliance with one that promised only consultations. Both agreements clearly implied American support for the *status quo* in the Pacific. The Nine-Power Treaty, which merely endorsed the Open Door for exploitation of the seemingly vast China market, served to distract critics from the realities of the power relationships being established. American participation in this informal system had one limitation: there could be no prior commitments that required the use of either economic or military coercion.

The Western Hemisphere, where the United States exercised increasingly hegemonic power, and the colonial world of Africa and southern Asia, where European colonialism was the dominant political system, were both to be disciplined and controlled by the Great Powers.[2]

The onset of the Great Depression in 1929 eliminated whatever slim chance there might have been for that inconsistent, regional, jury-rigged, Rube Goldberg-style[3] system to develop into a meaningful and long-term global structure. Moreover, Japan, Germany, China and the Soviet Union, all exiled for different reasons to the outer reaches of politics, soon mounted challenges that spelled the demise of the informal system that had spurned them. In the 1930s most nations withdrew into themselves, but none more so than the United States. Herbert Hoover's oft-expressed conviction that the Great Depression came to America from Europe, typified the reaction of a people who saw their success as the result of their own individual efforts. Embittered and cynical about their experience in and with Europe and the international community following the Great Crusade, Americans indulged in self-recrimination and vowed never again to try to 'save' Europe from itself.

The war between Adolf Hitler's Germany and most of the rest of Europe followed a series of challenges that began as soon as the Führer came to power in January 1933. Under his leadership, Germany broke out in less than a decade from the quarantine the other European powers had tried to impose after the First World War with the Versailles Treaty. He had not made it easy for Britain and France to oppose him. He rejected the Versailles system in increments, each relatively contained and thus unsettling rather than threatening. Rebuilding an air force, negotiating a naval agreement with the British, military reoccupation of the Rhineland – these all seemed legitimate actions for an independent state. Blatant but unofficial military intervention in the Spanish Civil War (1936–39) was more troubling, but then France and Britain hardly had clean hands in that arena. Union (*Anschluß*) with Austria in 1938, and demands for union with the Germans in western Czechoslovakia (the Sudetenland) masqueraded as corrections to ethnic inequities perpetuated by the First World War peace settlements.

The geopolitical pot of troubles was stirred by two consistent and consistently alarming Nazi policies. The first was Germany's aggressive economic action – autarkic policies of protectionism and bilateral trade agreements, which went directly against both American liberal economics (free markets) and the British imperial system, a system which was, in its own way, a world-wide commercial structure. The second was Hitler's increasingly brutal and callous treatment of Jews and his repression of organised Christian churches. Nazi persecution of Jews was infinitely more horrific than the regime's anti-Christian policies – there were no plans for a 'final solution' for Christians. But Hitler's treatment of the Christian churches, particularly the Roman Catholic and Lutheran Churches, alienated their European and American co-religionists – a far larger and politically more influential element than Jews. According to one German diplomat, Americans feared that Hitler was planning to replace Christianity with state-sponsored paganism, which caused 'doubt and wavering even among the Lutherans', who, with Catholics, comprised the bulk of German-Americans. Yet, without the threat posed by Hitler's aggressive policies and apparent military strength (grossly overestimated by all), western leaders would have shaken their heads, made the appropriate public expressions of concern, and then – as Winston Churchill did – claimed they could not intervene in the internal matters of other states.[4]

By 1938, perhaps somewhat earlier, Hitler's cautious, step-by-step overturning of the First World War peace settlement presented European leaders with a dilemma: the only way to prevent war was to go to war. Neither Britain nor France (nor the United States) was willing even to contemplate the possibility, nor – to hazard a guess – was the Soviet Union. Memories of the horror of the Great War were too recent and strong, while the Great Depression had reinforced the natural tendency of societies to focus on local, internal problems. At the same time, domestic instability made both France and the Soviet Union reluctant to become involved in external confrontations. In the mid-1930s, France had stopped its revolving door of governments only by settling on a weak coalition led by the Socialist, Léon Blum. In the Soviet Union, Stalin's anxieties had brought on the Great Purge, which crippled political, bureaucratic and military leadership.[5] In Britain, the government of Neville Chamberlain, though far from weak, was until the last equally reluctant even to consider military opposition to Hitler.

American isolationism in its common meaning is a misconception. The passage of legislation like the Neutrality Acts of the mid-1930s was, in fact, an admission that the United States was, either by choice or by fate, a player on the international scene. Those laws aimed to prevent big business (a ready villain in the midst of the Great Depression) from dragging the nation into war as had supposedly happened in 1917. The legislation prohibited aid, particularly arms sales and loans, to countries at war lest this draw the United States into the conflict. Underlying those actions was the belief that Europe had rejected American leadership after the First World War.

In fact, one of the great myths of the inter-war era is that the United States retreated into isolation and, by doing so, refused to play a part in creating a political or alliance structure that would have contained or prevented Hitler's war. There remain questions, serious questions, about the 1930s. Some will be answered, perhaps in the next decade or so, with the opening of the Soviet archives. But others can be answered only if we discard the conventional wisdom, bequeathed to us in large part by Franklin Roosevelt and his secretary of state, Cordell Hull, as part of their campaign to consign any and all opponents to the hell of extremism. By 1942, 'isolationist' was the dirtiest word in the American political lexicon. The classic neo-Wilsonian formulation of American isolationism in the 1930s is simple and simplistic: the United States refused to cooperate in the international system after the First World War, thus missing an opportunity to prevent Hitler's rise to power and preserve peace. The realist reformulation modifies that to read that the United States refused to foster or even consider a military alliance with Britain and France; *ipso facto*, the United States missed an opportunity to stop Hitler and prevent the Second World War.

Americans are no doubt affected by the myopia of nationalism, but it would be wrong to imagine that they are unique in this respect. All too often Europeans use isolationism as an epithet to describe American policies that fail to treat Europe as the centre of the geopolitical world. Too many studies of the inter-war period treat American foreign policy as an afterthought and then, in a few cryptic comments, leave the impression of United States culpability for what followed.[6] What was expected of American foreign policy? Was the United States expected to provide both leadership and backbone (Roosevelt's word) for a Europe traumatised by the memory of the First World War's horrors? Was it American policy that made the League of Nations weak, or would it be more correct to speculate that US participation would have made the League even less effective?[7]

But who was the true isolationist? The British prime minister, Neville Chamberlain, set a simple and absolutely self-defeating test for US intentions. If the United States was willing to make specific, presumably military commitments, then it was serious. Actually, American leadership was the last thing in the world an egotistical Chamberlain wanted. This was, after all, the man who pompously wrote his sister Ida, 'now I have only to raise a finger & the whole face of Europe is changed.'[8] Anything less than an unequivocal commitment on Roosevelt's part and the prime minister could (and did) label American initiatives as hot air. Chamberlain's test for Hitler was not nearly as rigorous. All the German leader had to do was toss off a few vague promises, incline an eyebrow (or moustache?), and declaim about his desire for peace. Chamberlain immediately responded with suggestions for conferences, and optimistic letters to his sisters. As for working with the Soviet Union, the most obvious ally against Hitler, Chamberlain would have no part of it.[9]

Any alliance against Hitler formed in 1938 or after would have had to be willing to force, or at least risk, a fight. Yet British and French (as well as American) diplomacy in those years was always guided by the belief that war was worse than its alternatives. Their disdain for Soviet proposals for a full-fledged military alliance, whether or not those proposals were sincere, highlighted Anglo-French unwillingness to consider such a step. No wonder Roosevelt repeatedly lectured the British on the need to stiffen their resolve. 'Good man' was Roosevelt's two-word expression of support for the Munich agreements of September 1938 – the appeasement approach that attempted to assuage Hitler's hunger by feeding him Czech territory. This did not reflect a liking for appeasement itself, but rather the president's desire that leadership in Europe should come from the Europeans. The previous February, Roosevelt had remarked to one of his ambassadors that if the police chief makes a deal with gangsters that prevents crime, he 'will be called a great man'. But if the gangsters break their word, 'the Chief of Police will go to jail'. Chamberlain seemed to be 'taking very long chances'.[10]

Perhaps American military commitments to fight in Europe could have prevented war, though deterrence failed to prevent the Japanese from attacking Pearl Harbor. But in an era when even the highly mechanised German army still used horse-drawn wagons to bring supplies to the Front, the burden for establishing a deterrent policy in Europe lay chiefly with the Europeans – France, Britain and the Soviet Union – not with a country on the far side of the Atlantic Ocean. Perhaps an American commitment would have shored up French morale and persuaded Chamberlain that the United States could be trusted in a crisis. But nothing the French did or Chamberlain said before 1939 suggests such an outcome. Whether an alliance would have prevented German aggression may be doubted; similarly for the claim that American support would have made the British and the French more courageous in their diplomacy. What is not questionable was the American attitude toward an alliance. The general public, Congress and most public leaders believed that alliances caused wars instead of preventing them, and they opposed any such arrangements for the United States.

The Munich agreements did not bring the 'peace for our time' that Chamberlain had predicted. In fact, the confrontation that lay behind the arrangement made all the participants aware that they had merely papered over the cracks, not reached a long-term solution. That awareness stimulated increased planning and spending on military preparedness, in Germany as well as among Hitler's enemies. By December 1938, Roosevelt had assigned his Treasury secretary, Henry Morgenthau, Jr, the task of coordinating US aid to the European democracies, as Britain and France both sought to buy aircraft and related equipment, and the Roosevelt administration sought to develop military production capabilities.[11]

In mid-February 1939, some six months before the war began in Europe, Roosevelt provided news reporters with a remarkably clear picture of the foreign policy he hoped to follow for the next few years.[12] Ostensibly speaking 'off the record' (which meant reporters could not quote him), Roosevelt, ever the liberal, linked economic and political freedom, telling the journalists, 'there are certain nations, about thirty or forty strong ... whose continued independent political and military and ..., let's say, their economic independence, ... acts as a protection for this hemisphere.'

'Suppose I say,' he went on, 'that the continued independence, in a political and economic sense, of Finland is of tremendous importance to the safety of the United States?' Then what about the Baltic states, Scandinavia, Greece and the Middle East? Deftly slipping to more immediate problems, he pointed out that Austria and Czechoslovakia had come off the list of independent nations. The independence of others, he argued, 'acts as a protection for the democracies of this hemisphere'. Even Senator Gerald Nye, the father of the neutrality legislation and Roosevelt's archetypal 'isolationist', understood that Roosevelt hoped to use Anglo-French power as America's 'first line of defense' – a different concept than a 'frontier'.[13]

Roosevelt had set his agenda. The spread of dictatorships threatened democracy – the code-word for American political liberty and economic opportunity. Back in 1937, in the wake of the Japanese attack on China, when Japan had ignored the Pacific peace structure and used military force to gain empire, he had spoken of preventing war by quarantining the dictators. He was apparently thinking aloud, for he had no plan and quickly backed away in the face of vocal opposition from what he called the 'isolationists'. Now, two years later, he advocated helping the British and French to quarantine (without using that word) the European dictators. The president admitted that such actions might be called 'unneutral'. But, he went on, the policy of the American government was to do everything it could to keep arms away from the Axis powers – Germany, Japan and Italy – while selling as much arms to the 'independent nations' as they could pay for.[14]

This was not the military globalism of Cold War America, or even the great power cooperation that Roosevelt himself would come to advocate. Rather it suggested a leader who recognised the limits of American power – limits imposed by domestic attitudes, by perceptions of the ability of the United States to influence events, and by common sense.

Hans Dieckhoff, the German ambassador to the United States in the late 1930s, was spot on when he warned his superiors in Berlin in March 1938 that 'the American Government, should it so desire, will encounter no insuperable difficulties in again pushing this country into the war at the psychological moment, just as in the [First] World War, and perhaps even more quickly.' He exaggerated more than a little when he wrote that one could recognise 'his master's voice' from London, but the overall point – that the United States was hardly isolationist – proved on the mark.[15] He seems to have recognised that there was considerable ground between isolation and intervention.

The German occupation of Prague in March 1939, a blatant violation of the Munich arrangement, along with Mussolini's move across the Adriatic Sea into Albania, not only prompted increased preparedness on the part of those threatened by Hitler, but also pushed Chamberlain to begin, ever so tentatively, discussions with Soviet leaders about some sort of mutual assistance arrangement. The negotiations never brought agreement. The Soviet Union continually changed its position; fear of Soviet intentions caused the Poles and Balts (Latvia, Lithuania, Estonia) to refuse promises of cooperation; and Chamberlain, who distrusted the Communists intensely, always found reasons to delay. He remained convinced that the Russians had no choice but to cooperate against Germany, despite reports of contacts between Berlin and Moscow.[16]

But Stalin had concluded otherwise. Following the First World War, the new Polish state had twice used military force to take territory at the Bolsheviks' expense, while the Baltic states had taken advantage of Soviet weakness to declare their independence after some 200 years of Russian rule. Stalin was determined to regain those lands. Munich, with its implied invitation to Hitler to move eastwards, destroyed any expectation Stalin had of developing collective security against Germany; the desultory British approach towards alliance negotiations merely confirmed that conclusion. Stalin made a virtue out of necessity and agreed to a pact with Hitler, gambling that the short-term benefits – time for the Soviet Union to rearm plus reacquisition of the so-called lost territories – seemed a better bet than relying on the British and French to become effective allies against Germany and also to agree to Soviet re-absorption of those lands.[17]

On 21 August 1939, rumour became reality when Berlin radio reported that Joachim Ribbentrop, the German foreign minister, was on his way to Moscow to sign the Nazi-Soviet non-aggression pact. Ten days later, on 1 September, German forces invaded Poland. Within two days, Britain declared war on Germany. Stalin delayed – cautious about German intentions, eager to present his actions as the recovery of his legitimate territory, and worried about the continuing military confrontation with Japan along the Mongolia-Manchuria border – but finally moved into eastern Poland a few weeks later in order to collect his part of the bargain with Hitler. 'It's the end of the world, the end of everything,' warned the American ambassador in London, Joseph Kennedy.[18] As Roosevelt had predicted, Neville Chamberlain, the chief of police, would have to go to jail or the political equivalent – lose his office. The only question was when.

British strategic assumptions were simple – and simply wrong. They assumed that Hitler's gaze was fixed on the Slavs to the east – especially the Ukraine. And they assumed that, if the Germans did attack in the west, France would hold out for a year, even two years, giving Britain time to do what Churchill had persistently advocated – rearm.

Ironically, Soviet and American assumptions were much the same. No one, least of all Stalin, thought the Nazi-Soviet Pact would survive for long, given Hitler's rants about the inferior Slavs. But analysts in both Washington and Moscow believed that the Germans had to take care of the problem closest to home, France. And France had already demonstrated, they thought, that while it might not be able to win alone, it could not lose. Thus Stalin, Roosevelt and Chamberlain all believed they had what every politician covets – the time to make tough decisions.

With the outbreak of war in Europe in September 1939, Roosevelt established a supposed neutrality patrol in the north Atlantic and arranged a Western hemisphere foreign ministers declaration setting up a 'safety belt extending outward from 300 to 1000 miles around the hemisphere, except for Canada', which had declared war on Germany. This meant American warships would enforce neutrality (that is, suppress German attacks on merchant shipping, including attacks on British vessels) in that vast area, freeing the Royal Navy for other tasks closer to home.

Roosevelt justified the neutrality patrol with the dual-level argument he had used earlier. That approach would continue as his explanation for the neutral-aid policies he adopted, at least until mid-1941. Every move served to protect 'the peace, the integrity, and the safety of the Americas', yet, as the President had proclaimed when the European war began, Americans were not expected to ignore their consciences and 'remain neutral in thought . . .',[19] as Wilson had appealed for in 1914. The best defence for the United States against the dictators was to help Britain and France.

Roosevelt used that same approach in fulfilling his private promise to the British to change what he labelled the 'so-called' Neutrality Acts, which prevented Hitler's opponents from purchasing war materials. But that was easier said than done. Even if the administration concluded that it had public support, it faced the threat of a filibuster in the Senate – and the Allies needed immediately the great 'psychological lift' that Chamberlain was requesting. How to do that without evoking American fears that they were being dragged into another unnecessary war?

The trick was to avoid names and speak in generalities. Roosevelt's appeal to Congress stated that the embargo gave 'a definite advantage to one belligerent as against another . . .'. No names, no call for aid to Britain and France – but everyone understood.[20] The press, and certainly the anti-interventionists, grasped the purpose: only the British and French were in a position to make effective use of the new procedures. The press, the anti-interventionists and the isolationists all did their jobs by pointing out the obvious. So did Roosevelt's supporters.

The public campaign against revision soon fizzled out, while Roosevelt mounted a counter-campaign that included creation of the cleverly named Non-Partisan Committee for Peace through Revision of the Neutrality Act. The committee, chaired by William Allen White, a nationally known newspaper editor from Kansas, later became the equally cleverly named Committee to Defend America by Aiding the Allies. Accepting Congressional advice to require that war materials be purchased only on the basis of 'cash and carry' (in non-American ships), the administration secured the passage of a revised Neutrality Act by solid margins on 3 November 1939. One columnist neatly summed it up: 'What a majority of the American people want is to be as unneutral as possible without getting into war.'[21]

Even as the White House fended off domestic opposition to benevolent neutrality, British efforts to make their blockade of Germany effective created problems for Roosevelt's campaign. The blockade, formally called 'contraband control' to assuage American sensitivities, aimed at preventing Germany from trading with the Americas. Little wonder that Churchill called the United States the 'greatest of all neutrals'. The system was complicated: neutral merchant ships had to be certified by a British consul abroad that their cargoes were not intended for Germany, directly or indirectly. Otherwise, they were subject to diversion to a British control port. In addition, the British blacklisted any company that traded with Germany – something Americans resented. The entire scheme had all too familiar echoes of how Americans thought they had been dragged into the First World War.

The British ambassador to the United States, Lord Lothian, reported in December 1939 general American sympathy for the Allies combined with a firm resolve to stay out of the war. But he also detected two ideas that threatened to pose problems for Britain. One was a kind of defeatism engendered by the absence of military victories – something that would worsen in 1940. The other, running counter to defeatism, was the expectation that Hitler had ensured his own destruction by making a deal with the Soviet Union that brought the two into direct contact over the corpse of Poland. That made a Soviet-German war inevitable, went the argument, a view reinforced by the Soviet attack on Finland, which inclined Americans to think they were not threatened and allowed them to focus on British trade regulations. Old suspicions quickly reasserted themselves, prompting Americans to conclude that the wily British were manipulating the blockade in their own economic interests.

At the same time, Chamberlain remained convinced that the Americans would not come to Britain's aid in time to make a difference – not an unreasonable conclusion. When, in January 1940, Churchill promised that 'no American ship should, in any circumstances, be diverted into the combat zone around the British Islands,' he went too far. The Chamberlain government, which to Churchill's dismay seemed all too willing to push the Americans into a corner, quickly forced a modification. At the same time, even Churchill underestimated Roosevelt's ability and commitment to deal with (and Hitler's ability to scare) the anti-interventionists. He pessimistically told Chamberlain that Roosevelt is 'our best friend, but I expect he wants to be re-elected and I fear that isolationism is the winning ticket'.[22]

On 9 February, the President announced that 'Under Secretary of State Mr. Sumner Welles will proceed shortly to Europe to visit Italy, France, Germany and Great Britain. ... Mr. Welles will, of course, be authorised to make no proposals or commitments in the name of the Government of the United States.' Given Roosevelt's frequent statements to the effect that Hitler was a 'nut' and a 'wild man', and that his assassination or overthrow by the German people was the only alternative to rearming Britain and France, the Welles mission seems to make no sense.[23] Yet, unless Welles, a friend of the Roosevelt family as well as a career diplomat, violated his instructions, the mission was much more than just a Roosevelt whim or a subterfuge to delay the expected German offensive. Even after visiting Hitler and Mussolini, Welles told the British War Cabinet that the only peace proposals that could work would have to begin with broad disarmament (a favourite Roosevelt proposal), while providing a 'sense of security to the Allies' without requiring 'the elimination of Herr Hitler'. Churchill told Welles that Britain 'must and should fight it to a finish', but privately Churchill and the Cabinet worried about the possibility of 'a patched up peace ...'.[24]

One explanation for the mission was that, with the 1940 nominations and presidential election coming up, Roosevelt wanted to blunt any accusations that he had not done everything reasonable to broker a peace settlement. This seems to contradict his forceful descriptions of Hitler as 'mad' and 'wild', but leaves open the possibility that hubris had overtaken the president and he had concluded that his continued leadership was essential for the nation, whatever the means. The other explanation is that Roosevelt, despite his misgivings and doubts about Hitler, believed it was his responsibility to make every effort to avoid what seemed almost inevitable – all out war. This option fits with the persistent American belief that Europeans could not resist the inclination to go to war over petty and selfish quarrels. The belief, often associated with 'Wilsonianism' though it predates Wilson, prompted Americans to think they could mediate the creation of a new and better international structure – a 'new world order' would be the phrase of an American president 45 years after Roosevelt's death.[25] Whatever Roosevelt's motives, and whatever Welles' diplomacy, it is clear that any compromise Roosevelt proposed would have been unacceptable to Hitler.[26]

The invasion of Denmark and Norway on 9 April 1940 ended the ominous quiet in western Europe – labelled the 'phony war' by isolationists – and brought the conflict a bit closer to the United States, physically and psychologically. Roosevelt remained unwilling to risk getting the wrong answer in a national debate on American policy towards aid to the Allies, but he told newspaper editors on 18 April that while his wife Eleanor was on a lecture trip she noticed 'that people were beginning to take their heads out of the sand', asking "What is going to happen *if*?" ... Before this Denmark episode and the Norway episode, there weren't nearly as many questions by the public.' As he did not have an answer to the question, he charged the editors to perform their 'very definite duty to start that thing going around the country'. Moreover, the possibility of the Nazis taking over Iceland and Greenland, both under the Danish monarchy, raised questions in the minds of reporters – and presumably other Americans. Once again, there were clearly good guys and bad guys, but no names were used.[27]

On 9–10 May 1940, Hitler's armies ignored the neutrality of the Low Countries – Belgium, the Netherlands and Luxembourg – in launching a major offensive that met with rapid success. Within a few days, the Germans turned to calculated war on civilians with the indiscriminate terror bombing of Rotterdam, forcing the Dutch to surrender. The Belgians, with an army larger than British ground forces on the continent, fought bravely, but outflanked by a swift German move through the supposedly impenetrable Ardennes forest (a lesson the Allies would have to re-learn during the German counter-offensive in 1944–45), they abandoned the fight by 18 May.

That was only the prelude to disaster for the Allies. A deadly combination of incompetent leadership, inadequate planning, lack of coordination, poor intelligence, and superior German tactics and strategy brought about the stunningly rapid fall of France.[28] By the time Churchill became prime minister on 10 May, the Germans had almost completed their move through the Ardennes. Three days later they broke the French lines at Sedan, crossed the Meuse River, then easily beat off poorly executed French counter-attacks. The battle for France was over, although it would take another month before organised resistance to the Germans ended.

Asked how Britain could hope to defeat Hitler, Churchill boasted that 'I shall drag the United States in,'[29] but that was whistling in the wind. Although the United States did not enter the fray formally until the Japanese attack on Pearl Harbor in December 1941 – two years and three months after the war in Europe had begun, and four and a half years after Japan's all-out assault in China – Roosevelt's re-election in November 1940 turned out to be a choice of a war leader or more precisely a leader who could keep America out of the war without allowing the war to be lost. Practically no one *wanted* to go to war; yet no one *wanted* Hitler to win. At the same time, a growing number of Americans (a majority by mid-1940) believed that defeating Germany would *require* that the United States join the fighting.[30]

Roosevelt played to the numbers. Whatever his own beliefs about entering the war, he avoided the question of direct involvement like the plague. His 'private' lobbying effort (what in later times would be called a political action committee) was led by the Committee to Defend America by Aiding the Allies. The name alone illustrated the strategy. His major aid programme before the election was a swap of decrepit First World War-vintage destroyers for valuable base rights in seven British territories in the Western Hemisphere; and in October 1940, just before the election, he pandered to national fears by promising that 'your boys are not going to be sent into any foreign wars,' never raising the question of whether American support for the Allies might force war on the nation.[31]

Roosevelt had been re-elected president in 1936 as a domestic problem-solver. Yet, in the years that followed, the international crisis demanded increasing attention. The cynical argument that Roosevelt welcomed and deliberately exacerbated relations with Germany and Japan in order to distract attention from his domestic failures is belied by the fact that the foreign crises were the work of the Germans and Japanese, not the United States. Nor is there persuasive evidence that Roosevelt had lost faith in the New Deal, even if he worried that the public might not share his view.

Did he believe, before the election of 1940, that the United States should and would enter the war? Who knows? He soon dropped his initial prediction in 1939 of a short war due to either a quick German victory or the collapse of the Nazi regime. Within a few months, he moved firmly, and publicly, towards a form of neutrality that favoured the Allies. But no evidence has surfaced to demonstrate that he actively and consistently lied to the American people about his ultimate intentions, and there are good reasons to conclude that he hoped the United States could (or would have to) fight a limited war, with only naval and air forces engaged against the Germans. Even after his re-election, Roosevelt told Cordell Hull, his secretary of state, and the American military chiefs in mid-January 1941, that the United States should be prepared to fight a defensive war in the Pacific, while the navy should prepare to convoy supplies to Britain. But the army should follow 'a very conservative' approach, he said, focusing on protecting Latin America.[32]

But not lying is not the same as telling the truth. Clearly, Roosevelt did not take the public into his confidence during the election campaign of 1940. He avoided and evaded awkward questions about how the United States could be neutral and still provide naval vessels and war supplies to one of the belligerents. The usual justification has been that Roosevelt, fearful of being told 'no' if he asked the public to endorse greater assistance to Britain, needed time to 'educate' Americans and their Congressional representatives.[33]

But the public, the president, and politicians in general follow conventions – accepted usages that provide what reporters call 'plausible deniability' for all parties. They use an adult version of the children's taunt, 'Ask me no questions; I'll tell you no lies.' Even the unsophisticated polls of the era (Roosevelt occasionally suggested questions for the pollsters to ask)[34] demonstrate that by mid-1940 respondents understood quite well what was at stake, but refused to ratify the hard decisions. That only illustrates the role leaders are expected to play: to make unpleasant choices and then if necessary take the blame for the consequences. What Americans wanted to hear in 1940 (and in subsequent crises) was not what they knew was the truth, but what they wished was the truth. In a sense, they wanted to be lied to.

The international crisis created by Hitler's conquest of western Europe led the Republican party to nominate Wendell Willkie, an avowed supporter of aid to Britain. Old-line leaders like Senator Robert Taft of Ohio, who had expressed a preference for a German victory rather than American involvement in the war, stood no chance of nomination (or election). Public opinion, as expressed in polls and through Congress, saw Hitler as a threat, which someone must deal with. However much the two presidential candidates avoided public candour, both Roosevelt and Willkie gave Americans exactly the foreign policy they believed they needed (according to the polls) – leaving the electorate to vote for their predictions, which were in fact their wishes.[35]

In spite of later claims, by colleagues and historians, that public opinion had limited Roosevelt's freedom of action, he apparently agreed with the majority of Americans. He understood that Britain and France were fighting America's war, but saw no need for the United States to be anything except what he later labelled 'the arsenal of democracy'. The collapse of French resistance in June 1940 made him willing to lend money, equipment and technical aid to Britain, culminating in what was virtually an economic declaration of war – the Lend-Lease Act of March 1941. But he remained convinced until late 1941 that a military alliance and full American participation in the war might be avoided.

Hitler's invasion of the Soviet Union made Roosevelt initially less optimistic, for it raised the spectre of a level of German strength that would necessitate American armed intervention. By mid-summer, Roosevelt had decided to bet on Soviet survival and committed the United States to sending aid. But the effect of indirect intervention would take time, and by the autumn of 1941 he had begun to speak and act in ways that indicated he believed direct intervention was necessary. In September and October, when German submarines attacked three US warships protecting merchant shipping bringing supplies to Britain, the administration seized the opportunity to expand the president's authority to take stronger action. Yet, in early November, he warned W. L. Mackenzie King, the Canadian prime minister, that a request to Congress for a declaration of war on Germany would lose overwhelmingly.[36] What was Roosevelt up to? There is no smoking gun, no diary entry or memorandum to explain his thinking. What all this suggests is that he had concluded that Hitler's Germany must be defeated, and that to accomplish this the United States must eventually enter the war. But deciding when, and how, could wait for a little while. The Soviet Union might survive – the Battle of Moscow had begun in early October 1941, but would not be decided in Russia's favour until early December. A German invasion of the British Isles had become unlikely if not impossible. So it seemed that Roosevelt once again had that cushion, that advantage so treasured by political leaders – time.

The Japanese attack on Pearl Harbor changed that with stunning suddenness. What historians have come to call the Pacific War was connected to the European conflict largely by the opportunities presented and fears created by the challenge Hitler posed. Japan's search for, even preoccupation with, gaining a colonial-style empire reached new heights by the 1930s. The Japanese military, especially the army, which dominated the government, had no qualms about using force to achieve its goals. The European colonial powers, which had long stood in its way, were increasingly distracted by the mounting crisis in Europe. When, in July 1937, Japanese expansion into China erupted into open but undeclared war, the Europeans expressed dismay but did nothing to restrain the Japanese army – nor did the Japanese government. China, torn by civil war and without effective leadership, posed little challenge to Japan's modern military forces. That left only the United States and the Soviet Union to block Japanese expansion. Stalin's regime, preoccupied with internal security affairs, sought only to prevent Japan from moving into Soviet Siberia. But the Americans were more troublesome, as they had been for the Japanese for most of the twentieth century. By the late 1930s, the United States seemed the only power standing in the way of Japanese goals. Americans were no more willing than the Europeans to consider a military response, but Roosevelt seemed eager to orchestrate sanctions against Japan. He mused about an economic blockade by all the major powers that would 'bring Japan to its knees within a year'. The sinking of an American gunboat, the USS *Panay*, in the Yangtze River in December 1937, brought only diplomatic protests from Washington, an official apology from Tokyo, and complaints from the isolationists about the fact that the warship was there in the first place.[37] Roosevelt's preference for economic pressure on Japan, reflecting but often more aggressive than State Department thinking, had been hinted at in his 'quarantine' speech of October 5, 1937. Over the following two years, that preference slowly but steadily became American policy as the administration abrogated Japanese-American trade agreements, put a 'moral' embargo on aircraft sales to Japan, and expanded its military presence in the Pacific. But Japan, committed to the incorporation of China into its economic and political sphere, continued its aggression undeterred.

Geopolitical considerations only buttressed the American determination to insist that Japan back off. Once Hitler's war broke out in Europe in September 1939, American attention shifted to that arena. The collapse of French resistance and the ensuing Battle of Britain – the struggle to prevent a German invasion of England – meant that the Americans no longer had the luxury of time. Then, in September 1940, the Japanese signed the Tripartite Pact with Germany and Italy. The pact was not, for the Japanese, an offensive alliance but rather a *pro forma* agreement that promised to allow them to do what they had done during the First World War – to expand their regional empire at the expense of the European colonial powers without having to confront them militarily. Officials in Tokyo wishfully assumed that America would turn to face the German threat first, leaving Japan to create what it euphemistically called its Greater East Asian Co-Prosperity Sphere. That they misread the American reaction is now obvious. That Washington misread the nature of the threat is equally clear.

While the Roosevelt administration exaggerated the threat of totalitarian encirclement (perhaps a conscious exaggeration on Roosevelt's part), it underestimated the intensity of the Japanese commitment to empire. Following the State Department's strategy (though Roosevelt often pushed for stronger measures), the administration assumed that, when push came to shove, Japan would not go to war against a power it could not defeat on the battlefield. Whatever the validity of American concerns about

Japan's seeming alliance with Germany, as well as long-standing Japanese-American conflicts over economic and commercial interests, misperceptions lay at the root of their war – for push did come to shove, and the predictions of both sides proved tragically wrong.

In an ironic prequel, concern about French Indochina (which included Vietnam) helped drag the United States into war. The new Vichy government in France signed an armistice with Germany and put collaborationist French authorities in charge of much of the French colonial empire. When, in the summer of 1940, the Japanese pressured Vichy to allow Japan to occupy the colony, the French quickly, if reluctantly, acquiesced. That posed a threat to British and American access to the resource-rich European colonies of Southeast Asia, and thus posed a threat to Roosevelt's policy, or rather wishful hope, that Britain might somehow contain the Nazi threat. Washington's response came in stages: a protest here, a complaint there, finally a threat that the United States would take it amiss if the Japanese moved further south. But its only immediate response was a misunderstood message from Roosevelt to Churchill, which seemed to predict a German invasion of Britain rather than the Japanese occupation of Indochina. (Churchill reacted with puzzled concern, but Anthony Eden, at his country home in South Devon on a stormy weekend, caustically reported that any German who tried to cross the Channel would arrive too seasick to fight.[38])

The details of Japanese-American policy for the 14 months preceding the Pearl Harbor attack on 7 December 1941, offer a lesson in the dangers of relying solely on military and economic deterrence. The United States continued to tighten the economic noose it had placed around Japan's neck, and to send diplomatic and military warning signals. The Japanese became increasingly anxious as their ability to fight a war was threatened by ever-more restricted access to raw materials, but continued to assume that, when push came to shove, the Americans would back off and focus on the European war. But the German attack on the Soviet Union in June 1941, instead of further distracting the United States, served to make Roosevelt even more concerned about Japan lest it seize the opportunity to move into Russian Siberia.

The Indochina prequel continued when, in July 1941, the Japanese moved into southern Indochina, menacing the American Philippine Islands as well as vital sources of Britain's war *matériel*. That only stiffened American resolve to get tough with Japan and force it to back away from confrontation. Economic sanctions already in place were heightened and tightened, prompting the Japanese to conclude that, if they were to fight, they must do so before their strategic supplies ran out. By August 1941, when Roosevelt met Churchill aboard a warship anchored off the British colony of Newfoundland, there was no room to manoeuvre left for Japan and the United States. Roosevelt held to the 'beat Germany first' strategy that Anglo-American military advisers had recommended early in 1941, but everyone seemed to understand that they were slowly but steadily slipping into war in the Pacific.

The sum of so many miscalculations and misperceptions was that the United States was stuck with a policy that had mistakenly assumed Japan would back down, while Japan developed a self-delusory war strategy that assumed the United States would be so disheartened by the Pearl Harbor attack that it would negotiate with Japan while focusing on the real threat, Nazi Germany.[39] Few wars in history have been generated by greater stupidity.

Notes

1. L. C. Gardner's *Safe for Democracy: The Anglo-American Response to Revolution, 1913–1923* (Oxford, 1984) provides a persuasive perspective for understanding the early twentieth century within the context of challenges to the existing political economies. The issue of sovereignty would not have arisen had the United States been able to dominate the international scene.
2. This typology owes much to the early works of A. Iriye, particularly *After Imperialism* (Cambridge, MA, 1969).
3. For the generations who missed the wonderful Rube Goldberg cartoons of the 1930s and 1940s, they invariably depicted a confused, elaborate, unnecessarily complicated structure (pulleys, gears, wheels, strings, chewing gum) aimed at accomplishing a simple task.
4. W. F. Kimball, 'Dieckhoff and America', *The Historian* 27 (1965), 230–2. A persuasive study of British overestimates of German strength is J. Kimche, *The Unfought Battle* (New York, 1968). See also E. R. May, *Strange Victory: Hitler's Conquest of France* (New York, 2000). Churchill's separation of external and internal matters is discussed in N. Rose, *Churchill: The Unruly Giant* (New York, 1995). See also D. Reynolds, 'Churchill and Allied Grand Strategy in Europe, 1944–1945', in C. F. Brower, ed., *World War Two in Europe: The Final Year* (New York, 1998), pp. 39–54.
5. This generally accepted characterisation of Soviet weakness must be balanced by such events as the Red Army's spanking of the Japanese in 1938.
6. One late Soviet-era book on the pre-war years argues that 'it was not until after the Second World War that the treachery of the Western powers came out fully. They used the Moscow talks as a means of pressure on Germany in their interests and negotiated with the Nazis behind the back of the Soviet Union from May to late August 1939.' Oleg Rzheshevsky, *Europe 1939: Was War Inevitable?* (Moscow, 1989), p. 152. The author goes on to claim that 'Much of the blame for the situation ... lies at the door of the US leadership. On August 16 [1939] Franklin Roosevelt sent the Soviet government a message counselling it to seek 'a satisfactory agreement' with Britain and France. However, the United States did not commit itself in any way, nor did it offer any assurances regarding the position of London and Paris. There is reason to

believe that by then Washington was certain the talks would fail.' D. C. Watt, *How War Came: The Immediate Origins of the Second World War, 1938–1939* (London, 1989), pays some attention to America's impact by inserting two chapters (of 32) on the US role, but only to prove that Roosevelt's pusillanimity ensured that US policy would not deter Hitler. Another English scholar, Christopher Thorne, went to the other extreme when he wrote that 'the neutrality laws clearly symbolized the unlikelihood of a commitment by the New World redressing the unhealthy balance within the Old.' From that point (p. 8) on, the United States and Franklin Roosevelt disappear from his study, *The Approach of War, 1938–1939* (London, 1967). Meanwhile, since the early 1990s, the pages of the journal *Diplomatic History* have been routinely filled with exaggerated self-criticism from American historians of US foreign policy about the 'parochial' nature of their field.

7. See, for example, I. Clark, *The Hierarchy of States: Reform and Resistance in the International Order* (Cambridge, 1989), p. 153.

8. W. R. Rock, *Chamberlain and Roosevelt* (Columbus, 1988), p. 32. 'Military isolationism' is the phrase used by C. Barnett, 'Anglo-American Strategy in Europe', in A. Lane and H. Temperley, eds, *The Rise and Fall of the Grand Alliance, 1941–1945* (London, 1995), p. 178.

9. The latest assessment is R. A. C. Parker, *Chamberlain and Appeasement: British Policy and the Coming of the Second World War* (London, 1993).

10. Rock, *Roosevelt and Chamberlain*, pp. 85–6 and *passim*. For British–Soviet relations in this period, see Parker, *Chamberlain and Appeasement*, pp. 222–45.

11. The best study of the American response to the Munich crisis and its aftermath is B. R. Farnham, *Roosevelt and the Munich Crisis* (Princeton, 1997). She argues that Munich and its aftermath gave Roosevelt's fears 'an immediacy that had been lacking'; p. 158. On US rearmament and use of European purchases to capitalise American war industry see T. A. Wilson, 'The United States: Leviathan', in D. Reynolds, W. F. Kimball and A. O. Chubarian, eds, *Allies at War* (New York, 1994), pp. 173–99.

12. R. J. C. Butow, 'The F.D.R. Tapes', *American Heritage* 33 (1982), 8–24. The transcript of the meeting is 'Conference with the Senate Military Affairs Committee, Executive Offices of the White House, January 31, 1939, 12:45 p.m.', President's Personal File 1-P, Franklin D. Roosevelt Library, Hyde Park, New York (FDRL).

13. Franklin D. Roosevelt, Complete *Presidential Press Conferences of Franklin D. Roosevelt*, 25 Vols (New York, 1972), # 523 [115] 3 February 1939; # 525 [140, 141], 17 February 1939.

14. Conference with the Senate Military Affairs Committee, 31 January 1939, PPF 1-P (FDRL), pp. 16, 17, 18. Nye as quoted in W. S. Cole, *Roosevelt and the Isolationists* (London, 1983), pp. 306, 307. The use of 'Axis' to describe the coalition is taken from the 1936 Italo-German agreement known as the Rome–Berlin Axis, after Hitler and Mussolini called their nations' relationship 'the axis on which the rest of the world would turn'.

15. The Dieckhoff quotes are from reports to the Foreign Office in Germany, *Documents on German Foreign Policy, 1918–1945*, Series D, Vol. I (Washington, 1949), # 440, pp. 689–90 and # 391, p. 605. For discussions of these issues that both agree and differ, see C. A. MacDonald, *The United*

States, Britain and Appeasement, 1937–1939 (London, 1981); Rock, *Chamberlain and Roosevelt*; P. Hearden, *Roosevelt Confronts Hitler* (De Kalb, 1987); R. Ovendale, *'Appeasement' and the English Speaking World* (Cardiff, 1975); W. I. Cohen, *Empire Without Tears* (Philadelphia, 1987).

16. A recent summary by a Russian historian is O. Rzheshevsky, 'The Soviet-German Pact of August 23, 1939', Society for Historians of American Foreign Relations *Newsletter* 22 (1991), 13–32.

17. Stalin's 'gamble' is persuasively described by S. Miner in 'Stalin's "Minimum Conditions" and the Military Balance, 1941–1942', in G. N. Sevost'ianov and W. F. Kimball, eds, *Soviet-U.S. Relations* (Moscow, 1989), pp. 72–87; and in S. Miner, *Between Churchill and Stalin* (Chapel Hill, 1988).

18. On the Soviet delay in occupying eastern Poland see G. Weinberg, *A World At Arms* (Cambridge, 1994), pp. 55–6. Kennedy is quoted in Dallek, *Roosevelt and American Foreign Policy*, p. 198.

19. The Roosevelt quotes are from R. Sherwood, *Roosevelt and Hopkins*, rev. edn (New York, 1950), p. 125; R. A. Divine, *The Illusion of Neutrality* (Chicago, 1962), p. 296. 'Feeding' is in J. R. Leutze, *Bargaining for Supremacy: Anglo-American Naval Collaboration, 1937–1941* (Chapel Hill, 1977), p. 46.

20. Quotes from Divine, *Illusion of Neutrality*, p. 289; S. I. Rosenman, *Working with Roosevelt* (New York, 1972), p. 191. See also *Presidential Press Conferences*, 14:135 (5 September 1939) and 14:149 (8 September 1939).

21. F. Kirchwey as quoted in Divine, *Illusion of Neutrality*, p. 312.

22. W. F. Kimball, *Churchill & Roosevelt: The Complete Correspondence*, 3 Vols (Princeton, 1984), I, C-5x, C-6x; Churchill's memo as quoted in M. Gilbert, *Finest Hour* (Boston, 1983), p. 117.

23. *Presidential Press Conferences*, 15:139 (9 February 1940); for Hitler as 'nut' and 'wild man', see Conference with Senate Military Affairs Committee, 31 January 1939, PPF 1-P (FDRL), pp. 4–5, 7–8.

24. F. Freidel, *Franklin D. Roosevelt: A Rendezvous with Destiny* (Boston, MA, 1990), p. 329; Gilbert, *Finest Hour*, pp. 191–2.

25. This is the argument of Reynolds, *The Creation of the Anglo-American Alliance*, pp. 69–72. In a different sort of 'Wilsonianism', the State Department warned Welles to keep in mind that 'history has shown the danger' of 'indicating that we are collaborating with the British for common peace terms.' State Department to Welles, 29 Feb. 1940, Welles papers, FDRL, box 155, 'memoranda, Jan–Feb 1940'. The Welles papers at the Roosevelt Library do not provide any unequivocal explanation of Roosevelt's intentions, and there is no documented and hence convincing explanation for the Welles Mission.

26. The British record of Welles's talks with them is revealing. See L. Woodward, *British Foreign Policy in the Second World War* Vol. I (London, 1970), pp. 164–72. For the day-by-day details of the Welles mission, see I. F. Gellman, *Secret Affairs: Franklin Roosevelt, Cordell Hull, and Sumner Welles* (Baltimore, 1995), pp. 166–202. Gellman dismisses the chance that the mission was a serious effort to arrange a peace settlement.

27. *Presidential Press Conferences*, 15:239–42 (9 April 1940); 15:265–6 (18 April 1940).

28. The latest study of the 'collapse' of France in 1940 is Ernest R. May, *Strange Victory*, in which May argues that inadequate intelligence analysis prevented

the French government from recognising German military intentions and from realising that the military balance actually favoured France.

29. M. Gilbert, ed., *Churchill War Papers*, Vol. II, *Never Surrender, May 1940–December 1940* (New York, 1995), Randolph Churchill recollection (18 May 1940), pp. 70–1.

30. J. MacGregor Burns, *Roosevelt: The Lion and the Fox, 1882–1940* (New York, 1956), repeatedly cites such public opinion polls; see, for example, pp. 399–400. For some examples of seemingly contradictory poll results, see Warren F. Kimball, *The Most Unsordid Act: Lend-Lease, 1939–1941* (Baltimore, 1969), pp. 57–8.

31. As quoted in Burns, *Lion and the Fox*, p. 449.

32. As quoted in Leutze, *Bargaining for Supremacy*, p. 219. Roosevelt's early predictions are in Reynolds, *The Creation of the Anglo-American Alliance*, p. 67. His hope that Hitler would be assassinated or overthrown was expressed as early as January 1939; Cole, *Roosevelt and the Isolationists*, p. 305.

33. This is the argument of historians like Arthur Schlesinger, Jr., Robert Dallek and Thomas A. Bailey, all seeming to agree with Burns's claim that 'Roosevelt was less a great creative leader than a skilful manipulator and a brilliant interpreter'; Burns, *Lion and the Fox*, pp. 400–4. Reynolds in *The Creation of the Anglo-American Alliance* finds that, until autumn 1941, Roosevelt continued to hope the United States could avoid all-out war.

34. M. Landecker, *The President and Public Opinion* (Washington, 1968), p. 123, n. 7.

35. This thesis is buttressed by the evidence in J. C. Schneider, *Should American Go To War? The Debate over Foreign Policy in Chicago, 1939–1941* (Chapel Hill, 1989), although, like most, he argues that public pressure 'forced' Roosevelt to move slowly. Taft's position is described in R. Shogan, *Hard Bargain: How FDR Twisted Churchill's Arm, Evaded the Law, and Changed the Role of the American Presidency* (New York, 1995), p. 110.

36. The three warships were the USS *Greer*, *Kearny*, and *Reuben James*. For the 'bet' on Soviet survival, see W. F. Kimball, *The Juggler: Franklin Roosevelt as Wartime Statesman* (Princeton, 1991), pp. 21–41. Roosevelt's comment to King is from D. Reynolds, *From Munich to Pearl Harbor: Roosevelt's America and the Origins of the Second World War* (Chicago, 2001), pp. 156–7.

37. A solid summary of Japanese policy formulation is M. Barnhart, *Japan Prepares for Total War: The Search for Economic Security, 1919–1941* (New York, 1987). The *Panay* incident is discussed on pp. 126–7, as is Barnhart's description of Roosevelt's musings about a blockade. The *Panay* was escorting some Standard Oil Company tankers, fleeing the outbreak of warfare around Nanking, China. The gunboat was there as part of a long-standing Anglo-American river patrol aimed at protecting their nations' interests and citizens. The British had been there since the 1840s; the Americans joined much later.

38. Kimball, *Churchill & Roosevelt*, I, R-11x/A (20 September 1940); R-11x/B.; A. Eden, *The Reckoning* (Boston, MA, 1965), p. 160.

39. There is a substantial literature on what Herbert Feis called *The Road to Pearl Harbor* (Princeton, 1950). As good a place to start as any is Jonathan G. Utley, *Going to War with Japan, 1937–1941* (Knoxville, 1985). W. Heinrichs, *Threshold of War* (New York and Oxford, 1988), traces the details of the final

American steps toward war, finding that Roosevelt assumed early on that war would come. The Pearl Harbor conspiracy thesis – the claim that Roosevelt knew about the Japanese attack in advance, but chose to say nothing so as to get the United States into the war against Hitler's Germany – seems destined never to die, despite the lack of evidence. The latest entry, as unpersuasive as its predecessors, is R. Stinnett, *Day of Deceit: The Truth about FDR and Pearl Harbor* (New York, 2000).

8 Poland

Anita J. Prazmowska

In the run up to the Second World War Poland briefly occupied a new and prominent role in international relations. Since the closing months of 1938 Poland's status had changed from that of Germany's partner in the destruction of Czechoslovakia to its probable next victim. In most European capitals the fear arose that Poland would provoke Germany by a hasty or imprudent response to tensions in the Free City of Danzig. The perception of Poland as a victim rather than a player in the complex game of brinkmanship that marked the months preceding the outbreak of the war, has long persisted, encouraged not least by the provocative work of the British historian A. J. P. Taylor. In his study of the implications of the British policy of appeasement, Taylor suggested that by guaranteeing Polish security and hence the security of the Free City of Danzig, Britain encouraged Poland to become intransigent and that this caused the outbreak of the Second World War.[1] While Taylor's apportioning of responsibility for the outbreak of the Second World War to the British policy of appeasement has been extensively debated, the general assumption has persisted that small states were at best passive, at worst opportunistic in their responses to the impending European conflict. The main reason for this is that the Second World War is still seen as the consequence of the breakdown of the Versailles order in which smaller states, first Czechoslovakia and then Poland, played only walk-on roles. By implication, the study of the east European states' foreign policies appears to be unnecessary. To conclude that they were passive, lacking in foresight and generally inept, is an easily made assumption even now.

A closer look at Poland's situation in the run up to the war will show that the country's military rulers behaved not as helpless victims but as leaders of a Great Power, and conducted a complex foreign policy. They assessed the merits of closer association with Germany against the background of a general distrust of decisions made by the four Great Powers: Germany, Italy, France and Britain. Security considerations played a major part in their deliberations, and the roles of the two overbearing neighbours, Germany and the Soviet Union, were carefully debated. The military regime, generally known as the 'rule of the colonels', clearly did make a number of imprudent decisions. That they conducted policies which resulted in Poland being ill-prepared to fight an enemy from the West in 1939, overlooked the likelihood of a Nazi-Soviet *rapprochement*, and forged no useful political and military links with their neighbours are factors for which they were responsible. Nevertheless, the international situation was not of their making, nor could they substantially influence the evolution of Germany's eastern policy.

After the Munich conference, Polish observers initially hoped that war in Europe had been prevented. The German occupation of Prague was largely accepted as a *fait accompli*: nothing could be done about the fate of the now renamed Czecho-Slovakia. But since October 1938, when Ribbentrop told Josef Lipski, the Polish ambassador to Berlin, that Danzig would have to return to Germany, tension between the two countries increased. By March 1939 Poland had become the focal point of international attention. In spite of the great secrecy surrounding Polish–German relations, it seemed clear that Germany was determined to incorporate Danzig into the Third Reich. The Poles were determined to fight Germany if an attempt was made unilaterally to carry this out. Nevertheless, when war broke out on 1 September 1939, Danzig was not the cause. The total destruction of the Polish state had become Germany's main military objective, and the seizure of Polish territories the broader aim. British and French entry into the war likewise had nothing to do with the Danzig issue or even the defence of Polish security. For them, the issue was the European balance of power, which had tilted dangerously in favour of Germany. Both powers had at different times undertaken to defend Polish security and territorial integrity, France by the Franco-Polish Agreement of February 1921 and Britain more recently as a result of Chamberlain's unexpected declaration on 31 March 1939. Once Germany launched its attack, neither power could help Poland directly. But the fact that Germany was the aggressor and the beneficiary of aggression, forced both governments reluctantly but inevitably to enter the war.[2]

In the midst of the diplomatic, military and economic turmoil in the period immediately before the outbreak of war, Poland pursued its own vision of a stable eastern Europe, and in the process displayed a remarkable degree of independence due to the fact that it distrusted all the Great Powers and viewed their attempts to interfere in Poland's affairs as self-serving. However, Poland failed to build up any regional anti-German bloc and did not realistically assess its own military limitations. These were obvious shortcomings of the military regime's policies. Nevertheless any suggestion that Poland was responsible for the breakdown of relations with Germany, or even of the outbreak of the war by failing to accommodate German demands over Danzig, does not stand up to scrutiny.

Poland's regional policies were based on the assumption that both the Soviet Union and Germany should and could be kept out of eastern and south-eastern Europe. At the same time, the desire to be the dominant power in the region led Poland's leadership to assume that they could benefit from German aggression, most notably from the weakening of Czechoslovakia whose economic and political influence they resented. An antagonistic attitude towards French influence in eastern Europe, while to some extent justified by France's disturbingly inconsistent eastern policies, led the Poles to overestimate their own military capabilities and to ignore French attempts to build up anti-German unity. When in 1938 Britain, through its involvement in the Czech crisis, took over from France the role of guarantor of the east European balance of power, Poland refused to go along with the Munich decisions not least because it had been refused the status of an interested party. In the event, the desire to benefit from the destruction of Czechoslovakia proved too strong, and Poland assisted Germany in that policy without considering the broader consequences for its own future role in eastern Europe. At the same time Poland's unwillingness to consider the benefits of supporting the Soviet policy of collective security left it unprepared for the consequences of the failure of Moscow's efforts, which led directly to a *rapprochement* with Germany and joint action against Poland.

The dilemmas faced by Polish leaders had always been complex. In January 1934 Poland secured a major international *coup* by signing a Declaration of Non-Aggression with Nazi Germany. Josef Piłsudski, Poland's military dictator, hoped thereby to remove one of the main sources of instability in eastern Europe. Both sides agreed to maintain the territorial *status quo* and to negotiate on all contentious issues. Since Danzig was the most controversial unresolved problem between the two states, 1934 marked the starting point of a constructive period in Polish–German bilateral relations. So long as they agreed not to change the status of the Free City, this would signal their desire to avoid conflict. On the other hand, any open call for the City to return to the Reich would be seen in Warsaw as a provocation and would have an impact on the whole of relations between the two states.

During the First World War, President Wilson had supported Polish hopes for an independent state with access to the sea, and after the war Poland emerged from the wreckage of the three empires that had previously dominated the region. Nevertheless, the issue of access to the sea remained to be settled in the Versailles negotiations. While the French premier, Clemenceau, pushed for a strong Poland, including the Danzig city and port, notwithstanding the fact that the majority of their population was German, the British prime minister, Lloyd George, seeking to limit the extension of French power in eastern Europe, opposed this solution.[3] Eventually a compromise was reached with the creation of a Free City, initially controlled by the League of Nations and later made self-governing, albeit still under League authority.[4] In 1933 the Nazis won a majority in the Danzig Senate and most of the architects of the League came bitterly to regret the compromise solution, which complicated their relations with

Germany and Poland. For Germany the solution was simply to demand the return of the city. For Poland the matter was more complicated as the city's port lay at the mouth of the main navigable river which ran through the length of Polish territory. Polish leaders were determined that Germany should not have the city, even though they accepted that it could not be incorporated into Poland. Unfortunately for all sides involved, the League of Nations' commitment to the maintenance of the independence of the city decreased with time and by the1930s Britain, France and Sweden, the three League guarantors of the city's status, heartily wished the Poles and Germans would come to some mutually acceptable agreement. But while the Poles deeply resented the League's authority in the city, they did not want it withdrawn. Thus the situation in 1934 was particularly advantageous to them. They had obtained a commitment from Hitler that he would not seek a confrontation over Danzig; this in turn led to the scaling down of anti-Polish activities by the Danzig Nazis. At the same time, the League Commissioner remained in the city, which the Poles accepted as a form of insurance policy. The Poles took little interest in the introduction of anti-Jewish laws in the Free City, and showed little sympathy for the Danzig Social Democrats when anti-trade union laws were implemented by the Nazi Senate. Boosted by the confident assumption that Hitler's Germany shared their aim of destroying the Soviet Union, the Poles ignored the implications of the Nazis' consolidation of their control of the City. Thus, on the face of it, the Danzig Free City in 1934 ceased to be a source of irritation in Polish–German relations, and became a touchstone of new and constructive relations. This was a radical departure from the earlier state of affairs.[5]

By 1938 Poland had moved still closer to the German camp. The growth of German belligerence towards Czechoslovakia allowed the Poles to hope for a further improvement in German–Polish relations on the basis of a shared desire to destroy the country, and for the consolidation of Poland's position in eastern and south-eastern Europe. Polish–Czech relations throughout the inter-war period had never been easy. While the Czech occupation of the coal mining district of Teschen during the Polish-Soviet war in 1919 was ostensibly the main bone of contention, in reality the rivalry was more fundamental. Poland's wish to act as the power broker in the region, brought it into conflict with its southern neighbour. Czechoslovakia's pivotal role in the Little Entente, a general union with Romania and Yugoslavia, appeared to preclude the extension of Polish influence into the Balkans. Poland had historic ties with Hungary and opposed the Little Entente's anti-Hungarian objectives. At the same time France's obvious preference for Czechoslovakia on account of, among other things, its coking coal and its shared interest in bringing the Soviet Union into the European balance of power, conflicted with Polish objectives. Poland resented French economic ties with Czechoslovakia and in 1934 refused to become part of the French plans for an eastern Locarno. Sensing an opportunity to assist Germany in destroying Czechoslovakia in 1938, the Polish minister for foreign affairs, Josef Beck, assured Hitler that if Germany succeeded in obtaining the Sudeten region from Czechoslovakia, Poland would simultaneously press for the return of the Teschen region and support Hungarian demands for Ruthenia. All these plans went astray in September 1938 when, by his decision for direct talks with Hitler, the British prime minister, Neville Chamberlain, destroyed Poland's seemingly strong negotiating position. Having assured himself of British and French support for his demands, Hitler no longer needed Poland, especially as he did not want to see Germany's expansion to the east blocked by a strong Polish-dominated regional bloc.

For the Poles, October 1938 turned out to be not a triumph but a moment of reckoning. On 24 October Ribbentrop put a plan to Lipski wherein Poland would relinquish Danzig, and in return Germany would extend the 1934 agreement for another 25 years. To Warsaw, this was tantamount to an ultimatum; Poland was being reduced to the role of a subordinate partner, a role it disdainfully rejected. From October 1938 until August 1939 Beck and Poland's military leaders belatedly put in place plans for war against Germany. At the same time attempts were made to forewarn Hitler of the likely consequences of a breakdown of relations between the two states. The Poles declared themselves willing and fully able to fight Germany. Meanwhile, relations between the two communities in the Free City of Danzig and relations between the Danzig Senate and the Polish port customs and postal authorities deteriorated dramatically. A game of brinkmanship was pursued, with the fate of Danzig becoming the focal point of international speculation. With the exception of Germany, all European governments sought to avoid hostilities: none wanted Polish-German differences to erupt into a European war.

By the beginning of 1939 Poland's previous policy of building regional unity had already collapsed. After the Munich conference, Germany's standing among the east European and Balkan states increased. Hungary and Romania both chose to appeal to Germany to support their territorial ambitions, rather than to coordinate their actions with Poland, whose influence was clearly diminishing. Regional unity, a tenuous concept throughout the inter-war period on account of the proliferation of petty and not so petty territorial disputes, was now being built on the basis of political and economic dependence upon Germany. Poland was unable to counter this process, and thus found itself increasingly isolated.

More worrying still for the Poles was the extent of their estrangement from France, Britain and Italy. Beck unfortunately concluded that he needed increased assistance from France at the very moment when France was seeking to divest itself of its east European commitments in favour of direct negotiations with Germany and Italy. Since the latter had become a source of serious concern by the end of 1938, Paris hoped that improved Franco–German relations would have a positive influence on Mussolini. During the Czech crisis, Beck rejected all French attempts to discuss Czech security, but by the winter Beck felt the need to test communication lines with France. Unfortunately, he had not considered the consequences of his earlier actions and of French preoccupation with Italy. In January 1939, when he tried to re-open talks with the French in order to reaffirm its commitment to Poland, Paris rebuffed his approach. Britain, irritated by Beck's high-handed manner during the Czech crisis, also avoided talks. Even Mussolini, who hitherto could be relied upon to encourage the Poles to take a robust line against Germany, appeared to have changed his attitude. All three powers sensed that Danzig was likely to become the object of German demands. None wanted to support Poland, preferring to concentrate upon improving their relations with Germany. Sensing Poland's isolation and anxious about Germany's ultimate objectives, Beck reassessed Poland's priorities in February 1939. He and his advisers concluded that Germany must be warned not to push the Danzig issue. They continued to give priority to the maintenance of good relations with Germany. But just in case this did not work out and in order to strengthen their negotiating position, they decided to pursue a parallel objective, the improvement of relations with Britain and France.

During the second half of March 1939 the international situation briefly favoured the Poles. On 15 March German forces occupied Prague. Shortly afterwards, Slovakia declared independence, then became a German protectorate. The general sense of anxiety was compounded by the Romanian minister to London, who informed the British Foreign Office that Germany was pressuring Romania to subordinate its economy to German needs. If this were true, the British Foreign Office recognised, Romanian oil would fall under Germany's control, not only strengthening its hand but also increasing the likelihood of war. While the British anxiously sought confirmation of this report, new rumours circulated about a possible German *coup* in Danzig. With these disparate bits of information heightening the tension, the British Cabinet moved from ideas of a regional east European bloc with the aim of opposing Germany to a unilateral declaration of support for Poland and maintenance of the *status quo* in Danzig.[6] On 31 March the British prime minister, Neville Chamberlain, unexpectedly issued the declaration in the House of Commons. The commitment was badly thought out and bore all the hallmarks of a hasty response to German actions. Poland had not initiated the change in British policy. Beck had in fact refused to be drawn into the initial proposal for a regional anti-German bloc, disliking any association with the Soviet Union. When on 21 March Howard Kennard, the British ambassador to Warsaw, put to Beck the proposal of a Britain guarantee of Polish security, Beck made his acceptance conditional on it taking the form of a mutual guarantee. At the same time, he withheld details of his exchanges with Ribbentrop concerning Danzig, which he considered to be of no concern to the British. In any case he had no reason to believe that Britain would actually take military action to protect Polish interests. In effect, both sides had entered into the agreement solely in order to respond to Germany's unexpected and worrying initiatives.[7] In the coming months and in the run up to the war, relations between Britain and Poland continued as before. Neither side trusted the other, and each pursued its own distinct foreign policy aims. And although most European capitals accepted the inevitability of war, the two powers proceeded hesitantly with their preparations for war, evidently continuing to hope that diplomacy would defuse the conflict with Germany.

In the aftermath of the British declaration to defend Poland, the situation in Europe did not change dramatically in spite of the general feeling of crisis. Although Hitler denounced the Anglo-German Naval Agreement of 1935 and the Polish-German Pact of Non-Aggression of 1934, Poland continued to behave as if war could be prevented. Beck, while hoping for material benefits from his new-found association with Britain, never completely lost hope of returning to the negotiating table with Germany. The most obvious sign of Poland's determination to keep the door open was its refusal to negotiate with the Soviet Union. Any political agreement with that country would have carried the inevitable connotation of building a bloc against Germany. Poland therefore refused to have anything to do with the Franco-British talks with the Soviet Union. During his visit to London in April, Beck also resisted British efforts to draw Poland and Romania into a mutual assistance treaty directed against Germany. While Beck's inflated sense of self-importance and the general overestimation of Poland's military potential go some way to account for his resistance, he was clearly also motivated by the desire to avoid entanglement in any anti-German bloc.[8]

There were sound reasons for Poland's reluctance to embark on an anti-German policy. In spite of the 31 March declaration, Chamberlain's government did little to persuade the Poles that in the event of a German attack on Poland, they could count on British military support. On the contrary, during the Franco-British staff talks in April and May it became apparent that neither country was able or willing to provide direct assistance to the Poles and furthermore that neither would take action in the West to relieve German pressure on Poland. This much was communicated to the Poles during joint staff talks at the end of May. The Poles were bluntly told that no action was envisaged to aid them and that none would be considered, since priority must be given to the defence of the British Isles and communication routes with the empire. Nor would the Royal Air Force bomb German military installations, since this might lead to retaliatory raids on Britain.[9]

The Polish government was allowed to harbour few illusions about British intentions. In all contacts with the Poles, British military and political leaders stressed that they were not in a position to offer any aid. At the same time, Poland came under pressure to avoid provoking Germany by action in Danzig. What in particular alienated Beck were the constant attempts to gauge the state of diplomatic relations between Poland and Germany. Mindful of the consequences for the Czechs of allowing Britain to take over negotiations for the settlement of the Sudeten issue, the Poles were determined to keep Britain out of the picture. They steadfastly refused to divulge any information and only released what they wanted the British to know, which was very little. Britain's refusal of all Polish requests for aid made it impossible for the Foreign Office to force the Poles to be franker.

When Polish delegates came to London, they soon realised that they would have to compete with other foreign delegations, which were also seeking British assistance. In spite of Britain's recent political initiative, imperial defence remained the top priority and no concessions were made to its new ally. The Treasury responded unsympathetically to Polish requests for financial assistance to purchase war *matériel*, treating them, as the Poles noted, on purely financial grounds. The Poles had initially requested aid and credit guarantees amounting to £60 million, although they hoped realistically to obtain only perhaps £20 million. By the outbreak of the war, the Poles, who felt insulted by Treasury attempts to link their request for aid to financial contracts for British firms, had broken off talks. The Treasury in fact had hoped the Poles would react in this manner, and when the talks were reopened after the German attack on Poland, the Treasury did all in its power to reduce the sums made available to the Poles to £5 million, none of which was actually spent before the fall of Poland. A special delegation which arrived in London to purchase British military equipment was similarly left in no doubt by British military chiefs that their requests were likely to have a negative impact on Britain's own state of preparedness. While the latest military equipment was offered to Iraq and other strategically important countries, the Polish military delegation reported undisguised official hostility.[10]

Thus, notwithstanding the conclusion of the Agreement of Mutual Assistance between Poland and the United Kingdom on 25 August, the Poles knew that when the moment came to face the German army, they would do so alone. Even France, the country that had consistently shown an interest in the fate of the states east of Germany, indicated unwillingness to underwrite Poland's preparations against Germany. Beck had the reputation of being anti-French. He therefore faced an uphill struggle when at the beginning of 1939 he sought to reconfirm France's earlier commitment to Poland. In April, Juliusz Łukasiewicz, the Polish ambassador to Paris, opened talks with Georges Bonnet, the French foreign minister, to define the precise scope of the bilateral Military Convention. On 13 May he was joined by a high ranking Polish military mission, which arrived in Paris to discuss joint action against Germany. In both cases the results seemed to be promising. The French appeared to confirm their political commitment to Poland and undertook to support Poland with the full force of their military might. In reality, however, Georges Bonnet, the French foreign minister, and Maurice Gamelin, the chief of staff, avoided formally committing France to the defence of Poland by not ratifying the political protocol and by making the military undertaking dependent on the protocol. Both sides knew that the agreements were not worth the paper on which they were written.[11]

Nevertheless, Polish political and military leaders continued to speak as if French and British aid could be expected in the event of war. As military men, they undoubtedly knew how difficult it would be for the Western Powers to assist Poland in the event of a war with Germany. They were painfully aware that Poland's capacity to withstand a German attack was limited, although they estimated that fighting in Poland might last three months. What they were unable to comprehend was that Britain and France could plan for war against Germany without the need of Polish support. They assumed that the Western Powers would need an eastern front and that sooner or later they would accept that Poland was the only country capable of providing it. They were even less willing to consider the possibility that the Soviet Union might play a pivotal role in an eastern front. But while the British and French governments seemed reluctant to enter into commitments with the Soviet Union, their military advisers were suggesting a reconsideration of the Soviet Union's future role. In any case, British and French military chiefs regarded Poland's defeat as a foregone conclusion in the event of war, which they expected to be a long and economically exhausting conflict. The Poles, on the other hand, persuaded themselves that, if they managed to withstand the initial German onslaught, the two Western Powers would come to their senses and accept that they needed Poland. They would therefore take military action against Germany before Poland was defeated. These misapprehensions were not resolved before the German attack on Poland.

In August 1939 the fate of Danzig again provoked frenzied speculation as to Germany's next move and whether Poland would fight to prevent it being incorporated into Germany. But when war broke out, Danzig was not the issue. In fact, Danzig had ceased being the issue on 23 August, when the city's Senate voted for its incorporation into the Third Reich. Although Poles in the city fought to protect Polish property and rights, and notably to hold onto the main Post Office, the fate of the city had dwindled in importance. Both sides knew that the outbreak of war was only a matter of days. On 1 September the League high commissioner, Carl Burckhardt, left Danzig, thus confirming the League's impotence in the face of German action.

That same day the *Wehrmacht* attacked Poland from three directions: from the north-west through the Danzig Corridor, from East Prussia where the Third Army sped towards Warsaw, and from the south-west where two armies moved into the industrial triangle of Łódź and Kraków. Bombing raids on Polish towns, industries and communication routes compounded Polish military difficulties. The entry of Soviet troops into eastern Poland, in accordance with the Ribbentrop-Molotov Agreement signed ten days earlier, spelled the end of Poland. The Polish government, the military high command and the Catholic Primate of All Poland hurriedly left for Romania.

Reluctantly, first the British and then the French governments bowed to the inevitable and declared war on Germany on 3 September. No action was take either to assist Poland in the east or to distract the Germans by action in the west. The fight to defeat Germany had only just begun. The fate of Poland, in accordance with their earlier plans, was subordinated to the ultimate outcome of the war.

Notes

1. A. J. P. Taylor, *The Origins of the Second World War*, 2nd edn (London, 1961).
2. For a more extensive treatment of the dynamic of relations between the European Great Powers and east European states, see A. J. Prazmowska, *Eastern Europe and the Origins of the Second World War* (Basingstoke, 2000).
3. P. S. Wandycz, *France and Her Eastern Allies, 1919–1925: Franco-Czechoslovak-Polish Relations from the Paris Peace Conference to Locarno* (Minneapolis, 1962), pp. 46–8.
4. A. M. Cienciala and T. Komarnicki, *From Versailles to Locarno: Keys to Polish Foreign Policy, 1919–1925* (Lawrence, KA, 1984), pp. 59–90.
5. Ministry for Foreign Affairs, the Polish Government, *Official Documents Concerning Polish-German and Polish-Soviet Relations, 1933–1939* (London, 1940), docs 34 and 36.
6. D. C. Watt, *How War Came: The Immediate Origins of the Second World War, 1938–1939* (London, 1989), pp. 148–52.
7. A. J. Prazmowska, *Britain, Poland and the Eastern Front, 1939* (Cambridge, 1987), pp. 47–50.
8. Ibid., pp. 64–7.
9. Ibid., pp. 94–5.
10. Ibid., pp. 115–25.
11. M. Alexander, *The Republic in Danger: General Maurice Gamelin and the Politics of French Defence, 1933–1940* (Cambridge, 1992), pp. 306–11.

9 Czechoslovakia

Igor Lukes

Czechoslovakia's ascent from the ashes of the Great War, the charismatic founder of the new state, Thomas G. Masaryk, and the Czech-German crisis of the 1930s have attracted considerable attention. This chapter approaches the saga from a new perspective by stressing those aspects of Czech history in the inter-war period that contributed to the country's collapse just two decades after it had appeared on the map.

It offers five related arguments: (1) By failing to build bridges to Warsaw and Budapest at a time when it was possible to do so the Prague government contributed to its isolation. (2) The Czechs treated their minorities well above the European norm at the time, but they did not treat them well enough. (3) The Little Entente consumed a disproportionate amount of Czech diplomatic effort, but it turned out to be an instrument against secondary or even illusory threats. (4) Prague's alliances with Paris and Moscow linked Czech national security with countries that shared neither borders nor objectives and values. They created a false sense of security in very insecure times. (5) In the crisis of 1938 the Czechs repeatedly confused their allies and the British by asserting their readiness to resist the Nazis militarily, while also indicating that they were open to a political settlement of their conflict with Hitler. This strengthened the hand of politicians who were trying to avoid war by appeasing the Third Reich.

Czechoslovakia's Reception in Central Europe

When the Czechoslovak delegates returned from the Peace Conference in September 1919 with a map of the new country, the president, Thomas Masaryk, and the foreign minister, Edvard Beneš, had every reason to feel victorious. The new state acquired 21 per cent of territory of the former Habsburg Empire, 26 per cent of its inhabitants, and no less than 60–70 per cent of its industry. The Czechs got everything they could have desired.

But there were also problems. The new Republic included the so-called Sudetenland. This territory had always been part of the Czech lands.

However, the majority of the people who lived there in 1918 made clear from the start that they were Germans and wished to remain part of a German-speaking state. Allied support for such a scheme was non-existent and the Sudeten Germans became citizens of Czechoslovakia. Although this was initially considered a small issue, it grew into a major problem in the 1930s.

In addition to the Sudeten quandary, the new Republic had to deal right from the start with another issue, one that involved the Silesian territory around the town of Tesin/Cieszyn. Both Prague and Warsaw claimed the area on historical and ethnic grounds. The conflict grew into an open wound between the two countries. The Czechs seized it militarily. Eventually, a conference divided the area between the two countries: the coal mines went to Czechoslovakia and Poland obtained the agrarian territory.

Warsaw regretted the loss of coal deposits. But what the Poles resented the most was that the Czechs had seized the region while the Red Army was marching into Poland. It did not help that in August 1920 Prague declared itself neutral in the Russo-Polish war. When Allied officials intervened with Masaryk on Poland's behalf, he replied that Bolshevism had to be defeated by social reforms, not by force. The truth is that Masaryk and Beneš disliked the Poles, and they allowed their feelings to determine Czechoslovak policy.

The Czechoslovak border with Hungary was also delimited in accordance with Prague's desires. The Magyars had fought on the defeated side in the Great War and their pre-war treatment of minorities was harsh. Neither the Allies nor their neighbours were now inclined to be chivalrous. In fact, a very large chunk of Hungarian territory was divided among the country's neighbours, and Prague partook in the process, acquiring a small but fertile territory at Hungary's expense.

Masaryk's and Beneš's failure to appease Warsaw and Budapest proved to be a serious error. Having gained territory at their expense, Prague should have sought out occasions to be magnanimous. Friendly words, combined with benevolence in the commercial sphere, would have gone a long way. But Masaryk and Beneš added insult to injury when they lectured Allied diplomats about the 'reactionary' and 'feudal' character of the Polish and Hungarian political élites.

As if they were unaware of the danger of international isolation, Masaryk and Beneš also ostentatiously displayed their anti-Catholicism. They proclaimed their disdain for the 'reactionary' Church, as they embraced the Hussite tradition that derived its origin from the writings of Jan Hus, the fifteenth-century Czech religious reformer. Predictably, their views were not received with sympathy among such largely Catholic neighbours of Czechoslovakia as the Poles, Hungarians, Austrians and Bavarians. Worse still, this attitude undermined the foundations of the fragile relationship the Czechs had with their own minorities: both the Sudetens and Slovaks were overwhelmingly Catholic.

Czechoslovakia's Ethnic Composition

In 1921 the Republic had a population of 13.3 million. Of the total, there were 6,700,000 Czechs, 3,100,000 Sudeten Germans, 2,000,000 Slovaks, 746,000 Magyars, 76,000 Poles and other minorities. These numbers were troubling: Czechoslovakia was home to almost four million inhabitants who considered it an artificial and alien state.

It had initially seemed that the new state would be designed with a relatively weak centre and strong regional, ethnically based cantons. But if the Sudetens had received their own canton, their legislature would have formally severed the German-speaking provinces from Czechoslovakia. No canton for the Sudetens meant that autonomy had to be denied the Slovaks. After all, there were only two million Slovaks and more than three million Sudetens. Consequently, the concept of the new state becoming a central European Switzerland was never to be tested, and Czechoslovakia was administered strictly from the centre. As time passed, this was resented not only by the Sudetens but also by the Slovaks who yearned to increase their nation's international visibility.

It is not clear that the Prago-centric style of administration could have been avoided, at least not at the beginning. But it is obvious that its continuation throughout the inter-war period alienated the Sudetens and created separatist tendencies in Slovakia. This remains true even though the Prague authorities treated the minorities well. Their political representatives were chosen in democratic elections. The Prague government created new secondary and college-level educational institutions in Slovakia, and it invested as much in schools in the Sudetenland as it did in the Czech districts. Prague had set the highest standard in Europe with its policy on minorities, but the Czechs were also capable of being arrogant and tactless toward them. Therefore, the Sudetens, Poles, Hungarians and even the Slovaks never lost the sense that Czechoslovakia was a convenient hotel and not a permanent home. This was bound to have consequences at a time of crisis: people fight for their home even when it is engulfed in flames, but they evacuate a burning hotel.

Prague's Diplomacy: The Little Entente and the French Alliances

For some years, the Prague government saw no reason to fear its German neighbour. Masaryk and Beneš therefore focused their foreign policy on the two countries that represented a source of danger to Czechoslovakia: Austria and Hungary. And they sought out others who shared their perspective.

Prague's first ally was Yugoslavia, at the time known as the Kingdom of Serbs, Croats and Slovenes. Like Czechoslovakia, it feared Habsburg restoration and Hungarian revisionism. Therefore, in August 1920 Belgrade signed an alliance with Prague.

Romania was persuaded to sign an agreement with Prague that paralleled the Czech-Yugoslav treaty the next year. Bucharest feared Hungary and the Habsburgs, but unlike Prague and Belgrade, it was also concerned about Soviet Russia. This is why the Romanians had hoped to enlarge the triangle Prague–Bucharest–Belgrade by including Poland – as another country that had to keep an eye on the Bolsheviks. But Masaryk and Beneš torpedoed the idea of a central European pact that would include Poland. They both believed that Warsaw behaved irresponsibly towards Soviet Russia and that the Polish corridor was bound to provoke a conflict with Germany in the future. In June 1921 the diplomatic triangle Prague–Belgrade–Bucharest was completed when Romania signed an agreement with Yugoslavia.

The Hungarian press poked fun at the new diplomatic grouping by calling it the Little Entente. Thus was born one of the major instruments of Czech foreign policy. It turned out to be effective in keeping down Hungary. Yet, in the long run, the Little Entente proved to be a conduit for energy expended in the wrong direction. The danger to the region would emanate from Germany and the Bolsheviks, not from Hungary and the Habsburgs.

France could not have watched the creation of the Little Entente with sympathy.[1] After all, its historical and still real source of concern was German, not Hungarian, revanchism. In late 1921 Paris began to press the Masaryk government for an alliance that would alleviate its fears of Germany. But the Czechs were reluctant to become pawns in French anti-German gambits. The matter had an important economic angle: Germany, not France, was Czechoslovakia's main business partner. And it was not smart for Prague to accept anti-German obligations by joining with the geographically distant France when it had a three-million strong German minority within its borders.

Impervious to such concerns, the French brought pressure to bear on Masaryk. The 1924 Franco-Czech Treaty, eventually signed in 1924, reflected the ambiguous feelings of Prague about this diplomatic instrument. It stressed 'Czechoslovak-French friendship', but it contained no formal military obligations aimed at Germany. Ironically, the very vagueness of the text caused many diplomats to assume – incorrectly – that the treaty had a secret military clause directed against Germany.

The Czechs had been reluctant to sign the 1924 agreement. But as Germany emerged from its post-war isolation it became imperative for Masaryk to weave Czechoslovakia into a system of collective security that would be guaranteed by the big powers for the benefit of all. The Locarno Pact of October 1925 decoupled eastern Europe from the rest of the continent and produced the appearance that German revisionism would be intolerable in the West, but that the eastern borders were not cast in stone. This made another Franco-Czech agreement necessary, but this time with a military clause against Germany. The new treaty, signed in 1925, contained an explicit statement that bound the two partners to assist each other if either were to become the target of German aggression. It became the linchpin of Czechoslovakia's security system until the end of September 1938.

Masaryk's and Beneš's domestic critics were quick to note that if one's property was on fire one needed to have neighbours who were willing to help with buckets of water. Even well-meaning friends in far away countries were of no help when the flames were raging. Of the allies that Prague had found so far, Yugoslavia and France had no direct access to Czechoslovakia, and the country's border with Romania was short and approachable only through rough terrain. At the same time, France was the largest country on the continent and its army was a desirable partner. It was now committed automatically to march in defence of Czechoslovakia against German aggression. This allowed Czech politicians to look at the future with confidence, and it added to Prague's sense of invincibility.

In the mid-1920s Prague felt itself to be on top of the world. The country had started to enjoy signs of internal stability and economic prosperity. In 1926 it became the first and only country in continental Europe whose government included representatives of a national minority when two Sudeten Germans became ministers. Moreover, the Czech economy was among the strongest in the world. Adolf Hitler was known at the time only to foreign policy specialists, Joseph Stalin was still clawing his way up the Kremlin pyramid of power, and Konrad Henlein, the future leader of the Nazis in the Sudetenland, was an obscure gymnastics teacher. Meanwhile, Czechoslovakia's security was guaranteed by France, the mightiest country in Europe. What more could anyone desire?

The Meandering Foreign Policy of Edvard Beneš: Prague, its Allies and Adolf Hitler

Let us start by looking at Czechoslovakia's relationship with the Kremlin. Masaryk and Beneš were of two minds when it came to the Soviet system. On the one hand, as socialists they were attracted to its official ideology. At the same time, they rejected such Leninist instruments as *coup d'état* and class struggle. They were, moreover, not at all amused when they learned that the first Soviet representatives who came to Prague in the summer of 1920 devoted most of their energy to running networks of spies. This had set Czech–Soviet relations back for years. While other countries established full diplomatic relations with the Kremlin, Prague held back. It was only in 1934 that Prague formalised its relations with Moscow. But once the Czechs and the Soviets started to communicate as representatives of sovereign states, their relations could hardly have been more cordial. In January 1935 the Czech Legation reported from Moscow that Soviet officials urged that Prague and Moscow sign a military treaty 'right now'.

After the Franco-Soviet Treaty had been signed in early May 1935, the Czech-Soviet treaty came into existence. Prague now had the 1925 treaty with France and the 1935 treaty with the Soviet Union.[2] The two bilateral pacts were linked via Article II of the Protocol of Signature attached to the treaty. It stipulated that the obligation to render assistance would become operational only after France had acted first. The Franco-Soviet and Czech-Soviet treaties provided a much-needed tranquiliser to the Prague political scene. The growth of the Third Reich made a profound impact in the Sudetenland. The Sudeten German political parties that had accepted the Republic as legitimate by serving in all Czech governments from 1926 onward began disintegrating as their members started joining the local Nazi organisation, the Sudetendendeutsche Partei (SdP). This is why the Soviet addition to the pre-existing Franco-Czech Agreement was so welcome. Exposed as it was to the growing Nazi threat, Czechoslovakia could still enjoy a sense of security because its territorial integrity was guaranteed by France, the Soviet Union and the Little Entente.

In 1935, at the age of 85, Thomas Masaryk realised he was no longer able to govern. He resigned and a short, but intense presidential campaign followed. The National Assembly elected Edvard Beneš to be the next president.

Masaryk died in September 1937, just as another ugly rumour started to circulate in Europe: in exchange for German reassurance regarding the finality of borders with France and Belgium, Britain would give Hitler a free hand in eastern Europe. The rumour exaggerated the reality behind it, but not by much. Lord Halifax told Hitler in November 1937 that the British did not expect the *status quo* with regards to Danzig, Austria and Czechoslovakia to last forever.

The European crisis accelerated further in early 1938. On 12 February 1938, Austria was bullied into signing an agreement with Hitler that paved the way for its own demise. Eight days later Hitler delivered a particularly vicious speech at the Opera House in Berlin. His most pressing job, he asserted, was to protect more than ten million fellow Germans who had been suffering for too long in Austria and Czechoslovakia. That same day, Anthony Eden in London announced his resignation as foreign secretary. The man who replaced him was the one who just three months earlier had given the Führer a green light for going after Austria, Czechoslovakia and Poland: Lord Halifax.

And Beneš, the man standing in the middle of the crisis? He told the German minister in Prague that if Berlin did not like the situation in

Czechoslovakia, he, Beneš, 'did not care'. He did not like Nazism, and he was not willing to hide it.

After Hitler occupied Austria in March 1938, all eyes were turned to Czechoslovakia. The next month proved to be dramatic. On 14 April Beneš learned that Paris was ready to take part in a conference of French, Soviet and Czech military specialists. Unfortunately, the French invitation came to Prague via the Czech Legation in Moscow; it was not an official proposal. Beneš replied that Prague would be happy to join whatever system was established directly by French and Soviet military specialists, but it was unwilling to take the initiative in this regard, supposedly out of respect for Polish and Romanian concern regarding the Red Army.

This would develop into a pattern of Beneš's behaviour during the crisis. First, he courageously denounced the ideology of Nazism to the German minister in Prague, but then he failed to accept the French informal offer of a military conference on the grounds that Paris and Moscow must make the first move. Yet it was Czechoslovakia, not France or the Soviet Union, that was being directly threatened by the Third Reich. How did he expect the French to march with him against Hitler if he was unable to show that the Czechs were determined to resist under any circumstances?

The second time the Beneš administration repeated the pattern of a strong stance without a follow up was during the so-called Weekend Crisis in May 1938. Prague responded to reports of alleged German military concentrations along the border by calling up reservists and military specialists. As became clear within days, Germany had not been preparing to attack Czechoslovakia. But as a result of its partial mobilisation, the Prague government now had 383,000 men deployed along the border with Germany. The next day, Beneš said in a speech: 'We're ready for everything.'

The measures executed by the Czech army made a good impression. Of course, the Nazis roared with anger. But they learned that Czechoslovakia was no Austria. Certainly, Prague now looked like a warmonger to its numerous critics in London. But they disliked the Czechs so intensely that the May crisis could hardly have made things worse. Importantly, too, the partial mobilisation of the Czech army potentially strengthened whatever anti-Hitler elements one could still find in Germany. There is, finally, evidence that it favourably impressed Polish military officers, and it most definitely stabilised the domestic scene in Czechoslovakia by re-establishing law and order in the Sudetenland. Yet, once again, Prague had failed to maintain the momentum and initiative *vis-à-vis* Berlin. Within a few weeks, in response to interventions from the British Legation, it began to decrease its military presence along the borders with Germany, thus signalling that a compromise obtained through a settlement was not out of the question. This encouraged the view in France and Great Britain that the Czechs could be brought to their knees by political pressure.

An initially strong stance against Germany followed by a loss of Czech initiative was detectable for the third time in connection with the Runciman mission. In July Lord Halifax proposed to dispatch Lord Walter Runciman to Prague in order to investigate the crisis in the Sudetenland. This was, of course, an internal Czech affair. Beneš was therefore entirely justified when he turned down the proposal. But he then buckled under British pressure and agreed to 'invite' Runciman. This was a fatal error. Those who sought to avoid war at all cost focused on the illusion that a solution of the Sudeten problem equalled peace. Unfortunately, Beneš now gave the appearance of believing in this chimera.

Members of the Runciman mission arrived in early August. They spent the next six weeks travelling throughout the border region; some members of the delegation developed the habit of extending their arms in the *Heil Hitler* salute. Runciman's findings, presented a week after the mission had returned to London on 15 September, could hardly have been worse for Beneš. The solution, Runciman asserted, required Czechoslovakia to cede its Sudeten territory to the Third Reich. Then, the Prague government was to 'remodel' its foreign relations, and enter into the zone of influence of the Third Reich. Finally, Prague was at that point to sign a commercial agreement with Berlin.

Runciman could legitimately claim that the majority of the Sudeten Germans wished to become part of the Third Reich, and that it made no sense to drag Europe into a war because the post-war peace treaties created an unbridgeable gap between their nationality (German) and citizenship (Czechoslovak). But it was disheartening for the British to suggest that Czechoslovakia become a vassal of the Third Reich.

The fourth manifestation of the pattern described above is seen in Beneš's treatment of the Franco-British proposal of 19 September. When the French and British ministers arrived at the presidential castle in Prague to demand that Czechoslovakia surrender the Sudetenland to Hitler, Beneš was just having a conference with a political confidant. The president was complaining that he was under pressure from London and Paris to give up the Sudetenland. This meant handing over democrats, socialists, and Jews to Hitler's *Gestapo*. It would be 'a massacre [and] barbarian anti-Semitic murder'. This, Beneš assured his friend, he would never do. In line with this sentiment, Beneš treated the two envoys curtly. They were told the next day that their proposal was unacceptable. Unwilling to take this as the final answer, the two envoys returned at 2:15 a.m., 21 September, with more threats – formulated personally by Lord Halifax in London – and armed with a French ultimatum that Paris would not abide by its obligations toward Czechoslovakia if Beneš chose to resist Hitler militarily. Beneš was stunned but started to reconsider. He still had no answer at noon when the two diplomats showed up yet again, demanding an immediate reply to their ultimatum. But at 5 p.m., Prague officially accepted it.

In the evening on 21 September, only hours after the Czechs had accepted the ultimatum, they had to deal with other demands on their territory. The Polish minister and his Hungarian colleague went to the Foreign Ministry and demanded a re-examination of the divisive territorial issues that had poisoned Prague's relations with Warsaw and Budapest.[3] A Czech foreign service officer suggested this was not the time to deal with these problems; he asked for patience. The Polish envoy declined. He pointed out that Czechoslovakia had seized the Tesin/Cieszyn territory when the Bolsheviks stood outside Warsaw. The Polish and Hungarian interventions added to the precariousness of Prague's position.

Beneš's tendency to take a strong initial stand followed by a reversal is evident, finally, in the series of events that took place between the Godesberg summit (22 September) and the conference at Munich (29–30 September). Having secured Prague's acceptance of the Franco-British ultimatum that Czechoslovakia surrender the Sudetenland, the prime minister, Neville Chamberlain, expected his meeting with Hitler at Godesberg to be brief and easy. He was taken aback when the Führer announced that diplomacy had achieved nothing. He was going to take what he wished by force. At one point, Hitler jumped up and shouted: 'The Czechs must be annihilated.' His behaviour contributed to the message sent jointly by London and Paris to Prague while the Godesberg summit was under way. It said that Great Britain and France could no longer 'take the responsibility of advising [Prague] not to mobilize'.

As we have seen in the context of Beneš's failure to accept the informal French proposal in April 1938 for military consultations with Prague and Moscow of April 1938, the president was reluctant to be in front of his allies. But he was most happy to mobilise on their advice. Much like the partial mobilisation of May 1938 had done before, the general mobilisation of 23 September gave the Prague government the illusion of success. Within a few days, the Czech army had well over a million citizens in uniform. The mobilised soldiers stood ready to defend the Republic. Beneš thought he now had the initiative and that his system of alliances was finally producing results. The Führer's demands from Godesberg were brought to Prague just as the general mobilisation was at its most feverish. No one in London believed they were reasonable. Prague declared them 'absolutely and unconditionally unacceptable'.

Many Czechs thought that the failure of the Godesberg summit, the general mobilisation of the Czech army, and, finally, the declaration had erased Prague's previous acceptance of the Franco-British ultimatum. The presidential castle was transformed into an armed camp. Beneš felt energised: 'If we withstand [Hitler's attack] for three weeks and if France and the Soviet Union intervene we will have won.' Both the Soviet minister, Sergei Alexandrovsky, who remained in close contact with Beneš throughout the

September crisis, and the German Legation in Prague reported that Beneš was determined to go to war – with his allies – against the Third Reich.

On 27 September, the president was still full of fighting spirit. Although he had just received a panicky note from the British that a German attack could be expected within 14 hours (28 September at 2 p.m.), Beneš calmly told the government that a 'superhuman effort' was being made to form a defensive line against the *Wehrmacht*. Should Germany attack, Czechoslovakia would defend itself, he asserted.

But Berlin, London and Paris had not forgotten that on 21 September Prague had formally accepted the Franco-British ultimatum. When it transpired that Hitler had invited Chamberlain for yet another summit, to take place in Munich on 29 September, the Europeans automatically assumed that the conference would merely determine the size of Hitler's conquest. The Franco-British negotiators were so unprepared to engage the Führer on specifics that the size of his booty was dictated exclusively by him. And when the Munich protocol and map became available in Prague, Beneš, the man who impressed others just days before as a warrior standing in the middle of a military encampment, could only repeat: 'Unbelievable, unbelievable.'

France, the main pillar of Beneš's diplomatic concept had crumbled. Prague was completely abandoned. And Moscow? Archival documents make clear that there was every reason to be sceptical about the possibility of Soviet military assistance – with or without France. Prague learned in August 1938 from an excellent source that sympathy with Hitler's Germany was growing rapidly within the Kremlin. 'I was told categorically,' testified the source, 'that there was no hope whatsoever for the Soviet Union to come to Czechoslovakia's assistance.'[4]

Minister Aleksandrovsky's deceitful behaviour on 30 September was the final straw. Beneš told the Soviet envoy at 9:30 a.m. that France had abandoned him. Was there any hope of a Soviet unilateral involvement on the side of Czechoslovakia, without France? Beneš needed to know as soon as possible. According to Soviet records, Aleksandrovsky cabled the question only at 11:45 a.m. that day. The Soviet positive reply arrived in Prague on 3 October, more than 60 hours after Beneš had accepted the Munich agreement and more than 30 hours after the Czech army had evacuated the defensive perimeter in the Sudetenland. It was therefore worthless.

For the fifth time in 1938 Beneš buckled under pressure. The mobilised army deployed in the field and the gas mask he had placed on his desk a week before were now forgotten, overridden by the Munich agreement. Under its terms Czechoslovakia lost 41,000 square kilometres, almost 5 million citizens (of whom 1,250,000 were Czechs and Slovaks), a large portion of its economic potential, and its vitally important line of fortifications. With Beneš's prodding Prague accepted the verdict just six hours after its receipt, on 30 September, at 12:30 p.m. There is every reason to be sceptical about the hypothetical course and outcome of the Czech-German war that the Munich agreement had prevented. But it is impossible to dismiss the argument that for the Czechs to fight Adolf Hitler was a moral necessity, even if it made little sense militarily.

Edvard Beneš resigned the presidency in early October 1938 and watched Europe sliding towards the war from his new post, a teaching position at the University of Chicago. Events did not allow him to stay there for long.[5] By the time the Second World War broke out, Beneš had returned to active politics. His diplomacy was mightily assisted by the thousands of Czechs and Slovaks who followed their president into exile. Having been denied the right to defend their country in the autumn of 1938, they fought Hitler wearing various allied uniforms. Notably, some 1500 flew in the Czech section of the Royal Air Force. They fought with determination and courage.

Beneš was pleased with the outbreak of the Soviet-German war in June 1941. It created a situation, he told a colleague, that he had hoped to have in place in September 1938: the Soviet Union, Great Britain, France, Czechoslovakia, Poland and Yugoslavia were all arrayed against the Third Reich. He believed that such an alliance made victory over Germany inevitable.

He was right. But the Czechoslovakia that reappeared on the map of Europe in 1945 balanced precariously on the fault-line between western Europe and the zone the Kremlin had carved out for its empire. It would take but a tiny pressure for it to fall behind the Iron Curtain. In February 1948, just 22 months after the defeat of Adolf Hitler's Germany, Czechoslovakia would be prostrate before Joseph Stalin. And the cruel mill-stones of central European history kept turning.

Notes

1. P. S. Wandycz, *France and Her Eastern Allies, 1919–1925: French-Czechoslo-vak-Polish Relations from the Paris Peace Conference to Locarno* (Minneapolis, 1962).
2. P. S. Wandycz, *The Twilight of French Eastern Alliances, 1926–36: French-Czechoslovak-Polish Relations from Locarno to the Remilitarization of the Rhineland* (Princeton, 1988).
3. A. Cienciala, 'The Munich Crisis of 1938: Plans and Strategy in Warsaw in the Context of the Western Appeasement of Germany', and M. Ádám, 'The Munich Crisis and Hungary: The Fall of the Versailles Settlement in Central Europe', in I. Lukes and E. Goldstein, eds, *The Munich Crisis, 1938: Prelude to World War II* (London, 1999), pp. 48–81 and 82–121.
4. The Archives of the Ministry of Interior, 305-740-1. Roman Jakobson to Prokop Maxa, 13 September 1939.
5. D. C. Watt, *How War Came: The Immediate Origins of the Second World War, 1938–1939* (New York, 1989).

10 The Neutrals

Neville Wylie

To include a discussion on the neutrals in a book investigating Europe's descent into war in September 1939 might seem rather perverse. How can states that tried to stay aloof from the war be held in any way responsible for its outbreak? The choice between peace and war surely lay with the Great Powers, whose statesmen paid precious little attention to the wishes of the Czechs, let alone those of their small, neutral neighbours. Yet, for many contemporaries, the concept of neutrality was far from irrelevant to the diplomacy of the 1930s. The drift towards neutrality in the mid-1930s inevitably affected the complexion of European politics at a time when the international system was already strained by the demands of the revisionist powers. 'Far from discouraging war,' insisted Quincy Wright, America's leading international lawyer of the time, 'neutrality has tended to encourage aggression of the strong against the weak. Neutral rights have themselves provided the basis for disputes which have drawn non-participants into war.'[1] This chapter tests these claims by investigating three areas in which the neutrals might be held to have contributed to the destabilisation of the international system before 1939: their 'rejection' of collective security, their influence on the operation of the European balance of power, and finally their impact on western defence planning after 1936.

The Neutrals and the League of Nations

Before turning to the events of the 1930s, mention should be made of the chequered development of neutrality over the preceding decades. European neutrality reached its apogee at the end of the nineteenth century, when the process of codifying and expanding the rights and duties of neutrals culminated in the fifth Hague convention on the rules of war in 1907. Well before this date, however, neutrality had been recognised as an acceptable form of international behaviour. Since 1815 responsibility for managing the international system had lain with the Great Powers. Europe's smaller powers were therefore not only expected to remain neutral in the affairs of the Great Powers, they were also actively encouraged to do so by the championship of 'permanent' neutrality for Switzerland (1815), Belgium (1830) and Luxembourg (1867), and the promotion of Scandinavian neutrality. The venerable position which this 'traditional', juridical form of neutrality had acquired by the turn of the century did not, however, long survive the outbreak of war in August 1914. The rights of small states and neutrals were quickly forgotten as the mentality of 'total war' took hold in the war counsels of the belligerent powers. The war in fact began with a violation of Belgian neutrality, and over the next four years the neutrals had their ships requisitioned and torpedoed and their economies subjected to increasingly severe blockade restrictions.[2] By 1918 the edifice of traditional neutrality and the assumptions that underpinned it – mutual respect for international law and the existence of an inclusive and balanced international system – lay in ruins.

The prospect of neutrality recovering its former status after the return of peace was dealt a serious blow by changes in the nature of international relations. The establishment of the League of Nations in 1919, an organisation whose legitimacy hinged on its universal membership and the concept of collective security, inevitably called into question the validity of neutrality as a maxim of state policy. The Kellogg-Briand Pact of 1928, which resurrected the medieval doctrine of 'just war' and outlawed the use of force in international affairs, accentuated the trend. Henceforth no state could be neutral in a war against aggression, and the neutrals' traditional claim to the moral high ground – based on their ability to provide humanitarian and political assistance to *both* belligerent sides – consequently lost much of its force.[3] The League also had a deleterious effect on the peacetime role of neutrality. By offering small states a measure of theoretical equality with the Great Powers, and a permanent forum for airing their views, the League reduced the appeal of neutrality for those smaller and weaker states that might, in other circumstances, have found neutrality appealing. This was particularly the case for the new successor states in central and eastern Europe, none of whom wished to mark their arrival on the international stage by accepting restraints on their sovereign rights.

Despite its tarnished image, neutrality did not entirely disappear after 1919. Switzerland's historic attachment to neutrality was recognised when it joined the League in 1920, and throughout the subsequent decade, the 'former neutrals', whose international profile had been sharpened by their activities during the war, frequently collaborated inside and outside the *Palais de Nations* to further their common interests. International disarmament was a *cause célèbre*, as was the promotion of economic cooperation, either through their own endeavours – such as the free-trade arrangements for the 'Oslo' states after 1930 – or through their active participation in international conferences.[4] While most of these activities were not directed towards recognisably 'neutral' goals, they did give the 'former neutrals' a distinctive identity on the international stage. The one initiative that related to the status of neutral rights was the repeated attempt of the Scandinavians and other small powers to amend Article 16 of the Covenant that dealt with their obligations towards collective security. It should be noted, however, that from the outset, the objective was not so much to resurrect the concept of neutrality, but rather to ensure that in a future war, they would be free to follow their own national interests. Individual state sovereignty, not neutrality, was the issue at stake.[5]

The 'former neutrals' relationship with the League was always therefore an ambiguous one. Although all but one voluntarily renounced neutrality in 1919, their commitment to collective security was never whole-hearted and entailed compromises which were justified only so long as the League retained the support of the majority of the international community. The charge then, that in trading in the League's promise of collective security for the doubtful 'salvation of neutrality' (to quote the Soviet foreign minister in 1936, Maxim Litvinov), Europe's small states were naïve, stupid or both, overlooks the fact that their support for the League had always been contingent. Moreover, their final outright rejection of Article 16 in July 1936 should not be seen as a panicked reaction to Mussolini's defiant gestures in Abyssinia, but rather the culmination of efforts over a decade and a half to amend this article so that it better reflected the interests of the smaller powers.

The event that precipitated a re-evaluation of the small powers' position within the League came in 1935 with the Italian invasion of Abyssinia and the League's abysmal effort to apply sanctions on the recalcitrant regime in Rome. In the early stages of the crisis the small powers were determined to see Italy held to account for its unprovoked attack. As Dutch foreign minister A. C. D. Graeff remarked four days before the sanctions debate opened, the issue was 'a matter of life and death' for an institution which was still reeling from its failure to deal with Japan's aggression against Manchuria, three years before. Considerable effort was made to galvanise the League's activities over the autumn of 1935. Correspondence between the small powers reveals that, while most were anxious to see the sanctions policy work, many feared that far from preventing war, sanctions might actually provoke a general war in which they were likely to suffer as much as anyone else.

The small powers' hopes for a successful outcome to the crisis evaporated over the winter of 1935/36, as Britain and France sought their own way out of the crisis and let the League's sanctions policy slowly unravel. The former neutrals' response to this set-back – a joint declaration on 1 July 1936 – has been judged by some historians as representing a 'significant change in their foreign policy'.[6] The declaration castigated the League for the inconsistent way in which the Covenant had been applied, with some articles, such as those on disarmament, almost completely ignored, and others applied in an arbitrary or half-hearted fashion. Until the international community agreed to abide by the rule of law and reinforce the League's hand in resolving international disputes, the signatories would not consider themselves bound by the provisions of Article 16.

The ditching of Article 16 and what was in effect the abandonment of collective security by the 'former neutrals' in July 1936 attracted a great deal of criticism. In a widely read book published in early 1938, a long-standing member of Britain's delegation to Geneva rounded on those 'small States who risk nothing at all', and whose 'moral fervour and determination to carry out the Covenant to the letter varied noticeably in proportion to their geographical proximity to the scene of action.'[7] There is little doubt that in renouncing collective security, the neutrals weakened one of the core elements of the League system. Yet, as Ger van Roon, the leading historian of the Oslo states, notes, the declaration was 'first and foremost a *reaction* ... to the failure of the League and its member states, notably the major powers, to call a halt to acts of aggression and to achieve collective security'.[8] Western Powers' vacillation had already been demonstrated when details of the Hoare-Laval pact were leaked to the press, and while some statesmen, such as Anthony Eden, were still prepared to champion the League's endeavours, most had, like Neville Chamberlain, long since dismissed them as the 'very midsummer of madness'.

The international response to Mussolini's invasion of Abyssinia provided conclusive proof that Europe's fate lay in the hands of the Great Powers, not with righteous civil servants in Geneva. Above all, it showed that the experiment in liberal internationalism begun in 1919 was at an end. The return to neutrality was a symptom, rather than a cause of this process. Indeed, the neutrals' July declaration and the events that preceded it did not signal their complete disengagement from the League. With the exception of Switzerland and the new nationalist government in Spain, the 'former neutrals' tried to retain 'one foot in each camp'. As one senior Dutch diplomat noted in early 1938, although Article 16 was 'dead and buried ... it must not be forgotten that burial involves the idea of resurrection'. This was the tenor of a declaration made in Copenhagen on 23 July 1938, in which the seven neutrals[9] reiterated their opposition to Article 16, but confirmed their desire to remain in the League. What is surprising is not so much the re-emergence of neutrality after 1936, but rather the neutrals' commitment to an international society based on the principle of pooled sovereignty, whether in the shape of a regional economic grouping, such as the Oslo pact, or, for all its faults, a universal institution such as the League. When peace returned to Europe, it was noticeably the 'former neutrals', the Dutch and Belgians, who led the way in promoting European integration.

The neutrality that took shape in Europe from the middle of 1936 had a number of distinctive features. For most aspirant neutrals, neutrality was not some lofty refuge, isolated from the world's events, but rather a strategy enabling them to engage actively in international affairs without simultaneously running the risk of alienating their powerful neighbours in Berlin and Rome. In short, what these states sought was 'non-alignment' or 'neutralism', not neutrality. It was only with the onset of the Czech crisis in the summer of 1938 that 'non-alignment' hardened into a policy of neutrality. At no time, however, did this represent a flight back to the passive, impartial neutrality of the nineteenth century. As Russia's summary expulsion from the League in December 1939 shows, the 'neutrals' remained perfectly willing to take dramatic – if selective – action on the international stage.

Paradoxically, the one 'neutral' to come out of the sanctions crisis with the least credit was Switzerland, the most traditional and respected of them all. Berne's membership of the League had never sat comfortably with the Swiss. A referendum on joining the League in 1920 had been won by the slenderest of margins, and thereafter, despite official enthusiasm, public support had been fragile at best. Although Berne initially voiced its support for the League in 1935, as the sanctions began to affect Switzerland's large business interests in northern Italy, popular, and increasingly official, sympathies moved sharply against the League. Berne was not prepared to sacrifice its amicable political and commercial relations with the Italians on the altar of collective security, and over the winter of 1935/36 it deftly drew on its 'obligations' as a neutral to dilute its application of the League sanctions.[10] Despite these endeavours, however, the crisis had a profoundly unsettling effect on the Swiss. Attacked from both sides and unable to persuade anyone to take its neutrality as seriously as it wished, Berne increasingly came to see the virtue of returning to Switzerland's traditional form of 'integral' neutrality. Although this change of policy was only confirmed in early 1938, the federal authorities began embracing an increasingly neutralist position from the first days of the sanctions crisis. This ultimately entailed returning to full political neutrality, but also disengaging from international projects – such as those on behalf of refugees – and bringing the work of the country's humanitarian agencies into line with official government policies. Berne's discouragement of any criticism by the International Committee of the Red Cross of Italy's use of chemical weapons in Abyssinia foreshadowed its dramatic veto of the Committee's appeal on the Holocaust, six years later.[11] In the minds of most Swiss diplomats, the war effectively began in 1936.

The Neutrals and the European Balance of Power

It was not collective security that failed to keep the peace in September 1939, but rather Europe's traditional system of balance of power. As Neville

Chamberlain belatedly acknowledged in February 1938, 'the League as constituted today is unable to provide collective security for anybody.' 'Small weak states,' he wisely concluded, ought not to 'delude themselves' that the League was capable of defending them against aggression.[12] If the neutrals were at least implicated in the demise of collective security, can the same be said for their involvement in the balance of power? Did the emergence of neutrality in the late 1930s destabilise international politics and, as Quincy Wright claimed, draw states into conflict when they might otherwise have remained at peace? Despite the ease with which neutrality coexisted with balance of power politics in the nineteenth century, historically neutrals have had a hard time preventing others taking advantage of the absence of an overarching hegemon and encroaching on their interests. Politics, like nature, abhors a vacuum, and in refusing to subordinate their political freedom to the patronage of a Great Power, neutrals inevitably perpetuated the kind of weak political structures that are likely to excite the predatory instincts of their neighbours.

Neutrals have tried to overcome this vulnerability by seeking safety in numbers. This was common practice in the eighteenth century, and reached its apogee during the Napoleonic Wars when Russia lent its support to a succession of 'leagues of armed neutrality'. By 1939, two distinctive regional groupings fitted into this historical pattern: the 'Oslo group', forged in 1930 and consisting of Scandinavia and the Low Countries, and the Balkan Entente, created in 1934 and comprising Romania, Yugoslavia, Greece and Turkey. Neither succeeded in keeping the war from their doors: all but one of the 'Oslo' states succumbed to foreign invasion during the Phoney War, while Balkan neutrality disintegrated over the spring of 1941. In both cases, the blocs lacked political cohesion and agreement on basic priorities. In the Balkans, member states agreed on the need to contain Bulgarian territorial ambitions, but disagreed on how to achieve this or how to respond to the blandishments of external powers – the Soviets, Germans, Italians or Hungarians. Significantly, the Entente turned down Bucharest's suggestion that they make a *joint* declaration of neutrality in September 1939. By contrast, the Oslo states enjoyed greater political homogeneity, were committed to a defence of the established order and had all experimented with neutrality in the recent past. It was the Oslo states which coordinated the activities of the 'former neutral' lobby in Geneva and articulated the distinctively 'small power' political agenda in the 1920s and early 1930s. Nevertheless, the deterioration in international politics from 1935 quickly revealed gaps in the alliance that only expanded over time. In a nutshell, the members' political, economic and security interests were simply too diverse to be accommodated under one roof. Furthermore, those members with the ability to gain leadership of the group – the Belgians and Swedes – were ultimately unwilling to mortgage their own security for the benefit of all.[13]

Merely recognising the weaknesses of regional neutrality by 1939 does not in itself explain the neutrals' role in the events leading to war in 1939. Neither bloc was specifically designed to cope with the problems that beset European politics in the late 1930s. The sole rationale of the Balkan Entente was to defend the post-war territorial settlement in the Balkans. Its members could afford the luxury of being indifferent towards developments in western Europe, but none could be neutral towards events that impinged on the politics of their region. In these circumstances, it is doubtful whether 'neutrality' is an appropriate term for Balkan politics at all. The Western Powers counted on the benevolent neutrality of the Entente in a future European war, but while they valued its role in pacifying a notoriously turbulent region, they did not consider it a suitable vehicle for advancing western interests at a wider European level. Moreover by the late 1930s, the Entente's ability to hold the ring in the Balkans had noticeably declined. The growth of German and Italian revisionism naturally encouraged the Bulgarians and Hungarians to press their own territorial claims. The West's response – offering guarantees to Romania and Greece and strengthening their ties with Turkey – may well have given the Axis, especially Italy, reason to pause, but their actions ultimately had the effect of diminishing Greek or Romanian interest in building regional security or neutrality through the auspices of the Balkan Entente.[14] The Balkans might thus have been a source of friction for the major powers before the outbreak of war in 1939, but in no sense can it be argued that it was Balkan 'neutrality' that fuelled this instability. During the 1930s, none of the states of the region claimed to be guided by considerations of neutrality, nor did any of them genuinely aspire to this goal.

A similar conclusion might be drawn for the Oslo group. Like the Entente, the problem of German revisionism was not uppermost in the minds of its leaders when the organisation was created in 1930. For the first five years of its existence, member states used the period meetings to discuss mutual economic difficulties, and it was only in 1935 that the group began to turn its attention to political matters. By 1938 all members were anxious to remain neutral in the coming conflagration, but only amongst the Scandinavians did a clear sense of 'regional neutrality' take hold.[15] This was by no means an unrealistic objective. Scandinavian neutrality survived the Great War, and there was every prospect of repeating the feat after 1939. There were clearly ominous signs: Moscow's unremitting hostility towards Finland, the German navy's designs on Norwegian bases for its future operations in the North Atlantic, and Britain's increasing fascination with Swedish iron ore as Germany's potential Achilles heel. But the importance of these issues lay in the future. The possibility of military operations in northern Europe featured in neither the British nor German war plans in 1939: such ideas as there were remained the preserve of a handful of staff officers or retired admirals.

It would be wrong to assume that the events of the inter-war period had no bearing on Scandinavia's fate once war began, especially in the case of Finland.[16] In retrospect it is clear that having long been accustomed to life at the margins of international politics, after 1918 Scandinavia became increasingly integrated into Europe's political, cultural and commercial affairs, and could no longer insulate itself from the convulsions of its neighbours. But it is equally apparent that neither the individual nor the collective efforts to 'neutralise' northern Europe in the latter half of the 1930s significantly affected the foreign policy calculations of the major states or obstructed those which sought a peaceful resolution to Europe's problems. Like Balkan 'neutrality', Scandinavian neutrality dominated the politics of Phoney War, but it had little influence on the politics of peace.

All Neutral on the Western Front?

Where 'neutrality' most obviously affected the European balance of power was Belgium's decision, in March 1936, to renounce its 1920 military accord with France and embark on a policy of 'independence'. The reasons for Belgium's action and its wider political and military significance have long intrigued historians. Why did Belgium seek refuge in a policy that had proved so disastrous 22 years before, and at a time when Hitler's aggressive ambitions in western Europe were becoming increasingly difficult to ignore? Moreover, was Belgium's reversion to neutrality responsible for sapping French confidence and military preparedness in the years leading up to the débâcle of 1940? In order to understand Belgian actions after 1936, it is vital to appreciate the fact that Belgian foreign policy was driven as much by internal political considerations as it was by Brussels' reading of the international situation. The prospect of France lurching to the left, realised in June 1936 with the election of a popular front government, and its new affection for the Soviet Union as evidenced in the Franco-Soviet treaty concluded the previous year, made Belgium's attachment to French coat-tails particularly irksome for the youthful king Leopold III and his court. But jettisoning the French alliance was justified primarily by the need to diffuse mounting anti-French sentiment in the country and prevent Flemish extremists splitting the country apart.[17] Belgian's declaration of 'independence' in March 1936 was, moreover, precisely that: a determination to blaze its own trail and not allow itself to be bound by the actions of a government in Paris that seemed set on a collision course with Belgium's southern neighbour. The declaration implied neither a return to strict neutrality nor an admission of political impotence. Indeed, once Belgium could no longer rely on French arms, it became easier for the government of the day to press the case for military rearmament.[18]

Those who hoped that Belgium's policy of 'independence' would enable it to walk tall on the international stage were to be disappointed. Within two years, 'independence' had mutated into 'neutrality'. Initial signs were, however, encouraging. By early 1937, Brussels had achieved its goal of slipping free from French tutelage without apparently compromising its own security. In April, Paris and London agreed to release Belgium from its obligations under the Locarno Treaty and Article 16 of the Covenant, while reaffirming their commitment to defend Belgium in the case of an invasion. Six months later, the circle was closed when Berlin gave an assurance that Belgium's territorial integrity would be respected in all circumstances.[19] Yet, while Belgian diplomats were pleased with their efforts, the paper guarantees proved insufficient on their own to secure Belgium's integrity. Belgium's hopes of reducing international tension by promoting constructive discussion of Germany's territorial claims – leaving it in possession of the Rhineland if necessary – ultimately collapsed under the weight of Hitler's insatiable territorial demands in central and eastern Europe. As the major powers edged closer to war, Belgium found itself increasingly marginalised. Leopold's forlorn appeal for peace on 22 August 1939 was ignored in Berlin, while his equally implausible offer of mediation with Queen Wilhelmina of the Netherlands in November only resulted in causing irritation in the belligerent capitals.[20] 'Independence' opened the door not to greater involvement in international affairs, but precisely the opposite, to neutrality. Having publicly committed himself in October 1936 to an 'exclusive and integral' Belgian foreign policy, Leopold and his senior military adviser, General Robert van Overstraeten, found it easier to embrace an increasingly restrictive concept of neutrality than admit failure and accept the domestic political consequences of restoring its links with France.

Paris was rightly alarmed by Belgium's return to neutrality. Belgium had been a valuable ally since 1918, a steadfast supporter of the Versailles settlement (joining France in its occupation of the Ruhr in 1923) and a military ally, prepared to help France overcome the problem of defending its vulnerable, low-lying north-eastern frontier. It was Belgium, therefore, that bore the brunt of western criticism of neutrality after 1936. In one celebrated outburst in late 1939, France's commander in chief, General Maurice Gamelin, railed against the Belgians as 'thoughtless and short-sighted mediocrities, traders whose perspectives have been distorted by business!'. Historians have tended to echo these sentiments. According to P. M. H. Bell, Belgium's policy was 'illogical' since it merely aggravated 'the instability of western Europe and played into the hands of Germany'.[21]

Such a view of Belgian neutrality assumes that western defence was not only faced with a 'hopeless dilemma' after 1936, but was in some way destined to lead to the chaos and confusion that occurred in May 1940. It ignores, however, the fact that after 1936 Paris remained master of its own destiny. The decision against extending the Maginot line northward along France's border with Belgium was a deliberate one, and taken after prolonged and serious deliberation. Cost was a major consideration, but underlying France's commitment to the concept of 'forward defence' was the belief that in the end, 'the coming of war would frighten the Belgians into asking for help'. As Robert Young observes, although there was 'more than a trace of ambiguity in French official perceptions of Belgium after 1936', Paris was none the less generally sanguine in its assessment of the military situation.[22] The 'guarded optimism' that characterised Gamelin's pre-war attitude towards the Belgians was based on the belief that he could compensate for loss of the Franco-Belgium alliance by drawing on the covert assistance of General Edouard van den Bergen, the Belgian chief of staff. In practical terms this secret channel, which was opened in late 1936, was unquestionably valuable, and delivered into French hands an enormous amount of technical data on Belgium's military effort. Gamelin held similar talks with francophile elements in the Swiss army, with the object of securing their consent to French intervention if Switzerland fell victim to German aggression.[23] With the benefit of hindsight, however, it is clear that in the case of Belgium, Gamelin confused van den Bergen's 'act of private defiance' for official government policy, and erroneously assumed that his secret discussions would blossom into official staff talks once war began. Leopold's retention of neutrality in September 1939 – and his increasingly strict observance of neutrality thereafter – 'signified nothing less than the collapse of French hopes for a secure defence of the Allied north-western flank'.[24] But it must be stressed that these were problems of September 1939. Before this date western planners mistakenly believed that they had the measure of the problem and judged France's situation accordingly. The hostility that Gamelin and his colleagues showed towards the Belgians once war began attests not just to the seriousness of France's predicament, but also to the extent to which Leopold's decision had exposed the deluded nature of French thinking over the preceding years.

Belgium's position might also be judged more charitably if we take account of the attitudes of the government in London. The security of the Low Countries had always been an important factor in Britain's strategic outlook towards the continent. Unlike Paris, however, London did not believe that Belgium's actions in 1936 necessarily prejudiced Britain's military or political interests. The chiefs of staff tellingly noted after Leopold's speech in October 1936 that 'an effective Belgian neutrality would be greatly to our advantage'. Indeed, there was considerable common ground between the goals of Belgium's 'independent' foreign policy after 1936 and British diplomacy towards the continent before the spring of 1939. London's unwillingness to embrace a continental military commitment mirrored Belgium's own reluctance to entertain any overt military agreements.[25] At a political level, too, although British policy-makers were frequently exasperated by Leopold's malleability and reputed pro-German sympathies, the two countries shared the same basic aim of preventing French provocation of Germany from upsetting their efforts to find a negotiated solution to Europe's problems. Belgium was thus a valuable adjunct to Britain's policy of appeasement. So too, intriguingly, was the concept of neutrality itself. Rather than viewing neutrality as a spectre undermining western security, Britain, adopting a distinctly nineteenth-century approach, saw it as a potential panacea for European diplomacy. Flushed after his meeting with Hitler at Berchtesgaden in mid-September 1938, Chamberlain horrified his French partners by suggesting that the current crisis might be eased if Czechoslovakia adopted 'a position of neutrality somewhat similar to that taken up by Belgium'. The gulf in views over neutrality is shown in the French reply, which bluntly reminded the prime minister that the 'neutralisation' of Czechoslovakia, like that of Belgium, would merely result in 'depriving France of a capital element in her security'.[26]

It took the war scare of early 1939 to convince London that neutrality was less benign than it had assumed. Reports of Germany's aggressive intentions towards the Low Countries, Switzerland and the countries of south-eastern Europe revealed how much the 'neutrals' had become a part of Britain's rapidly expanding agenda on the continent. The West's attitude towards the neutrals during the first half of 1939 shows very clearly how the actions of these countries had come to influence the operation of the international system by the last days of peace. A distinction should be drawn between the Balkan 'neutrals' and the neutrals of western Europe. For the former, Germany's occupation of Prague in March, coupled with its mounting commercial involvement in the Balkans, called into question the West's long-held assumption that it could rely on the benevolent neutrality of its traditional allies – the Romanians, Yugoslavs and Greeks in the coming conflict. More important for the purposes of this study, however, is the fact that the very vulnerability of these states seemed to endanger the European balance by tempting Germany into overplaying its hand. Indeed, such was Britain's concern that these states might fall under German influence that, overnight, it resolved to reverse its traditional policy towards the continent and dispatched security guarantees to Bucharest and Athens.

Although the western European neutrals were implicated in the war scare of early 1939, they did not represent as great a threat to the balance of power in Europe as those countries of south-east Europe, despite their vital importance to western security. By early 1939 the political preferences of these states were unequivocal. There was little real danger that Hitler would be tempted to use Germany's position to inveigle or cajole western Europe's neutrals into the German orbit. On the contrary, although Germany's relations with most neutrals were strained, Hitler actively *promoted* neutrality in the months leading up to the war, cynically offering the western neutrals non-aggression pacts as a sign of his good faith.[27] For the British and French governments, any German aggression against either the Low Countries or Switzerland could only be conceived as part of a broader attack on the western powers, and 'an attempt by Germany to dominate Europe by force'.[28] Whether the neutrals were the first line of western defence – as in the case of Belgium – or an advance trip-wire to signal Germany's aggressive intentions, the western neutrals were therefore fulfilling essentially the same role they had performed since the early nineteenth century. As Stratford Canning said of the Swiss in 1847, a traditional neutral could not 'be enfeebled, convulsed, or mutilated ... without suggesting dangerous fears or guilty hopes to the great monarchies which nearby surround it'. The West might therefore have hoped to entice Belgium off the fence, strengthen their military ties with Holland and Switzerland and include them all in their proposed mutual security arrangements with the Soviets, but the existence of neutrality cannot in itself be held responsible for the collapse of the European balance by the late summer of 1939.

At one level then, the road to war in September 1939 – leading from Versailles to Danzig via the Rhineland, Munich and Prague – passed the neutrals by. Yet, as we have seen, the attention shown towards the neutrals once the war began was to some degree foreshadowed by their involvement in European politics while the continent was still at peace, most notably in the first half of 1939. At no time during the 1930s were the Great Powers entirely free to disregard the interests of these small states. The re-emergence of neutrality by 1936 compounded the difficulties facing the international system in Europe, cluttered the diplomatic landscape, and provided the clearest sign yet of the League's redundancy as a peace-keeping organisation. But while the neutrals' part in the origins of the war needs to be appreciated, it would be wrong to judge their conduct unduly harshly, even with the benefit of hindsight and the knowledge of their ignoble activities in the war that was to follow. The neutrals were clearly an integral part of the European picture, at times they were even part of Europe's problem, but they were not part of its cause.

Notes

1. Q. Wright, 'The present status of Neutrality', *American Journal of International Law* 32 (1940), 409. There is no single work that deals with the neutrals in the 1930s: some of the results of the latest research are given in N. Wylie, ed., *European Neutrals and Non-Belligerents during the Second World War* (Cambridge, 2001).
2. G. Best, *Humanity in Warfare: The Modern History of the International Law of Armed Conflicts* (London, 1983), pp. 246–9; and R. MacGinty, 'War Cause

and Peace Aim? Small States and the First World War', *European History Quarterly* 27 (1997), 41–55.
3. For a treatment of these issues, see S. C. Neff, *The Rights and Duties of Neutrals: A General History* (Manchester, 2000).
4. See neutral actions at the Genoa Conference of 1922: C. Fink, *The Genoa Conference* (Chapel Hill, SC, 1984), pp. 113–16. A. Fleury, 'The Role of Switzerland and the Neutral States at the Genoa Conference', in C. Fink, A. Frohin and J. Heideking, eds, *Genoa, Rapallo and European Reconstruction in 1922* (Cambridge, 1992), pp. 201–16.
5. N. Ørvik, *The Decline of Neutrality, 1914–1941*, 2nd edn (London, 1971), pp. 119–44.
6. Ørvik, *The Decline of Neutrality*, p. 177. The 'former neutrals' consisted of Denmark, Finland, Holland, Norway, Spain, Sweden and Switzerland.
7. A. C. Temperley, *The Whispering Gallery of Europe* (London, 1938), pp. 208, 319.
8. Emphasis added. G. van Roon, 'Neutrality and Security: The Experience of the Oslo States', in R. Ahmann, A. M. Birke and M. Howard, eds, *The Quest for Stability: Problems of West European Security, 1918–1957* (Oxford, 1993), pp. 273–4. See also his *Small States in Years of Depression: The Oslo Alliance, 1930–1940* (Assen, 1989).
9. Finland, Sweden, Norway, Denmark, Belgium, Holland and Luxembourg.
10. J. F. L. Ross, *Neutrality and International Sanctions: Sweden, Switzerland and Collective Security* (Westport, CT, 1989), pp. 87–114.
11. R. Baudendistel, 'Force versus Law: The International Committee of the Red Cross and Chemical Warfare in the Italo-Ethiopian war 1935–1936', *International Review of the Red Cross* 322 (1998), 81–104. J.-C. Favez, *The Red Cross and the Holocaust* (Cambridge, 1999), pp. 87–9.
12. Hansard, House of Commons, 5th Series, Vol. 232, p. 227, Neville Chamberlain statement, 22 February 1938.
13. A common Belgian-Dutch approach was ruled out because of poor relations between the two countries. Stockholm tried to help ease Soviet–Finnish relations over the issue of the disputed Åland islands.
14. These events are analysed by D. C. Watt, *How War Came: The Immediate Origins of the Second World War, 1938–1939* (London, 1989), pp. 271–311; and G. Gorodetsky, *Grand Delusion: Stalin and the German Invasion of Russia* (New Haven, 1999). For Romania, see R. Haynes, *Romanian Policy towards Germany* (London, 2000); and D. B. Lungu, *Romania and the Great Powers* (Durham, NC, 1989).
15. P. Salmon, *Scandinavia and the Great Powers 1890–1940* (Cambridge, 1997).
16. J. Hiden and T. Lane, eds, *The Baltic States and the Outbreak of the Second World War* (Cambridge, 1992).
17. For a full analysis of Belgian politics, see D. O. Kieft, *Belgium's Return to Neutrality: An Essay in the Frustrations of Small Power Diplomacy* (Oxford, 1972).
18. In December 1936 national service was extended from 12 to 17 months.
19. For a discussion of German–Belgian relations, see P. Klefisch, 'Belgien und Deutschland 1930–1940', in Centre de recherches et d'études historiques de la

Deuxième Guerre Mondiale, ed., *1940 Belgique, une société en crise, un pays en guerre* (Brussels, 1991), pp. 141–58.

20. Watt, *How War Came*, pp. 561–6.
21. P. M. H. Bell, *The Origins of the Second World War in Europe*, 2nd edn (London, 1997), pp. 237, 238.
22. R. J. Young, *France and the Origins of the Second World War* (London, 1996), p. 63; A. Adamthwaite, *Grandeur and Misery: France's bid for power in Europe, 1914–1940* (London, 1995), p. 208.
23. These are frequently overlooked by historians, but were a vital component in French defence planning. See G. Kreis, *Auf den Spuren von La Charité. Die schweizerische Armeeführung im Spannungsfeld des deutsch-französischen Gegensatzes 1936–1941* (Basle, 1976); W. Gautschi, *General Henri Guisan. Die schweizerische Armeeführung im Zweiten Weltkrieg* (Zurich, 1989, French trans. 1991), pp. 113–40.
24. M. Alexander, *The Republic in Danger: General Maurice Gamelin and the Politics of French Defence, 1933–1940* (Cambridge, 1992), pp. 208, 202–9.
25. It was the British rather than the Belgians who were most reluctant to conduct military talks after 1936. See M. Kent, 'British Foreign Policy and Belgian Neutrality, 1936–1940', in J. Nevakivi, ed., *The History of Neutrality* (Helsinki, 1993), pp. 173–85; M. L. Smith, 'Britain and Belgium in the Nineteen thirties', in *1940 Belgique, une société en crise, un pays en guerre*, pp. 85–111; and B. Bond, *Britain, France and Belgium, 1939–1940*, 2nd edn (London, 1990), pp. 21–34.
26. *Documents in British Foreign Policy, 1919–1939* 3rd Series. Vol. II, no. 928, pp. 393–5, Record of Anglo-French conversation held at 10 Downing Street, 18 September 1938.
27. Only Denmark took up the offer.
28. Public Record Office, Cabinet papers, CAB 23/97, statement by Neville Chamberlain, Cabinet minutes 3(39)1, 1 February 1939.

11 China

John W. Garver

China's weakness was an important factor permitting and encouraging Japan's empire-building on the continent of Asia in the 1930s. To a significant extent, the Japan-American collision that finally resulted on 7–8 December 1941 in global war arose out of conflicts between Tokyo and Washington over Japan's effort to subordinate China. To the extent that China's weakness encouraged rather than deterred Japanese aggression, the train of events leading first to Sino-Japanese and then to Japanese-American war must be traced back to China's weakness. Stated differently, a power vacuum on the continent of Asia combined with the global crisis of capitalism that began in 1929 to prompt Japan down the road of expansion and ultimately produce the Asia-Pacific component of what became the Second World War.

China's decline goes back at least to the mid-nineteenth century. The decline was sufficiently advanced by the 1890s that China tottered on the brink of partition and loss of national independence. This dire situation led patriotic Chinese to increasingly radical and revolutionary solutions. The republican institutions that replaced the imperial system in 1911 failed to take root, however, and China slid into still deeper fragmentation. Its weakness and fragmentation increased after 1915, when the death of Yuan Shi-kai ended the last effective central authority in China. For over a decade China lacked an effective national government. Local authorities vied for foreign support.

The promulgation of the Open Door notes by the United States in 1898–1901, and later the Nine-Power Treaty concluded at Washington in 1922, were efforts to manage China's weakness and decline. (The nine parties to the treaty were Japan, the United States, Britain, France, Italy, Belgium, the Netherlands, Portugal and China.) In essence the treaty pledged all signatories to refrain from taking advantage of China's weakness by carving out exclusive spheres in China to the prejudice of the other powers and China's territorial and administrative integrity. As we shall see, Japan's assault on these arrangements was a major origin of the Japan-US war that began in 1941.

The nadir of Chinese strength was reached in the early 1920s. By that time the seeds of China's national regeneration were, however, already apparent. The First World War stimulated rapid economic development in China, but that country still lacked political institutions capable of unifying it and mobilising a substantial portion of national wealth for national defence. The reorganisation of Sun Yat-sen's Nationalist party with Soviet assistance in the early 1920s, and the success of the party's Northern Expedition in 1925–27, restored a significant measure of central authority. The decade between the transfer of the Republic's capital to Nanjing in 1927 and the outbreak of the Sino-Japanese war in 1937 was a period of rapid Chinese economic and political development. With German, American and Italian assistance, large strides were made in industry, transportation and communications, and a modern military was created under German patronage. Chiang Kai-shek used his increasing assets to further central control. In 1929–30, for example, his forces defeated those of the north-western warlords, Feng Yuxiang and Yan Xishan.

But while China was growing stronger, it was still far weaker than its rivals. Its defeat by the Soviet Union in a brief but intense war in 1929 over the Soviet-owned Chinese Eastern Railway in Manchuria was testament to this. So too was Chiang Kai-shek's policy of non-resistance, when elements of Japan's Kwantung Army (the main Japanese army garrisoning Japan's sphere of influence in southern Manchuria) seized control of Manchuria in September 1931. Chiang and other leaders of the Central government knew that if they went to war with Japan, their forces would be quickly overwhelmed, and their northern cities occupied. The extremist Japanese officers in the Kwantung Army understood this too.

It is an interesting counter-factual exercise to ponder what might have happened if China had had another decade to strengthen itself before Japan struck. What would have been the correlation of forces between Japan and China if, let us say, the 'golden age' of Nationalist rule had begun in 1917 rather than in 1927. With an additional decade to unify the nation, develop its infrastructure, defence industry and military forces, would China have been able to deter the expansionist adventure of the Kwantung Army extremists? Would greater Chinese national power have induced the higher authorities in Tokyo to rein in the extremists rather than extending *post hoc* approval to their successive *faits accomplis*? The answer must remain mere conjecture, but there is little doubt that China's weakness in 1931 encouraged the Japanese actions that took Asia and the world down the road to war.

Chinese Resistance to Japanese Aggression

Once Japanese forces seized Manchuria, Chinese policies of political and diplomatic resistance to Japanese aggression, and the patriotic passions that drove those policies, began to play an important role in the global polarisation that culminated in the Second World War. Here we encounter another intriguing problem of historical causation. Chinese of nearly all political persuasions in the early 1930s were convinced that economic forces governed world politics.[1] When Japan seized Manchuria, they therefore assumed that because Japan's actions posed a direct challenge to the commercial interests of the United States and Britain, those powers would intervene, sooner rather than later, to thwart Japan's moves. They assumed that Moscow would act, not on the basis of economic motives, but out of the concern for security threats posed to the Russian Far East by Japanese occupation of Manchuria. None the less, they expected that the Soviet Union too would soon enter the conflict with Japan. Shortly after the Mukden Incident, Chinese leaders, diplomats and journalists started advocating the formation of a US-British-Soviet-Chinese coalition to confront Japan and contain its imperial expansion. Over the next decade, Chinese representatives at all levels repeatedly told every American, British, Soviet, German and any other foreign representative who would listen to them that Japan's actions against China constituted a grave threat to international peace, law and morality, as well as to the economies and security of the rest of the world. All the powers, but especially the United States, Britain and the Soviet Union, should therefore work with China to thwart Japan's actions. This was in fact approximately what later transpired.

To what extent did Chinese advocacy of an anti-Japanese coalition contribute to the formation of such a coalition? Were Chinese arguments and warnings persuasive – especially perhaps in American ears? Or did their advocacy of such a coalition exacerbate Japanese paranoia and encourage Japanese actions to separate China from third powers, thereby provoking the antagonism of the United States? Akira Iriye argues that China's pedagogic efforts had little effect. The decisive factor driving the United States and Britain toward support for China against Japan in the 1930s was the course of Japanese policy itself.[2] As the decade proceeded, Japanese actions constituted an ever-clearer and more direct challenge to the multilateral system based on the Nine-Power Treaty. That treaty had pledged the signatory powers to uphold China's independence and integrity, equal economic opportunity within China's boundaries, and to give assistance to China's efforts to develop a stable system of government.[3] In essence, it had pledged its signatories to work together to assist in the development of a modern state in China and to abstain from unilateral actions detrimental to China's administrative integrity. Yet from September 1931, Japan was set on a course of unilateral action, with its policy process dominated by ultranationalists who regarded cooperation with the Western Powers as the route to Japanese decline and submission.

While China assiduously courted Western Powers, Japanese leaders increasingly concluded that cooperation with the international community would stifle their effort to create a vital, autonomous economic zone in East Asia. Moves in that direction by the Kwantung Army in late October 1931, when it expelled Chinese forces from Manchuria, led to a decisive shift in American policy. For the first time, the United States began cooperating with the League of Nations in support of China against Japan. For the first time, American leaders also began to consider economic sanctions against Japan because of its violations of the Nine-Power Treaty. These deliberations would not mature into policy for another decade, but the mental die was already cast.[4] Subsequent Japanese actions confirmed these early American suspicions. The creation and recognition of the Japanese puppet regime of Manchukuo in 1932, the declaration in 1934 of Japan's 'special responsibilities' to maintain peace and order in East Asia, the 1935 anathema on western support to China, Tokyo's rejection of a proposed Anglo-Japanese loan to China to stabilise China's currency in 1935, the establishment of Japanese puppet regimes in North China and Inner Mongolia in 1935–36, and finally the attempt to crush China through military means in 1937, convinced American leaders that Japan was seeking to dominate the whole of China. They became progressively more concerned about the implications of this for American interests in Asia.

China's continual anti-Japanese exhortations to American representatives in the 1930s probably played a minor role in bringing about the increasingly anti-Japanese cast of US policy. Americans were familiar with China's propensity to play off one foreign power against another. They were also preoccupied with domestic affairs, constrained by strong isolationist sentiment in Congress, and reluctant to come into conflict with Japan for the sake of Chinese interests. United States trade with Japan far exceeded comparable trade with China. Yet, in spite of these misgivings, Japan's repeated and increasingly sweeping challenge to the Nine-Power Treaty system in China pushed American leaders toward the conclusion that Japan had to be opposed since the consequences of acquiescing in Japanese domination of China were unacceptably high.

But if China's hectoring played a minor role in the evolution of American policy, its refusal to accept Japan's terms was a vital precondition for the harder American policy that emerged. China's Nationalist government refused to recognise or accept the new *status quo* created by Japanese actions in China's north-east. It worked to mobilise international pressure against Japan's actions, and adamantly refused to recognise Manchukuo, despite Tokyo's insistence. Chinese military forces sometimes resisted Japanese advances – in Manchuria in late 1931 and at Shanghai in early 1932. The Nationalist government also sought to thwart Japanese efforts to create 'autonomous' governments in parts of north China in 1935–37. It also refused to comply with Japanese demands to keep the Soviet Union at arms length and cease trying to align with the Western Powers to counter Japan's various moves.

Nanjing also pushed forward with measures to prepare China for eventual war with Japan. The Yangtze River, including its mouth near Shanghai, was fortified. A significant industrial base for supplying the defence forces was built in China's interior. A high-quality, modern army of nearly 400,000 troops was built with German advice, training and equipment. The Central government also worked assiduously to strengthen its control in various interior regions that would constitute the vital rear area in an eventual war with Japan. By late 1935 anti-Japanese sentiment in China was becoming intense, accelerating the process of internal unification against Japan. These trends confirmed the arguments of Japanese ultra-nationalists that bold measures were essential to protect Japan's position in China. They also created the possibility that the United States and Britain might support the Central government's resistance to Japan.

The Effect of China's Protracted War of Resistance

The war between China and Japan that began on 7 July 1937 would continue for eight long years and end with Japan's surrender in August 1945. China's tenacious conduct in this protracted war of resistance against Japanese domination had a major effect on the international situation during 1937–41. By tying down large numbers of Japanese forces and inflicting heavy losses on them, by eroding Japanese fiscal, material and military strength, and by diverting the attention of Japan's leaders and planners, China created a new strategic situation in East Asia. China became an important element of the global strategic situation. With Japan bogged down in an open-ended, costly and essentially unwinnable war in China, important new options opened up for Japan's rivals in Moscow, Washington and London. The haemorrhaging of Japan's military and economic resources in China also limited its ability to undertake forceful moves elsewhere. Leaders in Moscow and Washington quickly became cognisant of the new strategic situation created by China's protracted war against Japan, and for the first time began to support Chinese resistance.

China's protracted resistance against Japan had another effect as well. Tokyo, increasingly desperate to end the attrition of its strength in China, took increasing risks in an effort to force China to capitulate. Convinced that foreign support was the crucial factor enabling China to continue its war, Japan set out to sever China's international supply lines through Southeast Asia. Those moves contributed substantially to the coming of the Japan-US war.

When Japan's leaders decided upon war with China in July 1937, they did not expect it to last long. The chronicle of China's wars over the previous century encouraged this expectation. Between the first opium war in 1839–42 and the Sino-Soviet war in 1929, China's longest conflict was the second opium war of 1856–60, which lasted 48 months; the six other wars during this period were far shorter.[5] In contrast, China's anti-Japanese war of resistance from July 1937 lasted 97 months. China's defeats in earlier wars had also invariably resulted in its acceptance of part or all of the terms demanded by the victorious power. China's largely non-military response to Japan's moves between 1931 and 1937 encouraged the Japanese impression that China still had no stomach for a long war.

Japanese observers certainly noted the intense anti-Japanese nationalism sweeping across China by 1935–36, bringing anti-Japanese boycotts, demonstrations and assassinations. If some of those observers concluded that Chinese opinion was changing fundamentally and that Japan should therefore act with greater circumspection than in the past, such caution found no place in the ultra-nationalist atmosphere that prevailed in Japan by 1937. Japanese policy remained premissed on the expectation that after suffering several hard defeats at the hands of Japan's Imperial Army, China's leaders would come to their senses and cooperate with Japan rather than opposing it and inflaming anti-Japanese sentiments within China.

From July 1937 until October 1938 Japan poured more and more forces into China in the elusive search for victory – a process not dissimilar from the later American quest for victory in Vietnam.[6] Its armies pushed deeper and deeper into China, placing more and more of Chinese territory behind Japan's front lines. Several divisions of the Imperial Army were deployed to overwhelm Chinese resistance around Beijing and the surrounding regions. When Generalissimo Chiang Kai-shek launched an offensive against Japanese positions in Shanghai in August 1937, additional Imperial Army forces were deployed to overwhelm Chinese resistance there, then to push up the river to the Chinese capital at Nanjing. In the battle of Shanghai, Chiang Kai-shek lost the better part of his modern army. The fall of the lower Yangtze valley also cost Chiang a region that had provided 85 per cent of his government's revenue. Yet, instead of capitulating, China's government withdrew further west to a new provisional capital at Wuhan in the central China province of Hubei. Nor did the savaging of Nanjing after its fall break Chinese determination. On the contrary, Japanese barbarity only hardened Chinese resolve.

When Chinese resistance continued into 1938, Japanese planners drew up plans for another hoped-for knock-out blow. Additional Japanese forces were sent to China for a push south from Beijing along the main north-south rail line centring on the city of Xuzhou in north-west Jiangsu province. Xuzhou fell in April 1938, but still China resisted. The Imperial Army also suffered its first major defeat during the Xuzhou campaign, at Taierzhuang, when two Japanese divisions were mauled. Japan's strategists next targeted Wuhan, the provisional capital and industrial city in central

China. A push up the Yangtze River resulted in the fall of Wuhan in October 1938 after several months of bitter fighting and heavy Japanese causalities. Despite losing their last major industrial centre, China's government and military forces retreated further west and continued their resistance. A new provisional capital was established at Chongqing in Sichuan province. The central basin of Sichuan was protected by extremely rugged and essentially roadless mountain ranges to its east. With each Chinese retreat before Japan's advance, key personnel and equipment were evacuated westward to strengthen continued resistance.

After October 1938 Japanese forces in China did not resume large-scale offensive operations until 1944. By 1939 Japanese leaders fully recognised the quagmire they had blundered into in China. Nearly a million Japanese troops had failed to compel China to capitulate and were now forced to stand continual guard against possible Chinese counter-offensives. Guerrilla resistance was also spreading behind Japanese lines, as Mao Zedong's Communist forces fanned out to organise 'Anti-Japanese base areas' across north, central and south China. Moreover, Moscow and Washington showed increasing willingness to assist China, making the once-remote spectre of a Chinese-Soviet-American combination against Japan increasingly likely.

China's leaders too made a decision for war in July 1937. At that point, only the small minority opposed to war with Japan seem to have envisioned the sort of protracted war that actually developed. Most pro-war leaders, including Chiang Kai-shek, seem to have anticipated a relatively short war. For Chiang, the possibility of a protracted war seems to have been a fallback position in case things did not go as he anticipated. He expected early Soviet-American-British intervention to end the Sino-Japanese war on terms acceptable to China.

The idea of China relying on its vast area and population to wage a protracted war was, however, scarcely new in 1937. At the time of the first opium war, similar ideas were advocated by some Chinese literati as an alternative to the Qing/Manchu policy of compromise in face of superior British military power.[7] Similar ideas were again bandied about around 1900 when the Qing court decided to throw its support behind the Boxer attacks on foreigners. As the crisis in relations with Japan deepened in the 1930s, various individuals and groups – including but not limited to the Chinese Communist party – promoted this strategy as the route to national salvation. Mao Zedong understood very clearly that such a protracted war would create favourable conditions for the expansion of Communist power.[8] Chiang Kai-shek too was aware of the advantages that a protracted war offered the Communists. Largely for this reason, it was his least desired course. If the powers did not act as swiftly as he expected, China could resort to this option, but Chiang appreciated the domestic dangers of pursuing such a course.

American Support for China and Japan's Response

The Soviet Union was the first power to begin supplying substantial material assistance and solid political backing for China's war of resistance against Japan.[9] A Soviet-Chinese non-aggression treaty signed in August 1937 provided the basis for robust Soviet support to China, which continued until the autumn of 1939 and played a major role in sustaining Chinese resistance. Such support, along with contemporaneous Soviet support to anti-fascist Republican forces in Spain, also helped convince many Americans and British of the viability of a Soviet-Western alliance against the emerging revisionist bloc of Germany and Japan.

From another perspective, however, Soviet support for China in 1937–39 led not to the Second World War nor the greater Asia-Pacific conflagration that erupted in December 1941, but to Soviet non-participation in that conflagration until the very last days of fighting in August 1945. Soviet assistance to China during 1937–39 was partly intended to deter a Japanese attack on the Soviet Union itself. Stalin reasoned that with large armies tied down in China, Japan would be less likely to attack Soviet Siberia. This calculation proved correct. China's tenacious war of resistance against Japan, plus several sharp defeats of Japanese units administered by Soviet forces along the Manchurian border, and Germany's defection from its anti-Soviet partnership with Japan in August 1939, combined to discourage Tokyo from embarking upon war with the Soviet Union. Then, as Tokyo moved toward confrontation with the United States and Britain in 1941, it guaranteed stability on its northern front by concluding a neutrality agreement with the Soviet Union in April 1941.[10] This treaty guided Soviet policy until the Yalta conference of February 1945, when Stalin agreed to enter the war against Japan 90 days after Germany's defeat. To the extent that China's war of resistance against Japan helped persuade Tokyo of the prudence of reaching a *modus vivendi* with Moscow, it determined Soviet neutrality in the Asia-Pacific component of the Second World War. The consequences of this, in turn, were wide ranging. Had Tokyo decided to join Germany in an attack on the Soviet Union in 1941, as Berlin demanded, Soviet resistance might have been overwhelmed.

The United States emerged as China's backer only in 1938, after nine months of tenacious Chinese resistance had convincingly demonstrated its determination and ability to confront Japan. Within the Roosevelt administration, treasury secretary Henry Morgenthau was the leading advocate of aid to China. In March–April 1938 he pushed through the first American support for China – the purchase of 50 million ounces of Chinese silver so that China could acquire military supplies – explaining that, 'Anything we can do to help China in its resistance to Japan thereby strengthens our defence against possible enemies.'[11] Western appeasement of Hitler at the Munich conference and the fall of Wuhan in the autumn of 1938 strengthened the aid-China lobby in Washington. Shortly before the first American loan to China in November – a $20 million credit secured by future Chinese deliveries of tung oil – the State Department's Stanley Hornbeck explained its rationale. It was 'Better to have Chinese soldiers continue to fight Japan and to take now the small risk of an attack by the Japanese on ourselves, than to take the risk of a stronger Japan.' Further loans of a similar size were made in March 1940 and July 1940, and a much larger one ($100 million) in November 1940. With American financing, and top-level directives to make vital war material available to Chinese government purchasing agents, ever-increasing supplies reached what Chinese propagandists were pleased to call 'Free China'.

Japan's fatal push into Southeast Asia from 1939–41 was decisive in the escalation of conflict between Tokyo and Washington. Although the most important objective of Japan's push south was to secure control over the resource rich areas of Sumatra, Borneo, New Guinea, Malaya and Cochin China, a second objective was to force China to capitulate. Japanese leaders believed that foreign assistance – from the Soviet Union, the United States and Britain – was the critical factor in enabling China to continue its war against Japan. By 1940 they succeeded in cutting Soviet assistance to China, when Moscow aligned with Nazi Germany and moved towards the April 1941 neutrality agreement with Japan. British and American support were another matter.

There were two main routes by which Anglo-American supplies reached China in 1939–40. One was through the port of Haiphong in French Indochina and up the railway paralleling the Red River to Kunming in Yunnan province, China. The other was through the port of Rangoon in British Burma and up the rail line to Lashio in north-east Burma, then along the Burma road to Kunming. If these routes could be closed, western support for China would be stopped and, cut off from its Anglo-American backers, China would be compelled to come to terms with Japan – or so Tokyo's strategists calculated.

Japan's first moves toward Southeast Asia were the occupation of the Chinese island of Hainan in February and the Spratly Islands (nominally part of French Indochina, but also claimed by China and not effectively occupied by anyone) in March 1939. These moves led Washington to notify Tokyo in July of the cancellation of the 1911 treaty of commerce. Abrogation of the treaty cleared the way for American economic sanctions and constituted a major American warning to Tokyo not to move further South. Japanese military occupation of northern Indochina in mid-1940 provoked American economic sanctions against Japan. Impatient with French equivocation in the face of Japanese demands to shut the Indochina-China border, Japan bombed the Indochina rail line in April 1940. The Indochina government thereupon promised to suspend shipments of munitions over the line. This was not enough for Tokyo, which demanded complete termination of all commerce between China and Indochina, plus the stationing of Japanese military observers to ensure this cessation. On 20 June 1940, two days after France capitulated to Germany, the Indochina government accepted Japan's demands. Washington responded by announcing the first economic sanctions against Japan.[12]

Tokyo was dismayed that its repeated victories over Chinese armies had failed to force China into submission. Tokyo's view of the situation was embodied in a statement of 'Principles for Coping with the Changing World Situation', adopted by a General Staff-Army Ministry conference on 3 July 1940. The memorandum began: 'The empire, faced with changes in the world situation, will endeavour to settle the China Incident as quickly as possible ... and will seize the most opportune time to solve the problem of the south.' 'Solving the problem of the south' was a euphemism for seizing Dutch and British colonies in Southeast Asia. Article 1 of the 'Essential Points' outlined by the memorandum read: 'In its policy toward the China Incident, Japan will exert every effort to bring about the prompt submission of the Chongqing regime and will make special efforts to block acts of assistance by third parties to Chiang Kai-shek.'[13]

Prior to its closing in mid-1940, the Haiphong route had carried 42 per cent of all China's foreign supplies, while the Burma Road had carried 31 per cent.[14] After the Indochina route was closed, only the Burma Road remained as a conduit for 'assistance by third parties to Chiang Kai-shek'. Anticipating that the short war he had initially hoped for might evolve into a protracted war in which foreign supplies became crucial, Chiang had ordered work to begin on a road from Kunming to Lashio in December 1937. The road opened for operation in January 1939 and quickly became China's main supply line to the outside world.[15] In 1938 the British government had agreed to build a rail line from northern Burma into China's Yunnan province. The line was not built, but work on turning the Burma Road into a hard-surfaced, all-weather road was expedited. London also granted China credits to buy trucks for the road. By the spring of 1939, 1000 tons of supplies per month were transiting the Burma road. Before the Japanese occupation of Burma closed the road in January 1942, the maximum monthly flow reached 18,000 tons.

In June 1940, after the fall of France, Tokyo demanded that Britain close the Burma Road. London sought Washington's support over this issue. With no support forthcoming, and with German preparations under way to invade the British Isles, London complied with Tokyo's demand. The Burma Road was closed for five months. After the decisive failure of German air offensives in the Battle of Britain in September, however, London's position became stronger. The Americans also became more willing to associate with Britain against Japan, following Tokyo's alliance with Germany in September. As a result, Britain reopened the Burma Road in October 1940.[16]

During the 14 months before the start of the Pacific war, increasing quantities of American-financed war material flowed to China over the Burma Road. When Tokyo made its decision in early November 1941 for war with the United States, Britain and the Netherlands, closing the Burma Road and thereby knocking China out of the war ranked only behind seizure of the 'southern resource areas' as Tokyo's war objective. Among Japan's opening moves in the expanded war was a drive by two Japanese divisions in January 1942 from Thailand (by then a Japanese ally) into Burma to shut the Burma Road. Fighting was heavy. Chiang Kai-shek ordered nine Chinese divisions (about 60,000 soldiers) to advance into Burma to help hold China's vital link to the outside world. Anglo-Chinese efforts to hold Burma soon collapsed before Japan's swift blows. By May 1942 the Burma Road was again closed. It would remain closed until, through American efforts, a new route was opened through upper Burma in early 1945.[17]

China's protracted war of resistance against Japan, its tenacious refusal to surrender and determination to continue fighting, was a major factor drawing Japan into Southeast Asia, and therefore into confrontation with the United States and Britain. On the other hand, strengthening China's resistance to Japan was one means used by Washington and London to hinder Japan's seizure of the rich petroleum resources of Sumatra and Borneo. A paucity of oil was a strategic Axis vulnerability. Had the rich oil resources of Southeast Asia been shifted to the Axis side of the emerging global balance, the Allied cause would have been severely disadvantaged.[18]

The Status of China and the Coming of the Japan-US War

Profound disagreement over the status and future of China formed the core of Japan-US differences up to 1941. The American position in China was exemplified by the Four Principles presented by US Secretary of State Cordell Hull to Japan's ambassador, Kichisaburo Nomura, in April 1941. The Hull-Nomura talks continued for nine months, right up to the beginning of Japan's offensives on 7–8 December. Three of Hull's Four Principles dealt with China. The first called upon Japan to respect the territorial unity and sovereignty of all nations in East Asia. The second called for support of the principle of non-interference in the internal affairs of other countries. The third set out the principle of equality, including commercial opportunity.[19] These terms can be traced directly to the Open Door notes issued by Secretary of State John Hay in 1899–1900. They also capped a decade of American opposition to Japan's efforts to undo the Nine-Power Treaty system in China.

Japan responded to Hull's Four Principles by calling for American assistance to compel Chiang Kai-shek to come to terms with Japan on the basis of several broad principles of its own. The terms laid out appeared general and innocuous. American analysts assumed, however, that the Japanese army in China would determine their actual content. Japan also called upon the United States to enter into a separate and secret agreement to cease aiding Chiang Kai-shek if he refused to come to terms with Japan. Washington accepted neither demand. In essence, Washington wanted China to remain independent of Japanese domination and open, diplomatically and economically, to all powers. Tokyo in turn wanted to establish Japanese hegemony over China as a core element of a new Japanese-dominated New Order in East Asia.

As Tokyo moved towards a decision for war with the United States in November 1941, it advanced another set of terms regarding China. Again Washington rejected them. After finally deciding for war if Washington did not accept its terms by 26 November, an Imperial Conference drew up Japan's final terms regarding China, to be placed before Hull and the American government. Japanese units were to be stationed in North China, Mongolia and Hainan Island for a 'necessary period'. Nomura was instructed to reply to a possible American query that such a period would be 'about twenty-five years'. Japanese forces would begin to withdraw from China once a peace agreement had been reached between China and Japan (in other words, once China had accepted Japan's terms). Withdrawal of Japanese forces from China would be complete 'within two years of firm establishment of peace and order' in China. Japanese forces would be withdrawn from Indochina once there was peace between China and Japan. Tokyo agreed to accept the principle of equality of commercial opportunity in China, if it were also adopted in all other parts of the world. In the protectionist world of the 1930s, this was out of the question. The United States was also required to persuade Chiang Kai-shek to make peace with Japan. These terms were unacceptable to the United States. The final American response to Tokyo's proposal, on 26 November, called for the complete withdrawal of all Japanese military forces from China and Indochina, and for Japan's agreement to a non-aggression treaty with all countries in the region.

Japan's objective in China was the antithesis of that of the United States. Tokyo sought to bring China and Manchuria into a Japanese-led economic and military bloc. Such a bloc, Tokyo's planners believed, would possess resources and markets adequate to guarantee Japanese prosperity, and provide sufficient strength to resist coercion by the United States. For the United States, the creation of such a bloc would severely restrict American economic interests in East Asia, and threaten the security of US territorial possessions in the Pacific. It would thus go a long way towards excluding the United States from East Asia and the western Pacific.

There was also the question of how China and its resources would weigh in the global balance. If China and its resources were integrated into a Japanese-led East Asian bloc, and if that bloc remained aligned with the Third Reich, the resources of East Asia would augment those of Nazi-dominated Europe. Had the Soviet Union then collapsed before a German, or possibly German-Japanese, onslaught, the resources of all Eurasia might be combined in a bloc hostile to the United States. Preventing this was a strategic imperative, as Sir Halford J. Mackinder had pointed out in the nineteenth century and MacKinder's student, Nicolas Spykman, explained to Americans in the 1930s and 1940s. Refusing to concede Japanese control over China's resources and keeping China under Chiang Kai-shek fighting against Japan was a way of foiling German and Japanese efforts to construct a vast Eurasian bloc with the potential to overawe the United States.

Notes

1. Y. Sun, *China and the Origins of the Pacific War, 1931–1941* (New York, 1993).
2. A. Iriye, *The Origins of the Second World War in Asia and the Pacific* (London, 1987).
3. W. King, *China At the Washington Conference, 1921–1922* (New York, 1963).
4. Iriye, *Origins of the Second World War*, p. 14.
5. The first opium war of 1839–42 lasted 37 months, the Sino-French war of 1884–85 lasted 18 months, the Sino-Japanese war of 1894–95 lasted nine months, the fighting against Russia in 1900 lasted two months, against the other powers in the same year 11 months, and the Sino-Soviet war of 1929 lasted four months. The Conflict Catalogue, database of global inter-state conflict being developed by Peter Brecke, School of International Affairs, Georgia Institute of Technology.
6. On the military aspect of the Sino-Japanese war see D. Wilson, *When Tigers Fight: The Story of the Sino-Japanese War, 1937–1945* (New York, 1982); Pu-yu Hu, *A Brief History of Sino-Japanese War (1937–1945)* (Taipei, 1974); F. F. Liu, *A Military History of Modern China, 1924–1949* (Princeton, 1956).
7. J. M. Polachek, *The Inner Opium War* (Cambridge, MA, 1992).
8. T. Katakoa, *Resistance and Revolution in China: The Communists and the Second United Front* (Berkeley, 1974). The classic study of this is C. Johnson, *Peasant Nationalism and Communist Power* (Stanford, CA, 1962).
9. J. W. Garver, *Sino-Soviet Relations, 1937–1945: The Diplomacy of Chinese Nationalism* (New York, 1988).
10. G. Lensen, *Strange Neutrality: Soviet-Japanese Relations During the Second World War 1941–1945* (Tallahassee, no date, 1972?)
11. Y. Sun, *China and the Origins*, pp. 134–5.
12. H. Feis, *The Road to Pearl Harbor* (New York, 1965), p. 66.

13. C. Hosoya, 'The Tripartite Pact, 1939–1940', in J. W. Morley, ed., *Japan's Road to the Pacific War: Deterrent Diplomacy: Japan, Germany, and the USSR, 1935–1940* (New York, 1976), p. 207.

14. I. Hata, 'The Army's Move into Northern Indochina', in J. W. Morley, ed., *Japan's Road to the Pacific War; The Fateful Choice: Japan's Advance into Southeast Asia, 1939–1941* (New York, 1980), pp. 155–208.

15. Dian Mian, 'gonglu zai kangri zhanzheng zhong de lishi zuoyong', (Historic role of the Burma Road in the anti-Japanese war), Zhonggong dangshi wengao niankan, 1986 (Almanac of materials from the Chinese Communist Party archives), (Beijing, 1986), pp. 384–450.

16. On Britain's efforts to cope with the simultaneous German threat in Europe and Japanese threat in Asia see B. A. Lee, *Britain and the Sino-Japanese War, 1937–1939: A Study in the Dilemmas of British Decline* (Stanford, CA, 1973); N. Clifford, *Retreat From China, British Policy in the Far East, 1937–1941* (London, 1967); P. Lowe, *Great Britain and the Origins of the Pacific War: A Study of British Policy in East Asia, 1937–1945* (Oxford, 1977).

17. On the Burma campaigns see, C. F. Romanus and R. Sunderland, *China-Burma-India Theater: Time Runs Out in CBI* (Washington, DC, 1959); B. W. Tuchman, *Stilwell and the American Experience in China, 1911–1945* (New York, 1971).

18. D. Yergin, *The Prize; The Epic Quest for Oil, Money, and Power* (New York, 1991), Part III, *War and Strategy*, p. 303–88.

19. Feis, *Road to Pearl Harbor*, p. 178. The fourth principle provided for the non-disturbance of the *status quo* in the Pacific except by peaceful means. In plain language, this meant that Japan would not take action in support of Germany under the terms of the Tripartite Treaty of September 1940.

PART TWO:
THEMES

12 Political Science Perspectives

Robert Jervis

For political scientists, the international relations of the 1930s represent not only a horrifying episode in history, but a case that exemplifies and tests alternative theories of international politics.[1] Although international historians and political scientists share a common subject, they approach it quite differently.[2] Most historians would shudder to consider the immediate origins of the Second World War as a 'case' of something rather than historical phenomena to be understood in their own right; for political scientists, they can only be understood as a case because the very notions of explanation, understanding, and cause-and-effect relations involve comparisons to other situations. The relationships between the case and broader theories flow in both directions. That is, we both use our theories to help understand the case and we use the case as evidence for the validity of the theories, with the danger of circularity being overcome by looking at many aspects and instances.

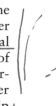

How Not to Use Theory and Evidence: Misuses of the 1930s

There is more questionable circularity in the way political analysts and policy-makers have used the 1930s to provide guidance for contemporary policy, especially during the Cold War. The 'lessons' drawn from the 1930s are that it is dangerous to try to appease aggressive dictators, that democracies must maintain their unity and strength, and that peace can be maintained only by a robust military posture and a willingness to rebuff hostile challenges. This is a problematic understanding of both the Cold War and the 1930s, in which each draws on the other. But to the extent that it is an accurate interpretation of the 1930s, the parallel analysis of the Soviet Union and policy prescriptions gains psychological if not logical plausibility.[3] Thus, to the extent that Hitler could be seen as an unappeasable aggressor and the Allied leaders as weak and blind, so Stalin and his successors seemed a similar threat who could be contained only by force or threats of force. But a parallel between the two eras requires a strained reading of the 1930s. Hitler could have been stopped earlier by a war that the Allies might have fought on more advantageous terms,[4] and Allied resistance might have triggered a military *coup* against him, but he could not have been peacefully contained. It is strange that the post-war theory of deterrence was built on the lessons learned in a conflict in which deterrence was not possible.

Analyses of post-war international politics similarly pointed to the dangers that a dictator's appetite could grow with the eating, that failures to stand firm in one encounter would lead others to expect climb-downs later (one crucial aspect of the domino theory), and that wars are likely to occur when challengers underestimate the defenders' resolve. But the attribution of these processes to the 1930s is false. Hitler's appetite long pre-dated his coming to power, let alone his attack on Poland. His successful coercion of the Western Powers increased his domestic support and convinced his sceptical generals of his wisdom, but did not change his own outlook. Furthermore, setbacks, most obviously when Britain and France stood firm against what they mistakenly believed was imminent German aggression against Czechoslovakia in May 1938, enraged Hitler rather than teaching him that he could not proceed. The domino theory also does not apply: the 'dominoes' that fell in Europe (Austria and Czechoslovakia) were economically and militarily significant, unlike the Third World countries that were the battlegrounds of the Cold War. The closest analogy to the latter was the Italian conquest of Ethiopia, and while the British and French behaviour in this instance may have been a blunder, it had little influence on Hitler's image of them. The United States may have been right to fight in Vietnam, but one cannot support this conclusion by reference to what might have stopped Hitler.

Even if the 1930s cannot give much guidance to what leaders did or should have done after the war, the Cold War has deeply affected scholarship on the 1930s. It is perhaps disturbing but not startling to learn that historians' views about events long past are likely to be influenced by contemporary political issues.[5] For example, political preferences are clearly discernable in the debates about whether Britain and France failed to oppose Hitler because they were more worried about the Soviet Union and in arguments about whether the Soviet Union ever was sincere in its professed willingness to join a coalition against Hitler. Taken purely as an abstract proposition, it is not illogical to argue that Stalin was willing to cooperate with the Western Powers against Hitler but that, once Hitler was eliminated, he would return to his own expansionist plans. Similarly, one could believe that while fear of the Soviet Union played little role in the Western Powers' policies in the 1930s, it was their staunch anti-Communism rather than Stalin's aggressive behaviour that animated their post-war stance. These views contain such strong political and psychological tensions, however, that they are rarely held. Rather, those who explain western behaviour in the 1930s by material weakness and/or failure to understand Hitler are likely to believe that the Soviet Union would not have been a reliable ally and was a dangerous adversary during the Cold War. Debates about international history are then rarely 'merely' about the history itself. Blaming the Soviet Union for failing to act against Nazi Germany fits nicely with seeing it as aggressive after the war; the belief that Britain and France preferred Hitler to Stalin and the argument that the West was responsible for the Cold War similarly make a nice package. Since the Cold War is still psychologically and politically salient in the West, many views about the 1930s have important political implications and political roots.

Politics and psychology similarly help explain a pattern of beliefs about the role of the Soviet Union and the Western Powers during the 1930s. Most of those who read the evidence as indicating that the Western Powers wanted to turn Germany eastward also believe that Stalin sincerely sought a coalition with the West. Conversely, those who believe that western calculations were driven by misperceptions of Germany usually attribute the breakdown of negotiations with the Soviet Union in August 1939 to Stalin's greed.[6] What is interesting is that blaming either the West or the Soviet Union leads to exonerating the other side; no one argues that neither the West nor the Soviet Union sincerely desired to recruit the other to the anti-German coalition. Just as analysts rarely see both the Western Powers and the Soviet Union as expansionistic during the Cold War, so scholars want to see at least one country as following a praiseworthy policy in the 1930s.

This does not mean that everyone is an ideologue, that there is no truth about the past, or that our views of the 1930s are nothing but a reflection of our psychological needs and political preferences. But it does mean that the arguments are a product of more than the evidence about the 1930s. Even those who think that eras are so different from one another that generalisations are impossible and that theories can only distort our understanding are strongly influenced by their general beliefs and conceptual frameworks. Nowadays all but the most naïve empiricists understand that facts cannot speak for themselves.[7] Intelligibility requires that they be made to speak, that they be put into some order and produce an account of some coherence. Indeed, it is a bit flip but not unreasonable to say that intelligibility requires manipulation.

Here the ground-rules for the discipline of history are somewhat different than for political science. The former places a higher priority on an accurate description of what happened than on a tight explanation for why this was so, let alone one that holds in other cases. Because political scientists seek more rigorous explanations with links to higher level theories, they are more willing to adopt accounts that do less than full justice to the history. This is not to say, of course, that they can force the story to conform to anything they like, but the discipline does permit the heuristic treatment of cases to show how, when seen in a certain light, they exemplify and even bolster a theoretical understanding. Political scientists are not allowed to torture the historical record in order to get it to say what they want, but they are allowed to see whether a mild working over will make it speak to the relevant theories.

So it is not surprising that when political scientists come to examine the origins of the Second World War, they find the events to be consistent with the general arguments they had already developed. For example, John Mueller has given us a stimulating argument that rich, highly developed countries will not fight each other because the high costs of doing so outweigh the likely benefits. The First World War showed how high these costs were and later technologies only increased them. The Second World War then should not have occurred, and the only way Mueller can explain it is by seeing Hitler as both an extreme aberration and a necessary condition for the war.[8] Without denying that there is much to this claim, it is worth noting that it is the only explanation for these events that is consistent with Mueller's general argument. In the same way, those who believe that the central determinant of world politics is whether the system is bipolar or multipolar, most notably Kenneth Waltz, attribute the Second World War to the fact that the system's structure made it difficult for the powers to join in blocking Nazi Germany.[9] By contrast, those whose theory of international politics generates an expectation that states will join with rather than balance against the most powerful state see 'bandwagoning' dynamics as central to the politics of the 1930s.[10] Similarly, scholars who are predisposed to be sceptical about the ability of democracies effectively to combat aggression see the Western Powers' domestic systems as the explanation for their failed policies, while those with a more sanguine view of the capabilities of democracies come up with quite different explanations.[11] In none of these cases did the scholar's general theory grow out of his or her examination of the 1930s. Rather, the view of the 1930s followed chronologically and psychologically the development of a general analysis of world politics.

Levels of Analysis

There are so many theories of international politics that might explain the Second World War that it requires some simplifying device to order them. Of course, there are many ways to categorise theories, all of which impose some distortions and exclusions, but one that is almost universally recognised, if not preferred, is through what is called levels of analysis. Inspired by Kenneth Waltz's *Man, the State, and War*,[12] it groups explanations for foreign policies and international outcomes by what are posited to be the main causes or independent variables.[13] Some theories assume they reside in the international system itself, others stress the domestic sources of foreign policy, and still others focus on decision-makers and the decision-making process.

Levels of analysis is not a theory, but a way of grouping theories. Furthermore – and this is much of its value – it does so in a way that indicates what kinds of evidence and counter-factual assertions are relevant to probing the validity of the arguments. Thus, theories that stress the importance of variables at the level of the international system imply that if these were to change, the outcome would change but that differences in the states' domestic systems and decision-makers would not produce a different result. Theories at the domestic level similarly imply that changes of domestic politics would have been highly consequential and that changes at the other levels either could not have occurred in the absence of different domestic politics or would not have had much effect. Decision-making arguments, although not denying the importance of the factors impinging on the leaders, argue that simple stimulus-response models will not do, that a state's foreign policy is mediated if not caused by the leaders' values, beliefs and perceptions, and that in many instances a different policy would have been adopted if those in power held different views.[14]

This does not mean, however, that there is only one theory at each level. Even the incomplete list I will give reveals the diversity of arguments that reside on a particular level. It also should be noted that we can develop arguments that combine independent variables from different levels. It might be convenient if one level were crucial for most cases, or even dominated any single case, but there is no reason to expect the world to be arranged so simply.

The International System

The starting point for most theories of international politics is that the system is anarchic, not in the sense of being chaotic, but in the sense of lacking a sovereign that can make and enforce laws. As a result, international politics is a self-help system, and the most fundamental cause of wars is the lack of a strong mechanism to prevent them. Furthermore, through the operation of the security dilemma many policies that are designed to increase a state's security have the effect – often unintended – of making others less secure, thereby exacerbating if not creating tensions and conflict.[15]

This general perspective, which is associated with the school of thought known as Realism, yields a number of different but related perspectives on the 1930s. The variant that has recently become known as Offensive Realism sees world politics as a struggle for power and dominance because superior position brings with it control over international outcomes and protection against others' inevitable attempts to dominate.[16] World history is then a succession of conflicts among major states that seek to maximise their power, and we see a dreary but necessary pattern of the rise and fall of leading states and empires, usually accompanied by wars.[17] The states that are most likely to disrupt the international system are those that are strong enough to make the attempt and yet are situated in a vulnerable political and geographical space. The Second World War exemplifies the processes involved. We can best understand it as the second act of the First World War, a view that, as we will see, is vigorously disputed by those who examine the domestic roots of foreign policy.

While not denying the horrifyingly unusual aspects of the Nazi regime, Offensive Realism argues that German foreign policy was quite familiar. In both the first part of the century and in the 1930s, Germany was a rising power that had been denied a share of influence, prestige and territory (in Europe and abroad) proportionate to its material resources. Furthermore, it was surrounded by actual or potential enemies who were likely to move against it as their power increased. Germany would then fight its neighbours unless and until it dominated, was permanently crippled, or somehow (an outcome not really imagined until it occurred) was deeply integrated with them. The more specific causes of the Second World War are to be found in the way the First World War ended. Although this seemed a decisive defeat for Germany, the territory and reparations that the Allies exacted only further embittered Germany without crippling its power. As the country made its inevitable recovery, the old ambitions and incentives predictably returned.

Defensive Realism argues that the world is not quite as harsh as that portrayed by Offensive Realists. Many states are satisfied with the *status quo*, do not strive for unilateral advantage, and seek security through cooperation and conciliation. But the security dilemma creates major problems. *Status quo* states can neither identify one another with a high degree of certainty nor be sure that those who are currently benign will remain so. Being frightened, making 'worst case' assumptions and deciding that it is better to err on the side of overestimating others' hostility can create the hostile environment that the state fears. This is a plausible picture of what happened both before the First World War and, to a lesser extent, in the 1920s. Here France (and at times Britain) was driven more by fears of a resurgent Germany than by the hopes for a peaceful Europe. The French therefore sought to maintain the temporary military advantage they had gained in 1918. Instead of conciliating the new German regime, they sought a harsh peace (although the insistence on high reparations initially came more from Britain) and subsequently acted on the assumption that a Germany that regained its strength would inevitably become sharply revisionist.[18] The fact that this nightmare came true owes at least something to the misguided policy. Had the Allies been more understanding of the German position, they might have trimmed Germany's borders less severely and re-integrated it into normal relations, as the victorious powers did with France after the Napoleonic wars. A Germany with fewer grievances, even if it had greater strength, might have been much less willing to support rabidly nationalist leaders and so might have been willing to accept – or at least not fight against – the *status quo*.

With sufficient imagination, one could make a similar argument for the 1930s, but to do so would mistreat the historical record more than even political scientists are allowed to do. A second-order implication of Defensive Realism is relevant, however. Although many leaders are insensitive to the security dilemma and quick to assume that others are arming for offensive purposes, more perceptive ones understand that the adversary may be acting out of fear of them. They will then opt for a policy of conciliation and what in the 1930s was called appeasement, a term that did not have its current pejorative connotation, but instead denoted a policy that sought to bring peace to a situation. Because British, and to a lesser extent French, leaders in the 1930s were sensitive to the security dilemma, and predisposed to believe that Hitler feared encirclement by hostile powers and sought only limited goals, they concluded that a policy of containment would lead to a spiral of unnecessary conflict. Thus awareness of the dangers implicit in the security dilemma can lead to policies that embody the opposite danger – treating an aggressor as though it could be conciliated. Leaders, especially Neville Chamberlain, committed errors not because they were naïve or foolish, but because they were sophisticated about the possibility that others might see them as aggressive and that an excessively forceful stance could produce war. Defensive Realism, then, stresses that there is no one certain route by which statesmen can make their states secure and that assessment of the other side is crucial because while failing to appreciate that the other side may be driven by fear can increase conflict, empathy if misplaced can lead to an equally disastrous outcome.

A third variant of Realism, Structural Realism developed by Waltz, shares with Defensive Realism the assumption that states seek to maximise security rather than power and that the security dilemma can cause wars. It also shares with Offensive Realism a belief in the strong resemblance between the two world wars. But for Waltz at least, the similarity is not that they represented one common struggle as much as it is that they both displayed the results of multipolarity and the alliance dynamics it generates.

Only superficially are the causes of the wars very different, with the first being a case in which the leading members of opposing alliances (Germany and Britain) had relatively few direct conflicts of interest, but were drawn into war by disputes between their weaker partners (Austria-Hungry and Russia), while the failure to contain Hitler was caused by the inability of Britain, France and the Soviet Union to develop a concerted policy. But, Waltz argues, both of these policy failures can be traced to the crucial fact that multipolar systems require even the largest states to rely on allies. Before 1914, this meant that peaceful states had to follow their more bellicose partners lest the latter leave them isolated and vulnerable; in the 1930s, this meant that each of the potential allies could try to shift the burden of blocking Hitler to the others (what is known as buck-passing).[19] Had the system been bipolar in either case with Germany and Britain being the two dominant states, their relations would have been hostile but they could have stayed at peace, as the United States and Soviet Union did during the Cold War. Before 1914 they could have forced their allies to refrain from fighting or, failing this, could have stayed out of the war; in the 1930s Britain would have had no choice but to mobilise her resources to contain Germany.

Although the alliance dynamics associated with bipolarity cannot provide a full explanation for the Second World War, the 1930s does provide clear evidence for buck-passing. Because Britain saw French power as at least equal to German and geography put France on the front lines, Britain believed that France had no choice but to bear the main burden of the anti-German coalition. Britain then had the luxury of trimming its defence spending and enforcing a division of labour whereby France supplied the bulk of the ground forces and Britain specialised in air power. These calculations are not the figment of some political scientist's imagination; they can be clearly found in the records of British deliberations. Furthermore, Britain's progressive abandonment of appeasement and increased commitment to France in the aftermath of Munich were the result less of the increased fear that Hitler would continue expanding until he was stopped than Britain's decreased faith in France's willingness and ability to contain Germany without concerted British assistance.[20]

Soviet policy is also explicable in terms of the expectations that others could and would do the dirty work of fighting Hitler: Stalin signed the neutrality pact with Germany on the premise that the Western Front would hold and he understood the disastrous implications of the fall of France.[21] Clearly, Soviet and British decision-makers miscalculated, and one can argue that this needs to be explained by a theory of decision-making. But the reply is that these errors are characteristic of the ambiguities and incentives created by multipolarity. An examination of the details of the leaders' thinking would be interesting, but would distract us from the essential causal variables that operate on the system level.

Domestic Sources of Foreign Policy

Theories that focus on the international sources of states' behaviour treat states as billiard balls: they are bouncing off one another and the differences in their internal composition are not consequential.[22] The obvious rebuttal is that states differ one from another in their domestic societies and politics in ways that affect their foreign policies. Although the international system rarely can be ignored – indeed, it is often partly responsible for the state's domestic regime[23] – foreign policy is rooted in domestic goals, world-views and politics, with the result that different types of states will react differently to the same external environment.

As with theories at the systems level, there is a profusion of competing kinds of explanations here, each of which privileges a different aspect of domestic politics. Thus Marxists see as crucial whether the state is capitalist, socialist or communist; Wilsonians say that what matters most is whether a country is democratic or not; others look at foreign policy as the by-product of partisan struggles to gain power at home.

In the case of inter-war politics, most theories of domestic sources start with the peculiar history of Germany. Late to unite into a single country and develop economically, it welded a capitalist economic system on to a pre-modern social and political system and followed a distinctive domestic path or *Sonderweg*. The result was incoherence and tensions at home that produced expansionism abroad. Germany could only be governed by incompatible coalitions united solely by the desire to maintain domestic order, keep middle-class values in check, and suppress the workers' socialist tendencies. There was a consistency in German foreign policy, then, not because of geopolitical constants, but because of the fundamental characteristics of its domestic regime; abnormal international behaviour was caused by an abnormal domestic regime. This is not to argue that Hitler's Germany was just like Kaiser Wilhelm's, let alone like the Weimar Republic. But lacking the social integration of a well-functioning modern society, Germany was prone to produce demagogues, to accept the uniting rhetoric of extreme nationalism, and to adopt foreign policies that could please disparate domestic audiences at the cost of multiplying foreign enemies.

Perhaps the sharpest debate revolves around the links between Hitler's domestic policies and what he did abroad. While in no way excusing his genocidal dictatorship, some historians, including A. J. P. Taylor, argue that the two realms were essentially separate and that there is no need to consider Hitler's racist ideology and his quest to eliminate inferior races when we are explaining his foreign policy.[24] This perspective, consistent with Realism, is wildly misleading for many scholars (myself included despite my Realist leanings) who argue that the First World War and the Second World War were radically different.[25] The former, like many other wars, was about power and security. The Nazis fought the Second World

War for very different objectives: not for the German state, but for the Nazi conception of the Aryan race. Domestic and foreign policy cannot be separated because they were twin manifestations of the same racist impulses. Many foreign observers saw this, and the perception of Germany as unappeasable was accelerated by *Kristallnacht*, the brutal attack on Jews in Germany in November 1938. The Holocaust was not a by-product of the war, but the objective for which it was fought.

Realists argue that security is the first goal of states. After having achieved this, they may seek a wide range of other goals, including expansion, but only desperation will lead statesmen to put their state at risk. This picture simply does not fit Nazi Germany, however. At any point in the 1930s, Germany could have ceased the quest for expansion and remained secure within its borders.[26] Instead, security was sacrificed in the attempt to dominate, and dominance was sought in order to serve interests framed in terms of race, not the German state.

The current concern with human rights abuses has brought into sharper focus the fundamental challenge to Realism presented by Nazi Germany; regimes that oppress their own citizens are prone to disrupt the international system. Dealing peacefully with the rest of the world requires a spirit of compromise, an ability to understand others' interests and outlooks, and the willingness to settle for limited objectives. Leaders of dictatorial regimes are likely to lack these characteristics. They cannot brook any opposition and, if they hold totalitarian ideologies, seek drastically to remake their societies. It is not likely to be an accident that regimes that were so murderous at home – most obviously Hitler's Germany and Stalin's USSR – were most destructive of the international order. Nor is it an accident that they failed in the end because the central control imposed by dictators creates enormous inefficiencies and inhibits the formation of an accurate picture of the world by penalising, if not killing, those who bring bad news.[27]

Realists do not – indeed cannot – accept this line of argument and point to counter-examples. Mao Zedong strove to remake Chinese society and was as murderous as any leader in the twentieth century, but pursued a cautious foreign policy. The other side of this coin is that the well-integrated and pragmatic British polity of the late nineteenth century, although moderate in its policy toward Europe, led the way in transforming world politics through the acquisition of colonies. And while many in the United States view its Cold War policies as peaceful and stabilising, citizens of Guatemala, Iran and Vietnam would disagree. The United States was not behaving in a particularly American, democratic or capitalist way, Realists argue, but was just a typical Great Power. Thus it is not surprising that during the inter-war era the United States did not try to save the world for democracy and humane values, but instead stood aside as long as it could, only providing major assistance to the Allies when France fell and the Western Hemisphere was threatened and joining the war only when it was attacked.

Parallel to the argument that dictatorships, especially totalitarian ones, are prone to disrupt the international system is the liberal claim, most closely associated with Immanuel Kant and Woodrow Wilson, that democracies usually follow benign foreign policies. The variant of this perspective most popular now is the 'democratic peace' thesis, which holds that democracies rarely if ever fight each other and can cooperate with each other relatively closely.[28] The causal mechanisms are several, ranging from institutional restraints that make it difficult for democracies to fight, to normative considerations favouring compromise and inhibiting conflict with states sharing similar values, to the incentives confronting democratic leaders and the resulting advantages they gain from making their promises and threats credible.[29] This view implies that if Germany had remained democratic, there would have been no war even if its power had grown. This thought experiment obviously cannot be carried out, although the claim is certainly plausible. It strongly clashes with Realism, especially in its Offensive variant, and casts doubt on the practice of treating states as though they were all alike.

Several other aspects of the diplomacy of the 1930s cast doubt on the more ambitious liberal claims, however. First, the assertion that the Western Powers were unable to reach an agreement with Soviet Russia because of incompatible social systems and strong anti-Communism in the West is undercut by the fact that Britain's relations with France and the United States also were rocky. Neville Chamberlain felt – with good reason – that the United States was unreliable and that France was simultaneously impulsive and weak-willed. Close ties to the former, then, were impossible and ties to the latter might only encourage dangerous adventures. In none of the Western Powers, furthermore, did democracy produce a dispassionate assessment of perils and opportunities, enlightened and honest public debate, a willingness and ability to mobilise resources for foreign policy goals, and decision-making that drew on diverse talents and perspectives. Thus while Chamberlain was no dictator, he had such a powerful mind and arrogant self-confidence that he could never be persuaded and only rarely be overruled and forced to bow to the preferences of colleagues and the general public.[30] The intelligence, openness and steadfastness of democracies were a major reason for their success in the struggle with the Soviet Union during the Cold War;[31] their democratic systems may also explain much of their behaviour in the inter-war years, but the story is not the same one.

An account of the general nature of their democratic regimes does not exhaust the possible domestic sources of their foreign behaviour. We may also need to turn to more detailed domestic politics. France was deeply divided throughout much of the inter-war period and issues of foreign policy were highly politicised in affecting and being affected by divisions between left and right. In Britain, the Labour party exerted some influence by opposing both government policy and greater rearmament, calling instead for a heightened commitment to the League of Nations without the military force that could have backed it up.[32] We cannot understand these (or perhaps any) foreign policies mainly in terms of external concerns and calculations.[33] Politicians above all want to gain and maintain power. Domestic politics is the means by which this is done and only in moments of gravest crisis, if then, should we expect calculations of domestic power to be submerged.

This is true for dictatorships as well as democracies. Stalin's horrendous purges, especially of the military, make little sense as external security policy. But they are quite intelligible in terms of maintaining his domestic power. Indeed, the possibility of war may have increased Stalin's incentives to see that loyalty rather than competence was the main criterion for military leadership; in a war, military leaders would inevitable gain greater power and if the war went badly, the military was the obvious group that could overthrow him.[34] Although Hitler worried less about a *coup*, his generals incessantly, if ineffectively, plotted against him and might have acted if the Allies had stood firm before 1939. Even without a coherent opposition, the country fielded numerous interests and factions, which Hitler's method of governing did little to curb.[35] But rejecting the implausible claim that the economic strains of rearmament required Hitler to go to war[36] we can argue that domestic politics played less of a role in German foreign policy than it did in other countries.

Marxist theories also focus domestically, but on the class interests and class struggles that are supposed to determine foreign policy. It is not the interest of a partisan faction, let alone of the country as a whole, that foreign policy serves, but the interest of the ruling classes. This implies that a different class structure would have produced a different foreign policy and that socialist states would have resisted Fascism. The argument is usually made most strongly for Britain, and involves two complementary claims. First, British policy was designed to ensure the continuation of the British economic and social system, which was less than fully stable. The growth of German power on the continent was a small price to pay for maintaining the capitalist order, which both had ties to Nazi Germany and would be greatly harmed by full-scale mobilisation.[37] The British élite's fear of the working class also played a role by contributing to an exaggerated fear of German bombing. The wildly inflated estimates of British vulnerability to air attacks were a product not only of technical errors, but also of the belief that the working class was not likely to take punishment and make sacrifices for a country in which they had so little role in governing. The second basic claim is that British leaders conciliated Germany because they realised that conflict would benefit the Soviet Union, which they saw as the greater danger to British power and the prevailing social order.

Appeasement made sense because it could turn Hitler east, a goal that grew out of the structure not of the international system but of British society.[38]

A quite different perspective on the domestic sources of foreign policy stresses that public opinion can support or hinder effective policy. France in the 1930s is often held up as a poster child for the proposition that a divided country cannot develop a coherent and sustained foreign policy. Governments changed rapidly and were hostage to the possibility not only of vehement parliamentary opposition, but also of street violence. This experience is at odds with the Realist proposition that the external environment, especially when it is threatening, is sufficiently compelling to override internal differences. Even in Britain, where stability was much greater, the political spectrum narrower, and the intensity of differences much less, domestic differences inhibited foreign policy effectiveness. It would have been difficult for Chamberlain to take a hard line before 1939, even had he wanted to, and in the last nine months of peace public opinion, now turned against appeasement, hemmed him in and prevented him from continuing the search for agreements.

Solid domestic support is particularly important when foreign policy requires sacrifices and the mobilisation of domestic support and resources. Excluding this consideration distorts calculations of national power. Thus it would seem obvious that the balance of power between Britain and France on the one hand and Germany on the other moved steadily in the latter's favour throughout the 1930s. In this reading, it would have been much better for Britain and France to have fought earlier.[39] But as long as public opinion was unconvinced of Germany's aggressiveness it was not willing to support a belligerent foreign policy or a large military build-up, with the attendant costs in terms of budget and conscription. If these states had gone to war earlier, their publics would have been divided on the wisdom of this course of action and been more susceptible to demoralisation and Axis propaganda and subversion. (Support from the United States and the Dominions also would have been much less.) By the same token, it is hard to believe that Britain would have held out in the dire circumstances following the fall of France had the population not been convinced of the horrific nature of the Nazi regime.[40] Indeed, in other cases leaders may exaggerate or stimulate conflict with one country in order to mobilise domestic resources for a variety of purposes.[41]

Decision-Making

Theories of decision-making are no more homogeneous than are those at the other two levels of analysis. Some stress that different individuals reach different decisions under the same circumstances; others point to commonalties in the way people think and decide. Both help explain the appeasement policy.

Almost all accounts agree that some French and many British leaders misperceived Hitler, thinking that his aim was only to revise the most objectionable parts of the Treaty of Versailles. Part of the explanation for this lies in the ambiguous nature of the evidence available to them. Only hindsight makes the pattern in Hitler's policies appear clear; until he moved against the non-German parts of Czechoslovakia in March 1939 one could easily believe that his aim was only to embrace all Germans within the Reich. Indeed, Hitler was quite conscious of the need not to appear aggressive, and much of the success of his policy is attributable to his astute use of deception. But also important was the fact that British and, to a much lesser extent, French leaders were predisposed to accept a benign image of Hitler because they had come to believe that the First World War had been a mistake, growing out of the security dilemma, and that the Allied policy of containing Germany instead of reassuring it had caused rather than prevented the war. There is a natural tendency for people not only to learn from the past but to over-learn and to see a current situation as matching the most salient case from recent history. Above all, then, Allied leaders were determined to avoid repeating the errors that had led to the previous war. They succeeded, but the result was to bring on a war through the opposite causal mechanism of inappropriate appeasement.[42]

Another cognitive mechanism explains why people were so slow to readjust their beliefs in light of changing German behaviour: people assimilate new information to their pre-existing beliefs.[43] None of us can be 'unbiased' information processors because information can only be interpreted in light of concepts and expectations. These processes lead to cognitive inertia as we routinely and even subconsciously ignore much information that our knowledge tells us should not be there or should have a certain meaning. In most situations, this bias serves us well, but it misleads us (and allows others to deceive us) when our beliefs about the world and images of other actors are inaccurate. Thus the benign image of Hitler was hard to dislodge. Many of his actions showed his aggressiveness only to those who already believed him to be so. Although we still know too little about the sources of political and psychological predispositions, we do know that they strongly influence perceptions and that the British policy is only explicable in terms of the predispositions of its leaders.

A related reason why Allied leaders were slow to recognise the threat Hitler posed was that he was – fortunately – unique. This was not widely understood at the time. Nazi Germany was seen as a difficult state, but not as a wildly abnormal one. Indeed, observers lacked a readily available intellectual category into which Germany as we now see it could have been fit. Their cognitive processing was neither unusual nor pathological. It is sensible to require extraordinary evidence before one reaches an implausible conclusion. Just as doctors are rarely quick to diagnose obscure diseases, so the Allied leaders were understandably slow to appreciate what they faced.

The biases discussed in the previous paragraphs are purely cognitive. They stem from the fact that people confront a complex and ambiguous world armed with only limited intelligence and information-processing abilities. We must then employ shortcuts to rationality and make radically simplifying assumptions. This is the only way we can form a coherent view of our environments and act in the face of the contradictions and limitations in the evidence and the great uncertainty about what the results of our actions will be.[44]

People are also subject to what are called motivated biases: what we think and how we think is influenced by emotions and needs.[45] We are not only prone to see what we expect to see, we feel pressures to see what we need to see in order to accommodate psychological and political pressures. Excessively threatening stimuli will not be readily perceived; established positions become psychological commitments as well as political ones; people often construct a subjective world that is much more comfortable than a cold reading of the evidence would lead one to expect. The most important kind of motivated bias operating in the 1930s was the resistance to facing value trade-offs. Because people want to avoid conflict between important values, they are prone to believe that the course of action that they favour is not only best overall, but is superior to the alternatives on many logically independent dimensions. In the 1950s and 1960s, for example, those who favoured a nuclear test ban believed that it would further American security interests, could be verified, and that testing posed a serious threat to public health. Opponents disagreed not just on one or two of these points, but on all three of them. This may seem puzzling, because the points are not necessarily connected. That is, it is quite possible that testing did indeed kill hundreds of thousands of innocent people but that a ban would not have served world peace or would have been susceptible to cheating. Yet almost no one espoused such a view.

In the 1930s, western decision-makers similarly sought to maintain three principal values: the maintenance of social stability with the attendant requirement of minimising tax burdens, preventing any state from dominating the continent, and preserving the peace. The last-mentioned loomed especially large because of the memories of the First World War. Indeed, it dominated in the sense that few decision-makers could squarely confront the idea that war might be necessary. The belief that the only way to maintain security was to arm and threaten war would have brought to the fore a sharp conflict between values, and it was much more comfortable to believe that a policy of safeguarding the domestic economy and paying due heed to Germany's legitimate grievances would keep the peace.

Motivated biases also play important roles within the government. Although we tend to think of intelligence as informing government decisions, causation often runs in the opposite direction. The incentives are less pressing in democracies than in dictatorships, but even in democracies intelligence services are prone to report what is likely to be accepted. Thus in the 1930s British and French intelligence, although sometimes skewing the analysis to try to produce desired outcomes, was generally guided by policy. The fact of a common correspondence between what was being reported about German intentions and capabilities and the position adopted by the British and French governments would seem at first glance to show the influence of intelligence, but a closer examination of the timing and processes reveals the operation of motivated bias.[46]

A decision-making perspective points not only to the importance of the way people think, but also to individual leaders' beliefs, values and personalities. It is not true, as many forms of Realism and other structural theories imply, that all decision-makers behave the same way in the same situation or that, as theorists of domestic sources have it, decision-makers passively reflect the characteristics of their states and the interplay of domestic interests. Rather, leaders often lead; they take the initiative and differ significantly among themselves. Thus, while there were many reasons for Britain to adopt appeasement, a good deal of the policy must be attributed to the skills and beliefs of individual leaders, especially Neville Chamberlain.

Most importantly, we cannot write the history of the 1930s as though Adolf Hitler were a normal German leader. Although most Germans wished to overturn parts of the Treaty of Versailles, few other than Hitler and his hand-picked lieutenants were willing to risk the destruction of the country in order to dominate Europe. Similarly, few would have made racial values rather than traditional national ones the loadstone of policy. It is telling that Taylor's portrayal of a 'normal' Hitler falters when it comes to his invasion of the Soviet Union: Taylor simply throws up his hands and says that at this point Hitler lost his senses.[47] But it is more convincing to see the invasion as the logical culmination of Hitler's thinking because the very point of gaining victory in the west was to be able to move east and racially purify Europe.[48] The terrible irony here is that the Nazi ideology not only drove their policy, but cost them the war. If they had treated the inhabitants of the Soviet Union humanely, they would have been welcomed as liberators and could have destroyed the Soviet Union, thereby making their regime invincible for the foreseeable future. But they could not do this because it did not fit with their principles and values. The outcome of the war as well as its origins, then, can be traced to the world-view of German leaders.

Political Science offers no single explanation for the diplomacy of the 1930s; instead it opens up a variety of perspectives. It also offers a way to order the various explanations, relates them to discussions of other cases and broader theories, and points to the kinds of evidence that will support or undermine conflicting claims. We are unlikely ever to settle on a definitive account of this fascinating and deeply disturbing era, but we may be able to enrich our understanding by thinking in terms of conflicting theories and what they lead us to expect from the history.

Notes

1. A more complete treatment would include events in East Asia as well as Europe. To keep this essay focused, however, I will examine only the latter and will also slight the role of the United States.
2. For discussions, see the Symposium on History and Theory in *International Security* 22 (1997), 5–85; C. Elman and M. Fendius Elman, eds, *Bridges and Boundaries: Historians, Political Scientists, and the Study of International Relations* (Cambridge, MA, 2001).
3. For discussions of how decision-makers draw lessons from history and how these lessons influence policy, see E. R. May, *'Lessons' of the Past* (New York, 1973); and R. Jervis, *Perception and Misperception in International Politics* (Princeton, 1976), ch. 6.
4. See, for example, W. Murray, *The Change in the European Balance of Power, 1938–1939* (Princeton, 1984).
5. J. Combs, *American Diplomatic History: Two Centuries of Changing Interpretations* (Berkeley, 1983).
6. See M. Carley, *1939: The Alliance that Never Was and the Coming of the Second World War* (Chicago, 1999) and the reviews of this book posted on H-DIPLO list on 21 February 2000 and the subsequent discussion, archived at http://ww2.h-net.msu.edu/~diplo/
7. There are many ambiguities and problems in T. Kuhn, *The Structure of Scientific Revolutions* (Chicago, 1962), but both psychologists and philosophers of science accept the basic point that evidence will be seen very differently by people who have different mental frameworks.
8. J. Mueller, *Retreat from Doomsday: The Obsolescence of Major War in the Modern World* (New York, 1989).
9. K. Waltz, *Theory of International Politics* (Reading, MA, 1979).
10. See, for example, R. Kaufman, 'To Balance or to Bandwagon? Alignment Decisions in 1930s Europe', *Security Studies* 1 (1992), 417–47.
11. R. Kaufman, *Arms Control During the Pre-Nuclear Era: The United States and Naval Limitation Between the Two World Wars* (New York, 1990); A. Groth, *Democracies Against Hitler: Myth, Reality and Prologue* (Aldershot, 1999).
12. New York, 1959. For a different way of ordering theories that purport to explain the Second World War, see K. Nelson and S. Olin, Jr., *Why War? Ideology, Theory, and History* (Berkeley, 1979), ch. 5.
13. I am putting aside the argument that the foreign policies of individual states and the outcomes that follow from the interactions of these policies have to be explained by quite different theories: see the debate between C. Elman and K. Waltz in *Security Studies* 6 (1996), 7–61; for the centrality of the concept of interaction in international politics, see Waltz, *Theory of International*

Politics, and R. Jervis, *System Effects: Complexity in Political and Social Life* (Princeton, 1997).

14. For a discussion of the implication of levels of analysis for how theories can be tested, see Jervis, *Perception and Misperception*, ch. 1.

15. Ibid, ch 3; Jervis, 'Was the Cold War a Security Dilemma?', *Journal of Cold War Studies* 3 (2001), 36–60.

16. Good examples of offensive realism are D. Copeland, *The Origins of Major Wars* (New York, 2000); and J. Mearsheimer, *The Tragedy of Great Power Politics* (New York, 2002). For the differences between offensive and defensive realism, see J. Snyder, *Myths of Empire: Domestic Politics and International Ambition* (New York, 1991); C. Glaser, 'Realists as Optimists: Cooperation as Self-help', *International Security* 19 (1994–95), 50–90; R. Jervis, 'Realism, Neoliberalism, and Cooperation: Understanding the Debate', *International Security* 24 (1999), 42–63.

17. See, for example, R. Gilpin, *War and Change in World Politics* (New York, 1981); P. Kennedy, *The Rise and Fall of Great World Powers* (New York, 1987).

18. The latest thinking on the Treaty of Versailles can be found in M. Boemeke, G. Feldman and E. Glaser, eds, *The Treaty of Versailles: A Reassessment after 75 Years* (New York, 1998); also see the insightful review essay on this book by M. Trachtenberg, 'Versailles Revisited', *Security Studies* 9 (2000), 191–205.

19. Waltz, *Theory of International Politics* , ch. 8; T. Christensen and J. Snyder, 'Chain Gangs and Bucks Passed: Predicting Alliance Patterns in Multipolarity', *International Organization* 44 (1990), 137–68. My own view is that the development of the pre-First World War alliances is a good example of the way in which limited agreements can generate positive feedback that changes the interests of the states and gives them greater incentives to work with their partners: *System Effects*, pp. 243–52.

20. See, for example, M. Howard, *The Continental Commitment: The Dilemma of British Defence Policy in the Era of Two World Wars* (Harmondsworth, 1974), chs 5–6. The French continued to worry that Britain might desert them, however: see R. Young, *In Command of France: French Foreign Policy and Military Planning, 1933–40* (Cambridge, MA, 1978); A. Adamthwaite, *France and the Coming of the Second World War* (London, 1977).

21. R. Tucker, *Stalin in Power: The Revolution From Above, 1928–1941* (New York, 1990), chs 21–2.

22. A. Wolfers, *Discord and Collaboration* (Baltimore, 1962), p. 19, also see p. 13.

23. P. Gourevitch, 'The Second Image Reversed: The International Sources of Domestic Politics', *International Organization* 32 (1978), 881–912; for an interesting application, see Brian Downing, *The Military Revolution and Political Change: Origins of Democracy and Autocracy in Early Modern Europe* (Princeton, 1992).

24. A. J. P. Taylor, *The Origins of the Second World War*, 2nd edn (New York, 1966).

25. G. Weinberg, 'The Second World War: A Different War', in Elman and Elman, eds, *Bridges and Boundaries*, ch. 8.

26. For a strong dissent and the argument that eventually the Soviet Union would have grown strong enough to menace Germany, see Copeland, *Origins of Major Wars*, ch. 6.

27. D. Lake, 'Powerful Pacifists: Democratic States and War', *The American Political Science Review* 86 (1992), 24–37; Ralph White, 'Why Aggressors Lose', *Political Psychology* 11 (1990), 227–42. But Ernest May shows that Hitler's conquest of France rested on an accurate reading of how his adversaries would behave: *Strange Victory: Hitler's Conquest of France* (New York, 2000). For an earlier argument that 'totalitarian systems ... [face severe] limits on rational calculation and analysis', see G. Almond and G. Bingham Powell, Jr., *Comparative Politics: A Developmental Approach* (Boston, MA, 1966), pp. 312–13.

28. For summaries of this literature, see B. Russett, *Grasping the Democratic Peace* (Princeton, 1993); and J. Lee Ray, 'Does Democracy Cause Peace?', *Annual Review of Political Science*, Vol. I (Palo Alto, 1998), pp. 27–46. For an extension of this argument which includes high levels of trade and common membership in international organisations as additional independent variables, see J. Oneal and B. Russett, 'The Kantian Peace: The Pacific Benefits of Democracy, Interdependence, and International Organizations, 1885–1992', *World Politics* 52 (1999), 1–37.

29. See, for example, B. Bueno de Mesquita, J. Morrow, R. Siverson and A. Smith, 'An Institutional Explanation of the Democratic Peace', *American Political Science Review* 93 (1999), 791–808; and K. Schultz, *Democracy and Bargaining in International Crises* (New York, forthcoming).

30. For a discussion of Chamberlain's influence over his Cabinet colleagues, see C. Hill, *Cabinet Decisions on Foreign Policy: The British Experience, October 1938–June 1941* (Cambridge, 1991), chs 2–5.

31. See, for example, J. L. Gaddis, *We Now Know: Rethinking Cold War History* (New York: 1997); T. Risse-Kappen, *Cooperation Among Democracies: The European Influence on U.S. Foreign Policy* (Princeton, 1995).

32. G. Lanyi, 'The Problem of Appeasement', *World Politics* 15 (1963), 316–28.

33. See, for example, M. Cowling, *The Impact of Hitler: British Politics and British Policy, 1933–1940* (Cambridge, 1975); for an analysis of an earlier episode in these terms, see R. Brown, *The Fashoda Crisis Reconsidered: The Impact of Domestic Politics on Foreign Policy in Africa, 1893–1898* (Baltimore, 1970).

34. Stalin also used, if not created, the war scare of 1927 in order to consolidate his power and implement desired domestic programmes, which were needed in part to contend with long-term foreign threats: A. Ulam, *Expansion and Coexistence: The History of Soviet Foreign Policy, 1917–67* (New York, 1968), pp. 164–7; R. Craig Nation, *Black Earth, Red Star: A History of Soviet Security policy, 1917–1991* (New York, 1992), pp. 60–8.

35. E. Peterson, *The Limits of Hitler's Power* (Princeton, 1969).

36. See the exchange between T. Mason and R. J. Overy in *Past and Present* 122 (1989) 205–40.

37. S. Newton, *Profits of Peace: The Political Economy of Anglo-German Appeasement* (Oxford, 1996).

38. See the material cited in note 6.

39. Murray, *The Change in the European Balance of Power*, is an excellent study that is flawed by its neglect of public opinion.

40. As it was, many in the Cabinet wanted to negotiated peace: P. M. H. Bell, *A Certain Eventuality: Britain and the Fall of France* (Farnborough, 1974);

Hill, *Cabinet Decisions on Foreign Policy*, ch. 6; John Lukacs, *Five Days in London: May 1940* (New Haven, 1999).

41. T. Christensen, *Useful Adversaries: Grand Strategy, Domestic Mobilization, and Sino-American Conflict, 1947–1958* (Princeton, 1996).
42. May, *'Lessons' of the Past*; Jervis, *Perception and Misperception*, ch. 6.
43. Ibid., ch. 4.
44. For a good summary of much of the relevant psychology, see S. Fiske and S. Taylor, *Social Cognition*, 2nd edn (New York, 1991).
45. I. Janis and L. Mann, *Decision Making: A Psychological Analysis of Conflict, Choice, and Commitment* (New York: 1977); R. Ned Lebow, *Between Peace and War* (Baltimore, 1981); R. Jervis, R. Ned Lebow and J. Gross Stein, *Psychology and Deterrence* (Baltimore, 1985). For an excellent discussion of how psychological models can be tested with historical evidence, see C. Kaufmann, 'Out of the Lab and Into the Archives: A Method for Testing Psychological Explanations of Political Decision-Making', *International Studies Quarterly* 38 (1994), 557–86.
46. W. Wark, *The Ultimate Enemy: British Intelligence and Nazi Germany, 1933–1939* (New York, 1985); P. Jackson, *France and the Nazi Menace: Intelligence and Policy Making, 1933–1939* (Oxford: 2000).
47. Taylor, *Origins of the Second World War*, p. 260. Many scholars argue that the quality of Hitler's judgment deteriorated after the start of the war (see, for example, May, *Strange Victory*, p. 463), but they see greater continuity is his goals.
48. See his well-known comment to the commissioner of Danzig, Carl Burckhardt, in 1939: 'everything I undertake is directed against Russia. If those in the West are too stupid and too blind to see this, then I shall be forced to come to an understanding with the Russians to beat the West, and then, after its defeat, turn with all my concerted force against the Soviet Union.' Quoted in K. Hildebrand, *The Foreign Policy of the Third Reich* (London: 1973), p. 88. Also see R. Overy with A. Wheatcroft, *The Road to War* (London, 1989), p. 45.

13 Ideology

Alan Cassels

What Is Ideology?

'Ideology has been dealt with in literally thousands of books and articles, but (as many other authors also conclude) its definition is as elusive and confused as ever.' So runs a recent authoritative statement on the subject.[1] Since ideology can and does mean different things to different people, it is incumbent at the outset of this essay to explain briefly how the word and the concept are being used.

One might begin by asking the question how ideologies differ from run-of-the-mill modes of belief and conviction. Many years ago the philosopher Isaiah Berlin offered one kind of answer in his witty book, *The Hedgehog and the Fox* (1953). Whereas the fox knows many little things, he wrote, the hedgehog knows one big thing. In this analogy the hedgehog is the ideologue who sees the universe driven by a single overriding natural law, at work perpetually and everywhere. He applies this law to interpret everything past, present and future. To cite two concrete examples, both of which loom large among the ideological factors operative in the approach to the Second World War, the Nazis asserted race to be a universal historical determinant, while Marxists viewed class relationships as an invariable law of history. Such monocausal world-views, accepted on faith with scant regard for empirical evidence, are cast in the same mould as those monotheistic religions in which every event is attributed solely to a divine master plan. Indeed, with the decline of traditional religion, especially in the West, ideologies have earned themselves the title of the secular religions of modern times. Simplistic quasi-religious ideologies brook no opposition. Their adherents tend to cling to their beliefs dogmatically, even fanatically. Utter certainty of historical inter-pretation gives a licence to pursue the dream of an ideal community not just by persuasion but by force. It is merely a matter of serving a higher power, an immutable natural law, and so the end justifies the means: 'One of the functions of ideology is precisely to suspend ordinary ethical considerations, and replace them by the prerogatives of the "historical mission".'[2] Abso-lutist or total ideologies are a visible mark of ruthless totalitarian regimes.

The image of total ideology has left its stamp on popular consciousness. To call someone an ideologue is to imply a rigidity of view and probable intolerance of alternative opinions. In everyday discourse, however, the word ideology has expanded its meaning far beyond the narrow compass of Isaiah Berlin's hedgehog. It is now often employed to designate more general belief systems which imbue the thought and conduct of a group, but without the fervour and ferocity of the totalitarian species. One writer has described ideologies as 'mental frameworks' which 'social groups deploy in order to make sense of, figure out and render intelligible the way society works'.[3] In other words, ideologies are present in all societies serving to simplify the complexities of the world, but patently not all societies find answers in a universal prescriptive law. Conservatism and liberalism, for instance, are specimens of non-totalitarian ideologies. They supply values and principles as springboards to action, but do not themselves amount to structured, self-contained doctrines. Both conceptions of ideology – the inflexible and the more adaptable – will be encountered below in discussing the origins of the Second World War.[4]

Choosing to treat ideology as a broad church, however, raises one distinct problem. That is whether to include nationalism in the category of ideology. Nationalism is certainly akin to other ideologies, sometimes shading into racism and imperialism, and it has demonstrated all too frequently its capacity to inflame passions and breed intolerance in the worst ideological fashion. Yet the acknowledged ideologies possess one characteristic which nationalism does not share; they are all ecumenical, unrestricted by place or ethnicity. Of course, it may be argued that the phenomenon of generic nationalism plays an ideological role globally, but self-evidently a specific national sentiment cannot. And it is precisely this particularist nationalism, always prominent among the causes of modern war, that one is reluctant to term an ideology. Moreover, nationalist feeling within one country becomes inextricably linked to, because it is presumably supportive of, the pursuit of national self-interest, which is arguably the obverse of ideology. For these reasons, and for clarity's sake, nationalism will *not* be included here in the catalogue of ideologies prevalent between the world wars. Rather, ideology will be limited to those 'mental frameworks' that patently and avowedly steered policy beyond mere national concerns and narrow self-interest. In this scenario a supranational ideology was sometimes employed to further nationalist ambitions, but as often as not it worked at cross-purposes to *raison d'état*.

Ideology and International Affairs in Historical Perspective[5]

The word ideology, or *idéologie*, came into use during the French Revolution to describe a coterie of intellectuals who aspired to redesign society along Enlightenment lines. Although the *idéologues* themselves made no impact on international affairs, it was the French Revolution that injected ideology (in the modern sense) into the practice of interstate relations. The revolution's philosophical thrust was summed up in the Declaration of the Rights of Man issued by the French National Assembly in August 1789 and expressly addressed 'to all mankind'. Hence, when the forces of the *ancien régime* moved against revolutionary France, the French responded with a 'crusade for universal liberty' and dispatched their armies to bring the rights of man to neighbouring countries. The international conflagration that broke out in 1792 has been called the 'first war of doctrine'. Furthermore, the crusade's early success on the battlefield owed much to a populist frenzy deliberately whipped up by revolutionary administrations in Paris; it inaugurated the nation in arms and a citizen army whose faith in the revolutionary cause translated into a reckless bravery and unexpected military victories. This cocktail of popular nationalism and supranational ideology was a far cry from the dynastic politics and mercenary armies that had been the norm before 1789. The French Revolution showed the potential that existed for a state authority to use ideology as a medium through which foreign policy issues might be transmitted to and perceived by a mass audience. However, the full exploitation of this resource lay more than a century in the future.

Meanwhile, revolutionary France, having injected ideology into international affairs, quickly found that the new weapon could backfire. Although many in the Low Countries, the Germanies and Italy had first welcomed French troops as liberators, attitudes changed as the inhabitants were forced to bear the costs of occupation, and later to contribute to the expenses of Napoleon I's campaigns. Uprisings under the banner of the rights of man were now directed against the French themselves. And in a wider perspective, the old order, which before 1789 had felt no need of self-justificatory theory, engaged in formulating its own ideological rebuttal of the French Revolution. It was expressed in practical terms at the Congress of Vienna assembled after the overthrow of Napoleon, 'child of the revolution', to return Europe to its pre-revolutionary state. By the Restoration of 1815 two broad but clearly distinguishable ideological groupings had emerged: those who applauded the French Revolution and its works confronted those who deplored it, left versus right, liberals against conservatives. The former's strength resided in western Europe where the concerns of a rising urban middle class were best served by parliamentary representation and a code of civil rights. By contrast, in agrarian eastern Europe a more traditional and hierarchical social system based on deference and prescriptive rights still held sway.

This ideological schism between western and eastern Europe shaped international affairs throughout most of the nineteenth century. Thus, in the years of further revolution, 1830 and 1848, the eastern European monarchies of the Habsburg Empire, Prussia and Russia, guided by the Austrian arch-conservative, Chancellor Metternich and his successors, presented a fairly solid anti-revolutionary front. But in Great Britain and much of western Europe liberals and radicals were accorded a sympathetic hearing and asylum. After 1870 and the unification of Germany Chancellor Bismarck, in imitation of Metternich, struggled to hold the three eastern European empires together on the basis of the monarchical principle and common ideological opposition to republican France. Only after Bismarck's forced resignation in 1890 was the ideological divide crossed. In a diplomatic revolution autocratic Russia joined republican France and liberal Britain in a triple entente encircling the Central Powers of Germany and Austria-Hungary. This alignment of powers that went to war in 1914 therefore crossed the accepted ideological boundaries. None the less, the First World War, with each passing year, witnessed an exponential and portentous application of ideology to the war aims of all the combatants.

The groundwork had been laid in the previous half-century, which saw a growing tendency to dress up conventional foreign policy interests in an ideological guise, above all that of Social Darwinism with its reverberations of imperialism and racism. In the English-speaking milieu the watchwords of the 'white man's burden' and 'manifest destiny' enjoyed broad currency. The French were always a prey to dreams of Napoleonic 'gloire', and in recently united Italy the political classes cultivated the myth of a third Rome. The Germans' longstanding sense of mission to dominate and civilise the racially inferior Slavs to the east met its equal in the Russian intelligentsia's fascination with a hyperbolic pan-Slavism. But more important than the presence of these ideological myths was the fact that they often gained the standing of widespread popular beliefs. In a democratic revolution that swept over much of Europe in the closing decades of the nineteenth century, millions of workers became integrated into their respective national communities as never before, partly through extension of the franchise, partly through the state's provision of embryonic welfare services. The process was expedited by corollary developments – the growth of state education, the appearance of a popular press and, in most countries, the introduction of a term of obligatory military service. These were all in one way or another educative agencies through which ideologies, hitherto largely the preserve of intellectuals, percolated down throughout society. The French Revolution had briefly hinted at the affinity between mass politics and ideology; the pre-1914 international anarchy and subsequent conflict served to drive home the point.

Almost from the start the First World War took on the character of a total war. While Jane Austen had been able to write her novels without a mention of the Napoleonic wars she was living through, between 1914 and 1918 total war demanded the energies of whole populations, male and female, civilian as well as military. In order to sustain morale for such gigantic war efforts, it was thought necessary to find an idealistic purpose for which to fight. So Britain and France, conveniently ignoring the nature of their Russian ally's regime, claimed to represent liberal democracy opposed to German military authoritarianism. For their part, the Central Powers claimed to be defending European civilisation from the incursion of Asiatic and Slavic barbarians. Lengthening casualty lists and deepening wartime misery guaranteed that, to revive flagging spirits, these messages would be sounded with ever increasing stridency.

In 1917, wartime ideologies crystallised around two charismatic figures. First, President Wilson led the United States into war, not as an allied power but as an associate, thereby affirming that his country did not consider itself bound by the secret territorial deals that the Allies intended to put into effect at war's end. In other words, the United States was to fight disinterestedly for a set of moral principles that were expected to inform the post-war world. More exactly, Wilson's credo was that the victory of democracy and national self-determination would see competition in the international arena replaced by conciliation, and old-fashioned warfare give way to collective security embodied in a league of nations. This Wilsonian vision of a brave new world, although short on empirical or historical credibility, had an enormous impact on mass opinion, as evidenced by the rapturous reception the American president received in Britain, France and Italy on the eve of the Paris peace conference. Moreover, it was not only in the victor nations that Wilson's message struck a chord. Germany and the other defeated states, for entirely pragmatic reasons, seized on his promise of a peace based on justice and reconciliation in the hope of evading the victors' vengeance. At the same time that Wilson was providing inspiration in the West another ideological star rose in the East. When the Bolsheviks under Lenin seized power in Russia, they took their country out of the war, publishing the secret treaties concocted among the Allies as proof that this was an 'imperialist' war. Lenin had grafted on to Marxism his own thesis that imperialism marked the final stage of capitalism. The ongoing war could thus be regarded as the harbinger of a world-wide proletarian revolution, and a Bolshevik Decree on Peace was explicitly addressed to 'the class-conscious workers' of Britain, France and Germany. At the close of the Great War international affairs revolved around the ideological clash of Wilsonianism and Marxism-Leninism.

In the short run, both Wilson and Lenin failed. Wilson was unable to obtain the sort of peace settlement that might have laid the foundations for an era of international goodwill, and the League of Nations did little to disrupt conventional balance-of-power politics. Nor did Lenin's world revolution come to pass. Nevertheless, Wilsonianism and Leninism lived on and, together with other 'isms', made ideology a prime ingredient of international relations in the period between the world wars.

Ideology in the Debate over the Origins of the Second World War

A useful approach to gauging ideology's contribution to the outbreak of the Second World War is to look at the series of historiographical debates about the inter-war foreign policies of the major international players. It can be shown that almost invariably the schools of thought split on the degree to which ideology was a motivating force in a particular national policy.

Nazi Germany provides an excellent case in point. That Hitler was an ideologue of the first order few would dispute, and it is but a small step to assume that the causes of 'Hitler's war' may be found in the Führer's 'political religion'.[6] Such, broadly speaking, is the position taken by those described as intentionalists. But scholarly consensus being a *rara avis*, the emphasis on Nazi ideology has been challenged, notably by the so-called structuralists or functionalists who prefer to dwell on the contingent circumstances surrounding Hitler's actions. (The same intentionalist–structuralist divide has given rise to an equally lively controversy in Holocaust studies.)

Nazi expansionist ideology did not spring fully formed from Hitler's brow. The Nazis appropriated and adapted what many Germans felt to be their historic destiny to conquer and colonise territory to the east. This fancy was fed by legends of the medieval Teutonic knights and by the more recent memory of the Treaty of Brest Litovsk that briefly, after Russia's exit from the First World War, enabled the Central Powers to annex vast swathes of the Russian empire. The German *Drang nach Osten*, moreover, had received the intellectual imprimatur of the Darwinian science of geopolitics. In his *Politische Geographie* (1897) Friedrich Ratzel had set forth the concept of *Lebensraum*, every nation's drive for its natural living space. In due course an *Institut für Geopolitik* was founded in Munich where Karl Haushofer, the institute's head in the 1920s, preached that Germany's *Lebensraum* lay in an eastwards direction. Nazism's deputy Führer, Rudolph Hess, was once a student under Haushofer. Although the connection with Hitler is tenuous, he undoubtedly imbibed notions of eastern *Lebensraum* that were circulating in Munich as he began his political career.

What Hitler brought to traditional nationalist obsessions was an extra measure of racism. All German geopolitical projects in the east, of course, were predicated on the Slavs' alleged backwardness and inferiority, and Hitler subscribed wholeheartedly to this conceit. He was fond of deliberately interchanging the words *Slawen* (Slavs) and *Sklaven* (slaves), and ultimately the Nazis came to apply the term *Untermenschen* (subhumans) routinely to the peoples of eastern Europe. But much more significant was Hitler's use of his visceral antisemitism as an additional rationale for pursuit of eastern *Lebensraum*. According to the history lesson he incorporated into his pseudo-autobiography, *Mein Kampf* (1925), 'for centuries Russia

drew nourishment from [the] Germanic nucleus in its upper leading strata' –
a vast inflation of a germ of historical truth. This segment of Russian society
having been swept away in the Bolsheviks' seizure of power in 1917, it was
supplanted, in Hitler's eyes, by Bolsheviks who were not just revolutionary
but also, and more ominously, Jewish. One of his favourite metaphors was
that of the Jew as a parasite preying on the body of a healthy nation.
Therefore, in the case of Russia, it was 'impossible for the Jew to maintain
the mighty empire for ever. He himself is no element of organisation, but a
ferment of decomposition. The Persian empire [sic] in the east is ripe for
collapse.' If one is looking for the ideological dynamo which drove Nazi
foreign policy, it is to be found here in his preoccupation with Bolshevism
and Jewry, his anti-Communism and antisemitism. It enjoined him to seek
Lebensraum at the expense of an enfeebled Russia: 'The right to possess soil
can become a duty if without extension of its soil a great nation seems
doomed to destruction,' he wrote in *Mein Kampf*. 'If we speak of soil in
Europe today, we can primarily have in mind only Russia and her vassal
border states' – words that the intentionalists take to be revelatory of the
Führer's political priority from first to last.[7]

The paramount role that the East assumed in Hitler's ideological vision
also grew out of his criticism of the pre-1914 German policies of *Weltpolitik*
and *Flottenpolitik*. By building a high-seas fleet in order to sustain a global
presence Wilhelmine Germany had alienated Britain. In contrast, Hitler
envisaged fulfilling his geopolitical aims in collusion with Britain, his race-
consciousness shoring up the conviction that two Anglo-Saxon powers
would see eye to eye. 'Germany would have to adapt herself to a purely
continental policy, avoiding harm to English interest,' he ordained. 'The
destruction of Russia with the help of England would have to be attempted.'[8] In a similar, though minor vein, he counted on bringing Italy back
into the German fold. This diplomatic reorientation would leave France,
whose hostility to Germany Hitler took for granted, in virtual isolation.

The year 1936 saw apparent progress made towards realisation of this
grand design. In October came announcement of a Rome–Berlin Axis
expressive of the two Fascist regimes' ideological empathy. More important,
however, was the conclusion three months earlier of an Anglo-German
agreement limiting Nazi Germany's naval construction. It accorded with
Hitler's current determination to put eastern *Lebensraum* ahead of world
power, and he viewed it as the harbinger of a firmer political understanding
by which London would give Germany a free hand in the east. Up to a point,
he was right. Although no further Anglo-German agreement was forthcoming, the Western Powers' appeasement allowed the Third Reich to
absorb Austria and Czechoslovakia, and cast a long shadow over the small
eastern European states. But when Britain in association with France balked
at Hitler's demand for the Polish Corridor, he was forced to improvise.
German overtures to the USSR resulted in the infamous Nazi-Soviet

Non-Aggression Pact of 23 August 1939, which flew in the face of years of rhetoric on the subject of Jewish Bolshevism. In reality, it was a purely machiavellian, temporary stratagem. Hitler never lost sight of his *Lebensraum* objective and, less than a year later, ordered his generals to prepare for an attack on the Soviet Union. Strictly speaking, then, 'Hitler's war' – that is, the war which he willed out of ideological conviction – did not break out until the Nazi invasion of Russian territory in June 1941. Contrariwise, the conflict with the West, especially Britain, which he provoked in 1939 by attacking Poland, was absent from the agenda sketched in *Mein Kampf* and elsewhere.

The discrepancy between Hitler's announced programme and the part he played in the outbreak of the Second World War is where all critiques of the intentionalist school begin. The seemingly unplanned onset of war in 1939 opens the door for counter-arguments to be mounted along two main lines: one is to discount the relevance of Hitlerian ideology, the other to discover structuralist-functionalist reasons for Nazi Germany's plunge into war. The former tendency is illustrated by those who would explain Hitler's policy in terms of an uncomplicated lust for power and prestige, coupled with a sharp eye for the main chance. A. J. P. Taylor in his notorious and quixotic *Origins of the Second World War* (1961) saw Hitler as an opportunist whose quest for power and dominion, not for himself but for his nation, was that of a traditional German statesman. Moreover, Taylor, who apparently had not read *Mein Kampf* before writing his book, evaded the issue of ideology altogether by stopping his account in 1939 – before the dogma behind the Führer's actions became inescapable. Yet another way of undermining the role of ideology is to diminish the status of the ideologue, Hitler himself, by suggesting that Nazi foreign policy was the consequence of interplay among various factions – other top Nazis besides the Führer, the Foreign Ministry, the military, and so on. This 'polycratic' interpretation suffers, however, from any firm evidence that Hitler was not in complete charge of foreign policy decisions. The most disputatious structuralist contention is that Nazi Germany was pushed into war in 1939 by looming economic and social problems at home. Tim Mason argued forcefully that rearmament had imposed such strain on the German economy that signs of social unrest were appearing by 1938–39, but that Hitler, haunted by memories of 1918, shied away from draconian measures against the workers. Instead, he found an answer in war to rekindle social harmony and conquest to feed Germany's economic needs: 'Nazi Germany needed war and conquest *in order to* go on rearming at a high rate.'[9] But once again it must be said that empirical evidence to support this view is very tenuous.

The intentionalist-structuralist debate has now more or less run its course and, if intentionalism has emerged slightly dented, it continues to be the dominant orthodoxy.[10] In actual fact, there was less of a gulf between writers of the two persuasions than appeared at first sight; a synthesis was always a credible option. A good example of the complementarity of ideas concerns the cumulative radicalisation of Nazi policy between 1937 and 1939 at home and abroad. On the one hand, this suggests that Nazi successes bred a self-perpetuating dynamism, the structural atmosphere which shaped Hitler's readiness to precipitate a second world war. Conversely, intentionalists can read in radicalisation a mark of Hitler's confidence that his star was in the ascendant, and that he could push forward eastern expansion even at the cost of antagonising Britain. In this sense, his invasion of Poland was not so much an aberration as an acceleration of his ideological programme. Doctrinaire belief and tactical manoeuvring were not incompatible: 'The broad ideological and geopolitical aspirations acted as permanent reference points or markers in the day-to-day conduct of affairs; on the other hand, Hitler acted like any politician in responding opportunistically to events or an altered set of conditions.'[11]

The notion that Hitler had carefully mapped out a 'blueprint for aggression' – the impression left behind by the post-war trials of Nazi war criminals at Nuremberg – may be summarily dismissed. None the less, some historians have observed in Hitler's policy a *Stufenplan*, a stage-by-stage approach to his ultimate goal. First, escape from the shackles of the Treaty of Versailles (rearmament and remilitarisation of the Rhineland), next the creation of a Nazified *Mitteleuropa* (the absorption of Austria, Czechoslovakia and western Poland), and then the climacteric push for *Lebensraum* (the assault on the USSR). But additional questions might be posed. Did Hitler's ambition really reach a stopping point with the continentalist goal of living space in the east? Or, in spite of his censure of the Kaiser's pre-1914 pretensions to a global strategy, did Hitler's own extravagant *Weltanschauung* perhaps extend to world dominion? Were this so, it would have involved challenging the two world powers, the British Empire and the United States of America. There are hints, particularly in Hitler's *Second Book*, written in 1928 but only published posthumously in 1961, that he looked ahead to an ultimate confrontation with the Anglo-Saxon powers. More material evidence took the form of plans for a high-seas fleet, conceived in 1938–39 as hopes for a British alliance receded to vanishing point, followed shortly by a contract for construction of the long-range Messerschmitt 264 known as the 'Amerika-bomber'. On the fall of France Hitler gave speculative heed to the French north-west African colonies as a launching pad for a cross-Atlantic operation.[12] And it should be remembered that Hitler's declaration of war on the United States after the Japanese attack on Pearl Harbor in 1941 was entirely gratuitous. Where once Hitler had expressed fear of the American colossus, his ideology eventually convinced him that it was mortally weakened by its race problem. However, these are all straws in the wind as far as a conscious Hitlerian resolution to push for world domination is concerned. He never drew up a comprehensive programme for global conquest as he did for the seizure of *Lebensraum*. How would Japan have been fitted into an Aryan universe? This and other questions remain moot, of course, because the Führer's failure to subdue Russia deprived him of the opportunity to demonstrate just how far his ideological megalomania might stretch.

It has already been remarked that governments in an age of mass democracy have shown a propensity to mould public opinion by means of ideology and ideological slogans. Since Hitler was a master of mass politics, it seems pertinent to ask to what extent he succeeded in persuading 60 million Germans to swallow the racist ideology that stood behind his expansionist schemes. Public opinion being notoriously difficult to calculate, it is not surprising that estimates vary. One authority concludes that, apart from the Nazi party faithful, 'admiration for Hitler rested less on bizarre and arcane precepts of Nazi ideology than on social and political values.'[13] But inquiries into the behaviour of ordinary German soldiers on the Eastern Front point in a different direction. Generally, these combat troops evinced not merely 'little reluctance', but rather 'much enthusiasm' in the execution of criminal orders and atrocities against Jews and Slavs. Here, on the battlefield, years of ideological schooling and military training appear to have created the ideal Nazi society (*Kampfgemeinschaft*) in which the 'perception of reality' closely matched Hitler's racist theories.[14] On a larger canvas, the German population maintained the war effort until the bitter end, although this probably owed more to residual patriotism than any ideological attachment.

Regardless of popular attitudes, the actual foreign and military policies of the Third Reich afford by far the best example we shall meet of the triumph of ideology over *raison d'état*. In the Second World War Hitler subordinated the very existence of Germany to the service of his 'political religion'. In *Mein Kampf* he had promised in absolutist terms, 'Germany will be a world power or there will be no Germany', foreshadowing where all-or-nothing allegiance to his ideology could, and did, lead.[15]

In the popular mind Hitler and Mussolini are usually lumped together. After all, they can both be characterised under the rubric of Fascist, and they were partners in the Axis and allies in the Second World War. In the realm of scholarship, however, much ink has been spilled in postulating a fundamental distinction between their two regimes. A cardinal point made by those of this persuasion is that, whereas Nazi Germany marched to the drummer of a racial ideology, Fascist Italy neither exhibited nor answered to any such single-minded belief system. (Mussolini's antisemitic legislation, it is generally conceded, was introduced in 1938 for tactical political reasons and, in any event, was indifferently enforced.) Mussolini nevertheless recognised the power of ideology well enough. He was in the forefront of opposition to what he saw as the spread of Communism through the Popular Front movement of the mid-1930s. Anti-Communism lurked behind his costly decision to intervene in the Spanish Civil War; Popular

Front success in French elections incurred his vituperative wrath; and he gladly signed an anti-Comintern pact with Germany and Japan. But the fact remains that the *Duce* proved quite unable to formulate a coherent ideology for Italian Fascism. The absence of a totalitarian ideology can be adduced to account for the inability of the Fascist regime to instigate the same emotional response in the mass of Italians as Nazism did among so many Germans.

Yet if Mussolini possessed no specific mono-causal world-view, that is not to say that he was not programmatic in his thinking. Once he embraced the cause of Italian nationalism at the outset of the First World War, its fulfilment became his unwavering, lifelong mission. Like Hitler, he appropriated and cultivated images of past national grandeur summed up in the myth of Rome. These harked back to the Rome of the caesars and the popes as inspiration to create a third Roman empire in the twentieth century. The newly dynamic Italy would find in the Mediterranean area its '*spazio vitale*', a rough equivalent of Hitler's *Lebensraum*. Of itself, an exclusionary nationalist sentiment and ambition, lacking by definition any supranational context, does not constitute an authentic ideology. But, on the other hand, the manner of holding and professing nationalist feelings can disclose an unmistakably ideological mentality. In which case one may be an ideologue without endorsing an explicit, rounded ideology, and Mussolini furnishes the perfect illustration.

Mussolini shared with Hitler an unquestioning faith in a Social Darwinian view of the universe. All life is struggle, especially so in international politics. There, a natural law of the jungle is operating to favour the strong and ensure that at any given moment some nations are on the rise and others in decline. Mussolini liked to dub the former virile and the latter effete. The strong element of natural law in Social Darwinism intimates that history is unfolding along predetermined lines. The sensation of swimming with the historical tide is symptomatic of the ideological cast of mind, and Mussolini's speeches and *obiter dicta* were peppered with references to '*destino*'. (Hitler too was wont to refer frequently to *Schicksal*.) Typical of the *Duce*'s mindset was his assessment of Italo–German relations a few months before proclaiming the Rome–Berlin Axis: 'Between Italy and Germany there is a common fate. . . . One day we shall meet whether we want to or not. But we want to! Because we must!'[16] This was political fatalism in lieu of *realpolitik* decision-taking.

The Mussolini–Hitler relationship forms the crux of the debate over the foreign policy of Fascist Italy. At one extreme stands an Italian historiographical school that claims, the Axis and later Pact of Steel notwithstanding, Mussolini never committed himself fully to Hitler until the very eve of entering the Second World War in 1940. Instead, behind his warlike talk, the *Duce* was playing the traditional Italian game of '*peso determinante*' (decisive weight) in the balance of power. To some extent, this is a riposte to the many English-language books which have depicted Mussolini as no more than a reckless opportunist and aimless adventurer who blundered into subservience to his German partner. But what both these interpretations overlook is Mussolini's fidelity to his dream of a third Rome, the force of his Social Darwinian creed and, above all, his ideological temperament. These attributes bring Mussolini as a politician much closer to Hitler than most writers have been prepared to acknowledge, and led him inexorably into the Nazi camp.[17]

The process began with the Ethiopian affair of 1935–36. Believing he had a green light from Britain and France to move on Ethiopia, Mussolini was incensed when the western states brought Italy's aggression before the League of Nations. Anger was soon mixed with contempt roused first by the Western Powers' deference to the despised League, and then by their pusillanimous avoidance of strong sanctions, which might have seriously impeded Italy's campaign in East Africa. With the conquest of Ethiopia accomplished by mid-1936, there was, objectively speaking, no reason why Fascist Italy should not have rejoined Britain and France in the Stresa Front established earlier to thwart Anschluß. (The union of Austria with Germany would put at risk Italy's hold over the German-speaking South Tyrol, the chief territorial prize won at the end of the Great War.) Yet not only did Mussolini refuse to return to Stresa, he told Hitler that he was tired of protecting Austrian integrity. An invitation to conclude Anschluß could hardly have been plainer, and well before its consummation in 1938 the Duce had thrown in his lot with Hitler. It was a clear choice of 'virile' Nazi Germany over the 'effete plutodemocracies', and also of Mediterranean spazio vitale over the security of Italy's own northern frontier.

In the immediate prelude to the Second World War Italian foreign policy was marked by a tug-of-war between two tendencies. On the one side, the advance of the Axis whetted Mussolini's expectations that the fantasy of a third Rome was within his grasp. Against this was the reality of Italy's economic and military weakness. On two occasions in 1938–39, during the Sudeten and Danzig crises, he was keen to take up arms against the western democracies, only to be forced to recognise Italy's woeful unpreparedness to engage in a major war. Undeterred, however, he pledged in the Pact of Steel to fight at Germany's side in any and every circumstance, and he chafed visibly at Italy's enforced neutrality after the outbreak of the Second World War. When at last Mussolini took his country into war in June 1940, it was in hope of picking up rewards in the wake of Germany's recent victories. Significantly, however, his announcement dwelled less on Italy's national interest and more on his perception of the Darwinian ideological contours of the conflict: 'An hour signalled by destiny is sounding .... This is a struggle between peoples fruitful and young against those sterile and dying.'[18] In Fascist Italy, as in Nazi Germany, life-and-death decisions were made in concordance with cosmic dogmas above and beyond conventional politico-strategic calculation.

Two totalitarian ideologies dominated the international scene between the world wars – Nazism-Fascism and Marxism-Leninism. In theory, Soviet foreign policy was dedicated to the furtherance of Marxism-Leninism and world revolution, and the Comintern, or Third Socialist International, was based in Moscow and served as a token of the Soviet Union's adherence to its revolutionary ideology. But when a global proletarian uprising failed to materialise after the First World War, Lenin set Soviet policy on the path of guarded but peaceful coexistence *vis-à-vis* the capitalist world, and by the Treaty of Rapallo with defeated Germany in 1922 the Soviet Union escaped the status of international pariah. In the meantime, the restriction of the 'Communist bacillus' to the Soviet Union bestowed on it the image of 'fortress socialism'. As such, it represented a beacon for radicals and revolutionaries everywhere, who were prone to translate promotion of Communist ideology into support of the national interests of the Russian state. Predictably, Moscow milked this confusion of aims to the utmost.

The ideological aspect of Soviet policy was thrust to the fore with Hitler's arrival in power in 1933. At issue was the matter of suitable allies to enlist in the fight against the menace of Nazism-Fascism. Hitherto, the Comintern had adamantly refused to cooperate with other left-wing elements; social democrats were contemptuously dismissed as class traitors and 'social Fascists'. But in Moscow they took seriously Hitler's rhetoric about *Lebensraum* in the east and, alarmed at Germany's revival, determined on a total reversal of policy. All Communist parties were ordered to join with 'social-democratic workers' in a united or popular anti-Fascist front while, on the diplomatic plane, the Soviet Union discovered an enthusiasm for collective security and made overtures for collaboration with Britain and France. The historiography of inter-war Soviet foreign policy hinges on one very simple question: Was the Soviet offer to work together with non-Communists and the western democracies genuine or not? That this problem assumed such prominence, at least in western scholarship, was due largely to the climate of the Cold War when all Stalin's behaviour was prejudged with suspicion. The partial opening of Russian archives through *glasnost*, it was hoped, would reveal some definitive answer, but so far this has not transpired. Therefore, historians are constrained still to fall back on the Soviet Union's actions in the series of crises leading up to 1939 as the most reliable indicator of Soviet motives.

The first Soviet attempts to reach across the ideological abyss to the bourgeois western states did not get very far. In 1934 the Soviet Union accepted an invitation to join the League of Nations and sit on its council, taking the place of Nazi Germany which had walked out of the League. Soviet representatives there spoke warmly of collective security, but were patently frustrated by the League's inability to check Mussolini's aggression against Ethiopia. A Franco-Soviet pact of mutual assistance, signed in 1935, proved equally disappointing mainly because the French shunned follow-up military talks. The following year, an uprising in Spain against an elected Popular Front government impinged directly on the new Soviet strategy. Intervention on the Nationalist side by Fascist Italy and Nazi Germany was matched by the Soviet Union on behalf of the Loyalists. But whereas the others sent military personnel and *matériel*, the most notable Soviet aid took the form of 'political advisors', many of whom were Communist refugees from Italy and Germany. Unfortunately, they expended considerable energy purging social democrats and other non-Communists from the Loyalist ranks. Although information of this betrayal leaked out slowly, the Spanish experience seriously undermined the cause of popular frontism. Furthermore, foreign intervention in the Spanish Civil War created the widespread illusion that the conflict was one between the two 'isms' – Communism or Nazism-Fascism. A growing impression that there was no choice other than Communism or Nazism-Fascism polarised opinion and obstructed attempts to find a middle ground.

There is little doubt that the make-or-break point in the Soviet Union's search for security by the collective route arrived in the Munich crisis of September 1938. The Soviet Union indicated it was ready to fight if Britain and France took the lead in resisting Hitler's demands on Czechoslovakia. Their capitulation at the Munich Conference could not fail to nourish the perennial Soviet suspicion that the bourgeois states' policy was to give Hitler a green light in eastern Europe and let him loose against Communist Russia. After Munich, it is fair to conclude, Stalin's trust in the Western Powers hit rock bottom, and an alternative security stratagem began to gain precedence. In the Kremlin there had always been a clique in favour of the German tie, a return to Rapallo, and now they had their opportunity to urge the merits of an interim *rapprochement* with Nazi Germany. A mark of their new ascendancy was a dramatic shift in May 1939 at the top of the Soviet Commissariat for Foreign Affairs; the cosmopolitan Maxim Litvinov, who had led the Soviet Union into the League of Nations and endorsed the principle of collective security, was replaced by V. M. Molotov, by repute antisemitic, anti-western and pro-German. Despite this ominous portent, it was not until August that the British and French cobbled together a low-level delegation for direct talks with the Russians, and it was in the midst of these forlorn negotiations that the Nazi-Soviet pact was announced on the 23rd. A Nazi-Soviet pact was, on the surface, an ideological travesty. A contemporary cartoon showed Hitler greeting Stalin with the words 'the scum of the earth, I believe?', to which Stalin responds, 'the bloody assassin of the workers, I presume?' It was an utterly pragmatic arrangement for each party, save in one respect. In Marxist-Leninist doctrine, both liberal democracy and Nazism-Fascism were but different manifestations of capitalism and, by leaving Britain and France to face Hitler alone, Stalin set up the prospect of an internecine war between imperialist states within the capitalist camp – just as Lenin had predicted capitalism would self-destruct through imperialist rivalries. It would be odd if such an ideological scenario did not occur to minds in the Kremlin. But as yet no documentation has been unearthed in Russia's archives to confirm such an ideological rationale behind the pact.[19]

The likeliest key to Stalin's foreign policy is not without ideological overtones, however, not in the sense of the propagation of Marxism-Leninism, but in the 'article of faith' that the capitalist world would, given the chance, 'renew their bloody assault on the homeland of socialism'.[20] This not unreasonable fear demanded that, at all costs, the hostile imperialist powers must be prevented from uniting, that the Axis and the Anglo-French bloc be kept apart. An implication, that most Sovietologists would now probably accept, is that the Soviet Union was sincere in tenders to the West for collective security, and evidence of Red Army manoeuvres at the time of Munich suggests that the Soviets were indeed prepared to fight Nazi Germany. When Britain and France refused to be wooed, self-preservation dictated a swing to Germany, the Nazi-Soviet pact gave the Soviet Union a breathing space and, by the division of Poland, a buffer zone while also obviating a possible two-front war against Germany and Japan.

Paradoxically, the Soviet preoccupation with the ideological antagonism of the capitalist world steered the Kremlin away from any doctrinal crusade of its own and towards non-ideological, balance-of-power tactics. The Soviet de-emphasis of its Marxist-Leninist ideology continued after the outbreak of war. In the darkest days of what Russian historiography refers to as the Great Patriotic War it was not Communist slogans but the old nationalist symbols of tsarist Russia that Stalin used to rally the populace. Where Hitler sacrificed his country for the sake of an ideological obsession, Stalin reversed the priorities.

Liberal democracy by its very nature is uncongenial to total ideologies. The ideal liberal society is one in which divergent beliefs and interests coexist, a pluralistic universe; it is the antithesis of the intolerant, conformist community prescribed by Marxism-Leninism or Nazism-Fascism. However, if we extend the definition of ideology to include those more inchoate 'mental frameworks', alluded to at the start of this essay, liberal democracies cannot be said to have escaped ideological influences in their foreign policy-making.

The focus of most studies of British foreign policy in the 1930s has been, naturally enough, on appeasement and its high priest, the prime minister Neville Chamberlain. The parameters of the discussion were laid down as far back as 1940 in a celebrated pamphlet, *Guilty Men*, which laid the blame for Britain's diplomatic débâcle squarely at the door of the Chamberlainites. Subsequent writings have centred on the severe constraints under which Chamberlain laboured, partly fiscal (a balanced budget demanded by orthodox economics in the Great Depression), partly strategic (the triple threat of Germany, Italy and Japan to a British Empire whose dominions were disinclined to combat). Still, the guilty men thesis resurfaces from time to time, and the battle of the books is unremitting.[21] However, preoccupation with the personal responsibility of Chamberlain and his fellow appeasers has tended to obscure a quasi-ideological phenomenon; namely, an attitude to war and peace fashionable in 1930s Britain that provided a backdrop to appeasement.

The influence of the American president, Wilson, was nowhere more keenly felt than in Britain, and at the heart of Wilsonianism were two assumptions. One was that the experience of total war between 1914 and 1918 had been so horrific as to render future war as an instrument of national policy invalid and that, furthermore, this lesson had been universally learned. The second was that, as the basic cause of the Great War had been the problem of national minorities, the way to peace was through the application of national self-determination. These same two precepts constituted the principled foundation of Chamberlain's appeasement policy, which is why A. J. P. Taylor could write provocatively that Munich was 'a triumph for all that was best and most enlightened in British life'.[22] Of Chamberlain's deeply felt repugnance for war there can be no doubt; every colleague testified to it. And his appeasement policy corresponded exactly to Hitler's ability to cloak his moves in the garb of national determination – the remilitarisation of the German Rhineland, the absorption of mostly willing Germans of Austria and the Sudetenland into the Third Reich. Conversely, the arrival of Nazi troops in Prague, with no self-deterministic justification, prompted the relinquishment, albeit reluctant, of appeasement. All of which does not mean that Chamberlain was consciously following Wilsonian doctrine. Rather, he reflected the popular ethos of the day. The relief of the majority of Britons at the avoidance of war at Munich was palpable, while the British public's recognition of the moral validity of national self-determination is encapsulated in the (possibly apocryphal) tale of the London cab driver who, at the time of the Rhineland crisis, opined that 'Jerry can do what he likes in his own backyard.' So Wilsonianism was belatedly and temporarily triumphant, although not without a touch of historical irony. Once it had been the democratic left that had preached the cardinal maxims of international conciliation and national determination; now it was a British Conservative government that put them into practice in the form of appeasement.

Conciliation through appeasement was the alternative to a balance-of-power strategy, which would have meant deterring Nazi Germany with the menace of a two-front war; in other words, responding to the Soviet overture for a collective security pact, a course Chamberlain rejected out of hand. Even after Hitler's Prague *coup* in March 1939 and the West's guarantee of Polish integrity, Chamberlain stayed obdurate: 'I am so sceptical of the value of Russian help that I should not feel that our position was greatly worsened if we had to do without them.'[23] What was plainly evident from this stubbornness was a profound and ideological antipathy to Communism. Chamberlain has been accused of harbouring a 'better Hitler than Stalin' mentality, in that his nightmare scenario seemed to be victory over Nazi Germany achieved with the aid of the Red Army, resulting in the spread of Communism westwards (as indeed happened after 1945).[24] It is interesting to compare Chamberlain's stance with that of the veteran anti-Bolshevik Winston Churchill. In 1939 the latter put *Realpolitik* ahead of ideology and campaigned vehemently for a 'grand alliance' with the Soviet Union. Similar advocacy came from all shades of the political spectrum and from within Chamberlain's own cabinet, and a Gallup poll indicated that 84 per cent of the British public favoured a military alliance with the Soviet Union. By August Chamberlain yielded so far as to authorise conversations with Moscow, but the delegation lacked plenipotentiary power and travelled by a leisurely sea route to Russia. If the mission's failure was not actually guaranteed, its success was highly unlikely. Once negotiations were joined, the Soviets raised more emphatically than ever their familiar prerequisite for an agreement – immediate access for Russian troops into Poland, Romania and the Baltic states on the grounds that these nations were subject to 'indirect aggression' by Nazi Germany. As a pre-emptive move against Hitler, this made geopolitical sense. But without any assurance that the Red Army would ever leave the countries it claimed to be protecting, the Soviet demand augmented Chamberlain's dread of the Communist bogyman. The Nazi-Soviet pact which frustrated grand alliance hopes reinforced his conviction that Stalin's purpose was 'to see the "capitalist" powers tear each other apart whilst they stay out themselves'.[25] This was the obverse of Stalin's fear of the West. Communist and anti-Communist alike, locked in an ideological symbiosis, suspected the other of plotting to use Hitler against his country.

Whether British appeasement owed more to Wilsonian idealism or less high-minded anti-Communism is open to argument, but no such uncertainty attaches to France, Britain's partner in appeasement. French anxiety about its security in the inter-war years stifled any regard for Wilsonian international morality and generosity. On the other hand, after the election of a Popular Front government headed by Léon Blum in May 1936, Communism became a much more immediate issue in France than in Britain. In London they spoke of 'better Hitler than Stalin', in Paris 'better Hitler than Blum'. The tension generated by the collision of philo-fascism and anti-Communism on the home front could not fail to affect foreign affairs. It certainly impeded fruition of the Franco-Soviet pact of 1935, and the next year Blum's wish to intervene in Spain on the Loyalist side was thwarted by the prospect of civil war erupting in France. The ideological fissures in French society had a sizeable hand in inducing a state of paralysis in foreign policy that consigned France to following the British lead. Some scholars have recently sought to establish an autonomous role for French pre-war diplomacy, but the consensus remains the damning judgement, 'they [the French] allowed others to forge their destiny.'[26] This was particularly true in the run-up to Munich: 'For most of the Czechoslovakian crisis Britain and France led essentially the same policy. But they did not do so in close cooperation, or in equal partnership. The British took [the] important initiatives.' In 1939 the same pattern held firm as 'the French were hustled into a position where their troops might be asked "to die for Danzig".'[27]

As for the actual Anglo-French declaration of war, it is popularly supposed that the decision was taken in order to destroy the evil of Nazism and defend liberal democratic values. Nothing could be further from the truth. It bears repeating that western political ideologies in the 1930s disposed London and Paris to appeasement designed to avoid war. Most serious historians are agreed that ideological belief had very little to do with the tardy resolution to stand up to Hitler. The ruling motivation, as in 1914, was geopolitical: 'Britain and France fought because they finally felt that Germany had gone too far ... Hitler was out to dominate the Continent.'[28] And again as in the First World War, ideological war aims, at least on the Allied side, were devised only after the fighting started.

The war that broke out on 3 September 1939 was, of course, no more than a European civil war. The Second World War, technically speaking, did not begin until over two years later with the participation of the United States and Japan. Up to 1939 the contribution of these two major powers to the coming of war was peripheral, but not inconsequential. Moreover, the relevance of both the United States and Japan derived from their national ideologies.

American foreign policy has historically functioned within the broad ideological framework of exceptionalism – a feeling of distinctiveness that sprang from the immigrant dream of creating a more virtuous society than those in the corrupt old world that had been forsaken. In the Puritan biblical metaphor, America was to be a city built on a hill that the rest of humankind could look up to. By the twentieth century the spirit of exceptionalism was pulling United States policy in contradictory directions. The need to avoid contamination by association with less upright members of the international community initially created a strong tradition of isolationism, but with time exceptionalism bred an urge, a duty even, to carry the blessings of the American system and values around the globe. This implied an interventionist foreign policy of the sort pursued by President Wilson. The dilemma posed was, in the words of one historian, 'whether domestic liberty could flourish alongside an ambitious and strongly assertive foreign policy'.[29]

Between the wars it was the old isolationist sentiment, fed by disillusion with Wilsonianism, that largely prevailed in American public opinion, and that administrations in Washington had to respect. During the 1930s President Roosevelt was torn between the two facets of exceptionalism, his true inclination a matter of historiographical debate. Vocal exhortations to resolve Europe's problems denoted a readiness to play a part in world affairs (and by the end of the Second World War he had become an open interventionist and patron of a thoroughly Wilsonian programme of international cooperation and conciliation). But in the prelude to the war it was lack of American action or firm commitment that had an impact on European affairs. Awareness of America's isolationist temper served, on the one hand, to encourage Hitler's belligerence and, on the other, to diminish the Western Powers' will to resist him.

Whereas American inaction can be listed among the origins of the Second World War, Japan's culpability resides in its international activism. As in Nazi Germany and Fascist Italy, ideology in Japan enjoyed official status. Indeed, since the Meiji restoration in 1868 Japan had offset its adoption of western technology by an ideological cultivation of the ancient precepts of filial piety, honour and obedience, especially to an emperor accorded a semi-divine character, all subsumed under the rubric of *kokutai* (national polity). The semblance of political religion was enhanced by the pervasive 'state shinto' religion, which preached the virtues and duties of *kokutai*. As an expression of the unique character and essence of the Japanese national community, *kokutai* carried within it the seed of race-thinking, and unquestionably a sense of Japan's superiority over its Asian neighbours motivated those behind Japan's incursions into China from 1931 onwards and its attempted subjugation of that country. In addition, Japan's imperialists were enamoured of the notion voiced by the German geopolitician Haushofer that the world was destined to be divided into several regional blocs, each dominated by one nation. Accordingly, their objective was to create a pan-Asian new order under Japanese control, to which they gave the name 'East Asian Co-Prosperity Sphere'. To one revisionist school of historical writing, this grandiose project was no more than a conventional *realpolitik* reaction to western, and above all American, economic moves to deprive Japan of its basic resources. Rational calculation may indeed have entered into Tokyo's decision-making, yet it is hard to ignore the ideological fervour with which Japanese imperialism was increasingly invested. The right-wing militants who came to dominate Japanese ministries deemed ideological conformity at home necessary to support expansion abroad, and in 1937 the Ministry of Education published *Kokutai no Hongi* (Principles of National Polity) and circulated two million copies. 'From around 1938,' writes a leading authority, 'the Japanese outlook on the world was becoming much more ideological.'[30]

In their militant imperialism Japanese governments demonstrated a kinship with the Axis states, a token of which was Tokyo's adherence to the Anti-Comintern Pact (which later evolved into the wartime Tripartite Accord). The effect on the European scene of Japanese penetration of the Asian mainland and general aggressiveness has already been noted. Japan comprised one-third of the triple threat to Britain and its empire which made appeasement of the Axis a preferred strategic option. Soviet alarm at Japanese machinations on the Russo-Manchurian border helped persuade Stalin to buy temporary security on his western front by the Nazi-Soviet pact. And finally, by shaking the entire Pacific balance of power Japan distracted America's attention from the European crisis.

Conclusion

Ideological thinking was a stock in trade of the aggressor states – Nazi Germany, Fascist Italy and Imperial Japan. In the most striking instance, German foreign policy under Hitler was constantly subject to the dictates of his racist *Weltanschauung*. Although Italian policy was not saddled with an equivalent doctrinaire burden, Mussolini acted as if it was; his fatalistic Social Darwinism bore the hallmark of a genuine ideologue. In Japan modern geopolitical doctrine was grafted on to the historic ideological statement of national identity. In contrast, the Soviet Union, supposedly in thrall to the most all-embracing of ideologies, turned away from Marxism-Leninism in the 1930s in favour of the *realpolitik* pursuit of Russian state interests. The liberal democracies were, in principle, unsympathetic to ideology, or at least to total ideologies, but were still swayed by less rigid belief systems – Wilsonianism, anti-Communism, exceptionalism. Clearly, ideology comes in multiple forms and is embraced with varying degrees of zeal. Nevertheless, as a generic phenomenon it had developed by 1939 into an integral and puissant factor in international affairs.

Notes

1. T. A. van Dijk, *Ideology: A Multidisciplinary Approach* (London, 1998), p. vii.
2. L. S. Feuer, *Ideology and the Ideologists* (New York, 1975), p. 83.
3. D. Morley and K.-H. Chen, eds, *Stuart Hall: Critical Dialogues in Cultural Studies* (London, 1996), p. 26.
4. Ideology is also interpreted in the broadest sense in P. M. H. Bell's excellent text, *Origins of the Second World War in Europe*, 2nd edn (London, 1997), pp. 154–5 and *passim*.
5. The brief synopsis which follows is developed in greater detail in my *Ideology and International Relations in the Modern World* (London, 1996).
6. Hitler's 'political religion' is the *leitmotif* of M. Burleigh's award-winning study, *The Third Reich: A New History* (London, 2000).
7. *Mein Kampf*, English translation R. Manheim (New York, 1943), pp. 654–5. A classic and succinct expression of the intentionalist position is K. Hildebrand, *The Foreign Policy of the Third Reich*, English translation (London, 1973).

8. Quoted in I. Kershaw, *Hitler,* Vol. I, *Hubris* (London, 1998), p. 247.

9. 'The Domestic Dynamics of Nazi Conquests', in J. Caplan, ed., *Nazism, Fascism and the Working Class* (Cambridge, 1995), p. 302; italics in the original. For the pros and cons of this thesis, see the exchange between Mason and R. J. Overy, 'Debate: Germany, "Domestic Crisis" and War in 1939', in P. Finney, ed., *The Origins of the Second World War* (London, 1997), pp. 90–112.

10. I. Kershaw, *The Nazi Dictatorship: Problems and Perspectives of Interpretation,* 4th edn (London, 2000), pp. 134–60.

11. R. J. Overy, 'Misjudging Hitler,' in G. Martel, ed., *The Origins of the Second World War Reconsidered,* 2nd edn (London, 1999), p. 103.

12. On Hitler's putative world-dominion ambition see N. J. W. Goda, *Tomorrow the World: Hitler, Northwest Africa, and the Path toward America* (College Station, TX, 1999); and M. Hauner, 'Did Hitler Want A World Dominion?', *Journal of Contemporary History* 13 (1979), 15–32.

13. I. Kershaw, *The 'Hitler Myth'* (Oxford, 1987), p. 10.

14. O. Bartov, 'Savage war', in M. Burleigh, ed., *Confronting the Nazi Past: New Debates on Modern German History* (London, 1996), pp. 129–32.

15. *Mein Kampf,* p. 654.

16. Quoted in R. H. Whealey, 'Mussolini's Ideological Diplomacy', *Journal of Modern History* 39 (1967), 435.

17. Two works that challenge the received wisdom and treat Mussolini and Hitler alike as programmatic thinkers are A. A. Kallis, *Fascist Ideology: Territory and Expansionism in Italy and Germany, 1922–1945* (London, 2000); and M. Knox, *Common Destiny: Dictatorship, Foreign Policy, and War in Fascist Italy and Nazi Germany* (Cambridge, 2000).

18. Benito Mussolini, *Opera omnia,* ed. E. Susmel and D. Susmel (Florence and Rome, 1951–80), Vol. XXIX, pp. 43–5.

19. Dmitri Volkogonov is the leading authority on the contents of the Russian archives and, apropos the Nazi-Soviet pact, writes that Stalin 'cast ideological principles aside' (*Stalin: Triumph and Tragedy* (London, 1991), p. 351). For the conjectural claim that Stalin intended by the Nazi-Soviet pact to set off a capitalist civil war and world revolution, see R. C. Raack, *Stalin's Drive to the West: The Origins of the Cold War* (Stanford, CA, 1995), pp. 21–8.

20. T. J. Uldricks, 'Debating the role of Russia in the Origins of the Second World War', in Martel, *Origins of the Second World War Reconsidered,* p. 135. In this bibliographical essay, Uldricks recommends J. Haslam, *The Soviet Union and the Struggle for Collective Security, 1933–1939* (New York, 1984) as the most balanced analysis of the subject.

21. R. J. Caputi, *Neville Chamberlain and Appeasement* (Selinsgrove, PA, 1999) is a historiographical survey of the extensive literature.

22. *Origins of the Second World War* (London, 1961), p. 189.

23. Quoted in R. A. C. Parker, *Chamberlain and Appeasement: British Policy and the Coming of the Second World War* (London, 1993), p. 236.

24. M. J. Carley, *1939: The Alliance That Never Was and the Coming of World War II* (Chicago, 1999) for anti-Communism as the root cause of appeasement.

25. Quoted in J. Charmley, *Chamberlain and the Lost Peace* (London, 1989), p. 185.

26. E. Weber, *The Hollow Years: France in the 1930s* (New York, 1994), p. 6.

27. P. M. H. Bell, *France and Britain, 1900–1940: Entente and Estrangement* (London, 1996), pp. 217, 224.
28. Bell, *Origins of the Second World War in Europe*, p. 341.
29. M. H. Hunt, *Ideology and U.S. Foreign Policy* (New Haven, 1987), p. 21.
30. A. Iriye, *Japan and the Wider World* (London, 1997), p. 77.

14 Economics

Robert Boyce

In view of the importance given to economics in the analysis of contemporary politics and international relations, it is remarkable how small a place it occupies in the literature on the origins of the Second World War. For every hundred books on, say, ideology, military plans and policies, intelligence, diplomacy and the personalities involved, scarcely one is published that directly confronts the economic issues. Of the many reasons for this situation, two may be singled out for mention. In the first place, the liberal conventions of historical scholarship place supreme value upon evidence, which in the case of international or diplomatic history means firsthand evidence of influence upon the decision-makers, whereas by and large economic factors exert only an indirect influence upon the making of foreign and defence policies. Second, and closely related to the first, is the negative influence of crude Marxist explanations of Hitler's rise to power in Germany, which began to appear in print even before he took office.[1] Based on the assumption that social classes behave precisely in accordance with their economic interests and that under capitalism big business exercises a hegemonic influence over the political system, Marxists presented Hitler as merely the cypher of German economic élites. The manifest inaccuracy of this interpretation served to underline objections to determinist, and particularly economically determinist, approaches to history. Yet to set aside economic factors is to overlook a number of extremely important, arguably crucial, aspects of the pre-war period. For, as the following chapter briefly indicates, the uniquely prolonged and severe economic crisis between the wars profoundly affected all the Great Powers, albeit in different ways, influencing their choice of leaders and even regimes, their levels of arms expenditure, their mutual relations, and ultimately their willingness or reluctance to contemplate war.[2]

The Political Impact of Recurrent Economic Crises, 1914–1931

Between 1914 and 1931 the world economy underwent recurrent economic crises, starting with the Great War itself and continuing with the post-war restocking boom and slump, the crisis in central Europe brought on by resistance to the Franco-Belgian occupation of the Ruhr, and the global crisis that followed the roller-coaster movement of the New York stock exchanges towards the end of the 1920s. The contrast with pre-war times could scarcely have been greater, when for over half a century most of the world had experienced almost uninterrupted growth, low or even negative inflation, stable exchange rates and steadily increasing foreign invest-ment – and this with modest levels of taxation and severely limited state intervention in economic affairs. This remained normality[3] for the post-war generation: the benchmark by which it judged current economic conditions and the competence of its political leadership. In parts of Europe, the dislocated markets, inflation and acute currency instability proved insupportable for existing regimes. Before the war ended, the combination of economic crisis and military defeat in Russia brought on two revolutions and the Bolshevik seizure of power. Throughout central Europe military defeat and economic breakdown brought revolution in 1918–19, and the economic crisis in Germany at the time of the Ruhr occupation in 1923 tempted both the Nazis and the Communists to organise *putsches*. In Italy the frustration of a costly military victory that appeared to bring no rewards, inflation and the difficulty of converting from a war to a peace economy led to the abandonment of a liberal parliamentary regime in 1922 and its replacement by a Fascist regime.

The four and a half years that began with the negotiations to end the Ruhr crisis were a time of relative stability, political as well as economic. Most of the internationally traded currencies were stabilised directly or indirectly on the gold standard and were made convertible. Trade barriers, erected or augmented at the end of the Great War, became the subject of numerous international conferences, and eventually tariff-building was halted and even reversed, while most non-tariff barriers such as import prohibitions, quotas and licensing, were almost completely removed. Foreign investment, which had been limited largely to Latin America and the British dominions since the war, was sufficiently reassured by these developments to return to Germany and elsewhere in Europe. But the economic consequences of the war and its aftermath were too recent to be forgotten. Employers remained deeply frustrated at the concessions made to organised labour in order to ensure its support during the war, and disturbed at the post-war growth of trade unionism, which eroded the prerogatives of capital and undermined their 'right' to manage. The middle classes as a whole regarded post-war levels of direct taxation – modest by present-day standards – as almost confiscatory and an attack on their personal freedom. Signs also appeared of resentment at the United States for apparently having done so well out of the war and for taking advantage of Europe's weakness by invading its markets and buying up much of its industry, particularly in the new and most dynamic sectors such as motor manufacturing, electrical power generation and equipment, aluminium smelting, office equipment, oil refining and distributing, and high-speed communications. The scale of American industry, exemplified in the mass-production assembly lines of the Ford Motor Company, and the vast potential of its domestic market comprising the 48 states, stood in stark contrast to European industry and markets, which had been further 'Balkanised' by the break-up of the continental empires, and added to the sense of European decline. Towards the end of the decade this prompted a spate of popular books including J. Ellis Barker's *America's Secret: The Causes of her Economic Success*, the Rt Hon. George Peel's *The Economic Impact of America*, André Siegfried's *America Comes of Age*, Jean Bonnefon-Craponne's *La pénétration économique et financière des capitaux américains en Europe*, Pierre Laurent's *L'impérialisme économique améri-cain*, Julius Hirsch's *Das amerikanische Wirtschaftswunder* and Oskar Sommer's *Amerika will die Zeit festbinden,* along with more provocative works such as Kadmi-Cohen's *L'abomination américaine*, Arnaud Dan-dieu's *Le Cancer*, Ludwell Denny's *America Conquers Britain*, Gustav Meyer's *Die Amerikanisierung Europas*, Lucien Romier's *Qui sera maître: l'Europe ou les Etats-Unis?*, Charles Pomaret's *L'Amérique à la conquête de l'Europe*, and J. L. Chastanet's *L'Oncle Shylock ou l'impérialisme améri-cain à la conquête du monde.*[4] Albeit different in each case, the underlying theme was that a second industrial revolution had occurred, transforming the optimal scale of production and creating the need for large, relatively homogeneous markets. This gave an enormous advantage to the United States as well as the Soviet Union, which was making great strides under the New Economic Plan to realise Russia's enormous economic potential. But it also put the writing on the wall for smaller countries and suggested that sooner or later the world would become dominated by five or six large blocs including a federated Europe, the British Empire, an American bloc extend-ing from North to South America, a Soviet bloc, and probably an Asiatic bloc dominated by either Japan or Russia. Such speculation acquired greater plausibility in the winter of 1928/29 after Herbert Hoover, the embodiment of aggressive American economic expansion, won the presidential election by a landslide and thereupon visited Latin America where he encouraged the idea of an American economic union.[5] A few months later, Aristide Briand, the French premier, announced France's support for the creation of a Euro-pean federation, placing economic integration to the fore.[6] At the same time, British Conservatives, having lost the general election in May 1929, moved rapidly towards a commitment to Empire Free Trade, a new euphemism for the policy of uniting the Empire on an economic basis.[7]

Meanwhile, however, nervousness continued at the spectre of renewed inflation and currency depreciation. The middle classes everywhere relied upon personal savings for their health care and security in old age, and during the Great War had patriotically subscribed to victory bonds.

Subsequently in Hungary, Austria and Germany inflation had destroyed their savings. The same was true only to a lesser extent in Italy, Belgium and France, where in seven years after the war inflation had threatened to run out of control. Thus the French franc, which since Napoleonic times was worth an unchanging 20f. = £1, slumped to 248f. = £1 in July 1926 before the rot was stopped and the franc was again fixed on gold at the sterling equivalent of 122f. = £1: barely one-sixth its pre-war value. Even in Britain, the only large European power to succeed in restoring its currency to its pre-war parity of £1 = $4.86, savers and investors had experienced the vertigo of witnessing the pound decline nearly 35 per cent to $3.22 between 1918 and 1920. This left the middle classes throughout Europe determined that, whatever happened, their governments must not allow the national currency to be undermined again, even if it meant cutting back on welfare and defence spending, restricting trade, intervening in labour contracts to reduce the cost of production, and if necessary setting aside normal constitutional procedures.[8]

Unfortunately, hardly had the gold standard been generally restored than a new economic crisis began, when in 1928 the accelerating bull market on Wall Street diverted American lending from Europe and drew European funds towards the higher returns available in America. The situation worsened when the United States Congress in late May 1929 signalled its determination to raise the American tariff substantially above its already record level. America, the world's largest exporter and greatest creditor, thus threatened the stability of Europe, which had come to rely upon dollar loans, and President Hoover seemed unwilling to intervene. This prompted a flurry of official protests from Europe and elsewhere, widespread displays of anti-Americanism, and a rapid recrudescence of protectionism when countries everywhere chose not to wait for the American tariff to be enacted into law before implementing their own defensive measures.[9] As interest rates rose, investment declined and unemployment soared, liberal states faced the unpleasant predicament of a sharp rise in expenditure on the 'dole' while tax revenue declined. Conventional wisdom demanded that they keep public spending within the limits of exchequer revenues, or inflation would result. Even a temporary retreat from 'sound finance' was likely to be interpreted as a sign of willingness to sacrifice currency stability and prompt the flight of short-term deposits to a safer home in some other financial centre. This had to be avoided since flight capital, largely a new phenomenon since the war, was now of sufficient magnitude to threaten the stability even of the strongest currency. In the circumstances, therefore, there was all too little the liberal states could do. Almost the only options open to them were to reduce public spending, retreat further behind pro-tective trade barriers, and intervene in the labour market in hope of restoring a new equilibrium between domestic and world prices. But action decisive enough to reassure the middle classes was bound to antagonise workers, who were confronted with the Hobson's choice of reduced wages and working conditions or unemployment. This provoked social conflict and in turn political crises, which drove voters increasingly away from the moderate parties towards the extremes of left and right. As early as 1930 the consequences for international relations were becoming clear. Liberal states that managed to weather the economic storm did so at the price of curtailing defence expenditure, limiting foreign commitments and where possible favouring their own trade within their empires or hinterland. The Fascist or militarist powers in turn responded by seeking scapegoats at home and abroad, reducing their foreign economic exchange so far as possible, and embarking upon aggressive imperialist adventures. Fifteen years of economic crisis thus set the stage for conflict and eventually another world war.

The Economic Background to Fascist and Militarist Aggression

The first serious breach of international peace came in September 1931 at the height of the international economic crisis, when Japanese forces began their subjugation of Manchuria. Since the war, Japan, under a succession of liberal governments, had relied upon international trade to support its rapidly increasing population on islands with distinctly limited natural resources. However, the rise of nationalism in China endangered a major outlet for its trade, and new American immigration restrictions added to the spectre of a world divided into exclusive blocs with doors everywhere closing to Japanese expansion. Leading industrialists, bankers and merchants, who by and large saw no alternative to participation in an integrated world economy, persuaded the Hamaguchi government to restore the yen to the gold standard in January 1930 and support League of Nations efforts to hold off a global retreat into protectionism.[10] But the new American tariff, which fell with particular force upon luxury imports such as woven silk, Japan's largest export commodity, aggravated the problems that accompanied the onset of the world slump.[11] Employer–worker relations came under intense strain, while peasants faced exceptional hardship. Agricultural prices had already declined by a third before the slump drove them down by another third. Emigration to the United States, an option in earlier times, was now closed. Two in five peasant families had relied upon silk production for money income, but the American market, which had absorbed nearly 90 per cent of exports, had practically vanished.[12] This caused widespread distress, and particularly in the region from which the imperial army traditionally recruited many of its troops.[13] Yet the need for tighter monetary policy and the loss of exchequer revenue reduced the government's capacity to cushion the impact of growing unemployment.

Indeed, with the exchange rate now fixed on gold, the government had little choice but to implement a policy of severe retrenchment: between 1929 and 1931 non-military expenditure fell by no less than 37 per cent.[14] As a result, respect for liberal government declined, especially among younger officers and students, many of whom turned to extreme nationalist and imperialist movements or secret societies. A *coup d'état* was attempted in March 1931 and four leading politicians or statesmen were assassinated in the next few years, creating a climate of fear within governing circles. In another act of impatience with the regime, officers of the Kwantung Army in Manchuria provoked an incident on 18 September 1931 in order to justify their seizure of the three Chinese provinces making up Manchuria and confront the Tokyo government with a *fait accompli*. Sidehara Kijūrō, the foreign minister, assured foreign diplomats that the military operation would soon be ended and the troops withdrawn. But the government's inability to address the consequences of the slump had so diminished its authority that senior military officers in Tokyo were prepared to connive with the rebels. Moreover, the politicians themselves were divided on the appropriateness of the Manchurian adventure. Only a few months earlier, Matsuoka Yosuke, a former diplomat and future foreign minister, had spoken in the Diet of the need for action. 'The economic warfare in the world is tending to create large economic blocs.' In the circumstances, he believed that Japan had no choice but to follow suit by the creation of a bloc comprising Manchuria, Mongolia and Russia's Maritime Province as well as Japan and its existing possessions of Formosa and Korea – a list to which others would soon add China itself.[15] The government's temporising brought it into conflict with an embarrassed Britain and an angry United States.

Despite the growing international friction, most Japanese businessmen remained convinced that the country could not afford to cut itself off from foreign markets. Japan's trade sharply recovered after the gold standard was abandoned in December 1931 and the yen was allowed to depreciate over 50 per cent against the dollar; indeed, so sharply that British, American, Dutch and other trading interests protested loudly at a Japanese 'invasion' of their markets.[16] With the encouragement of business, the Inukai and Okada governments continued to support international trade liberalisation up to the League-sponsored World Economic Conference in London in June 1933.[17] The failure of the conference and India's break in trade relations shortly afterwards further discredited the liberal ideas of politicians and big business, while strengthening advocates of a 'new order' in Asia.[18] In April 1934 the Japanese Foreign Ministry issued a statement asserting the right to 'protect' China from foreign interference: a sort of Japanese 'Monroe doctrine', which anticipated a new stage of imperialist expansion.[19] Having consolidated its grip on Manchuria, now renamed the independent state of Manchukuo, the Japanese army had extended its operations to Outer Mongolia and Jehol below the Great Wall before agreeing a truce with the Chinese nationalists in the spring of 1933. Relations remained extremely strained, however, and when in July 1937 a clash occurred between Japanese and Chinese forces at the Marco Polo Bridge not far from Peking, the Japanese government allowed the army to extend its sway over the whole of China. Preoccupied with domestic 'reforms' and European threats, the Soviet Union acquiesced in Japanese aggression, as did Britain and France. The United States, however, did not, and Franklin Roosevelt, the president, signalled his opposition in public speeches, diplomatic *démarches* and a proposal for secret naval conversations with Britain. Matsuoka, now foreign minister, sought to explain Japan's intentions to the United States in October 1940. Japan intended to construct 'a new order in Greater East Asia including the South Seas' for purposes of trade, development and emigration.

> This does not mean these areas are to be exploited and conquered, nor does it mean these areas are to be closed to the trade and enterprise of other countries. Japan has long tried to solve its population problem through emigration, trade, and enterprises abroad, but the various countries of Europe and America have nullified Japan's reasonable and peaceful efforts concerning its population problem since those countries have turned back Japanese immigrants to their great territory and have obstructed trade and enterprise.[20]

The American authorities, taking special note of the reference to 'the South Seas', regarded this as an aggressive rather than defensive stance, and allowed the confrontation to become rapidly more acute. Statesmen including Stanley Hornbeck, head of the Far Eastern division of the State Department, and Cordell Hull, the secretary of state, as well as Winston Churchill, the British prime minister, remained convinced that Japan would not be so 'irrational' as to attack the vastly larger, more powerful United States. But this was not how Japanese soldiers and statesmen viewed the situation. As James Morley writes, 'The Great Depression convinced [many] Japanese that the possibility of Japan's finding an acceptable place in any kind of world trading system was closed and that unless drastic action was taken, Japan would end up in a state of subjugation to the West not wholly unlike that of most of the rest of Asia.'[21]

If Italy embarked upon overseas imperialist adventures more belatedly than Japan in the inter-war years, it was partly because it had already succumbed to an anti-liberal Fascist regime. In a show of Fascist muscle-flexing, Italy restored the lira to the gold standard at a dangerously high exchange rate in December 1927, thereby immediately exposing the country to the same deflationary pressures that other countries with fixed exchange rates experienced when the world slump began in 1929.[22] The possession of dictatorial powers enabled the government to obscure the underlying weakness of the lira and rising unemployment. But with trade plummeting and economic output down by over 20 per cent (in current prices) between 1929 and 1931,[23] Mussolini became frantic to sustain the prestige of his regime.[24] On the domestic front he implemented grandiose public works schemes, crushed the remaining trade unions, pursued corporatism and industrial cartels, promoted ruralisation and extended political mobilisation.[25] He also cast about for success on the foreign front, especially once the international order was shaken by revelation of the Austro-German customs union scheme in March 1931 and by Japanese aggression in September. Glancing tentatively at Britain, Germany and even the Soviet Union for new alliances, he toyed with the idea of a Fascist International in imitation of the Socialist and Communist Internationals, turned to the crisis in the Danube in the hope of extending Italian influence, and in May 1932 he made bellicose speeches which undercut the conservative posture of his foreign minister, Dino Grandi, who he soon dismissed.[26] Always potentially dangerous, Mussolini now grew reckless. Describing Italy as a 'proletarian nation', and with little to show for his European manoeuvres, he returned to the longstanding dream of overseas empire. In January 1932 he sent Emilio de Bono, the minister for colonies, to Eritrea to look into means of extending Italian hegemony over Ethiopia.[27] In September 1932 General de Bono visited East Africa, and in December Mussolini called on him to prepare plans for an invasion.[28] But it was only in February 1934 that Mussolini decided to act.[29] As it happened, this was almost precisely the moment when national economic output, down nearly 30 per cent from its 1927 peak, reached the low point of the slump.[30] The Wal Wal incident in late 1934, when colonial troops from Italian Somaliland were allegedly fired on by Ethiopian forces, provided the excuse to proceed. Forces were steadily built up during 1935, and on 3 October a large Italian army in East Africa launched the attack. Contemporary domestic propaganda presented Ethiopia as the core of an imperial project that would solve Italy's population problem and yield up vast economic wealth. It may be doubted whether Mussolini and his comrades fully believed these unrealistic claims. Marginal as it proved to be in solving Italy's economic crisis, the Ethiopian adventure nevertheless had its origins in the economic slump, which left Mussolini increasingly concerned for his prestige. If he could not make the country rich, he would make it great through daring diplomatic or military initiatives.[31]

There was nothing inevitable about the steps that led from the Ethiopian war to world war four years later. Nevertheless, the conflict in East Africa prompted a diplomatic confrontation with Britain and France, which earned them Mussolini's scorn but also led him to forget the vital importance guarding Austria against German subjugation and to turn to Hitler for support. While potentially still able to step back from further aggression, Mussolini allowed his imperial adventure to alter the diplomatic landscape.

The League of Nations, having failed to address the world slump or Japanese aggression in East Asia, suffered a third crushing defeat and no longer counted for anything. More importantly, France's hopes of Italian support in the containment of Germany collapsed, leaving it demoralised and temporarily leaderless at the very moment when Hitler felt able to take greater foreign risks.

Although the Weimar Republic had survived ten years by 1928, it was if anything more vulnerable than ever to economic crisis. After the hyperinflation of 1923, which wiped out domestic savings, Germany's commercial banks had rebuilt their lending capacity by drawing in foreign deposits. On the eve of the world slump nearly 50 per cent of total deposits came from abroad, mostly from the United States and Britain.[32] These funds were particularly sensitive to interest rate differentials and other international factors. Thus, as early as 1928, the Wall Street boom exposed the German banking system to severe pressure. The resulting rise in German borrowing costs and reduction in credit also intensified existing industrial disputes, including a prolonged lock-out of workers in the Ruhr during the winter of 1928/29. This in turn reversed the downward trend of unemployment and threatened to divide the newly reconstituted 'Weimar coalition' government, comprised of the Social Democratic party (SPD), the Democratic party (DDP) and the Catholic Centre party, which included labour as well as employer interests. That was not all. The revival of the Weimar coalition under a Socialist chancellor and its support for the recently enacted unemployment insurance scheme, along with other concessions affecting the cost of labour, reawakened the apprehension of employers who increasingly favoured 'stronger' government. Similar apprehension soon spread throughout the middle classes. Having endured the collapse of the currency and destruction of their savings only a few years earlier, they were not prepared under any circumstances to tolerate a repetition. Now that the Reichsmark was restored to the gold standard, they expected governments to do whatever was necessary to keep it there. By the autumn of 1929 therefore the Müller government faced an increasingly acute dilemma, when rising unemployment and falling revenues pointed towards a serious budget deficit. Some reduction in unemployment provision was practically unavoidable if the deficit was to be addressed and confidence in the currency maintained. But this ran up against opposition from the Socialists within the cabinet, for whom fair treatment for workers was the *sine qua non* of their association with the bourgeois parties. Unable to resolve the dilemma, the coalition collapsed in March 1930. Heinrich Brüning, leader of the Centre party, whom President Hindenburg called on to form a government, doggedly pursued a compromise solution in which all classes shared the burden of adjustment.[33] But the slump was now acute, and as each day passed the burden of adjustment increased. In 1927 registered unemployment had fallen to a post-war low of 540,000, then rose to 2.3 million during the Ruhr lock-out in February 1929. Thereafter it declined some-what, but soon began to rise again, to nearly 3 million by December 1929, nearly 4 million by December 1930, over 5 million by December 1931, and over 6 million by January 1932 or more than 25 per cent of the labour force.

Hitler found it easy to exploit the growing crisis. In the first place, the growing army of unemployed offered fertile recruiting ground for his National Socialist party, which drew heavily upon these frustrated and often desperate men. Second, Hitler had already identified several scapegoats who offered a superficially plausible explanation for Germany's latest ordeal. One was the Allied powers, who had imposed the Versailles Treaty on Germany and still 'enslaved' it with reparations. Hitler gained unprecedented national prominence when Alfred Hugenberg of the Right-wing *Deutschnationale Volkspartei* (DNVP) invited him to join a public campaign against the New or Young Plan on reparations in July 1929.[34] Another scapegoat was international finance capital, allegedly Jewish-dominated, which exposed Germany to its blackmail. A third was the Marxists, who tempted German workers to betray their country in favour of the Socialist or Communist Internationals. Hitler also had ready-made appeal in rural areas, which had suffered acutely from the post-war decline in commodity prices, by his constant advocacy of autarky and protection for the farm community. In the relatively prosperous years after the Ruhr crisis he had made little if any progress politically. The Nazi vote in the Reichstag election of May 1928 was 810,000, down from the 907,000 it obtained in the December 1924 election and a mere fraction of the 1,908,000 it gained in the May 1924 election.[35] But once the world economic crisis began, Hitler's political fortunes soared.

Leaders of German big business by and large remained suspicious of Hitler and refused to bankroll his party.[36] Small and medium businessmen were, however, more enthusiastic and also much more numerous. In elec-toral terms, strong support also came from farmers and peasants. Still more significant, as Germany was now a largely urbanised society, was the support he obtained from the well-to-do classes. Despite the enduring belief that it was the lower middle classes, squeezed between the power of big business and the trade unions, which formed the core of his electoral support, detailed evidence from the four *Reichstag* elections between 1930 and 1933 leaves no room for doubt that in every substantial town in Germany Hitler's support rose in line with the average household income of electoral districts.[37] The reasons for this source of support are not hard to understand. Despite Hitler's outspoken hostility to international commerce and finance, he was equally loud in his defence of 'national' business and national interests. This refrain was bound to raise the suspicions of directors or managers of big business, practically all of which had a substantial stake in international markets, but it was increasingly congenial to the much larger number who owned or ran smaller businesses, which depended mainly upon the domestic market. It seems likely that his antisemitism (played down during the slump) also appealed more to the latter group. Even more important was his violent hostility to the two main Marxist parties, the Socialists and the Communists. Since the decision of the Comintern in 1928 to lurch sharply leftwards, Communist militants had again taken to the streets where they clashed with the Socialists as well as the Nazis. Perhaps unwisely, the Socialists, while in fact moderate and reformist, also continued to present themselves as revolutionaries. With unemployment rapidly rising, middle-class voters had good reason to fear that the Marxists would do well in future elections. In the circumstances, therefore, Hitler seemed a godsend. Here was a politician who was prepared to take the fight to the Marxists' camp, using many of their own techniques, while offering the appeal of national rather than international salvation. Notwithstanding his rabble-rousing style, he promised to reintegrate the working classes into the national community and end the social divisions that appeared to threaten the privileges of the middle classes. In the September 1930 Reichstag elections the National Socialists gained 18.3 per cent of the votes and 107 seats, up from 12 seats in 1928. This made them the second largest party in parliament after the Socialists. The Communists, the only other party to improve their position, managed only 77 seats in all. Before Hitler actually took power the National Socialists reached their zenith when, at the very trough of the depression, they obtained 37.4 per cent of the votes and 230 seats in the July 1932 Reichstag election. By this time unemployment had stabilised, and in the following months signs at last appeared of economic recovery. This was reflected in the results of the November 1932 Reichstag election, in which both the National Socialist and the Communist vote declined. But the recovery came too late to save the Republic. Shaken and divided by the economic crisis, leading conservatives installed Hitler in January 1933 as head of a coalition government, mistakenly expecting to keep him under control.

Paradoxically, one of Hitler's greatest advantages on becoming chancellor was his indifference to conventional economics. Confronted by economic crisis, leaders of the democratic powers accepted the constraints of balanced budgets, the operation of the gold standard and the prerogatives of capital, all of which severely limited their freedom of manoeuvre. Hitler, like the imperialists of Japan and Italy, dismissed the rules of the money economy as the ideological deceit of international financiers and instead concentrated on the real economy. While accepting that large-scale industry was necessary, he remained convinced that international trade and commerce unreasonably exposed the country to foreign influence. At the core of his thinking was the essentially anachronistic belief in the need for farmland to sustain a large peasant population uncontaminated by the cosmopolitanism of city life.[38] But he was also profoundly impressed by the global trend towards vast economic blocs and in particular the expansion of the informal

American economic empire. As he wrote in his *Zweites Buch* in 1928, if Germany wanted a place in the future world order and not become merely 'a second Holland or a second Szitzerland', it must act quickly, for 'with the American Union a new power of such dimensions has come into being as threatens to upset the whole former power and order of rank of the states'.[39] Germany must create its own empire by seizing 'living space' in Europe, the essential precondition for which was a nation unified and armed for a long war. He therefore demanded that the Reichsbank and Economics Ministry should remove existing financial constraints upon rearmament. With exchange controls already imposed by the Brüning government, this proved remarkably easy to do. Foreign creditors, some of whom faced insolvency if Germany ceased to service its debt, were willing to maintain and even extend lines of credit in order to discourage it from defaulting.[40] Similarly, foreign countries, especially those that depended upon the export of forest and farm products, willingly accepted German manufactures or credit in return for access to the German market.[41] Meanwhile, domestic wage and price controls and forms of rationing facilitated the pursuit of Hitler's priorities. Eventually a point was reached when the scale of imports required to sustain the rearmament programme exceeded even the credit obtained by Hitler's agents. This was followed by his decision to make war on Poland. The causal link, however, ran not from the economic predicament to aggression and war, but rather in the opposite direction.[42] Hitler as dictator was the most singular product of the world economic crisis. Yet, ironically, among the statesmen of the inter-war period none was so indifferent to economic policy or so unwilling to be governed by economic 'laws'.

The Economic Background to the Appeasement and Anti-Appeasement of the Democratic Powers

Britain's policy of appeasement had its origins long before the Great War and could scarcely be attributed simply to the world economic crisis.[43] Since the economic slump in Britain was briefer and shallower than in any other major power, except perhaps the Soviet Union, there might seem to be even less reason to seek an economic explanation for its foreign and defence policies in the 1930s. Nevertheless, it is hard to exaggerate the psychological impact of the slump upon Britain's political and business élites. While the slump itself was relatively mild, it followed a decade-long period that was generally perceived as one of crisis and 'depression', when tax levels, unemployment and real interest rates remained at record levels for peace-time. Those regions of the country where employment depended mainly upon the export of staples such as coal and textiles were devastated by the collapse of trade.[44] Moreover the slump culminated in a major financial crisis in the summer of 1931, which destroyed post-war efforts to restore sterling to its pre-war glory. Like its counterparts elsewhere, the second Labour government, which took office in June 1929, faced the impossible task of maintaining confidence in the currency along with its commitments to the unemployed. When it collapsed in August 1931, normal party politics were suspended – the only occasion in modern peacetime history when this occurred in Britain – and a non-party National government took office. When, despite these exceptional measures, sterling was forced off the gold standard, the government swiftly abandoned free trade and closed the capital market indefinitely to foreign borrowers. Not only did Britain's leadership of post-war efforts to reconstruct a multilateral economic system cease, its reluctance to share responsibility for European security sharply intensified.

The world economic crisis also brought Neville Chamberlain to the forefront of British politics, where he remained until the outbreak of the Second World War. Hitherto scarcely a contender for leadership, he emerged during the crisis as the sole front-bench Conservative confident of his grasp of economic issues. As the opposition spokesman on economic policy between 1929 and 1931, then chancellor of the exchequer from December 1931 under the ageing MacDonald and Baldwin, and finally as prime minister in May 1937, he gained an unchallenged ascendancy in the cabinet as the result of the crisis and his status as an economic expert. Despite his attachment to the memory of his father, Joseph Chamberlain, the champion of Imperial Tariff Reform, however, he proceeded cautiously when the opportunity arose to revive this policy at the Ottawa conference in 1932. Despite his origins in the manufacturing city of Birmingham, he displayed far greater preoccupation with financial issues than the real economy. While prepared to approve increased expenditure on rearmament, he insisted that it must not exceed the limit of budgetary and balance of payments stability. This he justified on the grounds that the economy was the 'fourth arm of defence', and that Britain could not fight a long war with a weak or unstable economy.[45] On the face of it, this was unexceptionable. But he was not prepared to interfere with savings and investments or impose physical controls on the markets by, for instance, curbing luxury imports, house-building and private consumption so as to release resources for rearmament.[46] His approach to economic policy reflected the views of the Treasury, the Bank of England and most of the City of London. And because of his dominant role within government, the Treasury extended its influence over British foreign policy and strategic planning.[47] The Foreign Office argued that the economic crisis made it incumbent that Britain should become more involved in Europe's crisis; the Treasury argued the opposite and prevailed.[48] As late as March 1939 the Treasury was prepared to oppose the expansion of the Territorial Army not only on financial grounds but because of its view of the deterrent effect upon Hitler.[49]

Chamberlain's approach to economic policy shaped and was shaped by his outlook on foreign affairs, which he shared with much of the British business community. In the first place, his chief preoccupation was domestic recovery; he was not a zealous imperialist, and he approached foreign affairs essentially as a peripheral problem to be disposed of in order to get on with issues closer to home. Limited in diplomatic experience,[50] he tended to judge foreign powers by their economic behaviour and shared the view of his closest adviser, Sir Horace Wilson of the Board of Trade, that international relations could be dealt with in much the same way as industrial disputes, by seeking a mutually acceptable compromise.[51] As he put it in 1937, he was sure a solution could be found if only he could 'sit down at a table with the Germans and run through all their complaints with a pencil'.[52] Thus he loathed France and the United States for accumulating two-thirds of the world's gold, which had resulted in severe deflation for the rest of the world and forced Britain into the humiliation of abandoning the gold standard in September 1931.[53] He blamed France for the rise of Hitler, claiming that it was responsible for driving Germany into crisis by its reparation demands.[54] His disdain for France intensified when its economic decline threatened to result in civil war.[55] But he grew to dislike the United States even more when President Roosevelt in April 1933 brushed aside his offer of currency stabilisation, then proceeded to wreck the World Economic Conference, threatened to smash the international monetary system by his gold-buying policy, and in 1934 embarrassed Britain by declaring it in default on war debts.[56] He was also intensely hostile to the Soviet Union, ignored signals from Moscow of its interest in an anti-fascist alliance, and agreed to conversations in the spring of 1939 only under strong pressure from colleagues. While there were, of course, good reasons for doubting Moscow's goodwill, his hostility bore a marked resemblance to attitudes in the business community where poor labour relations were commonly ascribed to Communist-controlled agitators.[57] In contrast, he respected Mussolini for ostensibly restoring order in post-war Italy, and blamed first Anthony Eden, his foreign minister, then France for turning Mussolini away from appeasement.[58] As for Hitler, while Chamberlain deplored his aggressive unilateral action he shared the view that Germany's extremism was largely the result of economic adversity, and conversely that economic recovery would restore it to the community of nations.

The effect of this economically oriented approach to foreign affairs was to reduce almost to nothing the possibility of a change in British foreign policy. In the first place it encouraged the assumption that Britain had three potential enemies and no worthwhile allies. As Chamberlain himself put it in 1937, 'there were limits to our resources, both physical and financial, and it was vain to contemplate fighting single-handed the three strongest Powers in contemplation.'[59] This was of primordial importance since with allies Britain could afford a robust policy of resistance to aggression, whereas alone it was virtually bound to pursue appeasement. While the existence of three potential enemies could scarcely be gainsaid, however, the lack of worthwhile allies virtually became a self-fulfilling expectation because of Chamberlain's disdain for France, the United States and the Soviet Union.[60] In the second place it exaggerated the differences between the democratic powers while minimising the distinctively aggressive character of the militarist and Fascist powers, which also encouraged appeasement. Chamberlain made little attempt at economically appeasing the dictators until political appeasement proved unavailing. But in November 1938 he encouraged industrial cooperation with Germany, which led to contacts between the Federation of British Industries and the *Reichsgruppe Industrie*, to a coal cartel, and to an Anglo-German business convention, which met on 15 March 1939, the day that German tanks rumbled into Prague. The sole practical result was to signal to Hitler that, notwithstanding firmer diplomatic language and rearmament, Britain did not intend to resist his aggression.[61]

No statesman appeared better equipped by experience to grasp the challenge of a world economic crisis than Herbert Hoover, who became president of the United States in March 1929. As a successful engineer who had lived and worked in China and England, director of the giant food relief programme in Europe after the Great War, and chief promoter of US trade expansion as secretary of commerce in the Harding and Coolidge administrations, he had travelled more widely and demonstrated a greater knowledge of business affairs than any other modern president. Yet, on taking office, he did little to counteract the disruptive effect of US protectionism and the overheated financial markets,[62] and after the slump began he preferred to blame other countries rather than joining them in multilateral reforms.[63] Colleagues had had to push him to propose a moratorium on inter-governmental debt in June 1931, when the international financial crisis threatened to bring down the banking system in the United States and Europe.[64] He saw the moratorium as a means of *limiting* American involvement in foreign affairs. But as it applied for only one year, it was scarcely in place before fears of what would follow unsettled the markets again. Hoover's reluctance to depart from the conventional economic wisdom of balanced budgets and self-clearing markets fitted nicely with his isolationist attitude towards Europe, which looked hopefully for American assistance. In his view, Europe did not need assistance except of a purely limited and temporary kind; rather, Europe should address its own problems by, for instance, abandoning reparations, after which each country should do its part by purging its economy of excesses.[65] In a similarly dogmatic way, he and Henry Stimson, his secretary of state, reasserted the principle of the Open Door or non-discriminatory trade, which placed the United States on a collision course with Japan when it subjugated Manchuria and asserted its hegemony over China. Hoover's belief in self-help created the impression of ineffectualness and indifference to the acute hardship endured by millions of Americans in the midst of the depression, and resulted in his decisive defeat at the hands of Franklin Roosevelt, his Democratic opponent, in the November 1932 presidential election.

Unlike Hoover or Chamberlain, Roosevelt claimed no expertise in economics, displayed far greater readiness to innovate in economic policy, and did not apply economic yardsticks to measure foreign countries or their leaders. However, he too displayed some of his predecessor's isolationist prejudices, such as a visceral suspicion of Britain and the large New York banks.[66] This predisposed him to pursue purely national solutions to the acute financial crisis that confronted him on taking office in March 1933. He thus casually misled the other democratic powers about his commitment to exchange rate stability, and in June he abruptly threw the World Economic Conference into utter confusion rather than allow the Europeans to pin him down on monetary policy. A few months later he unilaterally abandoned the gold standard and aggressively sought to devalue the dollar against gold. This infuriated Chamberlain as well as French leaders, who were struggling to sustain the by now seriously overvalued franc, and led both powers to default on their war debts.[67]

Largely in pursuit of trade, Roosevelt seized an early opportunity to normalise relations with the Soviet Union. This, however, brought negligible results because it virtually coincided with the start of the Stalinist purges and the termination of contracts to foreign consortia for large-scale development projects within the Russian empire. In the meantime the Wall Street crash and subsequent economic slump had exposed misdeeds in the American financial community. This revived claims that the Wall Street bankers had drawn the United States into the Great War in order to ensure repayment of their loans, and fed isolationist suspicions of 'internationalism' in New York and Washington. Roosevelt, his New York connections notwithstanding, shared some of the prejudice against Wall Street and was not prepared to risk his domestic reconstruction programme by resisting demands for greater isolationism. As a result, three Neutrality laws were adopted between August 1935 and May 1937, each one intended to ensure that the United States would never again be drawn into a foreign war on account of its commercial or financial interests.

The practical consequences of the Neutrality laws can be exaggerated, but not their indirect effect upon Congress and beyond. They helped persuade Roosevelt to proceed cautiously in face of the growing threat of another war in Europe. From youth he was rather anti-German, but he was also disdainful of France, which he regarded as decadent and corrupt, and he shared the isolationist tendency to exaggerate British financial and imperial strength. In order to ensure his influence within Congress he had appointed Cordell Hull, a prominent senator from Tennessee, as his secretary of state. While rather despising Hull for his provincialism, he allowed him to pursue his dogmatic approach to trade expansion based upon the negotiation of reciprocal trade agreements. This led to friction with Britain, which had adopted a tariff with imperial preferences in 1932 not least because of US protectionism, and now faced demands for reciprocal concessions that would restore the American advantage. Chamberlain, acknowledging the need for US friendship, reluctantly yielded,[68] but in East Asia the same policy led the United States inexorably closer to conflict with Japan. The United States traded little with China, less than with Japan, and invested little in its economy. For most of the inter-war period the Chinese economy had in fact stagnated under the weight of corruption, social conflict and war. Nevertheless Hull made it his personal crusade to oppose Japan's hegemony over China and surrounding territories. The American public, having turned in isolation away from Europe, looked instead for commercial opportunities in the Pacific region. Thus encouraged, the administration confronted Japan with the choice of abandoning its dream of empire or realising it through war.

France, in more subtle ways, was almost uniquely affected by the world economic crisis.[69] Having recovered quickly from the war and stabilised the franc at a competitive exchange rate, it entered the crisis relatively stronger than Britain, Germany or Italy, which misled its statesmen into hoping that they could ride out the storm without resorting to devaluation. It is easy now to belittle their conservatism, but no country that had experienced severe inflation after the war abandoned the gold standard until forced to do so.[70] When France finally did so in September 1936, this was still regarded as a daring decision. In the meantime, successive governments had defended the franc by intensifying trade protectionism, public economies and credit restrictions. While successful in avoiding devaluation, the cost of shoring up the franc included prolonged economic stagnation, severely curtailed rearmament and the revival of both Communist and fascist extremism. It is hard to say which one had the greater effect on French defence and foreign policy. The curtailment of rearmament – spending on arms declined 32 per cent between 1932 and 1934 and no coherent rearmament programme was introduced until 1936[71] – had a direct effect upon the operational effectiveness of the armed forces as well as intensifying conservatism among the high command and field forces. Economic stagnation discouraged manufacturers and industrialists from innovating or expanding their operations, leaving them less able to accommodate the large arms orders issued in the latter part of the decade. Political extremism, which from 1934 threatened to erupt into civil war, increasingly frightened investors who were already disturbed by the weakness of the franc. Their fears reached a peak when the Popular Front, a left-of-centre coalition of parties, took office in June 1936, and three months later it abandoned the gold standard.

The government's hopes that devaluation would release France from the prison of deflation and bring swift economic recovery were confounded by demands for industrial wage rises and an upsurge in the flight of capital, which threatened to produce a vicious circle of further devaluation, industrial unrest and capital flight. This led Edouard Daladier, the premier from April 1938, to give priority to inducing the return of capital by cautious fiscal policies and tough suppression of industrial strikes. As his foreign minister he chose Georges Bonnet, a politician with little experience of foreign affairs, but well respected in financial circles. Like Chamberlain, with whom he was on good terms, he seemed more anxious about the continuing domestic economic crisis and social turmoil than the external threat from Germany. Similarly, he intensely disliked the Soviet Union, which he associated with domestic labour militancy and socialist agitation.[72] In November 1938 Daladier succeeded in breaking a major strike and attracting back much of the flight capital, which enabled rearmament to be accelerated the following year. There was, however, a price to be paid in working-class resentment at the destruction of the Popular Front and continued social inequalities.[73]

In 1931 France appeared uniquely strong, alone capable of propping up the Austrian schilling, German mark and British pound sterling. In fact, however, France was by no means invulnerable to the world slump, and by 1933 Britain, its chief potential ally, and Germany, its chief potential enemy, were both recovering while France continued to decline.[74] By the summer of 1936 the other powers had comfortably surpassed pre-slump levels of economic activity, while France had only just reached bottom.[75] The divergent timing of their economic experience was enormously important, for it tempted both Britain and Germany to disregard France and to pursue unilateral policies which France was ill-placed to challenge. Once war became imminent, British as well as American and other statesmen recognised that France must contain Germany in the West if their own security was not to be threatened. But until then, with their own stability endangered, the slump had led them to focus their attention on domestic problems; notwithstanding the attention subsequently lavished on them by historians, foreign affairs remained a peripheral matter for the democratic powers until the eve of the war. Moreover, while grappling with economic problems and their social and political consequences, they blamed each other for pursuing irresponsible policies. This severely prejudiced their mutual relations and made it harder to cooperate on foreign policy issues. Thus while Britain and the United States retreated even further from involvement in European security arrangements, France retreated from eastern Europe and, lacking support from the other democratic powers, adopted a cautious policy of appeasement towards Italy, then Germany as well.

Conclusion

It would be as wrong to claim that the Second World War was caused exclusively by economic factors as it would be to claim that they played no part in the coming of war. None of the leading statesmen was wholly a prisoner of economic circumstances, none was obliged to act as he did. Nor were economic factors by and large immutable and objective facts. In each case the statesmen's response to economic circumstance was distinctive, reflecting national perspectives and priorities. None the less, economic factors played a constant part in shaping the behaviour of the major powers; and while their reactions to the economic situation were different in each case, there was a family resemblance in the behaviour of the dictatorships on the one hand and the democratic powers on the other. What makes the subject particularly important is that – unlike the First World War or the Cold War – the Second World War was the culmination of a lengthy crisis marked by the simultaneous collapse of both the international political system and the international economic system. Since the same statesmen struggled to address both aspects of this dual crisis, it is neither feasible nor desirable from the standpoint of historical analysis to attempt to examine the one without due regard to the other.

Notes

1. A good example is D. Guerin, *Fascism and Big Business*, rev. edn, trans. Frances and Mason Merrill (New York, 1973), first published in 1936 but drawing upon earlier publications.
2. A. J. P. Taylor, summarising the impact of the world depression, claims that 'faced with this storm, countries retreated within their own national systems, and the more industrialised the country, the greater was its withdrawal from the world.' 'The Second World War', the Creighton Lecture, University of London, 1972, p. 4. He was probably thinking of the United States, but, if so, his claim applies only to its relations with Europe and not with East Asia or Latin America. It was certainly not true of Germany.
3. We have Warren G. Harding, the aimiable but linguistically challenged post-war American president, to thank for the neologism 'normalcy': see R. K. Murray, *The Harding Era: Warren G. Harding and His Administration* (Minneapolis, 1969), p. 70, f. 72.
4. R. Boyce, *British Capitalism at the Crossroads, 1919–1932: A Study in Politics, Economics and International Relations* (Cambridge, 1987), pp. 101–19, 199–202 and *passim*; E. R. Beck, *Germany Rediscovers America* (Tallahassee, 1968), especially ch. 5; D. Strauss, *Menace in the West: The Rise of French Anti-Americanism in Modern Times* (Westport, CT, 1978), especially ch. 4.
5. Pierre-Etienne Flandin, vice-president of the French chamber of deputies, confidently anticipated that the trip would be the start of a 'huge imperialistic expansion'. United States, State Department records, RG59, M560, roll 30, Armour to Secretary of State, 25 December 1928.
6. M. Ray, 'Vers un Locarno européen', *Le Petit Journal*, 12 July 1929, p. 1.
7. On the anticipations of the 1920s, see Boyce, *British Capitalism at the Crossroads*, chs 4–5.

8. It may be noted here that the rise and decline of middle-class support for Fascism in France between the wars coincided precisely with periods of currency weakness and recovery. See the two works by R. Soucy, *French Fascism: The First Wave, 1924–1933* (New Haven, 1986); *French Fascism: The Second Wave, 1933–1939* (New Haven, 1995).

9. J. M. Jones, Jr., *Tariff Retaliation: Repercussions of the Hawley-Smoot Bill* (Philadelphia, 1934).

10. W. M. Fletcher III, *The Japanese Business Community and National Trade Policy, 1920–1942* (Chapel Hill, 1989), ch. 2.

11. A. Iriye, *After Imperialism: The Search for a New Order in the Far East* (Cambridge, MA, 1965), pp. 278–85.

12. Ibid., p. 219.

13. R. Storey, *Japan and the Decline of the West in Asia, 1894–1943* (London, 1979), pp. 139–41.

14. H. T. Patrick, 'The Economic Muddle of the 1920s', in *Dilemmas of Growth in Prewar Japan* (Princeton, 1971), table 7, p. 257.

15. A. Iriye, 'The Failure of Economic Expansion, 1918–1931', in B. S. Silberman and H. D. Harootunian, eds, *Japan in Crisis: Essays on Taisho Democracy* (Princeton, 1974), p. 265.

16. J. Halliday, *A Political History of Japanese Capitalism* (New York, 1975), p. 128.

17. Fletcher, *The Japanese Business Community and National Trade Policy, 1920–1942*, pp. 90–1. The breakdown of the conference evidently helped inspire Tota Ishimaru to write *Japan Must Fight Britain*, trans. G. V. Rayment (London, 1936), pp. 73, 113 and *passim*.

18. A. Tiedemann, 'Big Business and Politics Prewar Japan', in Morley, ed., *Dilemmas of Growth in Prewar Japan*, p. 285.

19. J. C. Grew, *Ten Years in Japan* (London, 1944), pp. 119–21.

20. Ibid., pp. 295–6.

21. J. W. Morley, 'The Pacific War: Some Interpretations, Old and New', in I. Nish, ed., *Interwar Japan*, Discussion Paper No. IS/89/187, Suntory-Toyota International Centre for Economics and Related Disciplines, London School of Economics, February 1989, pp. 4–5.

22. C. Vannutelli, 'The Living Standard of Italian Workers, 1929–1939', in R. Sarti, ed., *The Ax Within: Italian Fascism in Action* (New York, 1974), p. 141.

23. B. R. Mitchell, *International Historical Statistics: Europe, 1750–1993*, 4th edn (London, 1998), table J1, p. 911. The decline is stated in current prices, because while far greater than in real terms (adjusted for inflation/deflation), it probably corresponds closely to the perspective of contemporaries. S. La Francesca, *La Politica Economica del Fascismo* (Bari, 1972), p. 65, estimates the decline in *constant* prices between 1929 and 1932 at 33 per cent.

24. As D. Mack Smith writes, 'from 1930 onwards his speeches seem to have become less careful and more extravagant': *Mussolini's Roman Empire* (London, 1976), p. 29.

25. Renzo de Felice, *Mussolini il duce*, Vol. 1, *Gli anni del consenso 1929–1936* (Torino, 1974), p. 142 and *passim*.

26. Public Record Office, Foreign Office papers (hereafter PRO FO371 etc.), FO371/14365, C2355/230/18, Sir Ronald Graham to Arthur Henderson,

no. 187 'confidential', 14 March 1930; H. J. Burgwyn, *Italian Foreign Policy in the Interwar Period, 1918–1940* (Westport CT, 1997), p. 102; P. Milza, *Mussolini* (Paris, 1999), pp. 629–33; M. Knox, *Common Destiny: Dictatorship, Foreign Policy, and War in Fascist Italy and Nazi Germany* (Cambridge, 2000), p. 132.

27. De Felice, *Mussolini il duce*, Vol. 1, p. 416.

28. C. J. Lowe and F. Marzari, *Italian Foreign Policy, 1870–1940* (London, 1975), pp. 247–9.

29. De Felice, *Mussolini il duce*, Vol. 1, p. 418.

30. In June 1934 Mussolini himself vividly described the financial aspects of the crisis in a long letter to Guido Jung of the national bank: ibid., p. 140 n. 2. The actual timing of the slump is a matter of disagreement among economists, but see Mitchell, *International Historical Statistics: Europe*, p. 911, table J1.

31. Smith, *Mussolini's Roman Empire*, p. 64.

32. H. James, *The Reichsbank and Public Finance in Germany, 1924–1933: A Study of the Politics of Economics during the Great Depression* (Frankfurt, 1985), p. 179 n. 15. As James notes, the loss of American deposits was partly offset by the substitution of French depositions: ibid., p. 177.

33 W. L. Patch, Jnr., *Heinrich Brüning and the Dissolution of the Weimar Republic* (Cambridge, 1998), pp. 67–70 and *passim*.

34. A. Bulloch, *Hitler*, rev. edn (Harmondworth, 1962), p. 149; F. L. Carsten, *The Rise of Fascism* (London: Methuen & Co., 1970), pp. 134–5.

35. A. Milatz, *Wähler und Wahlen in der Weimarer Republik. Bundeszentrale für politische Bildung*, Heft 66 (Bonn, 1965), table p. 151. It is true that party membership was rising before May 1928, but the war veterans on whom it relied for its cadres were a steadily ageing group, and a party that speaks only to the converted ends up as an ineffectual sect.

36. H. A. Turner, Jr., *German Big Business and the Rise of Hitler* (Oxford, 1985). But see also the discussion in J. Hiden, *Republican and Fascist Germany: Themes and Variations in the History of Weimar and the Third Reich, 1918–1945* (London, 1996), pp. 120–3.

37. R. F. Hamilton, *Who Voted for Hitler?* (Princeton, 1982), Introduction, pp. 83, 90–1, 121, 198, 202, 206, 211 and *passim*. Milatz, *Wähler und Wahlen in der Weimarer Republik*, claims the key lay with the 'Kleinbürger- und Bauerntums', p. 133.

38. A. Hitler, *Mein Kampf*, trans. J. Murphy (London, 1939), pp. 126, 135–6, 201–2 and *passim*.

39. A. Hitler, *Hitler's Secret Book*, trans. S. Attanasio (New York, 1962), pp. 103, 108. Significantly, a few years earlier he was at least as impressed by the British Empire, which he called 'the greatest World Empire on this earth': *Mein Kampf*, p. 542, also pp. 127, 131–2, 524.

40. N. Forbes, *Doing Business with the Nazis: Britain's Economic and Financial Relations with Germany, 1931–39* (Ilford, 2001).

41 D. E. Kaiser, *Economic Diplomacy and the Origins of the Second World War: Germany, Britain, France and Eastern Europe, 1930–1939* (Princeton, 1980), ch. VI.

42. T. Mason and R. Overy, 'Debate: Germany "Domestic Crisis" and War in 1939', in P. Finney, ed., *The Origins of the Second World War* (London,

1979), ch. 4; M. Knox, 'Conquest, Foreign and Domestic, in Fascist Italy and Nazi Germany', *Journal of Modern History* 56 (March 1984), 53–4.

43. P. M. Kennedy, 'The Tradition of Appeasement in British Foreign Policy 1865–1939', *British Journal of International Studies* 2 (October 1976), 195–215.

44. Thus, even in July 1933, unemployment in Lancashire stood at 42 per cent: *Hansard*, 280 H.C. Deb 5s, col. 228 statement by Sir Herbert Samuel, 4 July 1933.

45. The phrase is from the introduction, prepared in the Treasury, to PRO CAB 24/273, C.P.316(37), Sir Thomas Inskip, 'Interim Report on Defence Expenditure in Future Years', 15 December 1937. R. P. Shay, Jr., *British Rearmament in the Thirties: Politics and Profits* (Princeton, 1971), p. 167, discusses the flaws in the argument. G. C. Peden, *British Rearmament and the Treasury. 1932–1939* (Edinburgh, 1979), p. 65, discusses its strengths.

46. S. Newton, *Profits of Peace: The Political Economy of Anglo-German Appeasement* (Oxford, 1996).

47. R. Boyce, 'Economics and the Crisis of British Foreign Policy Management, 1914–45', in D. Richardson and G. Stone, eds, *Decisions and Diplomacy: Essays in Twentieth-Century International History* (London, 1995), pp. 9–41; D. C. Watt, *Succeeding John Bull: America in Britain's Place, 1900–1975* (Cambridge, 1984), pp. 76, 85.

48. Thus, for instance, the Treasury opposed the Foreign Office argument for a comprehensive approach to the monetary, financial, commercial and security problems, which were set out in PRO CAB 24/255, C.P.301(31), 'Changing Conditions in British Foreign Policy, with Reference to the Disarmament Conference, a possible Reparations Conference and Other Contingent Problems', 26 November 1931. Continuing differences led Sir Warren Fisher, the permanent secretary of the Treasury, to propose that he should take over the Foreign Office as permanent secretary: Birmingham University Library, Neville Chamberlain papers, 7/11/29/19, Fisher to Chamberlain, 15 September 1936. This did not happen, but Chamberlain shared Fisher's hostility to the Europhiles of the Foreign Office: see for instance, ibid., 18/1/1020, letter to Hilda Chamberlain, 12 September 1939; ibid., 24 October 1937.

49. PRO T175104 Pt. 2, minutes by Bewley, 28 March 1939, Hopkins and Phillips, n.d.

50. Writing from the Lausanne conference on reparations in 1932, his first international conference, he naïvely described the French, German, Italian and Belgian delegates collectively as 'the foreigner': Neville Chamberlain papers, 18/1/789, letter to Hilda Chamberlain, 26 June 1932.

51. D. Dilks, ed., *The Diaries of Sir Alexander Cadogan, 1938–1945* (London, 1971), p. 53

52. K. Feiling, *The Life of Neville Chamberlain* (London, 1947), p. 319.

53. Shortly before sterling was forced off the gold standard he anticipated a German-style crash, with inflation running out of control and social crisis: *The Scotsman*, 12 September 1931, address to Unionist meeting, Dumfries, 11 September 1931. See also *Hansard*, H.C. Deb 5s, Vol. 256, col. 638, statement, 14 September 1931.

54. Neville Chamberlain papers, 18/1/764, letter to Hilda Chamberlain, 6 December 1931.

55. Ibid., 2/24A, diary, 19 February 1938; Feiling, *Chamberlain*, p. 323.
56. Neville Chamberlain papers, 18/1/785, letter to Ida Chamberlain, 5 June 1932, referring to the 'idiotic Yankees'; ibid., 18/1/809, letter to Hilda Chamberlain, 10 December 1932, on 'how the Americans let us down as usual'; ibid., 18/1/815, letter to Hilda Chamberlain, 4 February 1933, on America as 'a nation of cads'; ibid., 18/1/835, letter to Hilda Chamberlain, 10 July 1933, on Roosevelt's betrayal; ibid., 2/24A, diary entry 19 February 1938 on American unreliability. According to Sir Alexander Cadogan, permanent under-secretary of the Foreign Office in the later 1930s, Chamberlain had 'an almost instinctive contempt for the Americans and what amounted to a hatred of the Russians': Dilks, ed., *The Diaries of Alexander Cadogan*, p. 53.
57. 'As you know, anything that has to do with Russia raises my violent feelings.': Ramsay MacDonald papers, PRO 30/69/2/13, Chamberlain to MacDonald, 11 August 1933. On his opposition to an alliance, see R. A. C. Parker, *Chamberlain and Appeasement: British Policy and the Coming of the Second World* (Basingstoke, 1993), p. 236.
58. As Sir Eric Phipps, the British ambassador, warned Daladier in April 1939, 'Franco-Italian relations were the key to peace or war.' Parker, *Chamberlain and Appeasement*, p. 247, also ibid., pp. 121, 194, 206, 246.
59. Chamberlain to CID, 5 July 1937, quoted in David Carlton, *Anthony Eden, a Biography* (London, 1981), p. 106. See also F. McDonough, *Neville Chamberlain, Appeasement and the British Road to War* (Manchester, 1998), p. 47.
60. In December 1937 Chamberlain advised the CID, 'It would be a mistake to count too much on assistance from France or the United States in war': I. Colvin, *The Chamberlain Cabinet* (London, 1971), p. 67. In February 1938 the private secretary to the foreign secretary recorded, 'The Chiefs of Staff persist in regarding the problem as though we had three enemies – Germany, Italy and Japan – who all might attack us together and we should have no one to help us': J. Harvey, ed., *The Diplomatic Diaries of Oliver Harvey, 1937–1940* (London, 1970), p. 89.
61. Parker, *Chamberlain and Appeasement*, ch. 9; A. J. P. Taylor, '1939 Revisited', London, German Historical Institute, 1981, p. 6.
62. M. P. Leffler, *The Elusive Quest: America's Pursuit of European Stability and French Security, 1919–1933* (Chapel Hill, 1979), pp. 197–8.
63. H. C. Hoover, *The Memoirs of Herbert Hoover*, Vol. 3: *The Great Depression, 1929–1941* (New York, 1952), pp. 21, 26, 107; H. G. Warren, *Herbert Hoover and the Great Depression* (New York, 1959), pp. 128, 155; R. H. Ferrell, *American Diplomacy in the Great Depression: Hoover-Stimson Foreign Policy, 1929–1933* (New Haven, 1957), pp. 12–13.
64. Hoover Library, West Branch, Iowa, Presidential Papers Foreign Affairs, Box 1015, Financial, Moratorium, President's Diary of Developments 1931, 6 May–22 June.
65. Ibid., Box 1006, Financial, Correspondence 1931 June 11–20, Mills memo to the president, 18 June 1931. The following spring his secretary of state recorded, 'the President is so absorbed with the domestic situation that he told me frankly that he can't think very much now of foreign affairs.' Yale University Library, New Haven, Diary of Henry Stimson, 17 May 1932.

66. R. Boyce, 'Wall Street and the Spectre of the "Money Power" in Small-Town America before and after the Crash of 1929', in A. Capet, P. Romanski and A. Sy-Wonyu, eds, *États de New York* (Rouen, 2000), p. 29.

67. France had already stopped payments in December 1932, but it was Roosevelt's actions that ensured no further payments would be made.

68. Neville Chamberlain papers, 18/1/1029, letter to Hilda Chamberlain, 21 November 1937.

69. As Antony Adamthwaite writes, 'The effects of the world economic crisis did more to undermine French power than the material losses of the First World War.' *France and the Coming of the Second World War* (London, 1972), p. 5.

70. What E. P. Thompson called 'the enormous condescension of posterity', is evident in J. L. Kooker, 'French Financial Diplomacy: The Interwar Years', in B. M. Rowland, ed., *Balance of Power or Hegemony: The Interwar Monetary System* (New York, 1976), p. 126.

71. R. Frank [enstein], *Le Prix du réarmement français 1935–1939* (Paris, 1980), p. 38 and *passim*; J. Doise and M. Vaïsse, *Politique étrangère de la France: Diplomatie et outil militaire 1871–1991* (Paris, 1992), pp. 378–9.

72. Y. Lacaze, *La France et Munich: Etude d'un processus décisionnel en matière des relations internationales* (Berne, 1992), pp. 433–40; R. Frankenstein, 'The Decline of France and French Appeasement Policies, 1936–9', in W. J. Mommsen and L. Kettenacker, eds, *The Fascist Challenge and the Policy of Appeasement* (London, 1983), pp. 241–3.

73. T. Imlay, 'France and the Phoney War, 1939–1940', in R. Boyce, ed., *French Foreign and Defence Policy, 1918–1940: The Decline and Fall of a Great Power* (London, 1998), pp. 274–6.

74. J. Marseille, 'Les origines "inopportunes" de la crise de 1929 en France', *Revue économique* 31 (July 1980), pp. 648–84.

75. Mitchell, *International Historical Statistics: Europe*, p. 909 table J1. Before the French economy began to recover in the second half of 1936, gross domestic product was down from its 1929 peak by 12 per cent in constant prices and 41 per cent in current prices.

15 Peace Movements

P. M. H. Bell

At first sight, a study of peace movements may not appear central to an
examination of the origins of the Second World War when compared
to the ambitions of dictators, the deliberations of cabinets, or the plans of
general staffs. Yet such an appearance is misleading. A study of peace
movements brings us to the heart of a vital issue. In 1919, over much of
western Europe, and above all in France and Britain, the prevailing
sentiment was 'Never again' – no more war. If that feeling had continued to
prevail in these parliamentary democracies, where the support of public
opinion was necessary to go to war, there would have been no war in 1939,
or at any rate the conflict would have taken a very different form, with
France and Britain standing aside for some time. A crucial precondition for
the outbreak of war in 1939 was the transformation of the sentiment of
'Never again' into the reluctant but resolute acceptance of conflict that
actually obtained when war began.

The story of peace movements provides a key to that transformation.
The peace movements included the keenest opponents of war, gathered
together in organised form. This chapter examines the strength of these
movements in France and Britain, and asks how they ceased to carry
conviction, so that war came to be seen as necessary, even by most of its
strongest opponents.

What were the 'peace movements'? In the 1920s and 1930s there was a
good deal of confusion in the use of this term. In November 1933 a writer in
The New Statesman asserted with confidence that: 'In the sense of preferring
peace to war, we are all pacifists now.'[1] He was surely right; but within that
vague consensus of opinion we must make a vital distinction. Two very
different viewpoints stood out. There were: (1) pacifists, who believed that
war was always wrong, and must be unconditionally rejected; and (2) peace-
minded internationalists, who considered that war might have to be
accepted in extreme circumstances, but should be avoided if at all possible
by all the means available for international action – that is, conciliation,
arbitration or disarmament. Both types of peace movement will be
considered here. Absolute pacifists were few in number but ardent in their
convictions. Peace-minded internationalists were numerous, and wielded

considerable political influence through their support for the League of Nations and the cause of disarmament.[2]

This chapter concentrates on France and Britain, where peace movements were strongest. In Germany under the Weimar Republic there were a number of internationalist organisations, and also some small pacifist groups. The Nazis suppressed all these organisations shortly after they came to power in 1933. The law re-introducing conscription in 1935 made no provision for conscientious objection, and only a very few courageous individuals refused to undertake military service – which usually led to a death sentence.[3] The effects of peace movements on Weimar policy were negligible, and on Nazi policy nil. Outside Europe, there were significant American peace movements, which reinforced the already strong tendency towards isolationism and neutrality, and thus helped to remove a potentially salutary influence from European affairs. In the space available, however, it is best to concentrate on France and Britain, which illuminate our subject most effectively.

Peace Movements in France

In France, the climate of opinion summed up in the words 'Never again' affected almost the whole country. With casualties including about 1.3 million dead, France had suffered terrible losses, amounting to a demographic disaster, in 1914–18. War memorials, with their tragically long lists of the dead, stood as a constant plea against a repetition of such a calamity. In the 1920s, Poincaré on the centre-right and Briand on the centre-left shared the same purpose of avoiding another war, though they differed as to the best means of doing so. In the 1930s, no one could understand the policies of Daladier and Bonnet without remembering that both had been infantrymen in the Great War, and were deeply anxious to save the succeeding generation from the same experience. Within the army high command, Pétain and Gamelin had absorbed the same mental climate, and were defensive and cautious in their outlook – even generals did not want war.[4]

At an intellectual level, these convictions were reinforced by the arguments of 'revisionist' historians, to the effect that France had shared responsibility for the outbreak of war in 1914, and that the Treaty of Versailles had inflicted grave injustices upon Germany, which must be redressed in order to achieve a lasting peace. It is often said that between the wars French generals were obsessed with fighting the last war, and failed to look forward to the next. Much the same is true of members of the French peace movements, who looked firmly backwards towards the Great War and wanted to avoid repeating past mistakes. As will be seen, the same mentality was at work in Britain.

This all-pervasive revulsion against war was particularly strong in certain sections of French society. Among the peasants, the traditional backbone of the French army, there was a profound conviction that they had borne a disproportionate burden in the previous war, and that they could not afford to do so again. In October 1938 an editorial in *La Revue des agriculteurs de France*, under the heading '*Pour la Paix*', declared: 'The blood-letting of another war would this time go together with the destruction of our peasantry, and without the peasantry what would remain of France? A war won would be almost as disastrous as a war lost.'[5] In the previous month, during the Munich crisis, the journal's editorial board had appealed directly to Daladier to avoid war.

Before 1914, the *instituteurs*, the primary school teachers, had been standard-bearers of French patriotism; but after the Great War their main trade union, the *Syndicat National des Instituteurs* (SNI), became broadly anti-war and internationalist, with a hard-core minority of absolute pacifists. In 1938 the *Syndicat* included about 100,000 of the 130,000 *instituteurs* in France, who were respected figures in society, acting as secretaries in *mairies* throughout the land. They could mobilise widespread support, and during the Munich crisis, on 26 September 1938, the secretary-general of the SNI, André Delmas, published 'A Call to the Country: We do not want war', which its organisers claimed to have attracted 150,000 signatures in three days. (Daladier put the figure at no more than 80,000, but even that was impressive.)[6]

Organisations of *anciens combattants*, which also played a significant role in French society and politics between the wars, were broadly anti-war. Their most articulate and active members shared a sentiment which Antoine Prost calls 'un patriotisme pacifique', in reaction against the 'patriotisme belliqueux' of 1914. Many, perhaps most, were at least vague supporters of the League of Nations, and almost all seem to have admired Briand, whose heart-felt aspirations towards peace drew an instinctive response from those who had served in the Great War. A few became ardent pacifists in the absolute sense.[7]

Among French political parties, anti-war sentiment was strongest among the Socialist party, led by Léon Blum. In the 1920s and early 1930s most Socialists believed, with an almost religious fervour, that the key to peace lay in the League of Nations and disarmament. With the failure of the Geneva Disarmament Conference (1932–34) and the rise of Hitler, the Socialists split three ways: some were prepared to oppose Nazi Germany, even by rearmament and alliances; others continued to seek peace by means of concessions, even to Nazi Germany; and a small minority advocated absolute pacifism, claiming that even foreign occupation was preferable to war.

Revulsion against war was by no means confined to the political left. Many on the right also rejected war. When the Germans moved troops into the demilitarised zone of the Rhineland in March 1936, the French right-wing press agreed with the left that France must not go to war. Charles Maurras, leader of the *Action Française* and the very embodiment of right-wing patriotism, wrote: 'And first of all, no war. We do not want war ....'[8] Part of this right-wing sentiment arose from anti-Communism and fear that war would lead to revolution; some of it stemmed from sympathy with Fascism and Nazism; but whatever its roots, it added to the current of anti-war feeling.

There were also many organisations specifically devoted to the cause of peace. In 1936 the *Annuaire de la paix* counted over 200 'pacifist' organisations in France – though the word pacifist was used loosely.[9] Among these varied groups, the *Association de la Paix par le Droit* (APD) was one of the oldest and most influential.[10] It was not pacifist in the strict sense of rejecting the use of force in all circumstances, but sought to promote peace by advocating international arbitration, conciliation and disarmament, and therefore strongly supported the League of Nations, accepting that this might mean the use of sanctions, and even force if necessary. The membership of the APD at any one time was never large, varying between about 5000 and 7000 in the 1920s and 1930s; but the total who belonged at one time or another was much larger. Moreover, its members were drawn from influential groups in French society, notably teachers in universities, *lycées* and primary schools, and Protestant pastors – the influence of Protestantism in France has usually been greater than mere numbers might imply.[11] With the rise of Hitler, the APD, like the Socialists, split three ways. One of its leaders, Georges Scelle, argued from January 1938 onwards that the time had come to revive the old watchword 'if you want peace, prepare for war'; a small group moved in the opposite direction and took up an unconditional pacifist stance; while others, headed by Theodore Ruyssen, took a middle line, hoping to deal with Hitler by an ill-defined form of 'moral quarantine'.

In contrast to the APD, the *Ligue internationale des combattants de la paix* (LICP), founded in 1930, adopted from the start an absolute pacifist stance. The *Ligue*'s founder, Victor Méric, claimed a membership of 20,000 in 1933, though the actual number of subscriptions received that year amounted to only 7868.[12] But the group's significance was greater than either of these figures might imply, notably through the prestige of intellectuals and writers among its membership – for example, Félicien Challaye, who in 1934 published a striking book entitled *Pour la paix désarmée, même en face de Hitler*. (Challaye stuck to his guns, or rather to his rejection of guns, became a collaborator during the German occupation, and was tried and convicted after the Liberation.) The *Ligue* set out to encourage conscientious objection against conscription (which was allowed by French law in certain circumstances), causing some anxiety in the Ministry of War, not so much because of the numbers involved but through fear of the wider effects on morale in the country as a whole. In 1939, as war approached, the

Ligue's principal spokesmen held firmly to the line that peace must prevail over all other considerations, but they lost their following. Membership fell sharply, as most adherents decided that, however reluctantly, they would have to resist the advance of Germany and of Hitlerism.

Taken together, these different groups and currents of opinion formed a powerful combination, and it must be doubtful whether any French government could have led the country into war if this degree of opposition had been maintained. During the Czech crisis of 1938 Daladier felt the pressure of anti-war sentiment, especially from the peasants and *instituteurs*. Yet the following year the situation was transformed, and the actual outbreak of war revealed a virtual unanimity among the French people. The army was mobilised on 1 September 1939, and the reservists joined their units almost to a man – '*entre la résolution et la résignation*', as the prefect of the Rhône reported, in words which were true of the whole country. There were no anti-war demonstrations, and only a handful of individual protests. There was no repetition of the petition against war organised by the *instituteurs* in September 1938, and most of the *instituteurs* joined their units faithfully. The peasant organisations and journals (with only one exception, *La volonté paysanne*) supported the declaration of war. The principal organisations and newspapers of the *anciens combattants* had decided that enough was enough and Hitler must be stopped. The Socialists supported the war by a large majority. At the party congress at Montrouge as early as December 1938, Blum had gained a large majority for a resolution supporting the defence of France against any attack on its integrity, sovereignty and independence. (The vote was 4322 to 2837, with 1014 abstentions and only 60 for an 'integral pacifist' resolution.) In September 1939 only two Socialist deputies continued to advocate reconciliation with Germany rather than war. Even the pacifist *Ligue internationale des combattants de la paix* had very largely come to accept war. One of its leaders, Louis Lecoin, put out a leaflet headed '*Paix immédiate*', but it was disavowed by one-third of the signatories whose names were attached to it, and it had no visible impact.[13]

Virtually all the elements in the various French peace movements, which had been so strong numerically and had previously represented so fixed a cast of mind ('Never again') accepted war in 1939, reluctantly but determinedly. The reasons for this remarkable transformation, and its significance in the general question of the coming of the Second World War, will be discussed later. Meanwhile, let us turn to the corresponding situation in Britain.

Britain

In Britain, the climate of opinion was similar to that in France. In the Great War, the British suffered only about half as many casualties as the French – 723,000 killed as against 1.3 million, or 16 per thousand of the pre-war population as against 34 per thousand in France.[14] The numbers were smaller, but the shock was just as great, because the war was fought beyond Britain's shores and the stakes did not seem to be commensurately high. There was a widespread revulsion against war, and particularly against the sort of war represented by the Somme and Passchendaele. A new impulse was given to British peace movements, which already had a long history. For most of the nineteenth century peace movements had flourished in two main forms, those seeking to abolish war by international cooperation and mediation, and those – notably the Quakers – who professed absolute pacifism. In the 1920s and 1930s, these two strands became concentrated in support for the League of Nations on the one hand and the Peace Pledge Union on the other.

The League of Nations became a powerful magnet for the peace-minded, offering an escape from the alliances and secret diplomacy which (it was widely believed) had caused the Great War, and promising new hope for international cooperation and disarmament. A supporters' body, the League of Nations Union (LNU), was founded in November 1918, before the League itself came into existence, and became, in the words of its historian, 'the largest and most influential society in the British peace movement'. Its membership stood at 60,000 at the end of 1920, and reached over a million by 1932.[15] It crossed party boundaries, with the leaders of the main political parties normally serving as honorary presidents. Lord Robert Cecil, a Conservative, was the LNU's main leader; Oswald Mosley, while a member of the Labour party, was for a time its parliamentary secretary; and Violet Bonham-Carter provided a formidable Liberal presence. It was granted a royal charter in 1925. The LNU threw its weight behind the cause of disarmament, by Britain individually and more widely through the Geneva Disarmament Conference of 1932–34. After that Conference failed, and League economic sanctions failed to prevent the Italian invasion of Ethiopia, the LNU began to emphasise military sanctions as the best way to make collective security work. In principle, support for the League should always have included a commitment to the use of force if necessary, but in practice this was often ignored, and even strict pacifists had backed the League and joined the LNU. After 1935–36, this blurring of lines became more difficult, and numbers of pacifists began to leave the LNU.

The main rallying point for absolute pacifism in the 1930s became the Peace Pledge Union (PPU), founded by an Anglican clergyman, Dick Sheppard, who combined personal charisma and social respectability to a remarkable degree. On 16 October 1934 Sheppard published a letter in the press, calling on men to send him a postcard stating that they would be willing to support the following resolution: 'We renounce war and never again, directly or indirectly, will we support or sanction another.'[16] A meeting to carry this resolution was held on 14 July 1935, with an attendance of over 7000 at the Albert Hall. The appeal was extended to women in June 1936. The membership of the PPU (for which the only requirement was to sign the pledge) was never fully certain. One estimate at the end of 1936 was 118,000; the Union's own organiser put the figure at 87,000 in March 1937; and the highest membership, at about 136,000, was reached in April 1940.[17] These figures came nowhere near the mass support that Sheppard originally hoped for, but they were significant; and the movement gained the support of influential sponsors (including Vera Brittain, Aldous Huxley and Bertrand Russell), who helped to sustain its impetus when Sheppard himself died in October 1937.

Among the political parties, Labour followed a course very similar to that of the Socialists in France. In 1926 the Labour party conference adopted a resolution against war, including refusal to bear arms or to produce armaments. In 1933 the party conference passed a resolution 'to take no part in war and to resist it with the whole force of the Labour Movement', and raised the possibility of a general strike to prevent war.[18] From 1931 to 1935 the party's leader was George Lansbury, who was an absolute pacifist. A shift in policy began in 1934, when the executive committee presented a document on 'War and Peace', which attempted to reconcile support for collective security with opposition to war. At the party conference of 1935 Ernest Bevin launched a crushing attack on Lansbury for 'hawking your conscience round from body to body asking to be told what to do with it', and the conference voted by a vast majority to support war if necessary to carry out League sanctions against the Italian invasion of Ethiopia.[19] Lansbury resigned as leader, but for some time this shift was not translated into support for British rearmament. Up to 1936 Labour MPs voted against the annual service estimates in parliament, and in 1937 they changed their minds only to the extent of abstaining. As late as April and May 1939 the Labour party opposed the introduction of conscription. Thus Labour changed its views, but only slowly.

Three defining events were seen as representing the influence of peace movements in Britain: the 'King and Country' debate in the Oxford Union in February 1933; the East Fulham by-election in October 1933; and the 'Peace Ballot' of 1934–35. On 9 February 1933 the Oxford Union (whose prestige as a debating society and a nursery for aspiring politicians was still high) adopted by 275 votes to 153 the motion 'That this House will in no circumstances fight for its King and Country'. The main speaker for the motion was C. E. M. Joad, a well-known broadcaster and popular philosopher. This resolution attracted much attention in the press, and was widely regarded as a symbolic expression of pacifism among a generation of Oxford undergraduates. Yet its precise significance was uncertain, and the most careful accounts of the debate have come to agree that it was primarily a backward-looking protest against the events of 1914, and what was seen as 'the shrill patriotism of the popular press' at that time.[20]

The East Fulham by-election took place on 25 October 1933, transforming a Conservative majority of 14,521 at the general election of 1931
into a Labour majority of 4840 at the by-election. Some three years later,
on 12 November 1936, Stanley Baldwin (then prime minister) said in the
House of Commons that the East Fulham by-election had been decided 'on
no issue but the pacifist'. East Fulham, coming in the same year as the
Oxford Union debate on 'King and Country', thus came to signify a high
tide of pacifist sentiment. Yet its actual significance was less clear-cut.
Closer examination showed that the successful Labour candidate was not a
pacifist; that pacifism was by no means the only issue at stake in the
election; and that a crucial element in the result stemmed from the absence
of a Liberal candidate in a constituency with a substantial Liberal vote.[21]

The Peace Ballot was a large-scale vote on the League of Nations,
disarmament and sanctions, organised by the League of Nations Union and
conducted over several months from October 1934 to the summer of 1935,
with provisional results being published in June 1935. A questionnaire was
distributed over most of the country, with the pattern of coverage and
response varying with the strength of the LNU and the willingness of local
branches to take part. Despite such variations, the final result was
impressive, with a total of over 11 million responses. Among five questions:

> Question 1 asked   'Should Great Britain remain a member of the League
> of Nations?', to which the replies were: YES 11,166,818; NO 10,528;
> DOUBTFUL 12,138; NO ANSWER 216,759.

> Question 5 asked   'Do you consider that, if a nation insists on attacking
> another, the other nations should compel it to stop, by (a) economic and
> non-military measures? (b) if necessary, military measures? To these ques-
> tions the answers to (a), on economic sanctions, were: YES 10,096,626;
> NO 639,195; DOUBTFUL 27,369; NO ANSWER 862,705; CHRIS-
> TIAN PACIFIST 14,169. To (b), on military measures, the answers were:
> YES 6,833,803; NO 2,360,184; DOUBTFUL 41,058; NO ANSWER
> 2,381,485; CHRISTIAN PACIFIST 17,536.

The Peace Ballot was not a complete referendum involving the whole
electorate, nor was it a public opinion poll in the modern use of the term; but
the response was large, and the support for the League of Nations was
overwhelming. On the specific question of military sanctions (a disguised
form of words for war), the response was far from decisive. Nearly 7 million
were in favour (at least in principle); but a No vote of nearly 2.4 million showed substantial support for a sort of pacifism; while the 'Don't
Knows' amounted to another 2.4 million.[22] After the Ballot, the LNU
leadership hesitated, professing to adopt 'a vigorous policy of collective
security', but remaining unwilling to support even the tentative policy of
rearmament being put forward by the British government of the day.[23]

Each of these apparently defining events was thus, on close examination, less than definitive, but at the time the predominant impression was of the weight of the peace movement in Britain as a whole. The Oxford Union resolution seemed to symbolise the pacifism of the younger generation. Baldwin insisted that pacifism had decided the result in East Fulham, and he was haunted by the result for years to come. The Peace Ballot appeared to bear its significance in its very name. Coming together as they did in the space of just over two years, they seemed to confirm that peace movements held a commanding position in British politics and society.

Yet the same transformation came about in Britain as in France when war actually broke out in 1939. By that time, the League of Nations had clearly failed, and the LNU was losing influence and membership – only about 100,000 subscriptions were received in 1940.[24] The Peace Pledge Union secured an increase of members on the outbreak of war, but its effectiveness as measured in numbers of conscientious objectors to military service was very limited. In October 1939 only 2.2 per cent of those called up registered as conscientious objectors; in April 1940 the proportion was down to 1.2 per cent; and in July 1940, with a German invasion apparently imminent, it fell to a mere 0.5 per cent. (See Figure 15.1 overleaf.)

As for the Labour Party, on 2 September 1939 Arthur Greenwood, the acting leader in the House of Commons, made a strong speech in favour of war, and told Neville Chamberlain in private that he must deliver a declaration of war the next day. Only the Independent Labour party, with four MPs, opposed the declaration of war. Meanwhile, at Oxford a recruiting board for the three armed services was set up to appeal for recruits from the University. From a total of some 3000 eligible to serve, no fewer than 2362 volunteered at once.[25]

This acceptance of war among the members of the peace movements reflected the feeling in the population as a whole. The British went to war quietly, but with few doubts as to its necessity. A Gallup poll in the last week of September 1939 asked: 'Should we continue to fight until Hitlerism goes?', and received the answers: Yes – 89 per cent; No – 7 per cent; Don't Know – 4 per cent. The question was somewhat vague, but the answers showed a remarkable near-unanimity.[26] And indeed the British fought until Hitler was dead.

Reflections

This study of the strength and the sudden collapse of peace movements in France and Britain leads to an inescapable conclusion. The fact of such a reversal of opinion and sentiment, following much the same pattern in both countries, shows that the necessity of war was eventually felt to be

Figure 15.1 Conscientious objectors to military service, October1939–July 1940

Registration date	Total registrations	Number of provisional registrations as COs	% of COs
21 Oct. 1939	230,009	5073	2.2
9 Dec.	256,300	5490	2.1
17 Feb. 1940	278,289	5638	2.0
9 March	346,731	5803	1.6
6 April	335,909	4772	1.4
27 April	336,894	4218	1.2
25 May	348,991	3684	1.05
15 June	307,858	2387	0.77
22 June	355,105	2451	0.69
6 July	330,456	1898	0.57
13 July ·	342,367	1752	0.51
20 July	331,030	1669	0.5
27 July	380,087	2192	0.57

Source: R. Barker, *Conscience, Government and War* (London, 1982), p. 144.

overwhelming. The circumstances were such that war appeared unavoidable, even by those who had been most deeply opposed to it. The reasons for the transformation would require another study to elucidate fully, but the main outline is clear. First, patriotism still ran deep and strong in both France and Britain. The profound attachment of the French people to the soil of France proved even stronger than the widespread revulsion against war, and the number of those who were actually prepared to act on the belief that a German occupation was preferable to war proved to be small. The same was true of Britain. A historian of the University of Oxford, reflecting on the overwhelming proportion of Oxford students who volunteered in 1939, observed that 'The patriotism of 1939 was no less deeply felt than the patriotism of 1914, but it was differently expressed.'[27] The diminution in the number of conscientious objectors when the German army appeared on the French side of the Channel told its own tale. Second, even for those who still rejected the age-old pull of patriotism, the menace of Nazism became something that had to be resisted. For many on the left, the Spanish Civil War had put war in a new light, when it was fought for ideological reasons and to resist the advance of Fascism. Much more widely, the prospect of not simply a German but a Nazi domination of Europe was unacceptable. It was notable that C. E. M. Joad, whose speech in favour of the 'King and Country' resolution at Oxford was probably decisive in its acceptance, declared in September 1940 that, though he had been a pacifist as long as he could remember, he had come to think 'that there can be something worse even than war, and that is the Nazi domination of Europe'.[28] In this he was not alone. In 1939, and even more in 1940, patriotism and the rejection of Nazism pulled in the same direction.

In this connection, it was of the highest importance that in France Daladier, and in Britain Chamberlain, had so obviously done their utmost to preserve peace. In the 1920s there had grown up a school of thought in France that Poincaré had helped to bring about war, and he was often called '*Poincaré-la-guerre*'. In 1939 there was no question of crying '*Daladier-la-guerre*', and still less of calling Chamberlain a warmonger. If anything, there was a growing feeling that these two statesmen had gone too far to preserve the peace, so that the word 'appeasement' came to have ominous overtones. In fact, one of the effects of the policy of appeasement was an almost universal conviction in France and Britain that if Daladier and Chamberlain had failed to preserve peace, then war was truly necessary. This conviction came home to members of the peace movements (with the exception of a very few determined pacifists) as much as to the rest of the population.

There remains a further question. How far did the peace movements themselves contribute to the coming of war? In a direct sense, the answer is far from clear. It was sometimes said, for example, that the Oxford Union debate encouraged the aggressor states by convincing Hitler and Mussolini that the British were decadent and would never fight. The news of the resolution was in fact reported in Italy and treated as being the unanimous opinion of all students at Oxford and Cambridge, and then of the whole of British youth. This was the line taken by Fascist propaganda, and there is evidence that Mussolini himself believed it.[29] For Germany, by far the stronger and more dangerous of the Axis powers, the debate appears to have had no effect. Indeed, on 1 November 1933 the *Völkischer Beobachter* (the principal Nazi newspaper) published an article on the militarism of British youth.[30] Thus, in this instance, the direct effects occurred where they mattered least.

The indirect effects brought about by the peace movements are a different matter. There is a strong possibility that earlier and greater British rearmament might have helped to keep the peace, by deterring Germany from going to war. The peace movements were one (though not the strongest) of the influences inhibiting rearmament, and so contributed to the coming of war. More widely, one of the most significant elements in the origins of the Second World War in Europe was that German power was allowed to advance so far that, when it had to be stopped, it could only be halted by means of a general war. France and Britain in particular, through their policy of appeasement, permitted Germany to rearm, occupy the Rhine-land, destroy Austria and annex parts of Czechoslovakia – all unopposed, and even sometimes with their encouragement. The strength of the peace movements, and the weight of sentiment which they represented was one of the factors contributing to the policy of appeasement, and to the acceptance of the growth of German power. On the other hand, it formed only one aspect of the 'appeasement' cast of mind, which also flourished in circles far removed from the peace movements in either France or Britain.

The peace movements thus made only a limited contribution to the coming of war; but they still add much to our understanding of how the war came about. The peace movements in France and Britain were strong; the sentiments they represented ran broad and deep. The events and beliefs that transformed those sentiments had to be even more powerful, because only when that transformation had taken place would France and Britain go to war.

Notes

1. F. Hardie in *The New Statesman*, 18 November 1933, quoted in M. Ceadel, *Pacifism in Britain, 1914–1945: The Defining of a Faith* (Oxford, 1980), p. 146.
2. See the definitions set out in ibid., pp. 3–5; though Ceadel uses 'pacificist' rather than 'pacific internationalist'.
3. W. Wette, 'Ideology, Propaganda and Internal Politics as Preconditions of the War Policy of the Third Reich', in W. Deist et al., eds, *Germany and the Second World War*, Vol. I, *The Build-up of German Aggression* (Oxford, 1990), pp. 69–71, 74–7; P. Brock, 'Conscientious Objectors in Nazi Germany', in P. Brock and T. P. Socknat, eds, *Challenge to Mars: Essays on Pacifism from 1918 to 1945* (Toronto, 1999), pp. 370–9.
4. J.-L. Crémieux-Brilhac, *Les Français de l'An 40*, Vol. I, *La guerre: Oui ou Non?* (Paris, 1990). This book illuminates the whole question of public opinion in France, 1938–40.
5. Article, headed 'Pour la Paix', by P. Caziot, vice-president of the *Société des Agriculteurs de la France*, quoted in L. Mysyrowicz, *Autopsie d'une défaite: Origines de l'effondrement militaire français de 1940* (Lausanne, 1973), p. 337.
6. M. Cointet-Labrousse, 'Le Syndicat National des Instituteurs, le pacifisme et l'Allemagne, 1937–1939', in F.-G. Dreyfus, ed., *Les relations franco-allemandes, 1933–1939* (Paris, 1976), pp. 137–50; Crémieux-Brilhac, Vol. I, pp. 88–91.
7. A. Prost, *Les anciens combattants et la société française*, Vol. III, *Mentalités et idéologies* (Paris, 1977), pp. 78–119; for Prost's observations on 'un patriotisme pacifique', see p. 81.
8. Quoted in J. B. Duroselle, *La décadence, 1932–1939* (Paris, 1979), p. 171.
9. N. Ingram, *The Politics of Dissent: Pacifism in France, 1919–1939* (Oxford, 1991), pp. 1–2.

10. See ibid., pp. 20–32, for a survey of the APD.
11. Ibid., pp. 23–7.
12. Ibid., pp. 134, 142.
13. Crémieux-Brilhac, Vol. I, pp. 57–64; R. Gombin, *Les socialistes et la guerre: La SFIO et la politique étrangère de la France entre les deux guerres mondiales* (The Hague, 1979), p. 253.
14. J. Winter, *The Great War and the British People* (London, 1986), p. 75.
15. D. S. Birn, *The League of Nations Union, 1918-1945* (Oxford, 1981), p. 1 (quotation), pp. 25–6 (membership figures).
16. Quoted in Ceadel, *Pacifism in Britain*, p. 177.
17. Membership figures, ibid., p. 263.
18. Quoted in J. F. Naylor, *Labour's International Policy: Labour in the 1930s* (London, 1969), pp. 9, 58.
19. Ibid., p. 109. The vote was 2,168,000: 102,000, though these figures arose from the method of 'card voting', under which trade union leaders voted en bloc on behalf of all their members. A. Bullock, *Ernest Bevin*, Vol. I, *Trade Union Leader, 1881–1940* (London, 1960), p. 568, observes that the official report records Bevin as saying 'taking your conscience about', but some of those present heard 'trailing' or 'hawking', which carries more conviction.
20. M. Ceadel, 'The King and Country Debate', *Historical Journal* 22 (1979), 397–422; C. Hollis, *The Oxford Union* (London, 1965), pp. 185–91; B. Harrison, ed., *The History of the University of Oxford*, Vol. VIII, *The Twentieth Century* (Oxford, 1994), chapters by J. Winter, pp. 3–25, and P. Addison, pp. 167–88.
21. M. Ceadel, 'Interpreting East Fulham', in C. Cook and J. Ramsden, eds, *By-Elections in British Politics* (London, 2nd edn, 1997), pp. 94–111.
22. Birn, *League of Nations Union*, pp. 144–50 (including a full table of questions and answers); M. Ceadel, 'The First British Referendum: The "Peace Ballot", 1934–5', *English Historical Review* 95 (1980), 810–39.
23. Birn, *League of Nations Union*, p. 155.
24. Ibid., p. 201.
25. Addison, in Harrison, ed., *Oxford*, Vol. VIII, pp. 167–8.
26. PRO, INFI/261. The poll was taken by the British Institute of Public Opinion (Gallup) for the Ministry of Information. Its results were not published.
27. Addison, in Harrison, ed., *Oxford*, Vol. VIII, p. 168.
28. C. E. M. Joad, 'A Pacifist's Conversion', *The Listener*, 12 September 1940, p. 385.
29. D. Mack Smith, *Mussolini* (London, 1981), pp. 194–5.
30. Ceadel in *Historical Journal* 22, 421–2.

16 Armaments Competition

Joseph A. Maiolo

The moral is obvious: it is that great armaments lead inevitably to war. If there are armaments on one side there must be armaments on the other sides. While one nation arms, other nations cannot tempt it to aggression by remaining defenceless. ... Each measure taken by one nation is noted and leads to counter-measures by others. ... The enormous growth of armaments in Europe, the sense of insecurity and fear caused by them – it was these that made war inevitable.[1]

Sir Edward Grey's verdict on 1914 is a suitable starting point for any essay on the relationship between armaments and war. As British Foreign Secretary from 1905 to 1916, he had experienced firsthand the destabilising effect of the arms race on great power politics. After the war, the danger of 'great armaments' had been recognised. In 1919, the League of Nations called for the reduction of national armaments to levels consistent with safety and collective security. In 1925, when Grey published his memoirs, the post-war situation in Europe and Asia had stabilised enough for concerted efforts to begin. The Preparatory Commission for the planned World Disarmament Conference began its work in the following year. Hopes for a speedy outcome, however, proved ill founded. Seven years passed before the Conference convened. Discussions continued in Geneva well into 1934, but the advent of the Nazi regime in 1933 signalled the end of disarmament. The editors of the League of Nations *Armaments Year Books* had indeed recorded a steady rise in world arms spending from 1925 to 1930. The economic slump forced a reduction in arms spending from 1931 to 1933, but the steady upward trend resumed in 1934. In the 1939–40 edition, the editors explained the massive jump in arms expenditure in 1937–39 as evidence of 'the *state of mind* that prevailed in the world after the failure of the [Disarmament] Conference'. In what was to be their final statement on the subject, the editors remarked that, at the time of publication, 'some ten European and extra-European countries were at war'. Their statistical task had come to a gloomy end.[2]

The growth in world armaments recorded in the *Year Books* did not inevitably lead to the Second World War. As this volume shows, the war's origins are far more complex and contingent than any mono-causal explanation would permit. Most scholars reject the determinism of Sir Edward Grey's formula. Not all arms races end in war – the Cold War for instance – and not all wars are preceded by arms races.[3] Certainly, competitive military expansion was a precondition to the events of 1938–41, but war came in stages, starting in Europe and culminating in the Pacific. The role of armaments in these events and in the decisions for war is bound up in the wider complexity and contingency. Two recent studies of arms and the outbreak of the First World War, however, David Herman's *The Arming of Europe: The Making of the First World War* (1996) and David Stevenson's *Armaments and the Coming of War* (1996),[4] demonstrate that it is possible to disentangle arms competition from the broader causes of the world war. Interestingly, while there are plenty of good national and comparative studies of defence policies, armed forces and technology for the inter-war years,[5] there is no thorough study of the connections between arms races and the onset of the Second World War. This gap can be explained partly by the historiographical preoccupation with identifying culprits: the villains who armed early and plotted conquest and those who failed to prevent war by not arming early enough. It is also in part due to the reluctance of historians to adopt a systemic approach to the study of international affairs. To see how and why an arms race unfolds, one needs to reconstruct it as a process of reciprocal interactions, criss-crossing frontiers. The brief essay that follows makes no pretensions of comprehensiveness. Its purpose is merely to underscore some salient features of arms racing and the origins of the Second World War.

What Is an Arms Race?

The phrase 'arms race' generally invokes images of a competition in the number and power of weapons. Competitors 'race' in peacetime to win military superiority over rivals, who must respond or lag behind. However, the comparison with an athletic competition is misleading. Foot races have finishing lines: arms races do not. It was more by luck than foresight that the Committee of Imperial Defence proposed 1939 as the target date for the completion of Britain's industrial mobilisation plans and preparations.[6] To take another example, Hitler planned for a general European war in the mid-1940s, but provoked one over Poland in September 1939. It is also difficult to distinguish an 'arms race' from 'normal' military rivalry. States have always sought some measure of security and influence through the acquisition of armaments, and armed services are maintained with an eye on future military contingencies and likely adversaries. What turns routine force maintenance into an all-out arms race? If the answer is the profound forces that govern interstate antagonisms, then it may only mislead to apply the suggestive label 'arms race' on what is nothing more than a *symptom of more deeply rooted causes*. For these reasons and others, Colin S. Gray rejects the idea that there is a phenomenon *distinctive* enough to call an 'arms race'.[7] Less sceptical theorists locate arms races at the extreme end of a sliding scale that starts with 'the normal condition of military relations'. According to Barry Buzan and Eric Herring, competitors in an arms race go 'flat out or almost flat out' to procure arms.[8] As the graph below illustrates (Figure 16.1), the two world wars and the Cold War were preceded by steep rises in military spending. The arms budgets of the European Great Powers rose by 50 per cent in the crisis years 1908–13; in the late 1930s world military spending trebled; and in eight years of the early Cold War spending rose by 100 per cent.[9]

This fiscal intensity reflects a deeper psychological one. Competitors perceive themselves to be locked into a reciprocal and self-reinforcing cycle of actions and reactions. As David Stevenson puts it, 'arms racing is a *state of mind*, of deliberate emulation on both sides.'[10] We need not accept the view that an arms race is something akin to Frankenstein's experiment – the assembly of a ferocious military monster that overpowers its creators – to concede that an arms race is more than the sum total of defence policies.

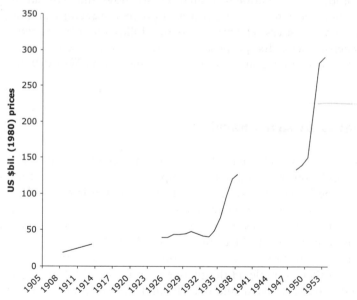

Figure 16.1 World military spending, 1908–1953.
Source: Adapted from M. Thee, ed., *Arms and Disarmament: SIPRI Findings* (Oxford, 1986), p. 18.

In other words, statesmen experience the push and the pull of armaments, yet the competition does not rob them of their freedom to make choices. A marginal note scribbled on Chamberlain's post-Munich air force estimates captures this interaction of human agency and arms race structure: 'It seems a strange result of the Prime Minister's policy of appeasement that we should be devoting so enormous a sum to the slaughter of civilians in other countries.'[11] Even neutrals on the arms race periphery are drawn into the game of deterring foes and attracting allies with targeted arms increases. In 1936–37, as Germany and Russia began to rebuild their Baltic fleets in earnest, the Swedish navy planned to build three heavy cruisers as a deterrent force: the Soviets would think twice before attacking Sweden for fear of tipping the cruiser balance in Germany's favour.[12] The key point is that political purposes govern arms races. States strive to achieve favourable military conditions for political ends. Competitors race to impose their will with threats or the use of force. Military measures substantiate threats and constitute the common currency in interstate bargaining. 'You should never menace,' Chamberlain wrote in September 1938, 'unless you are in a position to carry out your threats.'[13] This is why the process of competitive arms escalation, as Stevenson argues, is driven by recurrent and intensifying crises.[14] The steep upward climb in European arms spending in the crisis years of 1938–39 is indicative of this compelling incentive for arms racing. The trouble is that armed diplomacy and arms racing – as is the case in all the affairs of men – are not games of precision. Political effects contrary to what anyone originally intended may result. In May 1938, the Czech army partially mobilised in response to false reports of an imminent German attack. During the 'weekend' crisis, London and Paris issued warnings, while Berlin issued denials. The world press claimed that Hitler had been forced to back down. Angered by this humiliation, the Führer stepped up warship building against Britain and informed his military chiefs of his 'unalterable decision to smash Czechoslovakia by military action in the near future'.[15]

The Legacy of Total War and Arming in Depth

While arms races share common features, the inter-war race differed markedly from that of the pre-1914 period and the later Cold War. In the 1920s and 1930s, the most important influence on the goals of armaments planners was the Great War. The experience of mass industrial warfare transformed the accepted standard of national strength and erased the distinction between armies and societies. Before 1914, the Great Powers measured military strength by comparing the size of armies and navies and the money spent on them; after 1918, military men still counted soldiers and ships and compared defence budgets, but now they also worried about machine tools and the moral fibre of the civilian population. The yardstick of power had become a nation's ability to mobilise its whole economy and population for total war. Planning, industrial capacity and secure access to raw materials were the essentials. These keys to victory could not be improvised on the eve of 'the next' total war. An inescapable logic of all-embracing preparation and competition in peacetime cast a dark shadow on the conduct of inter-war international relations. To be sure, the reality of the two world wars fell short of the images of total war popularised by inter-war theorists.[16] Nevertheless, these grim projections provided a universal (and thus powerful) description of future war, and of what the powers had to do to be ready for Armageddon. In this way, the arms racing state of mind was an *inter-subjective or social construct*.

Not surprisingly, fear of the next total war was greatest in the states that were the least equipped to wage it. Seven years of war, revolution and intervention had left the Soviet Union physically devastated and industrially backward. In August 1920, the consequences were driven home by Poland's victory over the Red Army. In the aftermath, insecurity, Bolshevik ideology and visions of total war fused in the minds of Soviet officials, who faced the constant spectre of the capitalist powers combining to extinguish socialism. In the meantime, the Soviet Union had a brief respite during which to construct the industrial basis for machine-age warfare. In the 1920s, military planners called for the build-up of large, well-equipped armed forces backed up by centralised arms industries. One of the Red Army's best minds, Mikhail Tukhachevsky, envisaged massed tank armies and bomber fleets delivering crushing blows deep inside a foe's territory. He emphasised that 'industrial development shows us that we must fight a "cultured" war, that is with massive artillery, chemicals and so on – with all the ensuing strategic, organisational and mobilisation consequences.'[17] Stalin understood the relationship between industrial and military modernisation. His doctrine of 'socialism in one country' and his policy of crash industrialisation were linked to the medium-term need to deter Russia's western neighbours, Poland and the Baltic states, and, in the long run, to win the titanic struggle against the imperialist powers. 'We are fifty or a hundred years behind the advanced countries,' Stalin warned in 1931: 'we must make good this distance in ten years. Either we do it or we shall go under.'[18] In the shadow of total war, the Soviets *perceived* themselves to be in a *race* against time and an implacably hostile world order. Between 1928 and 1933, the period of the first Five-Year Plan brought conspicuous progress: Russia's growing arms industries delivered nearly 5000 aircraft, 10,000 tanks and armoured vehicles, 12,000 trucks and 17,000 artillery pieces. More importantly, defence plants were granted first call on skilled labour, raw materials and transport, while civilian industries were designed to convert quickly at the outbreak of war to tank, bomber and munitions production. By 1932,

Kliment Voroshilov, the people's commissar for military and naval affairs, could boast that 'the Red Army is capable of victoriously taking on the army of any capitalist country.'[19]

The Soviet policy of raising standing forces for current political-strategic purposes while readying the whole economy for a long war was typical of the way in which contemporaries understood 'armaments'. General Thomas, the man nominally in charge of coordinating the arms build-up in Nazi Germany, saw it this way: states had to strive for 'armaments in breadth' (front-line units and reserves) as well as 'armaments in depth' (economic endurance for a protracted conflict).[20] Once again, this view reflected a conventional reading of the lessons of 1914–18. Before the war, the European powers had devised offensive war plans to achieve swift victories. Since wars were expected to be short and conclusive, the land race revolved around extra men and matériel to ensure the successful execution of offensive plans. Between the two world wars, most professional military strategists were pessimistic about the prospects of quick victories, and deeply apprehensive about what another total war might bring. They agreed that if a rapid decision with standing forces in the opening engagements proved impossible, then the conflict would develop into a prolonged, attritional struggle between economies and societies.[21] How each of the Great Powers dealt with the dilemma of breadth and depth depended on a number of considerations, including the internal political and industrial obstacles to arms growth, access to raw materials, ideology and proximity to the central arms races. Broadly speaking, the United States, Britain and France hoped to arm enough to deter aggression without jeopardising the virtues of their liberal economies and societies; the Soviet Union, Nazi Germany, Fascist Italy and Imperial Japan raced (in theory at any rate) towards the total mobilisation of their economies and societies for the final show-down.

The British, for instance, saw no point in allowing arms spending to imperil domestic economic stability and overseas commercial relations indispensable to winning a long war. Economic strength deterred aggression, while signs of insolvency invited it. A balance had to be struck between acquiring the men and matériel to block the initial Nazi onslaught and husbanding the financial strength necessary to purchase overseas supplies and to raise capital abroad – what the Cabinet termed the 'fourth arm of defence'. At the end of 1937, the three armed service schemes were reassessed to reflect this breadth–depth relationship. Expanding the navy to ensure secure access to the empire and air defences to forestall a 'knock-out blow' from the Luftwaffe were priorities; preparing the army for continental war went to the bottom of the list.[22] In 1936, Léon Blum, premier of the Popular Front government, feared that France did not possess the breadth of modern weapons to repulse an attaque brusquée from across the Rhine. Contrary to expectations that Blum would champion reform, he prioritised a massive 14 billion franc, four-year arms programme over social and labour legislation (even at the price of his premiership), but soon discovered that French arms firms did not have the capacity in place to produce the required weapons on demand. He turned to a policy of nationalising key parts of the defence industries in order to put into place the depth necessary to generate breadth – a policy that did not pay off until 1939–40.[23] In both Britain and France, policy-makers underestimated the ease with which Germany overcame the industrial and skilled-labour bottlenecks that limited their own rate of rearmament. Even so, at the level of national policy, there were genuine political and psychological barriers as to how closely the democratic powers could emulate the totalitarians. As one Cabinet minister reflected, Britain could not match the arms drives of the totalitarian states 'unless we turned ourselves into a different kind of nation'.[24] Even the lifelong socialist Léon Blum once remarked that in 'attempting to oppose Fascism's bid for power ... one is too often tempted to follow in its footsteps'.[25]

It was true that the slump had stalled the initial French and (to a lesser degree) British armaments increases in response to the Nazi threat, while the Wehrmacht exploited the slack in Germany's depressed economy to steal a march in the arms race. But projecting the appearance of both breadth and depth proved easier than achieving them in reality. Hitler had intended from the moment he took power in 1933 to convert the German economy into a colossal engine for waging open-ended wars of territorial conquest and racial annihilation. Before he denounced the military clauses of the Versailles Treaty in March 1935, the top priorities for defence spending were infrastructure, training facilities and the industrial plant necessary for sustained armaments growth. His emphasis on depth resonated well with the concept of Wehrwirtschaft (war-based economy) that permeated German military planning. When the scale of rearmament began to strain German finances, Hitler rebuffed calls from the president of the Reichsbank for slowing rearmament and returning to the world economy through international trade. Instead, in September 1936, the Führer appointed Field Marshall Göring to head the Four-Year Plan. The production of vital raw materials and synthetic rubber and fuel were stepped up to render the Reich less vulnerable to maritime blockade. The consequent drive for greater weapons output and economic self-sufficiency (autarky) required closer integration of the civil and military economic spheres. Fears in London and Paris that the Nazis might seek war to escape from an impending economic crisis were misplaced. Wage and price controls kept inflation in check, while persuasion and coercion kept the workers in line. Controls on capital flows, trade and foreign exchange contained balance of payment problems. In 1938–39, the take-over of Austria and Czechoslovakia provided a fresh source of foreign exchange and raw materials. When European war came in 1939, Germany possessed impressive armed forces, but, as General Thomas complained, depth for total war was still three or four years away. The big war that <u>Hitler had planned for the mid-1940s came too soon</u>, and as a result the <u>Third Reich's armaments output stagnated</u>. The conduct and consequences of Hitler's foreign policy in 1938–39 destroyed his long-term ambitions for a total-war economy.[26]

Much the same can be said of Italy and Japan. <u>Mussolini</u> dreamt of a mighty and <u>self-sufficient economic basis for total war</u> to secure the Fascist state's place among the Great Powers. But Italy's <u>industrial backwardness</u> as well as the <u>dictator's owns failings</u> stymied the realisation of his vision. As in Germany, investment went first to <u>long-range programmes</u> to expand <u>production, infrastructure</u> and <u>autarky</u>. But <u>Italy was too dependent on seaborne supply</u> and <u>imported fuel</u> to be self-sufficient. <u>Poor planning</u> and a <u>lack</u> of coordination prevented the regime from exploiting Italy's full potential. <u>Mismanagement</u> plagued weapons design and manufacture. <u>Military spending trebled</u> after 1935, but most of this investment went on <u>Mussolini's adventures in Africa and Spain</u>, and not on in-depth preparedness or raising the fighting efficiency of the army.[27] In <u>Japan,</u> the dilemmas of <u>breadth versus depth, expansion versus consolidation,</u> likewise confounded policy-making. The <u>factional infighting</u> and <u>bitter interdepartmental rivalries</u> endemic within the policy-making élite aggravated the difficulty of pursuing a steady course. Many officials understood that the <u>twin goals of self-sufficiency</u> and <u>industrial growth</u> had to be coordinated. Japan required the <u>riches of northern China</u> and Southeast Asia to contend with the Soviet Union and the United States; but *time* was needed to construct the factories to convert these riches into warships, guns and bombers. The <u>Kwantung Army's conquest of Manchuria</u> in <u>1931</u> was a step towards autarky, yet the <u>aggressive move provoked the Soviets</u> into increasing their forces in the Far East. The Soviet menace in turn spurred <u>army hotheads</u> to press for immediate increases to standing forces to counter the Russians and to tighten Japan's grip on northern China. The <u>Marco Polo Bridge incident</u> in July 1937 constituted a decisive setback for those officers who grasped the need for time to prepare Japan for total war. As one leading advocate of autarky, Colonel Ishiwara Kanji, warned, '[China] will be what Spain was for Napoleon, an endless bog.'[28] As a result of the <u>renewed war in China,</u> Imperial Japan would become even more <u>dependent on overseas imports,</u> especially <u>American</u> imports, of critical <u>war materials.</u>

Arming in Breadth, Quantity and Quality

<u>Arming in *breadth*,</u> in particular the <u>rapid build-up and upgrading of forces</u> in the <u>late 1930s,</u> evolved into a number of *constituent* naval, air and air–land races. The <u>growth of navies</u> was <u>closely linked</u> to the breakdown of the <u>system of naval limitation by treaty</u> initiated at <u>Washington in 1922</u> and

reaffirmed at London in 1930. London, Paris, Washington and Rome all
signed the London Naval Treaty of 1936, but Tokyo refused to do so unless
it granted Japan tonnage equality with the United States and British fleets.
From 1937 a three-way race between these three seapowers ensued. Among
the medium-sized navies, a three-way race developed between Italy, Germany and France. Sadly for French admirals, who had benefited from
disproportionate funding in the late 1920s and early 1930s, the advent
of the Nazi menace diverted funds away from fleet expansion. As a result,
the French navy relinquished tonnage superiority over its two rivals. The
naval races only exerted influence on policy – and so the decisions for
war – through the strategic advice that admirals offered their governments.
In Britain, the Royal Navy backed appeasement of Germany because the
Admiralty knew that a premature European war would destroy its plan to
build by the mid-1940s a fleet sufficiently powerful to confront the Japanese
and German navies at once. The colossal American two-ocean navy
programme of 1940–41 helped to persuade the Japanese navy that it was
better to fight sooner rather than later. Ironically, Hitler had offered to limit
the size of the German navy to 35 per cent of the size of the Royal Navy
precisely because he believed Admiral Tirpitz's pre-1914 naval race had
been a prime cause of Britain's entry into the 1914–18 war against
Wilhelmine Germany. Hitler regarded the Anglo-German Naval Agreement
of June 1935 as a deal on spheres of influence: Britain was to turn away
from Europe and concentrate on its overseas empire; Nazi Germany would
proceed to build its continental empire free of British meddling. When
Chamberlain's interference in Hitler's expansionist programme became
more and more persistent in 1938–39, the Führer vented his anger by
demands for an ever more powerful German fleet.[29]

In Europe, the most dynamic competition was the air race between
Britain, France and Germany (see Figure 16.2 below). French and British
intelligence services had alerted politicians to Nazi Germany's covert air
rearmament well before Hitler unveiled the *Luftwaffe* in March 1935.
However, the Führer's announcement in effect fired the starting pistol.
Newspapers circulated scare stories of skies darkened with fleets of Nazi
bombers ready to rain down high explosives and poison gas on helpless
cities. Apocalyptic images of air warfare galvanised public opinion on both
sides of the English Channel behind greater expenditure on air forces.
Stanley Baldwin, the prime minister, who had earlier warned the House of
Commons that 'the bomber will always get through', in 1934 committed
the Royal Air Force to 'air parity' with the largest air force in striking
distance of Britain. Domestic opinion aside, the acceleration in the air race
was chiefly driven by diplomatic and strategic concerns. Airpower offered
a cost-effective deterrent. After a committee of top-level defence, treasury
and diplomatic officials had identified Nazi Germany as Britain's 'ultimate'
potential enemy in early 1934, Chamberlain, then chancellor of the

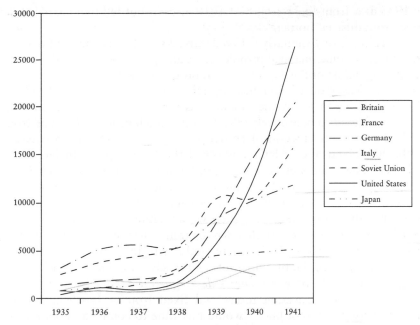

Figure 16.2 Military aircraft production of the Great Powers, 1935–1941.
Source: R. J. Overy with A. Wheatcroft, *The Road to War* (London, 1999).

exchequer, revised the committee's spending proposals to the benefit of the Royal Air Force. From then onwards, airpower – 'the most formidable deterrent to war' – played a pivotal role in his efforts to force Hitler to the negotiating table.[30] In the early stages of rearmament, when Germany was vulnerable, the Führer – always dangling promises of an air limitation agreement – exploited fear of bombing to deter France, Poland and Britain from concerted action. German airmen also reckoned that the *Luftwaffe* could gain a decade-long head start if they moved swiftly.[31] Considerations such as these encouraged decision-makers in all three capitals to augment 'front-line' air strength first. The more machines you had in the 'shop window', so ran the logic, the greater the political impact they would have.[32] Unfortunately, the 'shop window' of the French *Armée de l'Air* was rather bare. *Luftwaffe* planners were right to conclude that building an aviation industry from scratch provided them with a temporary edge in aircraft production. Thanks to a scarcity of orders in the 1920s, France's aviation industry had ossified. By the mid-1930s, when large orders were placed, the sector was too poorly organised and technically backward for mass production. Until the reorganisation of the air-frame industry that followed nationalisation in 1936, output lagged woefully behind demand. France's 1934 Plan I for air force expansion, for instance, called for the production by 1935 of a front-line strength of 1010 aircraft but fell two years behind owing to industrial bottlenecks.[33]

The French army similarly suffered setbacks in the first stage of the land arms race. Chronic financial turbulence resulting from efforts to defend the franc in the midst of the depression had produced defence cuts in 1931–35. The army was reduced and field exercises were cancelled. In 1933–35, as Germany began to lay the foundations for non-stop army growth, the French remained comparatively idle. Alarming intelligence on German troop levels, Hitler's introduction of conscription in 1935, and the occupation of the Rhineland a year later quickened the French pace. In late 1936, Daladier, then Blum's defence minister, launched an enormous scheme of military modernisation. Although the balance of trained formations, reserves and munitions favoured France until 1937, the high command knew that the more populous Reich would ultimately overtake them in armed manpower. To offset this demographic inferiority, French strategy pivoted on the defence. If the army could withstand another Schlieffen-like onslaught, then the full might of the French empire and France's allies could be brought to bear in a *guerre de longue durée*. In case of a surprise attack, the army's covering forces and fixed frontier fortifications (the much-criticised Maginot line)[34] would buy time to complete mobilisation. Considerations of armed diplomacy and deterrence also came into play. The 1936 arms drive would provide French politicians with the means to negotiate from a position of strength and dispel thoughts in Berlin of an *attaque brusquée*. Unfortunately, the 1936 orders for new weapons swamped the limited capacity of French manufacturing. Output eventually picked up, but the delay was *politically* demoralising.[35] Just as the production lag occurred in France, the arms build-up in Germany delivered the 'political power' Hitler had demanded in 1933. Although foreign observers overlooked the shortages of officers and arms that distressed German staff officers, the growth of the original 100,000-man force was still astonishing: the 1935 target of 36 infantry and 3 armoured divisions (520,000 men) by 1939 was reached three years early. The Four-Year Plan answered speculation in the high command about whether the pace would be slackened. 'The extent of the military development of our resources cannot be too large,' Hitler wrote, 'nor its pace too swift.'[36]

Hitler's Four-Year Plan memorandum identified the Soviet Union as the long-range target of Germany's in-depth war preparations, but available striking power and the army's operational planning were directed against the victims of the first stage of his expansionist project, Austria and Czechoslovakia. In 1937–38, General Beck, chief of the general staff, considered the army capable of an aggressive defence against France, if the *Wehrmacht* attacked Czechoslovakia, but feared that such a war might provoke the formation of an overwhelming coalition of Great Powers, including Russia.[37] Except as a bogyman with which to terrify foreign

statesmen, Hitler did not take the immediate threat from the Red Army
seriously. The Soviet Union, on the other hand, stepped up rearmament and
revised upwards wartime production goals for heavy weapons as the Nazi
menace developed. Soviet officials planned for war against a German-Polish
attack from the west and a Japanese attack in the Far East. In 1931, the
Kwantung Army's aggression had caused a crisis in Russian defence circles.
In order to deter Japan and insert a razor-sharp edge into negotiations with
the Japanese, the Soviets amassed powerful land and air forces in the Far
East. Both sides viewed the mid-1930s as a period of potential danger: 'if
we could deploy, say, 2000 aircraft,' Marshall Tukhachevsky wrote, 'then a
war in 1934 could be considered excluded'. The Japanese army could not
keep pace in this competitive build-up of men and machines. By 1938–39,
when whole formations of the Kwantung Army were wiped out in clashes
along the Mongolian-Manchurian frontier, Japanese army intelligence
estimated that the Red Army had accumulated nearly twice as many men,
five times the number of aircraft and more than ten times the number of
tanks than their own forces.[38]

The arms races of the 1930s were both *quantitative* and *qualitative*.
Before 1914, the European armies raced for more soldiers and weapons of a
similar type; before the Second World War, the rapid rate of technological
change compelled the powers to compete in hardware of increasing
sophistication, complexity and expense. The most striking advance was in
the air. All-metal monoplanes replaced wood and canvas biplanes. Between
1918 and 1935, engine performance increased from 225 horsepower with
speeds of 125 mph to 500 hp with speeds of 200 mph. By the eve of the
Second World War, front-line fighters such as the Messerschmitt Bf109 and
the Supermarine Spitfire had engines of over 1000 hp generating speeds in
excess of 350 mph, as well as increased flying ranges and improved
weapons. Likewise, from 1935 to 1940, the striking range and payloads of
bombers more than doubled.[39] In these circumstances, to lag behind was
crippling. Italy failed to make the qualitative leap of the late 1930s early
enough. The air force leadership remained wedded to the open-cockpit
biplane for fighters. The aero-engine industry could not design a good
water-cooled engine in the 1000 hp class necessary for high-performance
monoplanes. A reliable four-engine long-range bomber also proved beyond
Italy's reach. In the mid-1930s, the *Regia Aeronautica* had been an
imposing symbol of Fascist vitality; in June 1940, the month of Mussolini's
entry into the war, most of Italy's aircraft were obsolete.[40]

Technological change challenged military men to fashion new doctrines
and force structures.[41] How were the new weapons to be employed? Did the
'strategic' bombing of cities offer a new war-winning method to shatter
the will of enemy civilians? Should aircraft be used principally as adjuncts
to the army and fleet? In Britain, the squabble between the Royal Air Force
and the two older branches of the armed forces over the control and missions

of aircraft worked to the detriment of naval aviation and close army support. In France, doctrinal indecision resulted in a multi-purpose bomber, fighter and reconnaissance design that failed to live up to any of these tasks. Innovation, however, did not simply revolve around the quality of hardware. By 1940, the French arsenal included first-class tanks (the SOMUA-35 and Char-B), but the army did not devise the operational and tactical ideas to employ them aggressively. By combining tanks, motorised infantry and dive-bombers – all linked by radio – the German army innovated in the field of combined-arms doctrine and tactics (what was later dubbed *Blitzkrieg*). While technology was not an autonomous force driving the arms spiral, the timing of change could influence strategic postures. The coming of radar and the high-performance fighter in 1937–38, for instance, spurred the transition in British deterrence away from bomber parity to credible fighter defences. Recalling the pre-1914 race in all-big-gun dreadnoughts, the British Admiralty hoped to use diplomacy to forestall another qualitative escalation in warship design. The London Naval Treaty of 1936 as well as bilateral agreements with Germany and Russia in 1937 set agreed limits on gun size and tonnage in each warship category (battleships, cruisers, destroyers etc.), the object of which was to prevent technical one-upmanship.[42] In 1937, the Japanese navy made just such a bid for qualitative superiority by laying down in secret the first of two 'super' battleships of 69,000 tons, armed with 18-inch guns. However, as the Pacific war would show, the true innovation in sea power was in the development of aircraft carriers and carrier-borne torpedo and dive-bombers.

Armaments Competition and the Decisions for War

How did the arms races interact? The most important competitions were the air–land races between Britain, France and Germany in western Europe. The European naval races, military rivalry between Soviet Russia and Japan, and the Japanese bid for naval supremacy in the Pacific would not have sparked the global conflagration of 1939–41. It was only when the *core* arms competitions in Europe ended in a general war that new threats and opportunities emerged for the Great Powers on the periphery. The collapse of France in May–June 1940 was the turning point. The western Allies had 'won' the arms race in the sense of having stockpiled the most military hardware, but owing to failures in intelligence and a blunder in strategy, the *Wehrmacht* won an unexpected victory with superior all-arms doctrine and tactics and a bold strategy of breakthrough.[43] As a result of the Allied defeat, Washington launched a crash armaments programme, while Tokyo exploited the European calamity to penetrate further into Southeast Asia. In Europe, Mussolini, stayed out of the war in 1939 owing to military weakness and resource scarcity, but took the plunge in 1940. In July of that year, Hitler turned eastward to face the growth of Soviet armaments.

The coming of global war from 1939 to 1941, and the role of the peripheral arms races in progressively expanding the conflict, contrasted sharply with the sudden outbreak of world war in July–August 1914. Much of the explanation for this lies in the close proximity of the competitors in the pre-1914 arms races: France, Germany, Austria-Hungary and Russia shared land frontiers. But geography was not the only factor. The tight political grouping of the powers was also important. Before the First World War, the central land arms race was between the two great alliances: France and Russia versus Germany and Austria-Hungary. The pre-1914 growth of armies reinforced these alliances and drew in the most powerful detached player, Britain. Statesmen courted allies to ensure a preponderance of strength for the next diplomatic confrontation or, if it came to it, war. British and French staff officers informally discussed war plans, and the French offered to finance Russia's railway construction to increase the striking power of its ally. Before 1939, global armaments competition did not have a corresponding political effect. The Anti-Comintern Pact and the Rome-Berlin Axis (and even the Tripartite Pact of 1940) were smoke-screens to deter the *status quo* powers rather than the political foundations of a well-coordinated arms drive. Hitler regarded allies as pawns. All three aggressors, in fact, craved arms and autarky only to satisfy their *own* ambitions, not those of allies.

What appeared to be Axis coalition building did not encourage closer links between the *status quo* powers. The lessons of 1914 once again played a part here. Like many contemporaries, Chamberlain and Roosevelt believed that inter-bloc arms races had helped to cause the Great War. American neutrality laws were intended to isolate the United States from European entanglements and arms races. From anxiety of being forced into another European conflict, the British government refused to offer the French a concrete security commitment, and rejected proposals to prepare the army for another continental war. Without Britain, the French sought to reinforce their ties with the small powers of eastern Europe. To the great cost of French power, influence and prestige, however, shortages of skilled labour and machine tools made it impossible for France to encircle Germany with small allies deploying modern tanks and aircraft. Arms likewise played a role in forestalling a Franco-British-Russian military alliance. Stalin's purges of the Red Army in 1936–38 did little to promote confidence in Paris and London in the offensive power of the Soviet war machine; deep suspicion and ideological antipathy made close cooperation in armaments and war planning a step too far. Historians often place the burden of blame for this hostility on Paris and London, but the feeling was mutual. In 1934, for instance, when a French air mission visited Moscow to propose a much-needed exchange in aviation technology, Stalin barked that 'the French are *slithering* to us for intelligence. Our aviation interests them because it's well established that we're strong in that field.'[44] After Munich, Roosevelt hoped to contain Hitler at limited cost by supplying Britain and France with the means to bomb the Nazi regime into submission. 'Had we had 5000 planes and the capacity to immediately produce 10,000 per year, even though I might have had to ask Congress for authority to sell or lend them to the countries of Europe,' the President explained, 'Hitler would not have dared to take the stand he did.'[45] This belated containment strategy of arming allies crumpled with the *Wehrmacht's* triumph in June 1940.

To assess the impact of armaments competition on the onset of global war, we must turn to the connection between the arms balance and the decisions for war. Arms racing, to use George Peden's phrase, was 'a matter of timing'. Once the race took off, there was no way to erase the consequences of early decisions and restore initial conditions. The French discovered this when their arms makers could not produce on demand. The Russians paid a price by arming too early. Soviet production stagnated in the mid-1930s: by 1941, much of Russia's arsenal was obsolete.[46] More precarious still was the breadth–depth balance. Because long-term investments in industrial capacity were cut short in 1939–40, German and Italian arms output (and so striking power) stagnated in the first years of the conflict. Resource-poor Japan attacked the world's most advanced and self-sufficient economy before building up the depth of economic readiness required for the contest. As suggested at the start of the chapter, the problem of timing was compounded by the fact that no one could locate the finishing line (the coming of world war) in advance. Each of the powers strove to achieve conflicting political and military goals with competitive arms increases. No Great Power stood still for long. Germany may have stolen a march in 1934–35 and raced to fight and win a big war in the mid-1940s, but France and Britain set into motion their own countervailing defence programmes in 1936. When would they catch up?

How decision-makers calculated and acted upon competitive *trends* tells us much about the influence of the arms races on the coming of war. Generally speaking, a positive shift might encourage a foreign policy of firmness or war. Awareness that a temporary military superiority was ebbing away might encourage a policy of retreat or pre-emptive war. We do not need to dig too deep in the sources to find calculations of this sort – what in current jargon are called 'windows of opportunity' and 'windows of vulnerability'. In 1931, as the first Five-Year Plan began to show results in the output of modern weapons, some Soviet officials worried that the capitalist powers might launch a pre-emptive war against Russia.[47] Similarly, in 1933–34, Hitler and some of his officials wondered whether France and Poland might wage a preventive war against Germany. In the early phases of European arms races, thoughts of preventive wars revealed much more about the misperception of foreign intentions or the malicious intent of those who entertained them than the real intentions and policies of their potential adversaries. But as the arms races of western Europe intensified from 1936 onwards, perceptions of the shifting arms balance increasingly acted as *constraining* or *empowering* influences on decision-makers.

Turning to France and Britain first, the most decisive influence of the arms races on policy-makers was the transformation in outlooks that took place in 1938–39. Before Munich, a sense of inferiority characterised estimates of the arms balance. In 1936, huge defence programmes were undertaken by both Great Powers in order to present a credible deterrent. Blum, Daladier and Chamberlain all saw arms and preparations for a long war as powerful inducements for a general European settlement. French and British defence plans would peak in 1939–40. By then, the prospect of a show-down with Hitler and European war could be faced with some confidence. In the meantime, the Western Powers hoped to buy time for arms increases and avoid an early confrontation by pressing ahead with diplomacy. Britain, a global maritime power, was particularly anxious to reduce the triple threat: 'We cannot foresee a time,' wrote the chiefs of staff, 'when our defence forces will be strong enough to safeguard our territory, trade and vital interests against Italy, Germany and Japan simultaneously.'[48] In 1936–38, French and British intelligence also adopted a 'worst case' approach to estimates of the scale and pace of German military expansion. Crude stereotypes of Teutonic efficiency and German national character contrasted sharply with the frustrating bottlenecks experienced by British and French leaders in the completion of their own arms schemes. Accordingly, when the Munich crisis came, statesmen on both sides of the Channel sensed that they were passing through a danger zone. In another six or 12 months, things would be different – but for now war might spell disaster. More to the point, since French and British strategists planned to absorb the first German blow and then grind the Nazi war machine down through a prolonged struggle of attrition and blockade, they saw little that could be done in the short run to rescue Czechoslovakia: 'We can do nothing to prevent the dog getting the bone, and we have no means of making him give it up, except by killing him by a slow process of attrition and starvation.'[49]

Obviously, pessimistic military forecasts were not the only reason for Chamberlain's search for peace in 1938. Even so, the arms balance offered reasons for a negotiated settlement. In France, the full-scale overhaul of the aviation industry in 1936 brought aircraft production almost to a halt in 1937. At the time of Munich the *Armée de l'Air* possessed only 50 modern fighters. Uppermost in the minds of British and French officials was the fear that the *Luftwaffe* might deliver a 'knockout blow'. As we now know, these fears were exaggerated and reflected much deeper anxieties about social upheaval and the end of European civilisation. The *Luftwaffe*, though capable of a sustained attack on Paris, could not devastate London. Air intelligence in both states had produced accurate estimates of total German air strength, yet did not recognise that the number of serviceable machines was a great deal less. It is tempting to pillory French and British policy-makers for overrating German might. For those who lived through history, however, perceptions counted because they informed decisions. Perceptions also reveal much about the process by which arms competition *structured* contemporary expectations and outlooks. What was remarkable was how swiftly perspectives changed. After September 1938, intelligence from inside the Nazi camp spoke of Hitler's wild rage at the Munich agreement and of his determination to achieve hegemony by force; in response, Britain and France accelerated rearmament and began to cooperate in preparations for total war. In April 1939, the British Cabinet ordered conscription. Intelligence in both capitals now circulated balanced reports that underscored the Third Reich's strengths and weaknesses. The 1936 rearmament plans began to pay off. French aircraft production picked up, and British output started to outstrip that of Germany. French industry delivered armoured fighting vehicles, anti-tank guns and other heavy weapons in quantity. Even though the balance of forces in early 1939 had changed marginally (arguably for the worse on land), the positive upward trend in British and French rearmament and strategic confidence translated into robust foreign policies. In the wake of the German occupation of the rump Czech state in March 1939, London and Paris offered guarantees to Poland, Romania and Greece in order to build a barrier against further Axis expansion. In 1939, war planners were convinced that France and Britain could withstand the first German and Italian blows and triumph in the long run. This sense of gathering strength was empowering. In September 1939, despite the Nazi-Soviet Pact, Chamberlain and Daladier accepted war over Poland.[50]

The dynamic interaction of perceived shifts in the military balance and of crises can be found in Hitler's calculations as well. Rational military factors did not alone determine his actions, but the view that Germany's arms lead was a wasting asset was a theme he returned to often. At the Hoßbach conference on 5 November 1937, Hitler told his officials that the Reich's relative strength would decline after 1943–45. 'The world [was] expecting our attack and was increasing its counter-measures from year to year. It was while the rest of the world was still preparing its defences,' he had said, 'that we were obliged to take the offensive.'[51] Hitler wrecked his own preparations for a total war in the mid-1940s because he forced the pace of events in 1938–39. Each crisis *compressed* his timetable while *enlarging* his appetite for armaments. The imputation that he had backed down in the May Weekend Crisis of 1938 angered him into pressing ahead with the destruction of Czechoslovakia. Later that month, he declared that he would act while Czech, British and French defences were still inferior: 'English rearmament will not come into effect before 1941/42. French rearmament will also still last many years.'[52] To satisfy his growing lust for martial glory and violence, Hitler relished war with the Czechs. He dismissed General Beck's arguments that Paris and London would intervene. A swift and overwhelming blow would forestall outside intervention. However, the bloody end that he had craved was thwarted by Chamberlain's shuttle diplomacy and threatening mobilisations undertaken by the French army and British navy. At the last moment, Hitler *was* deterred.[53] He reacted once again by venting his fury with demands for weapons directed at the architects of Munich. In the winter of 1938/39, Hitler ordered a fivefold increase in *Luftwaffe* strength, a trebling of munitions output, and top priority for the navy's gigantic Z-Plan fleet (10 battleships, 15 battlecruisers, 55 cruisers, 8 aircraft carriers and 249 U-boats). Given the conflicting demands on Germany's limited industrial capacity, let alone the requirements for fuel oil and storage, these directives were unrealistic. Aware of the acceleration in French and British arms growth, Hitler warned of the *Wehrmacht* losing its lead in a few years. In September 1939, Hitler stubbornly ignored signals of Anglo-French determination to enforce the Polish guarantees. The Führer now refused to be deterred. '"Time" will, in general,' he said, 'work against us when we do not use it effectively.'[54]

For Japanese decision-makers as well, fears of a closing 'window of opportunity' weighed heavily on them by 1941. The Nazi victories in 1940 had opened up the chance to push southward in order to isolate China and to control or secure access to the resources of the French and Dutch empires. Aggressive Japanese moves into Indochina and Tokyo's adherence to the Axis alliance were met with an American oil and scrap-metal embargo. Although bilateral talks continued between Cordell Hull, the US secretary of state, and the Japanese ambassador in Washington, by July–August 1941 the Americans had turned to a policy of containment and coercion. Their hope was that the raw materials embargo would drain Japan of the means to wage war, while the formation of an anti-Japanese coalition in the region and the steady deployment of new B-17 'Flying Fortress' bombers to the Philippines would in the meantime deter Tokyo. As the secretary of war assured the president, 'these new four-engine bombers coming off the assembly line should constitute a great pool of American power applicable with speed and mobility to the respective spots where in the interests of our national strategy of defence it is important that such power should be applied.'[55] Alas, the Japanese were not deterred by the B-17 build-up. Instead, what focused minds in Tokyo in November–December 1941 was the drain of incessant war in China and dwindling stocks of war reserves. The oil embargo – in effect an armaments embargo in this era of *in-depth* preparedness – had set a timetable for Tokyo either to capitulate to American demands or resort to force of arms: 'As a result of the present overall economic blockade imposed by Great Britain and the United States, our Empire's national power is declining day by day.' The military balance was about to shift: 'From the standpoint of operations, if the time for commencing war is delayed, the ratio of armaments between Japan and the United States will become more and more unfavourable as time passes; and particularly, the gap in air armament will enlarge rapidly'. At the Imperial Conference of 12 November 1941, Premier Hideki Tōjō summed up the now-or-never rationale behind the decision to attack Pearl Harbor: 'Two years from now we will have no petroleum for military use. Ships will stop moving. When I think about the expansion of the American fleet, the unfinished China Incident, and so on, I see no end of difficulties ... I fear that we would become a third-class nation after two or three years if we just sat tight.'[56]

This chapter began by rejecting Sir Edward Grey's assertion that great armaments inevitably lead to war. In the 1930s, armaments growth worked in complex and contingent ways: both as a cause and a consequence of international conflict. To understand why Grey's assertion is not an ironclad law of world politics, one final question must be addressed: why did some states but not others launch aggressive wars when windows of opportunity appeared? After all, Wilhelmine Germany did not exploit Russia's temporary weakness in 1905 to start a European war on favourable terms, but ran a grave risk by doing so in 1914. France and Poland did not wage a preventive war against the Nazi regime in 1934. In the early Cold War, as Stalin raced for atomic weapons, the United States did not exercise its nuclear monopoly to stop him.[57] To reach the answer we need to see armaments competition as part of the larger clash of ideas. What were weapons for? Were they implements of a regulated system of security or tools for violent conquest, tyranny and revolution? Although statesmen everywhere were prepared to fight rather than surrender great power status, the experience of 1914–18 had prompted firm adherence to two conflicting standpoints. For those following in Grey's footsteps, war was no longer a legitimate means to alter the *status quo*. But for others, war was a *desirable* method to achieve diverse and far-reaching goals. Most significant of all in the link between arms and the coming of the Second World War, great armaments and total war dominated Hitler's dark visions of relentless revolution, expansion and racial annihilation.

Notes

1. Viscount Grey of Fallodon, *Twenty-Five Years, 1892–1916*, Vol. I (London, 1925), pp. 89–90.
2. League of Nations, *Armaments Year Book* (Geneva, annually 1924 to 1940). The quotations are from the preface to the final volume, pp. 3–9. My emphasis.
3. P. M. Kennedy, 'Arms Races and the Causes of War, 1850–1945', in his *Strategy and Diplomacy* (London, 1983), pp. 165–77.

4. For a review, see H. Strachan, 'The First World War', *Historical Journal* 43(2000), 889–903.
5. For example, see W. Murray and A. R. Millett, eds, *Military Effectiveness*, Vol. II, *The Interwar Period* (1988), *Calculations: Net Assessment and the Coming of World War II* (1992) and *Military Innovation in the Interwar Period* (1997).
6. G. C. Peden, *British Rearmament and the Treasury, 1932–39* (Edinburgh, 1979), pp. 66, 109.
7. C. S. Gray, 'Arms Races and Other Pathetic Fallacies: A Case for Deconstruction', *Review of International Studies* 22 (1996), 323–35.
8. Both quotes are from B. Buzan and E. Herring, *The Arms Dynamic in World Politics* (Bolder, CO, 1998), pp. 75–82.
9. D. Stevenson, *Armaments and the Coming of War in Europe* (Oxford, 1996), p. 3.
10. Ibid., p. 9. My emphasis.
11. The note, dated 29 October 1938, can be found in Public Records Office, Kew, PREM1/236 (hereafter PRO, PREM 1/236, etc.).
12. A. Berge, *Sakkundskap och politsk rationalitet. Den svenka flottan och pansarfartygsfrågan 1918–1939* (Stockholm, 1987), pp. 125–8.
13. K. Feiling, *The Life of Neville Chamberlain* (London, 1946), p. 360.
14. Stevenson, *Armaments*, pp. 10–11, 414–17.
15. D. C. Watt, 'Hitler's Visit to Rome and the Week-end Crisis of May 1938: A Study in Hitler's Response to External Stimuli', *Journal of Contemporary History* 9 (1974), 23–32.
16. General E. Ludendorff's *Der Totale Krieg* (Munich, 1935) was typical. For a discussion of total war, see R. Chickering, 'Total War: The Use and Abuse of a Concept', in M. Boemeke, R. Chickering and S. Förster, eds, *Anticipating Total War* (Cambridge, 1999), pp. 13–28.
17. See D. Stone's *Hammer & Rifle: The Militarization of the Soviet Union, 1926–1933* (Lawrence, KS, 2000); and L. Samuelson, *Plans For Stalin's War Machine, 1925–1941* (London, 2000), pp. 19–28.
18. The quote is from Stalin's speech to the leaders of industry, 4 February 1931, in *Collected Works*, Vol. XIII (Moscow, 1955), p. 41.
19. Samuelson, *Stalin's War Machine*, pp. 144, 201, and Stone, *Militarization*.
20. B. Carroll, *Design For Total War: Arms and Economics in the Third Reich* (1968), p. 46.
21. D. C. Watt, *Too Serious a Business: European Armed Forces and the Approach to the Second World War* (London, 1975).
22. G. C. Peden, 'A Matter of Timing: The Economic Background to British Foreign Policy, 1937–39', *History* 69 (1984), 15–28.
23. R. Frank[enstein], 'The Decline of France and French Appeasement, 1936–39', in W. J. Mommsen and L. Kettenacker, eds, *The Fascist Challenge and the Policy of Appeasement* (London, 1983), pp. 236–45; M. Alexander, *The Republic in Danger: General Maurice Gamelin and the Politics of French Defence, 1933–40* (Cambridge, 1992), pp. 110–41.
24. Peden, 'A Matter of Timing', p. 22.
25. P. Jackson, *France and the Nazi Menace: Intelligence and Policy-Making 1933–39* (Oxford, 2000), p. 107.

26. R. J. Overy, *War, Economy and Society in the Third Reich* (Oxford, 1994), pp. 178–256.
27. M. Knox, *Hitler's Italian Allies: Royal Armed Forces, Fascist Regime and the War of 1940–43* (Cambridge, 2000), pp. 23–49; V. Zamagni, 'Italy, How to Lose the War and Win the Peace', in M. Harrison, ed., *The Economics of World War II* (Cambridge, 1998), pp. 192–200.
28. M. Barnhart, 'Japan's Economic Security and the Origins of the Pacific War', *Journal of Strategic Studies* 4 (1981), 105–24, and his *Japan Prepares for Total War: The Search for Economic Security, 1918–1941* (Ithaca, NY, 1987).
29. S. Pelz, *Race to Pearl Harbor: The Failure of the Second London Naval Conference and the Onset of World War II* (Cambridge, MA, 1974); and J. Maiolo, *The Royal Navy and Nazi Germany, 1933–39* (London, 1998).
30. Peden, *Treasury*, p. 121.
31. W. Deist, 'The Rearmament of the Wehrmacht', in W. Deist, M. Messerschmidt, H. Volkmann and W. Wettes, eds, *Germany and the Second World War*, Vol. I, *The Build-up of German Aggression* (Oxford, 1990), pp. 480–90.
32. R. J. Overy, 'Airpower and the Origins of Deterrence Theory before 1939', *Journal of Strategic Studies* 15 (1992), 73–101.
33. Alexander, *Republic in Danger*, pp. 147–8, 154.
34. For a full discussion of this issue, see M. Alexander, 'In Defence of the Maginot Line', in R. Boyce, ed., *French Foreign and Defence Policy, 1918–40* (London, 1998), pp. 175–83.
35. Jackson, *Nazi Menace, passim*; Alexander, *Republic in Danger*, pp. 34–68, 111–27; R. J. Young, 'L'Attaque brusquée and its Uses and as a Myth in Interwar France', *Historical Reflections* 8 (1981), 92–113.
36. Deist, 'Wehrmacht', pp. 408–56.
37. W. Deist, *The Wehrmacht and German Rearmament* (London, 1981), pp. 96–101.
38. Stone, *Militarization*, pp. 184–209, 213; Samuelson, *Stalin's War Machine*, pp. 149, 155–8; A. Coox, *Nomonhan: Japan against Russia, 1939* (Stanford, CA, 1985), pp. 76–91.
39. J. Buckley, *Air Power in the Age of Total War* (London, 1999), pp. 107–24.
40. Knox, *Italian Allies*, pp. 43–4, 64–7; Zamagni, 'Italy, How to Lose the War', p. 193.
41. For thorough studies of these issues as well as the institutional, cultural and political factors that influenced the way in which armed forces adapted to technological change, see Murray and Millett, eds, *Military Innovation*; and H. R. Winton and D. Mets, eds, *The Challenge of Change: Military Institutions and New Realities, 1918–1941* (Lincoln, NE, 2000).
42. Maiolo, *Royal Navy*, pp. 11–56.
43. See K.-H. Frieser, *Blitzkrieg-Legende: Der Westfeldzug 1940* (Munich, 1996); and E. R. May, *Strange Victory: Hitler's Conquest of France* (London, 2000).
44. O. V. Khlevniuk et al., eds, *Stalin i Kaganovich: perepiska 1931–1936* (Moscow, 2001), Doc. nos 352–3, pp. 347–8. My emphasis.
45. C. A. MacDonald, 'Deterrent Diplomacy: Roosevelt and the Containment of Germany, 1938–1940', in R. Boyce and E. M. Robertson, eds, *Paths to War* (London, 1989), p. 309.
46. Stone, *Militarization*, p. 216.

47. Samuelson, *Stalin's War Machine*, p. 124.
48. PRO, CAB 53/34, 'Comparison of the Strength of Great Britain with that of Certain other Nations', 12 November 1937.
49. PRO, CAB 55/12, British Chiefs of Staff report, 'Military Implications of German Aggression Against Czechoslovakia', 19 March 1938.
50. W. Wark, *The Ultimate Enemy: British Intelligence and Nazi Germany, 1933–39* (Oxford, 1985), pp. 202–40; and Jackson, *Nazi Menace*, pp. 298–387, set out the change in British and French outlooks in 1938–39 more fully.
51. *Documents on Germany Foreign Policy 1918–1945*, Series D Vol. I, no. 19, pp. 29–39; J. Wright and P. Stafford, 'Hitler, Britain, and the Hoßbach Memorandum', *Militärgeschichtliche Mitteilungen* 42 (1987), 77–123.
52. J. Noakes and G. Pridham, eds, *Nazism, 1919–45*, Vol. II (Exeter, 1988), pp. 710–12, and (on the Czech defences)722.
53. R. J. Overy, 'Germany and the Munich Crisis: A Mutilated Victory?', in E. Goldstein and I. Lukes, eds, *The Munich Crisis, 1938* (London, 1999), pp. 191–215.
54. See Overy, 'A Mutilated Victory?' and his 'Germany, "Domestic Crisis", and War in 1939', in *War Economy and Society*, pp. 205–32. On Hitler's statements about French and British rearmament and time see: W. Carr, *Arms, Autarky and Aggression* (New York, 1972), p. 106; Noakes and Pridham, *Nazism*, Vol. II, pp. 731–2 (for General Thomas on the arms race), 741, 764; and C. Burdick and H.-A. Jacobsen, eds, *The Halder War Diary, 1939–1942* (London, 1988), pp. 24 (14 August 1939), 30 (22 August 1939), 62–3 (27 September 1939).
55. US National Archives, secretary of war, Henry L. Stimson, to the president, 21 October 1941, Record Group 107, file 'White House Conference', Box 11; and D. Harrington, 'A Careless Hope: American Air Power and Japan 1941', *Pacific Historical Review* 48 (1979), 217–38.
56. N. Ike, ed., *Japan's Decision for War: Records of the 1941 Policy Conferences* (Stanford, CA, 1967), pp. 131, 225, 238.
57. M. Trachtenberg, ' "A Wasting Asset": American Strategy and the Shifting Nuclear Balance, 1949–54', *International Security* 7 (1988–89), 5–49.

17 Intelligence

John Ferris

What is Intelligence?

Intelligence is the collection and analysis of information by a power, to enable it to make maximum use of its resources against rivals and potential enemies. Intelligence is not a form of power but a means to guide its use, whether as a force multiplier, or by helping statesmen to understand their environment and options, and thus how to apply force or leverage, and against whom. Intelligence is a rational activity, but its significance, like rationality itself, is limited. Intelligence shows what can be understood in the context of what cannot be known. It commonly addresses several related questions, which can be answered only in probabilistic terms, hence the uncertainty of any answer must be multiplied by that of others. Subjects under observation defy their observer through denial and deception, and alter their behaviour in response to that of the observer. They use intelligence to guide their actions – and so affect the behaviour of the observer. The truth is not just out there; through the use of intelligence powers may gain greater knowledge of the international environment – and alter it.

The specialist literature on intelligence and the origins of the Second World War is small but rapidly growing. The works of the first generation of intelligence historians often were highly commendable, but were written before the principal state archives were opened and bear the shortcomings of pioneering efforts. The authors struggled to discover evidence, to make sense of fragments, to create a context and a chronology. By and large, their work focuses too much on estimates of the military capabilities of other states as opposed to the intentions of their leaders, and the views of middle-level bureaucrats as opposed to the leading statesmen. It is coloured by the liberal materialism of our time, and fails to examine the intellectual foundation for perceptions or to link intelligence systematically to policy. It treats diplomacy purely as a function of cryptology – it should be so simple. By necessity, these authors aimed at the reconstruction of specific data sets rather than general explanation, and sometimes distorted the influence of intelligence on particular events while missing its systematic import.

Meanwhile, the general literature on the origins of the Second World War has incorporated intelligence in different ways. Virtually every work written before 1974, ignored it, sometimes at crippling price. Many subsequent works, and all the most significant ones, incorporate it as well as possible, albeit constrained by partial access to the evidence.[1] A tiny portion of the literature makes full use of the currently available record. The record is now large. Over the past decade, a mass of documentation has been released by the British government, and French records captured by the Red Army in 1945 have recently been acknowledged and released by the Russian Federation. As recently as 1980, intelligence barely ranked as a topic worthy of academic study: new work was written in a vacuum, almost without benefit of scholarship, while the relevant documents in the public domain were limited and often hidden. Now, studies of intelligence are numerous, and specialists are almost swamped in documents. The intelligence record is good for the United States, Britain, France and Italy, tolerable for Germany, and illuminating if incomplete for the Soviet Union, Japan and the more significant secondary powers. Intelligence can and should be incorporated into the written history of the war's origins.

The significance of intelligence is none the less far from obvious. The most common failing is what might be called the Bloomsbury syndrome: the acceptance of anecdote instead of analysis. The most dangerous one is the assumption of influence: because secret intelligence was available to a decision-maker, it must have affected his decisions; or because intelligence provided invaluable information, access to its records must transform our understanding of events. Such arguments are not necessarily wrong, but they can be established only by testing the evidence. What really matters about intelligence is not what it is but what it does. Ideally, in order to determine the function of intelligence within the evolution of any event, its importance must be established in relation to all other relevant factors. This is often difficult to do. Most academic students of intelligence would probably accept that the effect of intelligence depends upon its interpretation in the context of a set of conditions that govern expectation and usability. Decision-makers are not mere prisoners of perception, unable to learn from error or to change their minds. But they are usually reluctant to change their minds, and tend to interpret bits of information on the basis of preconception. Frequently, intelligence is difficult to assess. Intelligence services usually provide masses of material, often utterly irrelevant, of unknown accuracy, or on a tangent of relevance, drawn from the hearsay of thirdhand sources. A pre-existing body of ideas shapes the assessment of such material. These range from broad factors like social, political or religious schools of thought, to official doctrines about specific topics or the eccentricities of individuals. This process is prone to produce well-known errors such as mirror-imaging and best-case or worst-case logic. Where an intelligence service knows better than the power it is analysing what line of policy it should follow, then a mistake by that power may lead the intelligence service into error. Good intelligence may be unusable or be used counter-productively or invalidate itself. If an intelligence service accurately determines another power's intentions and forestalls it, the result may be a new and unexpected policy. Intelligence can fail by succeeding, or vice versa.

Intelligence affects tactics more than strategy. Intelligence on another power's bargaining position can often be applied immediately, and its effect can be gauged with precision. Greater problems occur with the broader aspects of intelligence. The answer to the question 'what can X do?', varies with the questions 'why?', 'against whom?' and 'where?', and with calcula-tions about the outcome affected by the interaction of luck, types of tactics, styles of diplomacy and untested pieces of technology. To uncover inten-tions is an even more ambitious undertaking. Statesmen frequently do not know what they may wish to do in the future; even where they are now sure, they may change their minds or have them changed. Policy – especially for the long term – is often formulated and executed in a Byzantine fashion, with different departments of state pursuing different, sometimes contra-dictory, ends. Even when they pursue the same ends, they may differ over the means. In order to assess the policies of another power, an intelligence service must identify which factions or individuals influence its policies on any given issue; calculate the range of outcomes of the struggle between them; and guess at the probabilities of the possible results – which might not occur for years ahead. The result is that powers usually understand the intentions and capabilities of other powers only in particular instances and in a fragmentary way. Intelligence usually provides first-rate informa-tion on second-rate issues, and second-rate information on first-rate issues. It rarely provides unambiguous statements by leading statesmen as to what they will do on a specific topic at a given date, but rather the views of middle-level officials. With data incomplete and analysis conjectural, it is always possible to find enough doubtful detail to derail any unwelcome assessment. Intelligence can have a chaotic effect; it may not help effective action, although it often does so. But rarely it strikes events like lightning; and it is impossible to know the consequences until afterwards.

Intelligence and Policy-Making

Between 1933 and 1941, intelligence was fundamental to the formulation of policy by the Great Powers. It provided as much information as did any conventional source, and was used by decision-makers in a fashion complex even by the standards for the genre. But whereas officials in all powers used intelligence to achieve their policies, the men at the top enjoyed remarkable autonomy on the great issues of state. In 1938–39 Edouard Daladier dominated foreign and defence policy in France, as did Neville Chamber-lain in Britain. In 1940–41, Winston Churchill controlled British policy toward the United States and Japan, while Franklin Roosevelt played fast and loose with the Constitution in his exercise of power. Their control over national policy matched that of Hitler, Mussolini and Joseph Stalin. Nor did any state handle intelligence by committee. Everywhere, assessment was confused and politicised, and these general problems aggravated specific ones. In Britain and France, bureaucrats and politicians wielded intelligence in internal struggles over policy. If this was also true in Italy, the United States and Germany, where men used intelligence to curry favour at the top, it was even more so in the Soviet Union, on account of the purges. But the intuition, or rather personal quirks, of men at the top governed the use of intelligence: the paranoia of Stalin, the megalomania of Chamberlain and to a lesser degree of Churchill, the self-satisfaction of Mussolini and Roose-velt, the self-delusion and desire to gamble for the highest of stakes of Hitler and key decision-makers in Japan. These men all thought they knew one another better than did their own advisors. Chamberlain projected his thinking on to men who thought differently, and sabotaged official policy by pursuing a private one. Experience at Munich led him to think Hitler was a man he could work with; meetings with 'umbrella men' led Hitler to believe he could make worms turn at will. Both were wrong.

These statesmen used intelligence to understand their environment and to alter it, and relied upon their own intuition rather than the estimates of their professional analysts. They were affected by ideology, whether the liberal democratic forms of Britain, France and the United States; the variants of social Darwinism, militarism and racism in Italy, Germany and Japan; or the Marxism-Leninism and militarist ideas in the Soviet Union. It has become common in the West to denigrate the importance of ideology in politics. The triumph of liberalism and liberal realism have made these ways of thought seem natural – meta-ideological – and all competitors as idiotic. As a result, liberal materialists have unconsciously projected their ideas on to the minds of inter-war decision-makers. Yet ideologies, the world-views they reflect or produce, and the clash between them, have seldom affected international relations as much as in the inter-war period. Ideas shaped the policy of every power and their understanding of others. In their analyses, contemporary liberals used concepts of economic self-interest and national and institutional character; racists used demographic determinism, crude social Darwinism and generalisations about 'races'; while Marxist-Leninists used economic determinism and crude forms of class analysis. A perceptual gap prevented statesmen from understanding each other's policy, especially since foreigners found it hard to take Hitler's ideology seriously. He did. Granted, even with mutual understanding the aims of statesmen would have clashed; but in the world as it was, misunderstandings about basic policy triggered mutual misunderstanding over day-to-day diplomacy. These circumstances were deadly for statesmen pursuing policies of bluff and deterrence and delicate forms of manipulation and influence, which hinged on the precise delivery and comprehension of signals. As a result, deterrence failed. It required an act of imagination to step out of one's own ideological framework to understand what was happening. Few leaders attempted the exercise, and none succeeded for long.

Thus British statesmen, drawn from a class that believed it set standards for all, assumed that no one could want to overthrow the world they had made. They treated their outlook and behaviour as universal norms, which they were not. They came from a political culture characterised by a willingness to limit gains, avoid recklessness and assess others by the standards of gentlemen, and by faith in progress and reason. Liberals, some of them Christian idealists or its secular offspring, liberal internationalists, regarded war as a misfortune or a disaster. Their challenge was to assess statesmen like Adolf Hitler, whose behaviour was governed by militarism, social Darwinism and classical racism, who played at madness and liberalism, loved war, and were prepared to gamble with the fate of their country. The result was incomprehension. Britons sometimes focused more on determining whether a statesman was a gentleman than the nature of his foreign policy. When Lord Halifax reported to colleagues on his first meetings with Herman Göring and Hitler, he spent much time describing their dress, making style the man; he broke with these Germans when their behaviour convinced him they were bad. British statesmen, like French ones, were not cowards or fools, but they had lost some of their elders' hard-edged realism and hard-won expertise. They did not fail because their intelligence was bad; they used intelligence badly because they failed as statesmen. In intelligence, wisdom is to information as three is to one. At the same time, these decision-makers were influenced by realism. Among them were hard realists such as Sir Robert Vansittart, and some liberal militarists such as Churchill. Precisely because such men focused on will rather than material, they understood Hitler better than their contemporaries or many later students of appeasement. Most British decision-makers were materialists who emphasised capabilities and rejected any risk of bluff. If Britain was weak and endangered, they argued, it must be cautious. Wrong, retorted Vansittart, caution would only signal weakness and create danger. He was right.[2]

Britain's policy failures illustrate the importance of reliable knowledge and the dangers of misperception and poor intelligence. American and French statesmen made equal errors of assessment between 1936 and 1941; Soviet, Japanese and Italian statesmen made even greater ones. The master of mistakes was Hitler; he who asked 'what comes next?' when Chamberlain declared war in September 1939; who in 1940 refused to concentrate on smashing Britain when it stood alone, but chose instead to start a second front against the Soviet Union; who in December 1941 declared war on the

United States, perhaps the only thing that could have brought it into the European war – all because of his beliefs. Yet Hitler's errors were typical of the Nazi inner circle, all of whom grossly misunderstood decision-making in Britain, overestimating the power of aristocrats and royals. His foreign minister, Joachim Ribbentrop, thought a cabal of Americans, freemasons and Jews ran Britain. Ribbentrop turned against Britain in part because he interpreted the abdication crisis as an anti-German *coup*; Rudolf Hess flew to Britain during May 1941 in the belief that discussions with a peer of the realm could turn Whitehall. The memory of Russia's poor military performance of 1914–18, multiplied by ethnocentrism and racism, prevented most German decision-makers from understanding the danger of invading the Soviet Union. Germans, assuming the United States would join Britain during any great crisis, continually referred to an 'Anglo-American power-sphere' or 'a corporation USA/England' as though the two were one, and held they would lose nothing from forcing Washington to side with London. Japanese leaders made precisely the same miscalculation. The Axis states thus transformed their misconceptions into reality.[3] Racists, social Darwinists and Marxist-Leninists misconstrued liberals as thoroughly as the liberals misconstrued them.

Assessing Intentions and Capabilities

Preconceptions and images – ideas of how the world worked and states behaved – also shaped assessment. These phenomena were complex. Where liberal materialists gauge the strength of a people and its army by looking first at economic strength or gross national product, then institutions, tactics and weapons, most observers of the 1930s looked as much to gross national willpower and 'national characteristics' as to any technical factor.[4] A standard category in American analysis was 'psychologic'. In their combat estimates, American general staff officers were trained to include such matters as, 'Racial Characteristics. A calm, temperamental, stoical or excitable people; war-like or peacefully inclined; strong or weak; bold or timid; intrepid or easily discouraged.'[5] Ideas about national *'mentalité'* or character shaped French assessment of Germany. In the Soviet Union the characteristics of classes and the morale of foreigners when fighting a proletarian army shaped military estimates; in Nazi Germany, estimates were shaped by the assumed influence of race.[6] Nor was this just a military phenomenon: when gauging the effect of their policies on a people and its leaders, statesmen too relied on ideas of national characteristics, what in August 1939 Ribbentrop termed 'his knowledge of the English psychology'.[7] Ideas about national character stemmed from observation of behaviour during sports, work or war, from the stereotypes of history and literature, from racist theories. They were surprisingly international: French, German and British ideas about Russian national character, for example, were similar, though not identical. Such stereotypes about nations (or class, gender and generations) have some explanatory power, but are acutely susceptible to over-generalisation and useless in predicting behaviour. They are also prone to errors of ethnocentrism; that is, the tendency to treat one's behaviour as the solution to universal problems, and shade all too easily into the territory of racism. None the less in the inter-war years they frequently led statesmen into specific, and often misleading, predictions in the absence of evidence, and to action based on these errors. An examination of two cases will illuminate these issues: the image of Britain as a power, and of the quality of Japanese armed forces.

Foreign perceptions of British power and policy stemmed from history, including a selective understanding of its military performance between 1580 and 1815. When condemning British leaders in 1939, Mussolini said: 'These men are not made of the same stuff as the Francis Drakes and the other magnificent adventurers who created the empire. These, after all, are the tired sons of a long line of rich men, and they will lose their empire.' Conversely in 1940, his foreign minister, Count Ciano, thought the British attack on the French fleet at Oran in July 1940 'proves that the fighting spirit of His Britannic Majesty's fleet is quite alive, and still has the aggressive ruthlessness of the captains and pirates of the seventeenth century.'[8] Foreigners believed Britain was always selfish and treacherous, but either strong or decadent – with nothing in between. These views were international and longstanding: in 1895 Kaiser Wilhelm II noted, 'England will at best only seek to exploit us and then leave us in the lurch at the opportune moment'; in 1935 a German ambassador mentioned 'the dreaded realism of the British'.[9] However unflattering, these views respected British power and its Realpolitik. Another set of images about Britain focused on its wealth, and therefore its weakness. In 1934 the Italian ambassador to Britain, Count Grandi, described the country as no longer a bulldog but 'a hippopotamus ... slow, fat, heavy, somnolent, weak in eyesight and even weaker in nerve'.[10] Images of Britain tended toward two poles – 'perfidious Albion' and a 'nation of shopkeepers' – and observers jumped from one to the other with the ease of exotic dancers. Mussolini thus explained the change in British policy following Hitler's annexation of Bohemia and Moravia: 'We must not forget that the British are readers of the Bible and that they combine mercantilism with mysticism. Now the latter prevails, and they are capable of going into action.'[11] These images produced a paradoxical and generally overlooked problem for British statesmen between 1815 and 1945. They were expected to be masters of machiavellianism or else the most decadent of rentiers, when in fact they were neither. British decision-makers had never been so cynical or venal as foreigners imagined. Yet failure to meet their expectations, or even actions which merely seemed inexplicable against them, were deemed perfidy in disguise, or evidence of rot. The problem was magnified because foreigners found British policy harder to fathom than that of any other power, in part because for generations Whitehall aimed to keep foreigners guessing, while so much of its policy hinged on deterrence. Unfortunately, the inter-working of British action and foreign archetypes obscured the signals on which deterrence rested, while failure to behave according to archetype produced cognitive dissonance. Hitler and Mussolini entirely misunderstood British policy between 1935 and 1938, fueling rage and mistaken policy between 1938 and 1941. The intelligence failures most crucial in shaping the road to the Second World War in Europe were those made about Britain.

During the 1930s, Germany, Italy and Japan confronted Britain while seriously misreading its reactions. Hitler thought the British Empire was in decline because it lacked population and ruthlessness – 45 million Caucasians ruling ten times their number of non-Aryans but unwilling to do so through fire and will.[12] Mussolini dismissed Britain because of its age and wealth – 'plutocratic and therefore selfishly conservative'; 'No one over 40 years liked to go to war. The decisive factor, finally, had been that England, as a result of the revival of her trade in the last few years, had become extraordinarily satiated, and satiated people did not like to risk anything.'[13] Foreigners measured British strength by the self-confidence of its rulers; they moved against it because they believed it safe to do so. 'The British Empire already is an old man,' said one officer of the Imperial Japanese Navy (IJN) in 1934. After Munich, leaders of other democratic powers endorsed the stereotypes. Daladier called Britain a 'frail reed' and Roosevelt complained it 'cringed like a coward'.[14] British leaders seemed uncertain, so their opponents thought Britain weak. In August 1939, no foreigner expected Britain to do what it did – fight unless its aims were met; in these circumstances, it had no choice but to act. Given the effect of its image, only a resolute policy – even of bluff and recklessness – would have served, and the sooner the better. Nothing would better have suited British interests in 1935 than to treat the Italians as they did the French fleet at Oran five years later. To borrow a phrase from Franklin Roosevelt, Britain had nothing to fear but fear itself.

It is commonly thought that western assessments of Japanese military forces were inaccurate, the result of racism. This is not so. Some foreign observers did claim that the Japanese suffered from poor eyesight or balance, which affected their military capacity, but western intelligence did not allow vulgar or scientific racism to dominate its assessments. The problem was not racism, but ethnocentrism; western observers treated their own approach to war as the universal basis for measuring military value. They gauged the quality of Japanese forces by their ability to fight western forces in western conditions rather than their own ability to engage the IJN or the Imperial Japanese Army (IJA) in East Asia. These forms of military ethnocentrism were the single greatest cause of western military intelligence failures, closely followed by the way foreigners linked assessments of Japanese combat potential to 'national character'. As Captain Bonner Fellers, later a senior intelligence officer under Douglas MacArthur, stated in 1935: 'The psychology of the Japanese soldier is the psychology of his people.'[15] For a combination of genetic and environmental factors, the Japanese were regarded as lacking aptitude for machines and the capacity for innovation, while having great endurance, obedience to hierarchy and organisational ability. Air and naval officers prized the first set of qualities far above the second, which led them to underrate Japanese pilots and sailors. Army officers prized both sets of qualities, which led them to respect the IJA's infantry but to criticise its artillery and armour.[16] To western observers, Japanese infantry and fighter pilots formed the opposite extremes of the spectrum; the former admirable, the latter incompetent, and for the same reasons. Observers drew less consistently from other sets of qualities: most saw the Japanese as well organised but prisoners to their preparations, unable to learn quickly or improvise, lacking individual initiative, courageous but prone to hysteria under stress. It should be added that a substantial body of Japanophiles downplayed such views and emphasised positive ones, seeing Japanese as uniquely quick to learn and to overcome errors.

Opinions differed about each Japanese service, and every estimate included negative and positive comments.[17] Foreign observers regarded the IJA with respect, though its reputation sagged from 1932–36 as the result of its mixed performance in China. French observers in 1931 declared the army to be an '*outil parfaitement dressé*' – a perfectly honed weapon – but they were less impressed by 1937.[18] Observers regarded the IJN as large but not quite first – or second – rate. Estimates of Japanese air forces were negative, though they rose before the Pacific War, when experts (but not commanders) began to rate them as good by western standards.[19] Assessment varied by country and institution. French and British observers were unusually positive about the IJA, and about services they had trained, the British about Japanese naval air forces, the French about Japanese army air forces; American and German officers in China, who identified with the country, were more negative about the IJA than were their colleagues in Japan. Western observers overstated the fragility of Japanese national morale and underrated their ability to adapt; they thought Japan weaker and more cautious than was the case, and underestimated the offensive power it could wield out of its area, although everyone recognised its defensive capacity at home. Yet western observers and staff officers were no less accurate in their assessment of Japanese military forces than European ones: they made comparable errors about Italy and greater ones about the Soviet Union. The errors stemmed partly from inaccurate preconceptions, but also from Japan's success in hiding its most modern equipment, especially aircraft. Japanese leaders were even less accurate in estimating their own power. But the effect of these estimates was far from simple. German soldiers rated the IJA lower than did their British or French counterparts, and Hitler applied racist thinking to military analysis more than other statesmen, but for strategic reasons he allied with Japan. The British army had good intelligence on Japan, analysed it extremely well, and had it accepted at high levels – but it was ignored in Malaya. So too with the American army and the Philippines, although in this case the intelligence and assessment were less good. The Royal Navy's mediocre assessment of its Japanese counterpart was saved by system and circumstances; its strategy, resting on bean counting of warships and a rejection of best-case planning, was not distorted by its underestimate of Japanese quality.[20] Similarly, the United States navy, with one exception – the failure to realise that Japan might dare to mount a surprise attack on the American main fleet at home. The United States and even more so Britain assessed Japanese air power poorly, which presaged disaster. Decision-makers thought they held an edge in air power over Japan, and assumed Japan's morale to be uniquely vulnerable to attack by air; they based their policies of deterrence and defence upon these assumptions, which betrayed them.[21] Otherwise, the errors about Japanese military power were irrelevant at the highest levels in London and Washington, where the great mistake was deeming Japan's statesmen too cautious to risk a war simultaneously against Britain and the United States, because it must lose such a conflict. While the latter assumption proved correct, the former was wrong.

Image and estimate shaped the policy of every state in complex ways. Between 1933 and 1941, far more than in 1905–14, decision-makers everywhere misunderstood the fundamentals of power and policy. German and to a lesser degree Italian strength was exaggerated, that of everyone else underrated, especially Japanese, Soviet and American. There were many reasons for this. Some stemmed from technical matters shaped by fallacies such as mirror-imaging. Intelligence of a statistical sort on GDP or numbers of battalions was fairly easy to collect, not so on qualitative or technological issues or – even more difficult – on how far and fast a state could rearm. The French overestimated the size of the German army because they misconstrued the calibre of its paramilitary formations, just as the British overrated the pace of Luftwaffe expansion because they assumed it must act like the Royal Air Force. British and French observers misread the evidence on the German army's ideas about operations because they could not believe Germans would wish to fight that way, or that such an approach could defeat them; German observers similarly misjudged the British Fighter Command. Again, the politicisation of intelligence had a consistently ironic effect. Hitler and Mussolini mistook military power more than any other statesmen. They got their own forces wrong because their subordinates deceived them. But British and French commanders deceived their own masters, overestimating their weaknesses as well as German power, which reinforced the Axis miscalculations.[22] Some failures of assessment stemmed from the interplay of images. British and French estimates rested on a stereotype of Germans that exaggerated their efficiency. When assessing combat power, Germans, Italians and Japanese fetishised willpower and spirit, assuming their races had both, but not their opponents. They underrated the significance of economics and organisation, and misunderstood American and Soviet strength. These failures in the estimation of power contributed in 1935–38 to uncertainty in Paris and London and to aggression and bluff in Rome and Berlin. In 1939 they contributed to the way Germany, Britain and France, and in 1941 Germany, the Soviet Union, Japan, the United States and Britain, all misconstrued each other's intentions and power. Thus military intelligence failures led them to enter wars of a kind none expected.

Diplomatic Intelligence and Codebreaking

Between 1933 and 1941, diplomatic intelligence was higher in quality than ever before and more widely distributed and more competitive. Here, spies were as good a source as any other. The mutual incomprehension on big issues could best be penetrated by acquiring documents from other states, through agents in place or by rifling the diplomatic bags of foreign governments while in transit. Despatches say more than telegrams. Codebreaking illuminated only a part of the picture: few leaders bared their heart over the telegraph or international telephone lines. The best documented codebreaking bureaus, the British Government Code & Cypher School (GC&CS), Germany's *Forschungsamt* and *Pers* Z, and the American army Signals Intelligence Service, provided material as valuable as that obtained by Italy and the Soviet Union through spies and document stealing. Human intelligence services varied in quality, with the United States weakest, the Soviet Union strongest, and the rest fairly equal. The average service was good, the best great.[23] Despite its later failures, during the 1930s the British Secret Intelligence Service (SIS) performed ably in western Europe, China and the Middle East, maintaining the quality of its networks while concentrating on procuring documents. The German *Abwehr* performed comparably well in western and central Europe, using Ukrainian nationalists, for example, against Poland. Through consuls, traitors and work with anti-colonial forces, Japanese intelligence learned what it wanted to know before 1942. Through masterly method, the French *Deuxième Bureau* illuminated its main target, Germany, as did Polish and Czechoslovak agencies. Italian intelligence did well against Britain and France. The greatest hoard of gems was acquired for Moscow by ideologues and mercenaries. Soviet intelligence acquired copies – sometimes in multiple form – of British telegrams and despatches from four sources in the Foreign Office and also from the agent who penetrated British establishments for Italian intelligence.[24] During 1939, Soviet intelligence had remarkable access to the secrets of all the Great Powers. It penetrated the German embassies in Warsaw and Tokyo (and thus also Japanese decision-making), the British embassies in Rome and Paris, and the Foreign Office's Communications Department; and probably acquired key correspondence from most embassies in Moscow through black bag jobs and chancery servants turned spies. Anglo-French negotiators in Moscow stayed in local hotels where their private discussions were no doubt bugged. Intelligence has shaped few events as much as Soviet decision-making on the Germano-Soviet Pact.

Less is known about diplomatic codebreaking. The cryptanalytical and intelligence personnel at the GC&CS rose from 80 to 200 members between 1934 and 1939, which was roughly similar to the expansion of the *Forschungsamt* and *Pers* Z, while in 1938–39 the Soviet OGPU's code-breaking section had about 100 members and that of the US army, 22 to 25.[25] Each week, on average, the GC&CS gave Whitehall 74 solutions of encoded telegrams from foreign governments, and read important diplomatic systems of perhaps 20 smaller powers as well as the United States, France and Japan. It had no access to German systems or to the diplomatic ones of the Soviet Union and Italy, but it did succeed against Italian military and colonial codes, some Red Army and Comintern traffic, and the military messages of Japan and many smaller states. The documentation on German codebreaking is less thorough – a sample comprising 0.0066 per cent of the *Forschungsamt's* output between 2 September 1938 and 2 September 1939. It provided more reports than the GC&CS, perhaps 604 per week in 1938–39, but most were intercepted telephone calls, something Britain did, but not through the GC&CS, or minor telegrams which the latter would not have bothered publishing.[26] Together, the *Forschungsamt* and *Pers* Z seem to have been less good at diplomatic codebreaking than the GC&CS, providing fewer solutions and cracking middle-level codes of only two major powers, Japan and Italy, though their success against most states in the Balkans was fundamental to the diplomatic battleground on which Germany chose to fight. American codebreakers beat just one major state, Japan, which in turn had little success against any great power. Italy read much military and some diplomatic traffic of most states in the Balkans and many in Latin America, Spain, the United States, France and Britain – more or less at the GC&CS's standard. Probably France did slightly better than Germany or the United States, though worse than Britain or Italy: it read some Italian diplomatic traffic, some minor British traffic, and broke the codes of Spain, Eire and Austria. The success of the Soviet Union is uncertain, although it probably rated above France and conceivably led the world in diplomatic codebreaking. Poland broke Germany's supposedly unbreakable encrypting machine, Enigma; other small states no doubt had successes.[27]

Other practices matched codebreaking in significance. Although every
state rifled the bags of foreign powers and tapped the telephones of foreign
embassies, Italy had a spectacular ability to seize documents, and Germany to exploit international telephone lines crossing its territory. The
Forschungsamt's ability to monitor telephone conversations to and from
diplomats in Berlin and on the European trunk lines that ran through its
territory, produced a triumph of communication intelligence. These technical successes, however, were not always useful to policy. Hitler did not
like to read telephone intercepts (as against solutions of telegrams), while
Göring, the *Forschungsamt's* master, did not freely share its output with his
rival, Ribbentrop, nor let his service cooperate with that of the foreign
minister. More generally, success in communications intelligence varied
with a power's ability to intercept and solve the relevant traffic. The Soviet
Union could intercept only traffic sent to and from embassies in Moscow or
on cables crossing its territory, weakening the value of its codebreaking
capabilities, as occurred for similar reasons to the United States and to Italy.
Britain controlled the bulk of intercontinental cables, giving the GC&CS
the same position in the world as the *Forschungsamt* had in Europe. These
two states appear to have gained the most communication intelligence in
the 1930s.

Security against espionage also varied. Far and away the strongest was
the Soviet Union, which was protected by ferocious counter-intelligence,
purges at home and great cryptography abroad; then Japan, with powerful
counter-espionage but poor cryptography, and Germany, where the situation was reversed; then perhaps Italy, with Britain, France and the United
States at the bottom of the list. The importance of insecurity is hard to
determine. In broad terms it is not always a problem, as when the credibility of a power's bargaining position must be signalled and believed to
have effect. Insecurity is a problem only when a power is bluffing, mistaken,
uncertain or fearful of pursuing a policy another power can disrupt, as was
true for the *status quo* powers of the 1930s. During 1939, Soviet penetration of British establishments shaped its reaction to a poor offer from
Whitehall and an attractive one from Hitler – indeed, it helped the Soviet
Union to procure the German offer. Yet security can be too much of a good
thing. The Soviet Union hid the virtual doubling of its military in size after
September 1939, which contributed to Germany and Britain underestimat-
ing its strength in divisions by 50 per cent in 1941. Security thus sapped the
deterrent posture Stalin thought he had established; he knew his state was
strong and assumed others did so, too. They did not, although Hitler might
well have attacked even had he known the real strength of the Red Army.

In the balance of intelligence and insecurity, each power had an edge
over some rival, led the world somewhere, and was beaten by another
power. Generally, each was stronger in intelligence than security, in attack
over defence, although the Soviet shield was formidable and the *katana*

dull. The United States and Japan stood at the bottom of the league table and the Soviet Union ruled the roost, but otherwise the intelligence services of the Great Powers, Czechoslovakia and Poland, were broadly similar in quality. In part, parity occurred because the central issue between 1937 and 1939 was central Europe, where a regional intelligence service could outclass a major one based outside the region, and the traffic of small states could betray the position of a Great Power whose own cryptography was impenetrable. (Through this means, Germany followed the details of the British strategy of guarantees in eastern Europe in the spring of 1939.)[28] In central Europe British intelligence was weaker than anywhere else and the German stronger. Again, the power of intelligence is difficult to define. If the Soviet Union led the world in collection, usually this stream died in dust; during the purges, spies abroad lost contact with their Soviet masters; in 1941 excellent intelligence did not save Stalin from error; only in 1939 did the Soviet Union use intelligence well, to serve a poor policy.[29] When combined with politicisation and paranoia at home and the effect of images, the stream of intelligence on British policy blinded the Soviet leadership to a greater danger. British intelligence, while less successful against the Soviet Union than vice versa, arguably aided policy as much. Japan was easily outweighed, yet in 1941 its foes failed and fell because Japan needed only simple knowledge for its attack, while the knowledge required for defence against it was hard to collect and harder to interpret. Altogether, diplomatic intelligence was of high quality, and balanced fairly equally between the Great Powers. As a whole it did not work systematically in favour of any one power against another, although it did have that effect in many specific instances.

The Intelligence Duels

This balance of intelligence can be seen as a series of individual duels, in which most countries defeated Japan and the United States, the Soviet Union whipped all comers except perhaps Poland, and Italy beat the *status quo* powers and smaller states but not its fellow revisionists. Generally, Great Powers defeated several lesser ones and small states were beaten by two or more Great Powers, with the Turks, Yugoslavs, Spanish Nationalists and Republicans defeated by most. This approach, however, is too linear to explain how knowledge affected the dynamics of international relations. In other words, the duels must be seen in systematic terms, where the result – or just the process – of each affected all the rest. In the 1920s, the revisionist powers were weak and isolated, most states supported the *status quo*, and the liberal order was backed with arms. France and Britain held the strategic initiative in diplomacy, determining the nature of the contest and thrusting the burden of uncertainty and the need to make the first move on to others, who had to guess their intentions and how to influence them. In such circumstances, revisionists might gain little from superior intelligence and lose with mere parity; even with poor intelligence, *status quo* powers could still pick the ground and the time to fight, at worst losing the occasional trick. With good intelligence they could see the cards in their opponents' hands, after having picked the game and the deck. From 1933, conversely, the liberal order became less cohesive and militarily weaker, the beneficiaries of the *status quo* declined to support it or each other. The balance of power ceased to work because no one tried to make it do so. Only the revisionists played power politics and they aimed to wreck the balance. They grew in strength and in number – Germany, Italy, the Soviet Union and Japan. Although the revisionists did not work closely together, when one shook the *status quo*, they all gained. It was easier for them to shake the system than for the *status quo* states to cooperate in its support. All states played a lone hand; even mere alignments were rare and weak. The system ceased to shelter its members, offering little support to any defender or impediment to any attacker. The power of the stronger party in any relationship or the system as a whole was multiplied, because the weak stood alone. The revisionists might use the most opportunistic of tactics and pursue any bilateral relationships they wished, because they wished to destroy the system; the *status quo* powers did not, and thus their tactics were constrained and their policies tangled. They searched for a diplomatic solution when there was only a strategic one, through the application of power. Each *status quo* power also faced a particular dilemma. The United States had little ability to affect events. French leaders feared they held a losing hand, doubting their ability to hold off Germany without foreign support, unsure how to meet its pressure, forced on to the defensive in central Europe, an area hard to defend, and trying to square the strategic circle through multilateral diplomacy. The British pursued an active and ambitious policy, aiming to solve every problem in the world at once through multilateral and liberal internationalist means. Until 1937, they could neither achieve this policy nor abandon it. They found themselves constantly responding to the initiative of the revisionist powers, defending their own interests while jettisoning those of the international system. British and French statesmen were thrown into uncertainty, sometimes believing every action had such unpalatable consequences that the easiest solution was to take none at all, on other occasions willing to prime the pump of better relations with Germany and Italy by paying them for the privilege of starting a bargaining process.

These problems were structural and psychological: they centred on intelligence or its absence. A reactive power needs better intelligence than a strong and active one. It must know the active power's intentions, the latter merely its own mind. This situation breeds tendencies such as uncertainty, guessing as to the active party's aims and the means to influence them, and worst-case planning. Between 1933 and 1939 the *status quo* powers needed outstanding intelligence. They did not have it. The GC&CS offered Britain little on the policy of Italy, Germany and the Soviet Union, and the SIS little on the Soviet Union and Japan. French military intelligence was good, but much of this advantage was lost to politicisation, while its diplomatic intelligence was weak until 1939. The United States had expertise against only Japan. Intelligence was slow to help *status quo* statesmen understand Hitler's and Mussolini's intentions and their willingness to act on them. They had to guess at these matters and did so badly; fears that they might guess wrong or bluff too far helped to queer their pitch. The inability to be sure of Hitler's intentions until 1939 or of Mussolini's until 1940 crippled decision-making and let Germans and Italians manipulate France and Britain. Britain assessed far more accurately the aims of Japan, the one revisionist state whose diplomatic traffic the GC&CS still mastered; had Britain penetrated Italian codes in 1937–38 as in 1923–26, Mussolini could not so easily have manipulated Chamberlain. France got Italy right only at the turn of 1938–39, when codebreaking demonstrated Italian hostility.[30] Intuition and translations of foreign newspapers gave Hitler and Mussolini a better picture of policy than their opponents received through secret sources – of Stalin in 1941 as much as Daladier in 1938. The limits to intelligence were part of the problem of the *status quo* powers – and an improvement would have mattered; it might have been the only means to tear blinkers from eyes when vision still mattered, and to let statesmen understand how far deterrence and concession could or did work. Instead, they stood divided and on the defensive, weaker than the revisionist powers in intelligence and security, unable to choose the ground of battle, and made to play to their weaknesses. The key battleground became central Europe where the position of the *status quo* powers was weakened and that of the revisionists strengthened because the imbalance of power multiplied that of intelligence. The revisionist powers often forced the *status quo* powers to play on their ground, against their strong suit, sometimes in a contest where one trick took the game – most notably Germany in 1938–39, and the Soviet Union in 1939. They could win simply by disrupting the *status quo*, somehow, somewhere. France and Britain had to defend specific interests without upsetting the whole.

Intelligence and the Coming of the War

Between 1933 and 1941, diplomatic intelligence shone most on secondary issues, but still illuminated the heights. In 1936–39, Germans and Italians easily monitored French and British relations with central and south-east

European powers, casting light on the diplomatic battlefield from all sides. During the Munich crisis, the *Forschungsamt* listened as the highest Czech leaders broke their hearts and the secrets of Prague, Paris and London over the telephone; it learned how foreign counsels were divided, that Britain and France aimed to avoid war and were pushing Czechoslovakia to capitulation. This material was immensely valuable. It compromised Britain's policy of keeping everyone guessing, and the credibility of France. It did not change German policy, but reinforced its thrust by enabling Hitler and Ribbentrop to realise they were winning and might gain more by a further turn of the screw.[31] During 1939, the traffic of Balkan states and the telephone calls of ambassadors in Berlin and Rome guided German and Italian diplomacy (the latter aided by access to confidential British and French documents), although it also led them into conflicting policies and internal disagreements. It led Hitler and Ribbentrop to think that Britain was bluffing, that determined action could break the log-jam in central Europe and the *status quo* in the continent without risk of war in the West. It led Ciano, Göring (and perhaps some of Ribbentrop's subordinates) towards different action and a cacophony of mixed messages, which reinforced Whitehall's belief that Germany was bluffing. Throughout, German success against low-security telegrams or telephone calls showed the mood of diplomats and statesmen. A few hours advance warning of foreign overtures enabled Hitler or Ribbentrop to prepare an effective response, something to which Whitehall attached real (or unreal) significance.[32] Intelligence was fundamental to the diplomatic tactics of Germany and Italy; less so to their strategy.

Between 1933 and 1938, conversely, the GC&CS's solutions of Japanese traffic steered Britain through dangerous water. Aided by the SIS, it revealed that, propaganda aside, the Axis was a fiction. These services uncovered the secret relations between Japan, Germany and Italy, showing clearly, if not comprehensively, the aims behind the Anti-Comintern Pact.[33] Whitehall used this intelligence to deduce the intentions of the hostile powers and their factions, no mean feat, given the confusion in these relations and the obscurity of the Pact. The Japanese and German factions that promoted the Pact did so to confuse other powers. The effect was contrary to their intentions. By monitoring discussions about it, Britain could determine the relations between Japan, Germany and Italy. In late 1938 solutions of Japanese traffic showed that Germany was pressing Japan to turn the Pact from a defensive alignment against the Soviet Union into an offensive alliance against Britain. This news sparked an anguished analysis of GC&CS solutions by the Foreign Office, and helped it understand Hitler's aims.[34] Although Britain lost access to major Japanese diplomatic systems in February 1939, it had a powerful means to analyse Japanese intentions through reports from other sources of the debate in Tokyo about Hitler's offer. This shaped its policy toward Japan, Germany and the Soviet

Union. The United States, the Soviet Union and Germany possessed similar information. Although the evidence is lacking, knowledge of this Japanese debate may well have confirmed to Hitler that Tokyo could not meet his needs. In turn Stalin was made aware of imminent danger and opportunity, and thus proceeded to the Nazi-Soviet Non-Aggression Pact – although it was only one strand of the intelligence available to Germany, and an even smaller part of the puzzle for the Soviet Union.

These successes were significant. There were others, yet at the highest of levels intelligence mattered less than incomprehension. Diplomatic intelligence aids bargaining and knowledge. It is easier to use it than to learn from it. In the circumstances, the effect was systematic: fighting on their ground and knowing their minds, the revisionist powers had better intelligence and acted on it opportunistically, while the *status quo* powers, ruled by uncertainty, were inferior in information and could use it less freely. In the winter of 1938/39, lessons derived from Munich combined with good and bad intelligence led British and French decision-makers to take a firm line, the only one justifiable in strategic terms, however poor its execution. But learning was neither easy nor linear. Much data and experience were needed to change any mind on any issue. Meanwhile, rivals at home and abroad also learned from experience, and changed their behaviour too, and so all lessons learned were invalidated before they could be applied. At the start of 1939, a flood of reports, including deliberate disinformation, enabled Paris and London to understand Hitler's aims; and Germans to think Britain hostile after Munich, when it was not, and act to make it so. Britons and Germans drew the same lesson, that if pushed to the limit, the other power would back down. Within this framework they interpreted intelligence, sent mixed messages, deployed leverage, and wrecked the other's application of these insights in the weeks before 3 September 1939. For equally dialectical reasons, in August 1939 Soviet policy stunned Britain, while Italian policy had the same effect on Hitler; 1941 was equally full of surprises, when Germany wrong-footed Stalin, and Japan caught out Roosevelt and Churchill.

One can reconstruct the logic behind decisions only by examining the data available to decision-makers. In the period 1933–41, this mirror illuminates the policy of statesmen with unique clarity, but the greatest reflection is of the state system. Intelligence was better than between 1904–14 and more widely distributed and used. Yet more large unintended events occurred before the Second World War than before the First. In the decisions for war, only Italy in 1940 and Germany and Japan in 1941 acted as they intended (though not with the hoped for results). In 1941 Americans, British and Soviets were more surprised than any leaders had been in 1914, while on 1 September 1939 neither Hitler nor Chamberlain expected war with each other. Reason, *raison d'état* and intelligence were poor guides for these statesman, because they viewed events and played the game so differently. Statesmen thought the state system was a machine where all one needed to create an effect was to pull a lever. In fact, the machine was baroque and broken. There were more levers to be pulled than in 1914, but with less certain effect and more people pulling away. Statesmen thought they were all playing a game with one set of rules; instead, each was simultaneously playing a different game with the same pieces. All thought they understood the world; in fact none did. The expectation of certainty proved to be a source of incomprehension. The more they thought they understood events, the more mistaken they were; the more they trusted their intuition or intelligence, the more misguided they proved to be. There was a striking correlation between good intelligence and failed policy between 1939 and 1941: Germany and Britain in 1939, the Soviet Union, Britain and the United States in 1941. Intelligence was not a tool for these statesmen: it was a broken saw whiplashing across the system. The path leading to the Second World War was strewn with accidents – and yet had they not happened, ultimately such a war still would have occurred because of differences between the interests of states. Interests and power were factors of the first order, with ideology, images and intelligence in the second rank. Yet the latter shaped the outbreak of the Second World War more than did the former. These events were not produced by rational policy informed by perfect knowledge. Instead, they stemmed from a series of accidents, which were rooted in mutual incomprehension. Ideology and image created incomprehension, which intelligence could not overcome; its success in acquiring data mattered less than its failure to penetrate preconception, or to help intention overcome accident. Intelligence most shaped the origins of the Second World War through its failure. A war that should have occurred by intention, did so by accident.

Notes

1. D. C. Watt, *How War Came: The Immediate Origins of the Second World War, 1938–1939* (London, 1989); G. Weinberg, The *Foreign Policy of Hitler's Germany*, Vol. II, *Starting World War Two, 1937–1939* (Chicago, 1980); W. Murray, *The Change in the European Balance of Power: The Road to Ruin* (Princeton, 1984), R. A. C. Parker, *Chamberlain and Appeasement* (London, 1993).
2. J. R. Ferris, ' "Indulged in all Too Little"? Vansittart, Intelligence and Appeasement', *Diplomacy & Statecraft* 6 (1995), 122–75.
3. H. H. Herwig, *Politics of Frustration: The United States in German Naval Planning, 1889–1941* (Toronto, 1976), pp. 196–97, 212–13; W. Deist, M. Messerschmidt, H. Volkmann and W. Wette, *Germany and the Second World War*, Vol. I, *The Build-up of German Aggression* (Oxford, 1990), pp. 559; J. Morley, ed., *Japan's Road to the Pacific War: The Final Confrontation* (New York, 1994), pp. 197, 215.

4. Useful accounts of military estimates and their impact on policy include J. Maiolo, *The Royal Navy and Nazi Germany* (London, 1998); P. Jackson, *France and the Nazi Menace: Intelligence and Policy Making 1933–1939* (Oxford, 2000); M. Alexander, 'Did the Deuxième Bureau Work? The Role of Intelligence in French Defence Policy and Strategy, 1919–1938', *Intelligence and National Security* 6 (1991), 293–333; and Antony Adamthwaite, 'French Military Intelligence and the Coming of War, 1935–1939', in C. Andrew and J. Noakes, eds, *Intelligence and International Relations* (Exeter, 1987), pp. 191–208; and the essays in E. R. May, ed., *Knowing One's Enemies: Intelligence Assessment before the Two World Wars* (Princeton, 1984); and W. Murray and A. Millett, eds., *Calculations: Net Assessments and the Coming of World War II* (New York, 1992). Works addressing the issue of 'national characteristics' in estimates include A. Barros, 'Le Deuxième Bureau évalue les forces allemandes: les dangers du sport et de l'éducation physique 1919–1928', *Guerres Mondiales et Conflits Contemporains* (forthcoming), and 'Finding Weakness in Strength and Strength in Weakness: French Intelligence and the German Air Menace, 1919–1928', in P. Jackson and J. S. Siegel, eds, *Intelligence and Statecraft: the Use of and Limits of Intelligence in International Society, 1870–1970* (forthcoming); and J. R. Ferris, ' "Worthy of Some Better Enemy?" The British Assessment of the Imperial Japanese Army, 1919–1941, and the Fall of Singapore', *The Canadian Journal of History* 28 (1993), pp. 223–56, and 'Student and Master: Britain, Japan, Airpower and the Fall of Singapore, 1920–1941', in B. Farrell, ed., *Singapore Sixty Years On* (Singapore, 2000); C. Bell, 'The Royal Navy, War Planning and Intelligence Between the Wars', in Jackson and Siegel, eds, *Intelligence and Statecraft*; and A. Best, *British Intelligence and the Japanese Challenge in Asia, 1919–41* (London, 2002).

5. Center for United States Military History, Carlisle Barracks, Carlisle, Pennsylvania, USA, AWCCA File 315-3 (hereafter AWCCA, etc.), United States Army War College, 1926 course, memorandum 18 January 1926, 'Intelligence Features of Specific War Plans'.

6. Service Historique de l'Armée de Terre, Château de Vincennes (hereafter SHAT etc.), 7N 2484, 'Le Deuxième Bureau, Son Role-Son Organisation-Son Fonctionement', 31 January 1927.

7. *I Documenti Diplomatici Italiani*, Ottava Serie: 1935–1939, Vol. XIII (Rome, 1953), p. 1.

8. M. Muggeridge, ed, *Ciano's Diary, 1939–1943* (London, 1947), pp. 9–10, 274.

9. N. Rich and M. H. Fisher, *Holstein Papers* (Cambridge, 1961), p. 551; N. Rich, *Friedrich von Holstein: Politics and Diplomacy in the Era of Bismarck and Wilhelm II* (Cambridge, 1965), p. 438; *Documents on German Foreign Policy* (hereafter *DGFP*), Series D, Vol. I, p. 1168.

10. M. Knox, *Mussolini Unleashed: Politics and Strategy in Fascist Italy's Last War* (Cambridge, 1982), p. 34.

11. Muggeridge, *Ciano's Diary*, p. 51.

12. *DGFP*, D, Vol. 1, p. 33; for broader accounts of German perceptions of Britain, see G. Waddington, 'Hassgegner: German Views of Great Britain in the Later 1930s', *History* 81 (1996), 22–39; Deist et al., *Germany and the Second World War*, Vol. I, pp. 548–9, 595–604, 627–32, 642–3, 711.

13. *DGFP*, D, Vol. I, pp. 3–5; R. Mallett, *The Italian Navy and Fascist Expansionism, 1935–1940* (London, 1998), p. 150.
14. Memorandum by United States Naval Attaché, Tokyo, 22 June 1934, Confidential US Diplomatic Post Records, Japan, Part 3, Section A, microfilm reel 18; Watt, *How War Came*, pp. 139; Jackson, *Nazi Menace*, p. 32.
15. Hoover Institution on War, Revolution and Peace, Bonner Fellers Papers, Box 1, Memorandum by Fellers, 1933, 'The Psychology of the Japanese Soldier', p. 30.
16. J. R. Ferris, ' "Worthy of Some Better Enemy?" ', pp. 223–56.
17. AWCCA, File number G-2, Number 4, 1936, Lecture by Colonel Burdett, 23 November 1935.
18. SHAT 7N 3333-1, 'L'Infanterie Japonaise', n. d. probably 1931; SHAT 7N 3334-1, 'Les Forces Militaires en Presence en Extreme-Orient', 'Conference fait à l'École Supérieure de Guerre', 21 April 1937.
19. J. R. Ferris, 'Student and Master: Britain, Japan, Airpower and the Fall of Singapore'.
20. Bell, 'The Royal Navy, War Planning'.
21. J. R. Ferris, 'The Singapore Grip: Preparing Defeat In Malaya, 1939–41', in I. Gow and Y. Hirama, eds, *A History of Anglo-Japanese Relations, 1500–2000: Military Dimensions* (Basingstoke, 2002).
22. W. Wark, *The Ultimate Enemy, British Intelligence and Nazi Germany, 1933–1939* (New York, 1985); Jackson, *Nazi Menace*. For German and Italian military services, see Knox, *Mussolini Unleashed*, pp. 32–3; Mallett, *Italian Navy*, pp. 180–1; Deist et al., *Germany and the Second World War*, Vol. 1, pp. 501.
23. The following are serious studies of the intelligence services of the major powers: D. Kahn, *Hitler's Spies* (New York, 1978); D. Porch, *The French Secret Services: Their History from the Dreyfus Affair to the Gulf War* (Oxford, 1995); C. Andrew, *Secret Service: The Making of the British Intelligence Community* (London, 1984); C. Andrew and O. Gordievsky, *KGB: The Inside Story of its Foreign Operations from Lenin to Gorchakov* (London, 1990); and C. Andrew and V. Mitrokhin, *The Mitrokhin Archive: The KGB in Europe and the West* (London, 1999); for Czechoslovakia, General F. Moravec, *Master of Spies* (London, 1975); R. A. Woytak, *On the Border of War and Peace: Polish Intelligence and Diplomacy in 1937–1939 and the Origins of the Ultra Secret* (New York, 1979).
24. Andrew and Mitrokhin, *Mitrokhin Archive*, pp. 55–110.
25. J. R. Ferris, 'Whitehall's Black Chamber: British Cryptology and the Government Code & Cypher School, 1919–1929', *Intelligence and National Security* 2 (1987), 54–91; D. Irving, ed., *Breach of Security: The German Secret Intelligence File on Events Leading to the Second World War* (London, 1968), pp. 21, *passim*; and D. Kahn, *Hitler's Spies*, pp. 178–81; 'Assignment of SIS Personnel, August-September 1938', RG 457, Historic Cryptologic Collection, Box 751, National Archives and Records Administration, College Park, Maryland (I am indebted for this reference to Dr. David Alvarez); memorandum by E. Petrov, 'Report on the Organization of Soviet Cipher Services (with particular reference to the Soviet State Secret Service Department (Spets Otdel)', 10 August 1956, A 6823/5, Australian Archives, National Office, Canberra.
26. This figure is calculated by adding together the different *Forschungsamt* reports in Irving, *Breach of Security*, and Public Record Office, London (hereafter

PRO), FO 371/21742, C 11002/1941/18 (in the former case, identified by a 6 figure number).

27. C. Andrew, 'Déchiffrement et diplomatie: Le Cabinet noir du Quai d'Orsay sous la Troisième République', *Relations Internationales* 5 (1976), 37–64; P. Jackson, 'Intelligence and the End of Appeasement', in R. Boyce, ed., *French Foreign and Defence Policy, 1918–1940* (London, 1998); Ferris, 'Whitehall's Black Chamber', and 'The Road to Bletchley Park: The British Experience with Signals Intelligence, 1892–1945', *Intelligence and National Security* 17 (2002), pp. 53–84; D. Alvarez, 'Left in the Dust: Italian Signals Intelligence, 1915–1943', *International Journal of Intelligence and Counterintelligence* 14 (2001), 231–53, and *Secret Messages: Codebreaking and American Diplomacy 1930–1945* (Lawrence, KS, 2000); D. Irving, *Breach of Security*; and D. Kahn, *Hitler's Spies*. Evidence on the Soviet side is fragmentary, though useful material is included in *The Mitrokhin Archive*. Andrew and Mitrokhin, p. 69, indicate that the Soviet Union solved some traffic from every Great Power and many smaller ones, but the nature and significance of this success is uncertain. They claim that 'No Western SIGINT agency during the 1930s seems to have collected so much political and diplomatic intelligence.' This claim is dubious. Given the limited Soviet ability to intercept traffic, agents probably gave it more telegrams than codebreaking did. The GC&CS, with roughly similar success against systems and more access to traffic, probably solved more significant telegrams than Soviet codebreakers, while Italy perhaps was in the same league as the Soviet Union as regards the combination of codebreaking and black bag jobs.

28. Irving, *Breach of Security*, pp. 55–120.

29. Watt, *How War Came*; and Andrew and Mitrokhin, *The Mitrokhin Archive*, pp. 83, 107–8, 119.

30. Jackson, 'End of Appeasement', pp. 234–60.

31. A collection, not necessarily complete, of *Forschungsamt* intercepts of Czech telephone traffic during the Munich crisis are in PRO, FO 371/21742, C 11002/ 1941/18.

32. Irving, *Breach of Security*, pp. 55–120.

33. Aspects of this issue are discussed in Ferris, 'Vansittart, Intelligence and Appeasement', pp. 122–75; D. Dilks, 'Appeasement and 'Intelligence'', in D. Dilks, ed., *Retreat From Power*, Vol. I, 1906–1939 (London, 1981), pp. 155–7; G. Weinberg, *The Foreign Policy of Hitler's Germany*, Vol. II, 1937–39 (1980), pp. 282–3; A. Best, *Britain, Japan and Pearl Harbor: Avoiding War in East Asia, 1936–1941* (London, 1995); and J. Chapman's many works on the intelligence relations between the Axis states: for example, J. Chapman, 'Signals Intelligence Cooperation Among the Secret Intelligence Services of the Axis States, 1940–41', *Japan Forum* (1991), pp. 231–56.

34. Dilks, 'Appeasement and Intelligence', pp. 154–8.

18 Diplomacy and Diplomatists

Donald Cameron Watt

The record of the First World War did severe, if not permanent, damage to the standing and credibility of two of the traditional instruments of European governments and of the élites from which they were recruited. The first victim was the professional military, or, to be more accurate the generals and their general staffs. I have written elsewhere of the effect that this had on their role as advisers on policy to the European powers between the First and the Second World Wars.[1]

The second section of the ruling classes of the powers to be affected were the professional diplomatists.[2] They were held guilty of conducting their business in secrecy, signing treaties in time of peace which bound their countries to make war together on third parties, and in time of war to divide the rewards of victory, without the knowledge of the public or of substantial sections of their governments. This accusation was engendered on the radical wing of European opinion, especially in Britain, and migrated to America, in that curious way, described in the 1950s by the young Sir Lawrence Martin, through William Buckler of the American embassy in London, and Colonel House to President Wilson.[3] Wilson's call for 'Open Covenants, openly arrived at' became a key note in Wilsonianism; and the American president was quite happy with this.[4] But the idea originated with the British upper-bourgeois liberals of the Union for Democratic Control. And its roots in the reaction of European progressivism to a war which seemed to them to embody the worst aspects of European institutional conservatism and militarism made it immediately part of the European acceptance of the Covenant of the League of Nations and of the Treaty of Versailles which embodied it.

President Wilson's formulation was incidentally unwelcome to Lloyd George, whose style of negotiation was very much of the ambush mode, going public being for him a phenomenon of which the timing and the occasion were an essential part of the whole process. But the English habit of publishing copious Blue Books of diplomatic correspondence at regular

stages throughout the nineteenth century set an obvious precedent for
President Wilson's formulation. Bismarck for one complained about it and
the difficulties that it presented for his own more secret form of diplomacy.
Secure behind the barrier of the seas and naval control of the exits from
continental Europe to the oceans, Britain could afford to ignore this. It is a
measure of the increase in Britain's sense of insecurity in the first decade of
the twentieth century that the Liberal government of Campbell-Bannerman
and Asquith managed to entangle itself in the ambiguities of the Anglo-
French entente, with its staff talks that theoretically did not involve a
military commitment to France, the nature of which was concealed not only
from the Central Powers, but from the larger part of the Liberal Cabinet in
Britain into the bargain.

Both the military and the diplomatic services of the powers were,
of course, already under attack even before 1914 for the narrowness of
the social circles from which they recruited their members. The military,
supposedly, were institutionally stupid, giving rise to the quip that military
intelligence was a contradiction in terms, and that the British army in
France and Flanders consisted of 'lions led by donkeys'. As for the diplomats, it was not only in the United States that they were seen as frock-coated
'cookie-pushers', moving from one cocktail party to another, concerned
with matters of precedence as much as with matters of state, and, in the
London joke, 'playing [working] from eleven to four' (in the afternoon) like
the fountains in Trafalgar Square. It was none other than Gladstone who is
alleged to have referred to the diplomatic service as 'outdoor relief for the
titled classes'.

Partly, of course, this was a survival from the time when monarchs or
emperors as heads of states accredited their personal representatives to each
other's courts, and used diplomatic missions as a means of employing
persons who could be identified with their own courts for the purpose.
In part, this reflected the convention by which diplomatists appeared in
court wearing uniforms every bit as over-decorated as those of field-
marshals in full fig. Even the conventional clothes of a statesman or diplomatist offended the man who felt himself to be different. Hitler, for example,
sacked the German Foreign Ministry chef de protocol, who so mismanaged
the programme of his visit to Rome in May 1938 that he did not have time to
change out of the 'frack und cylinder' (morning coat and top-hat) in which
he had paid his respects to the civilian mayor of Naples, and found himself inspecting the Italian battle fleet in Naples harbour, dressed, as he said
indignantly, 'like a French minister-president' rather than the Nazi head
of state.

In actual fact, recruitment to the diplomatic services of the powers, like
that to the army general staff, had already been diluted a little by the degree
to which the increasing wealth of the professional classes even before 1914
had begun to make it possible for their sons to qualify for recruitment

alongside the sons of the nobility, both on grounds of private income and of education. Recruits to the British diplomatic service before 1914 included the sons of naval officers, of successful surgeons, even of the head of a Dominions (Canadian) university. In Germany, sons of Prussian land-owners not of the Junker class were already serving alongside the minor nobility. For this latter class entry was of course always possible without going through the process of examination, through the system of attach-ment to an embassy abroad by permission of its ambassador. In 1933 both the British ambassador in Berlin, Sir Horace Rumbold, and Konstantin Freiherr von Neurath, the German foreign minister, had entered their respec-tive services by this route, the latter having failed the normal entry exam-inations because his handwriting was of an almost legendary illegibility.

The gap was to be further narrowed in the British case after 1918 by two new developments, the direct recruitment to the Foreign Service in 1918 of those who had won commissions in the armed forces during the world war, many of whom had only reached that rank as a result of their completion of a university education. Lord Strang, who was to reach the position of permanent under-secretary in the British Foreign Office after the Second World War, was the son of what in Britain would be called a market gardener, and in the United States a truck farmer, who had been educated as a scholarship boy at University College, London. His close friend, the British ambassador to Iran in the 1940s, Sir Reader Bullard, presented an even more extraordinary case, being the son of a London dock worker, who had entered the Levantine Consular Service after qualifying at the Foreign Office-financed course in Oriental languages at the University of Cam-bridge,[5] and had been promoted from the Consular to the Diplomatic Service after catching the eye of his superiors as British consul general in Leningrad when relations with the Soviet Union were renewed by the Macdonald government in 1931.

Bullard and Strang were in charge of Soviet relations with Britain during the period in which the British ambassador was 'withdrawn for consulta-tion' as a consequence of the crisis in Anglo-Soviet relations in 1934 resulting from the Soviet security authority's attempt to make the British engineers of Metro-Vickers into scapegoats for the initial failure of the Soviet electrification programme. Strang's lack of any British middle-class guilt complexes towards the Soviet Union (and his private excoriation of Sydney and Beatrice Webb, the celebrated left-wing intellectuals who had recently returned with wide-eyed praise of the Soviet Union, in his cor-respondence with Bullard), may well have been one of the hidden reasons for the Soviet objections to his dispatch to Moscow in 1939 to take part in the abortive Anglo-Soviet negotiations for a pact to restrain Hitler.

During the inter-war period the rigid divisions between those who worked on the staff of the various foreign ministries and the diplomatic corps began steadily to disappear. Staff on missions or embassies abroad tended to work a three-year cycle, three years abroad, three years at home. It is noticeable that they came to play a much larger role in the development of policy during their periods at home than they could during their postings as junior secretaries to the embassies abroad. But the most important side of this development was to accentuate the transnational linkages and friendships that they developed with their opposite numbers in other embassies in the capitals to which they were posted.

This was of course particularly true of those 'embassies under siege' like Moscow, where social contacts with the indigenous citizens after 1932 were discouraged by the political police, or suspect when they were not. An example is the four-way friendship that developed between Charles Bohlen of the United States embassy in Moscow, Fitzroy Maclean of Britain, their Italian colleague and the young Johnny von Herwarth of the German embassy, as partners in tennis in the first instance, through which von Herwarth was able to give his American and Italian colleagues detailed and continuous reports on the progress of the Nazi-Soviet negotiations in the summer of 1939. Unfortunately for Great Britain, Maclean was posted away from Moscow in the spring of 1939. His successor, Armand Dew, seems to have been one of those diplomatists who never liked making friends with foreigners and rejected von Herwarth's overtures. (He was killed in an air crash on the way to the Yalta conference in 1945, so we will never know for sure.) Britain remained unwarned, until too late.

Such clusters of friendships were not uncommonly found in two other contexts. The first was in the regular annual meetings of the Council and the Assembly of the League of Nations, where national delegations tended to be headed by the foreign ministers of the powers (who changed with the changes in the governments of which they were members). Their professional advisers, who were not subject to such changes, included, year in year out, the same figures from the senior foreign ministry staffs of the powers. Second, and occasionally more frequent, were encounters at the meetings of the Preparatory Commission to the Disarmament Conference and of the Conference itself. Parallel with these were the Naval Disarmament conferences and their various preparatory meetings. The fact that so many of these meetings were in a sense adversarial in nature made the achievement of genuine social linkages between delegates from different powers difficult to achieve at the time, or identify retrospectively. Nevertheless, they happened.

The round of diplomatic receptions alone at such occasions ensured that the permanent experts of the powers in particular fields became known to the foreign ministry staffs of those powers with whom they dealt. The German deputy to the Four-Year Plan, Helmut Wohltat, was, of all things, the German representative on the International Whaling Commission, which met annually. It was through these contacts that he won the confidence of his British opposite numbers sufficiently to feel able to embark on that curious mission in June 1939, which led him to meet Mr Robert

Hudson, the junior minister for overseas trade, and advance proposals, which did much to confirm the Soviet view that Britain was still intent on appeasing Nazi Germany.

Perhaps the most remarkable of these transnational linkages was that established in Berlin in 1938 between Sir Nevile Henderson, the British ambassador, his French and Italian colleagues, André-François Poncet and Bernardo Attolico, and the state secretary in the German Foreign Ministry, Ernst von Weizsäcker, where, with various motivations but a common desire to avert the opening of war, the four men kept each other informed and worked to thwart von Ribbentrop and the war party. Von Weizsäcker was pursuing a more devious game of attempting to undermine the determination of Germany's opponents as well as that of Hitler's advisers. In a sense Munich and its aftermath represent his declared policy, the 'chemical dissolution of Czechoslovakia'; but he can claim very little credit for that outcome. The Munich agreement, to Hitler's subsequent and well-documented fury, resulted from Chamberlain making Hitler an offer which he could not refuse; not, that is, without it becoming clear to everyone, including the mass of the German people and his military, that the responsibility for war was entirely his.

Much the same pattern can be seen in 1939, though without the participation of the new French ambassador, M. Robert Coulondre. (M. François-Poncet, who was transferred to Rome in November 1938, failed to strike up the same rapport in Rome either with Lord Perth or his successor as British ambassador, Sir Percy Loraine). This cooperation did not manage to persuade Hitler that Ribbentrop's insistence that Britain and France were bluffing was mistaken, nor to outmanoeuvre Ribbentrop's determination on war.

What this evidence amounts to is to show that between sections of the European diplomatic and Foreign Ministry élites there developed parallel, if not common, attitudes towards international issues, especially those of war and peace, which were 'transnational' in Robert Aron's sense of the word rather than merely representing the policies of their political masters. In other cases, the national foreign ministries contained significantly powerful figures who worked against the policies of their governments; if not in alliance with their opposite numbers in other countries, at least with political and public opinion figures in their own. In Britain, the permanent undersecretary, Sir Robert Vansittart, ran his own intelligence service, and in alliance with the head of the press department in the Foreign Office briefed at least one of the private newsletters which flourished in Britain at a time when political control of the press was at its most active, in terms hostile to the assumptions and pictures of German activity given to the press by the advocates of appeasement. In France, Daladier, while premier, advised various foreign diplomatists to deal with Vansittart's counterpart, Alexis St Léger Léger, rather than with Georges Bonnet, his cabinet colleague and foreign minister. Bonnet celebrated Munich by transferring the head of the Quai d'Orsay's press department away from his post to the department dealing with the United States, and posting the most influential critic of appeasement at the Quai d'Orsay to the French embassy in Ankara.

Distrust of their diplomatists, and still more of their Foreign Ministries, was shared by Hitler and Mussolini with Chamberlain, who notoriously kept much of his contacts with Italy secret from his foreign secretary, Anthony Eden, using the so-called 'secret channel' constituted by the ex-MI5 head of the Conservative party's research division, Sir Joseph Ball, and the Maltese-born legal adviser to the Italian embassy in London. Attempts to use another member of the Downing Street staff, George Steward, the press adviser, in similar contacts with the German embassy in London, broke down on MI5's penetration of the embassy, and their consequent reportage to Sir Alexander Cadogan, Vansittart's successor, of every such contact. The fact that the German ambassador, Herbert von Dirksen, was cut out of the German decision-making process in matters of foreign policy, made the contacts pointless anyway.

Hitler's distrust of diplomacy and its practitioners was well illustrated in the summer of 1939, when the heads of the German missions to Warsaw, London and Paris were not allowed to return to their posts from their annual summer leave. Yet within the German Foreign Ministry there were career officials who not only regarded it as their duty to obey the policies of their Führer, but also identified themselves with his aims, where others who did not, or who felt that they could no longer exercise any influence to moderate them, were running for cover to appointments to embassies in neutral countries. Von Weizsäcker had himself posted to the Vatican, for example. Ritter, the ultra-nationalist German ambassador to Brazil, whom the Brazilians sent home in 1938, remained chief economic negotiator in the German Foreign Ministry until very late in the day. Gaus, the legal adviser, used his lawyer's intuition to purge the records of anything that could be used by the Allied prosecutors in the post-war war crimes trials; but he stayed with von Ribbentrop until the end. And there were the German Foreign Ministry career officials who indulged in treasonable relations with the Russian intelligence, or took part in the conspiracy to assassinate Hitler, men like Ulrich von Hassell or Friedrich Werner von der Schulenburg, the former ambassadors in Rome and Moscow. Others were purged under the 1935 Nuremberg racial laws.

The German diplomatic service, it has to be recognised, had to face its challenges from Nazism already battered by time and the effects of Germany's defeat in 1918. To a man its staff was revisionist and rejected the war-guilt clauses of the Treaty of Versailles. It was also deeply involved in maintaining the clandestine financing of Germanic institutions in the territories lost by the treaty. In 1933 only one of its senior diplomats joined the Nazi party. He was promptly given the sack; the foreign minister was forced, however, to reinstate him. He was to take his revenge by denouncing those who had Jewish blood or connections when the Nuremberg Laws were passed in 1935.

But the severest blow to its resistance to Nazification came from age and death. Of the ambassadors and senior departmental heads in service in 1933, one, von Prittwitz, the ambassador in Washington, resigned immediately. A second, Rudolf Nadolny, was engineered by the foreign minister, von Neurath, who saw a rival in him, into a conflict with Hitler on Russia and resigned. Two heads of departments fell victim to the Nuremberg laws, one partially Jewish and one with a Jewish wife. Two, von Hoesch in London and his colleague in Paris, Roland Förster, died in 1936. Bernhard von Bülow, the state secretary, reached the age of retirement that same year. All of these were persons of decided minds with followings among the younger members of the diplomatic service. Ulrich von Hassell, the ambassador to Rome, and his colleague in Beijing, fell as a result of their policies conflicting with those of von Ribbentrop.

Of these von Hoesch, von Hassell and Nadolny had been considered for the post of foreign minister in 1932 when von Neurath, also a professional diplomatist, had been appointed foreign minister. His confirmation in this post had been one of the conditions set by von Hindenberg when Hitler was offered and accepted the chancellorship at the end of January 1933. Von Neurath successfully saw off the first attempts by Nazi sympathisers to take over the Foreign Ministry in 1933–34. His conduct of German diplomacy during the Rhineland crisis of 1936 won him Hitler's admiration. But he was unable, deprived of von Bülow's iron, to stave off for long Ribbentrop's development of his position in Hitler's court. And both his nerve and his health were broken by the revelations contained in Hitler's address to him and the military leaders on 5 November 1937, making it easy for Hitler to persuade him to resign in favour of von Ribbentrop the following spring.

Of the remaining ambassadors, von Dirksen, transferred from Tokyo to London in 1938, von Welczeck in Paris and von Möltke in Warsaw were all removed from the circuit in 1939. Neurath's son-in-law, von Mackensen, von Bülow's successor as state secretary in 1936, took refuge in 1939 as ambassador in Rome, where he survived by keeping his head down. His successor was Ernst von Weizsäcker, who had joined the Foreign Ministry from the *Reichsmarine* in 1920. He ran the office efficiently enough to satisfy von Ribbentrop who, in any case, preferred personal diplomacy in dealing with his Axis allies, and was easily bored with routine diplomacy. He was a man who lived from *coup* to *coup* amidst Hitler's admiration and the unwillingly given applause of Goebbels's press. Von Ribbentrop had only joined the party in 1932. All the old hands from Göring downwards loathed him. But he fascinated Hitler.

Dirksen's replacement in Tokyo was the military attaché, General Eugen Ott. Ironically, he had originally been posted to Tokyo by the army to put him out of the reach of the SS who had him on their list as a potential target for assassination. The German attack on Russia finished the career of the only other senior member of the German Foreign Service capable of arousing the admiration and loyalty of his juniors, von der Schulenburg. Like von Hassell, he did not survive the failure of 20 July, 1944.[6] He was tipped for the post of foreign minister in the cabinet to be set up by the conspirators after Hitler's disposal, should they decide to approach the Soviets rather than the western allies for a separate peace.

The British Foreign Office was not without its quota of wide-eyed Wilsonians who saw injustice in the Versailles settlement and a moral case for the satisfaction of German complaints against its alleged inequity. This was obviously true of Sir Nevile Henderson and Lord Perth, the British ambassadors in Berlin and Rome at the time of Munich. It was also true of Mr Ashton-Gwatkin, head of the Foreign Office's Economic Department, although he did his best to conceal the fact after the war. Recent memoirs reveal that there were others. Apart from the Catholics in the service, there do not seem to have been any rabid Sovietophobes. But then there were not any open admirers of Soviet achievements either. The majority saw their duty as to carry out the policies of the elected government without opposition, once their advice had been tendered and ignored. The younger generation in the service, recruited from 1930 onwards, saw matters not only in terms of traditional British interests and enmities, as did, for example, so many of the generation which had lived through the war of 1914–18 (Vansittart for example), but also in terms of resistance to totalitarianism. They found no difficulty in 1944–45 moving from German to Soviet totalitarianism as the object of resistance.

Their mentors were Sir Alexander Cadogan himself, who moved from his initial acquiescence in appeasement to being Halifax's conscience and Churchill and Eden's manager of the Foreign Office; Sir Orme Sargent, Cadogan's deputy; and a brace of tough-minded British diplomatists who succeeded Perth and Henderson: Sir Percy Loraine in Rome and the so-called 'radical diplomat' who drank Molotov under the table and used pipemanship to court Stalin, Sir Archibald Clerk Kerr. Both, significantly, like Cadogan, had long experience outside Europe, where the weight of British prestige and local illusions of Britain's strength and power went with the post.

The one exception, Sir Robert Craigie, the ambassador in Japan from 1937–41, whose skills as a negotiator terrorised foreign naval experts in the naval disarmament conferences and avoided war with Japan in 1939, had no followers in the Foreign Office. He was totally wrapped up in his family, his formidable American wife and his son who was a permanent invalid. He was at odds with the doctrinaire Sinophiles of the Far Eastern Department; and Churchill had counted him as an enemy since the late 1920s. On the outbreak of war with Japan, the Foreign Office Far Eastern Department rubbished his final report, and he disappeared into privacy. His close family friendship with Neville Chamberlain's widow did not help either. Eden took his tone entirely from Churchill on such matters. His vanity in any case did not allow him to cultivate or encourage relations of equality of esteem with his diplomatists. Cadogan, who had served in China and been the object of Japanese air attack, saw no reason to intervene in Craigie's case. Membership in the House of Lords, a directorship of the Suez Canal Company, gifts of patronage conferred on other successful public servants, were not on offer. His memoirs do not disclose the degree of disagreement between himself and the Churchill government. The full scale of his achievement, not least in avoiding a war with Japan in July 1939 over the Tientsin concession, only became apparent when the archives and documents were opened to historical research.

The British ambassador in Washington from 1932–39, Sir Ronald Lindsay, was a former permanent under-secretary. He was however handicapped in making any significant entry into the Roosevelt court or impact on the president by the fact that his wife was a member of the most rock-ribbed of New York Republican families, the Colville Hoyts, from a milieu which regarded Roosevelt as a traitor to his class. In any case, Franklin Roosevelt, unlike his cousin, Theodore, was not an Anglophile, though he did not mind pretending to be, and managed to convince a number of gullible British friends that he was. Nor was his court remotely like that maintained by Theodore Roosevelt.

More to the point, he was fundamentally incapable of using professional diplomatists in any real way whatever. The comparison with Theodore Roosevelt's cultivation of the ambassadors in Washington during his presidency is particularly striking in this regard. He relied almost entirely on personal intermediaries. His first emissary, Norman Davies, was destroyed in 1937–38 by Cordell Hull, his secretary of state. In 1936–38 he twice used the Master of Elibank, whose friendship he had made in 1917–1918 when Elibank was assistant military attaché in Washington. Elibank's post-war recollections made much of this friendship. But one can judge its real value by the fact that there was no communication between the two men after Elibank left Washington, until he re-opened it on Roosevelt's election to the presidency in 1933. It was not until Harry Hopkins arrived on the scene that Roosevelt began to indulge in positive personal diplomacy instead of diplomacy by oratory. His own appointments to embassies were almost entirely rewards for electoral favours or studied insults, as in the appointment firstly of an obscure Southern judge and then of an active member of the Bostonian Irish Mafia as ambassadors to London, and of an equally obscure Southern historian as ambassador to Berlin. The only appointment which was intended to advance his own policies was that of his friend William Bullitt as ambassador to Moscow on the opening of relations with the Soviet Union in 1934. This was not a success. Bullitt was posted to Paris, where he became a bit of a maverick. His successor in Moscow was a populist millionaire who fell for Soviet propaganda hook, line and sinker, to the despair of his professional advisers. Thereafter, Roosevelt contented himself with a career diplomatist.

After the Second World War diplomatists suffered a renewal of the criticisms they had suffered after the First. In part this resulted from the decision by the British government on the one hand and the three western allies on the other both to publish their own diplomatic records and to publish selections from the captured German diplomatic archives. The American decision to prosecute selected German diplomatists as a follow up to the Nuremberg trial of the leading German war criminals reinforced this hostility. The British documents were published shorn of the internal minutes either of the Cabinet or the Foreign Office staff. As a result, apart from the occasional private letter or minute of conversation in London, the Third Series of *Documents of British Foreign Policy, 1919–1939,* which covered the last two years of peace, and was the first to be published, depicted foreign policy as a dialogue between selected ambassadors abroad, and the foreign secretary. Sir Nevile Henderson and Lord Perth thus emerged as silly self-deceived simpletons, telling London what it was assumed the appeasers wanted to hear. Henderson died before the publication began; and Lord Perth's ill-health left him in no position to defend himself. As a result they were demonised by the anti-appeasers led by Sir Lewis Namier, who were echoed by Anglophobe historians in America. The search for 'guilty men' in Fleet Street condemned all diplomatists equally, as élitist enemies of the British people, who, it was implied, had defied G. K. Chesterton and 'spoken' once and for all in the 1945 General Election. The release of the Foreign Office archives for the 1930s under a Public Records Act not passed until 1967, establishing a 30-year closed period, produced a small population of now ageing historians, for whom the picture is now in reasonable focus. This does not include the historians who produce programmes for the visual media. Research is now galloping after the years of the later Cold War, and there has been a revival of populism in the attempt to apportion the 'blame' for the failure of Anglo-Soviet relations from 1945 onwards on British élitist hostility to the Soviet system and to the British Communist party, on American subsidies for British writers against Communism and on the machinations of the Information Research Department, a Foreign Office agency involved in semi-clandestine propaganda against the Soviet system abroad. This populism has established itself in academe, and in repeated attempts to argue that a professional diplomatic service is an archaic survival rendered obsolete by modern communications technology and ease of travel. The Foreign Office in the 1930s still awaits a proper prosopographic investigation, an analysis of its internal factionalism and of the differing attitudes of the separate generations of recruits from pre-1914, from the 1920s and from the 1930s.

Professional diplomatists have, however, largely been freed from accusations of responsibility for their failure to turn back the tide of events that led to the outbreak of the Second World War. It is the policy-makers who ignored the reports from their diplomatists and from their intelligence services and who made proposals which related little to the pattern of events on the ground who are held to have earned the greater responsibility for what Winston Churchill called the 'avoidable war'. But there are those, the present writer included, who regard such a statement not as a legitimate historical judgement but as another piece of historical evidence of how the interpretation of the events of the inter-war years has developed since the political controversies of the 1930s and 1940s. To end on a personal note, we regard it as an obstacle to, if not a misuse of, historical research and understanding, to search for persons to blame, and if asked to name a conflict to which this soubriquet could be applied, we would never dream of including the Second World War.

Notes

1. D. C. Watt, *Too Serious a Business: European General Staffs and the Approach of the Second World War* (London, 1975).
2. There has been much less study of the contribution made by the diplomatists collectively to the events which led up to the outbreak of the Second World War, once the initial outburst of polemical studies digesting the initial publication of the British and German diplomatic documents for 1938–39 had passed. The work of Sir Lewis Namier in Britain and the Scottish and German émigrés, Gordon Craig and Felix Gilbert, in the United States is the most permanent memento of these years. Sir L. Namier, *Diplomatic Prelude, 1938–39* (London, 1946), *Europe in Decay* (London, 1948), and *In the Nazi Era* (London, 1948); G. Craig and F. Gilbert, eds, *The Diplomats* (Princeton, NJ, 1953).
3. L. W. Martin. *Peace without Victory: Woodrow Wilson and the British Liberals* (New Haven, CT, 1958). For the more general coincidence of Wilson's views with those of the various liberal strains in Europe, see A. J. Mayer, *The Political Origins of the New Diplomacy* (New Haven, 1959). Martin, later vice-chancellor of the British University of Newcastle, was a British citizen who graduated from an American university. Meyer was a Swiss who also graduated in the United States.
4. It should be noted that his rhetoric did not match his practice. He objected in the strongest terms to the proposal to publish the French minutes of the proceedings of the Council of Four, which did not see the light of day until after the Second World War.
5. There were in fact two parallel courses, one for the Levantine Consular Service, in Arabic, Turkish and Farsi, and one for the Far Eastern Consular Services in the Mandarin and Japanese languages. It is an extraordinary comment on the social

divisions of the period that both were only for two years, so that there could be no question of entrants qualifying as undergraduates in the University of Cambridge (and therefore as gentlemen). Originally, graduates were employed simply as interpreters. But in practice they were indistinguishable and were not distinguished from other members of the Consular services.

6. Much of this is based on two articles by the author and materials used in his book *How War Came: The Immediate Origins of the Second World War* (London, 1989); 'Nazi Leaders and German Diplomats', *Journal of Central European History* (1955); 'Hitler and Nadolny', *Contemporary Review* (1959). For the von Weizsäcker group, see R. A. Blasius, *Für Grossdeutschland – gegen den grossen Krieg. Staatssekretär Ernst von Weizsäcker in den Krisen um die Tschechoslovakei und Polen 1938/39* (Cologne, 1981).

19 Propaganda

Philip M. Taylor

The axiom that 'when war breaks out, the first casualty is truth'[1] belies the significant role played by propaganda *before* the outbreak of World War Two. Although more commonly associated during the inter-war years with the dictatorships,[2] recent research has uncovered significant propaganda activity, both at home and abroad, on the part of the democracies.[3] Many studies focus on domestic campaigns that served to forge national identities at a time when governments were just beginning to regard propaganda, defined in various ways, as an essential function of the peacetime state, although the difficulties of evaluating the impact of this propaganda are compounded by the absence of statistical or attitudinal data relating to public opinion. For example, the American Institute of Public Opinion Research was only founded in 1936 and the nearest British equivalent, Mass Observation, was not formed until 1937.[4] Research on propaganda has therefore tended to be top-down, with major areas of controversy forming around speculation, of necessity, about its effects or impact. None the less, it was between the wars that state propaganda conducted at both the national and international levels came to be a fact of everyday political and diplomatic life. Obviously the dictatorships embraced it more readily – and more visibly – as an essential element of their power. But the democracies also engaged in it, more reluctantly, slower and in less obvious, but in many respects more intriguing ways.[5] The degree to which this peacetime propaganda conflict contributed towards heightened international tension and misperception, and thereby to the outbreak of war in 1939, is the subject of this chapter.

Propaganda and Communication

If wars begin in men's minds, then the thought processes which influence decisions to go to war – whether rational or irrational, whether real or imagined – demand our scrutiny. Historians have traditionally been wary of multi-disciplinary analyses, yet any analysis of propaganda requires considerable borrowing from other academic disciplines. As a process of communication designed by the sender to influence both thought and behaviour on the part of its target audience, propaganda analysis needs a wide-ranging framework utilising methodologies from psychology and behavioural science,[6] sociology and audience research, political science and international relations, and what we now call media studies.

First, however, we need to discard some of the pejorative historical baggage that the word 'propaganda' has acquired during the course of the twentieth century. In democracies, especially, propaganda has become a dirty word associated with deception and lies or, at best, half-truths. There has always been a tendency, perhaps a self-delusory one, to believe that it is something which other people do, especially in totalitarian or authoritarian regimes. As such, it is branded as a form of Orwellian 'thought control', usually conducted by dictators who fear the free-flow of ideas and the open exchange of information and opinions that democracies purport to value as an essential political dynamic between government and people. Propaganda thus becomes a form of oppression and a system for maintaining political power: the triumph of coercion over persuasion, of power over public opinion. In doing so, it appeals to emotion rather than reason and is thus a powerful tool in appealing to 'the masses', who get caught up in a frenzy of sentiment at the expense of individual dissent. Such popular views of propaganda reinforce the notion that democratic governments do not engage in anything remotely like this, except perhaps in time of war out of necessity for the survival of the state. Rather, because democracies respect individualism, education and reason, they thus confine themselves to the conduct of 'publicity' or 'public information' campaigns based upon 'facts' to allow citizens to make up their own minds. In short, in democracies, we aspire towards 'the truth', whereas in non-democracies they deliberately tell 'lies'.

Conceptually and indeed historically, this is far from helpful. For a start, it fails to understand the nature of propaganda as a value-neutral process of persuasion. Propaganda is simply the process by which one individual or group tries to persuade another of the merits of its case. In itself, therefore, it is not a 'good' or a 'bad' thing; it is merely a form of communication between sender and recipient. For example, a letter sent through the post could contain propaganda, but this does not mean that the letter itself is propaganda. During the course of the twentieth century, there has been a revolution in which the forms – or media – of communication available to human beings have increased dramatically, from radio and (at first silent) cinema at its start to mobile phones and the internet at its end. Indeed, this is what distinguishes the twentieth century from every period before it. Communication via technology, *per se*, is also value-neutral; like propaganda, it can be used for good or ill. Consequently, we have in this century witnessed a corresponding increase in the presence of propaganda, as more and more people try to persuade more and more target audiences of the merits of their cases, utilising more and more communications media.

For a case to have merit, it needs to have credibility. For it to be credible, the case needs to be based upon common points of reference that the recipient can identify with, and thus accept. This is why many propaganda analysts maintain that propaganda is at its most effective when reinforcing pre-existing beliefs. These appeals may be emotional, but they can also be rational. Different forms of communication between sender and recipient, such as advertising, depend for their success upon their ability to achieve mutual identification. This brings us to a much more helpful concept, namely the notion of 'effective' or 'ineffective' forms of communication, including propaganda. Effective or successful communication does not, however, help us to distinguish between propaganda and other forms of persuasion. This is because such an approach places the emphasis on analysing the end process of the classic definition of communication as who says what, how, to whom, when and with what impact. Probably the most ambitious attempt at this was by the French sociologist, Jacques Ellul, in the late 1950s and 1960s as part of his analysis of the 'technological society'. It was Ellul's contention that propaganda was so prevalent in modern societies because people actually needed it as a structure for understanding the complexities of modern life when other frameworks, such as those provided by religion, were in decline.[7]

For our purposes here, we are going to add to the classic definition of communication a word which historians are only too familiar with: why? If we ask ourselves why the sender is bothering to make a case to a certain target audience, we begin to locate propaganda on a spectrum of persuasive techniques which includes advertising, public relations, political communications and even education. Therefore, we need to look at the question of *intent*. And it is here that we can, if we must, make our value judgements about propaganda. It may well be that propaganda benefits both sender and recipient at the same time. Propaganda can also be accidental. But if the intent of the sender is to benefit the recipient, even within Ellul's complex theories, then the process is *not* propaganda. For our purposes here, therefore, propaganda is designed principally to benefit the sender. As such, therefore, advertising designed to get people to buy a product, and thereby increase the profits of the company, would more accurately be labelled economic or commercial propaganda. Similarly, political communication designed to get people to vote for a particular political party is likewise political propaganda.

Within this framework, it becomes easier to accept the notion that democratic states can, and indeed, do conduct propaganda. This is not a good or a bad thing; it merely is. Whether that propaganda is effective or ineffective is largely irrelevant for purposes of identification of the process. But we do need to examine why governments of all varieties have increasingly used the growing number of available mass media with the intention of persuading audiences of the merit of their cases. If we look at these intentions, we not only find propaganda everywhere, but we can also perhaps accept more easily the notion of propaganda as a justifiable activity of the modern state – or indeed otherwise.

A working definition of propaganda therefore is as follows: the intentional dissemination of information and ideas, by whatever media of communication are available, to a recipient target audience with the objective primarily of benefiting the sender.[8]

The Legacy of the Great War Propaganda Experiment

The first scholars of propaganda[9] appeared during the inter-war period. They focused on wartime, and the Great War in particular, for it was then that centrally organised state persuasion came to be recognised as an essential weapon of war. It was the British who eventually came to be recognised as the masters of the new craft which, although some officials had reservations about it, had yet to acquire its demonic status. Having started the war with nothing that could be remotely described as a propaganda department, virulent anti-British German propaganda – particularly in the United States – prompted the creation of the War Propaganda Bureau at Wellington House under the direction of Charles Masterman.[10] Reflecting the still prevalent written media of the day, the focus of Wellington House output was on print materials – the press, pamphlets, leaflets and books. The target audience also reflected a prevailing view in the Whitehall of 1914, that the people who really mattered were the élite of American society. Hence, propaganda was directed at American opinion-makers (politicians, businessmen, journalists, educators and editors) rather than directly at mass American opinion and, to provide it with credibility, the most famous literary authors of the day – from John Buchan (who was actually in charge of British propaganda briefly in 1916) to H. G. Wells (who briefly headed propaganda directed at Germany in 1918)[11] – were recruited into the campaign to present the British case as both 'just' and 'justified'. The intention at first was not so much to bring the United States into the war on the Allied side as to ensure its continued neutrality. In order to achieve this, it was felt best to maintain the secrecy of Wellington House's existence and thus not allow any connection to be made between those writing on its behalf to an official British government propaganda campaign.

With the United States in the war from 1917 onwards, Wellington House went into decline. After the war was over, however, when those early propaganda scholars uncovered the sheer extent of its North American activities, there took root a belief that the United States had somehow been duped into the conflict by skilful British propaganda.[12] The covert nature of the British campaign at the time merely reinforced conspiracy theories, and

American isolationists seized upon the British wartime propaganda record to underscore the validity of their 'never again' position.[13] Meanwhile, others also damned Britain with faint praise for their skill at propaganda. Thus, for example, in defeated Germany, General Ludendorff rationalised military failure in 1918 by claiming that German soldiers had been 'hypnotised like a rabbit is by a snake'.[14] This gave rise to the myth that Allied propaganda, or more specifically British psychological warfare directed at combat troops, had been the root cause of defeat, not military incompetence. In 1924, Adolf Hitler devoted two chapters of *Mein Kampf* to this theme. Within ten years of the end of the Great War, propaganda as a legitimate persuasive process had been thoroughly discredited within democracies like Britain and the United States, not least following numerous revelations that the high-profile wartime atrocity stories – such as the infamous German 'Corpse Conversion Factory' – had been falsehoods.[15]

It is too readily forgotten that, on the domestic front, the British government had been highly reluctant to engage in propaganda. The wave of patriotism that greeted the outbreak of war in 1914 at first appeared to render it unnecessary. Patriotism, not propaganda, seemed to be doing the job anyway, as volunteers rushed to join the armed forces. Patriotic organisations seemed to spring up like spontaneous combustion, and it was only following the huge losses on the Western Front that the flood of volunteers dwindled to a trickle, requiring the introduction of conscription in 1916.[16] By then, especially after the Somme, there was a growing recognition that war weariness and the growing peace movement required more systematic attention, and when Lloyd George replaced Asquith in December 1916, one of his first tasks was to deal with the entire business of propaganda. As the war dragged through its third Christmas, the new prime minister established the National War Aims Committee to conduct home propaganda, and he systematised the early and somewhat haphazard organisation by creating a Ministry of Information and a Department for Enemy Propaganda in 1918. Significantly, Lloyd George turned to the press barons, Lords Beaverbrook and Northcliffe, to head up these organisations. Whereas British propaganda in the final year of the war was targeted more appropriately at mass rather than élite opinion, it was to have serious consequences for Britain's post-war attitudes towards propaganda as a responsibility of government.

None the less, as others were studying the British wartime experiment for peacetime applications, especially in the new Soviet Union, Fascist Italy and later Nazi Germany, the Great War had taught the victors that public opinion could no longer be ignored as a political phenomenon. It had been a Total War in which the entire resources of the nation – military, economic and psychological – had had to be mobilised over a four-year period in order to ensure survival. The mass of the population had been touched by the war to some degree, as the memorials to the fallen in the smallest of hamlets still testify. The press, for all their protests about being independent and their right to remain critical, had cooperated in the war effort to the extent that the sheer horror of the fighting had been kept from the public.[17] Indeed, most of the atrocity propaganda which fed the atmosphere of hatred towards 'the Hun' had emanated from Fleet Street rather than Whitehall. *The Times History of the War* may have proclaimed in 1920 that 'good propaganda probably saved a year of the war – and a million lives',[18] but the fact that it had been supervised by the men from the new world of mass press publicity threatened to give them power to sway the masses in the post-war period. They had to go back to Fleet Street, and the wartime propaganda machinery was dismantled as quickly as possible.

In Britain, the massive expansion of the electorate following the Representation of the People Acts of 1918 and 1928 meant that, henceforth, elected governments would stand or fall on the basis of their ability to convince the new mass of enfranchised voters of the merits of their right to govern. This was to be a responsibility for political parties, not for press barons. The parallel discrediting of the word 'propaganda' meant that such activity would need another label. The British may have had to resort to propaganda in wartime in order to assist military survival, but there was to be no room for similar forms of manipulation in peacetime. Instead, the British resorted to 'national publicity' in, for example, the pioneering efforts of the Empire Marketing Board to promote the merits of empire between 1926 and 1933.[19] In an age in which the people were just beginning to become political participants, the political parties began to see the need to get into the business of persuasion and developed their own *publicity* machinery for releasing information to the public, sometimes directly via their own publications, but more usually indirectly via the mass media.[20]

The Rise of 'Public Diplomacy'

It is often asserted that popular involvement in the Great War led to an increased popular interest in foreign affairs, partly as a reaction to the secret diplomacy that was widely held to be a cause of the catastrophe of 1914. Whether this was true or not (we simply do not have the public opinion data to test it), it was widely believed at the time and a prime motivating factor in what we would now term the opening up of government. Perhaps it was the media who believed this, especially after their experience of working with government during the war. Certainly, the triumph in Russia of Bolshevism with its internationalist ideological agenda brought an external threat closer to home, exacerbated by the new regime's emphasis on propaganda which was regarded as an essential weapon to 'spread the word' – and cinema images – about the legitimacy of the proletariat to govern the mass of the largely illiterate Russian peasantry: government by the people, for the people, in another socio-political context. This revolution from below, which saw the centuries-old Tsarist regime deposed, sent powerful shock waves through the rest of the world's ruling élites, who drew the conclusion that 'the masses' in their own countries needed either to be oppressed or to be persuaded. The road towards oppression was chosen by the dictatorships; persuasion was the route chosen by the democracies.

In the process of this realisation, especially following the advent to power in 1933 – quasi-democratically – of Adolf Hitler, certain distinctions began to emerge between the way democracies and dictatorships conducted propaganda. Apart from calling it something else, official democratic propaganda would have to operate within the context of a free media. By contrast, the Nazis, who set up a Ministry of Popular Enlightenment and Propaganda under Josef Goebbels in 1933, tolerated no such hostages to fortune.[21] As the regime usually credited as being the first true modern propaganda state, Nazi Germany ensured that every newspaper, every radio station and every cinema was under rigorous state control. Similarly in the Soviet Union, especially after 1928 as Stalin tightened his grip on power, state control of the media ensured a near monopolistic national and world-view amongst the population as a whole. Deviations from the official line were to be severely punished, and to avoid the potential ramifications of bolting the stable door after the horse had bolted, tight state censorship was enforced to ensure that alternative viewpoints, dissent or information that might undermine the credibility of state authority and legitimacy never reached the public domain.[22]

This is not to suggest that democracies eschewed censorship.[23] Apart from obvious issues of national security, for which in Britain there was a Defence of the Realm Act, there were varying degrees of tolerance towards what might be called artistic licence on the part of fringe or non-mainstream communicators. Where novels, poetry or productions in the theatre fell into such categories in the eyes of the dominant élite, there had been a long tradition of censorship, dating back almost to the invention of printing, and was embodied in laws concerning slander, libel and blasphemy. Censorship of the press varied from country to country; in Britain, it was largely confined to defence matters under the 1911 Defence of the Realm Act (D Notices). The relatively new medium of cinema created considerable concern not least because of its popularity amongst the 'working class' and young people (over 21) including females (until 1928 over 30) – the very people who had been recently empowered with the vote. Because the devastation of the Great War had effectively crippled the European cinema industry, films emanating from the New World gained an enormous opportunity to fill the entertainment vacuum. The ascendancy of 'Hollywood' in the 1920s worried many European governments because it was recognised that films could be influential in shaping attitudes – from the relatively trivial such as dress sense to more significant social, sexual and political attitudes. The French, concerned about the subjugation of national culture by outside influences, imposed a quota system on the import of Hollywood films while the British, fearful of the influence of Bolshevism especially after the General Strike of 1926, banned such Soviet masterpieces as *Battleship Potempkin* and *Strike*. The Nazis banned virtually every foreign film.

There was one serious technological threat to such attempts hermetically to seal off societies from outside influences, and this came in the form of radio. Films could be banned at their point of import, but broadcasting transcended the corporeal environment. As Lenin recognised, radio was 'a newspaper without paper – and without frontiers'.[24] Indeed, given the internationalist thrust of the Bolshevik revolution until Stalin resorted to 'Socialism in One Country', Moscow was the pioneer of this new medium of international propaganda, building the most powerful transmitter in the world in 1923 in order to spread the word that 'workers of the world unite'. Radio not only enjoyed the characteristics of transcending traditional geographic frontiers, it was also immediate, personal and required no literary skills. As the spread of wireless receivers grew world-wide in the 1920s and 1930s, it became an increasingly influential medium of international as well as national communication and provided the opportunity for governments to speak directly to the peoples of other countries. Despite growing concern about the content of such international radio transmissions, there was little that recipient countries could do except protest or resort to censorship in the form of jamming, which was expensive. In the 1920s, the British government became so alarmed at Radio Moscow's broadcasts aimed especially at the imperial colonies that it insisted upon clauses preventing 'subversive propaganda' being inserted into the 1921 and 1928 Anglo-Soviet Trade Agreements.

During the 1926 General Strike in Britain, there was also concern about Radio Moscow trouble-making in Britain itself, and there was an early attempt to jam its frequencies. It seemed to many that radio posed a significant threat to the traditional diplomatic principle that nations should not interfere in the internal affairs of other nations. The rise of international radio 'wars' in the 1920s and early 1930s prompted sufficient concern in Geneva where the League of Nations spent four unproductive years attempting to outlaw propaganda transmissions across frontiers. This was because no one accepted that what they were doing constituted 'propaganda' in what was becoming the accepted pejorative sense: they were merely transmitting their 'point of view'. With the rise of Fascism and Communism, however, this was being translated into ideological warfare in which democracy found itself on the defensive. The Nazis found an ingenious solution whereby only 'people's wireless sets' were sold to the public, tuned in to domestic frequencies only; listening to foreign broadcasts was eventually banned. Meanwhile, Nazi external radio was used as a form of psychological artillery fire, with reassurances to the Germans separated from the homeland by the Versailles Treaties that they had not been forgotten. With the Americans in isolation, and with the French consumed by domestic strife, it was left to the British, for all their reluctance to engage in peacetime propaganda, to do something to counter the growing influence of revisionist and extremist ideologies.

Against the backdrop of the Great Depression, however, only a few in Britain were convinced that propaganda – or 'national self-advertisement' as it was now being labelled – would be cost-effective expenditure. Indeed, the Empire Marketing Board fell victim to budgetary cuts and was closed down in 1933. But, in the years that followed, as the Nazis demonstrated to the rest of the world how much store they placed on projecting national revival and virility through press, radio and sound cinema, the pressure to do something more positive to counter accusations about decadent democracy and declining empire mounted. As one Foreign Office official argued:

> The emergence of the totalitarian state in Europe has presented us with new and urgent problems. To deal with them a new outlook is required. We are faced with competition on a formidable scale in many parts of the world, and that competition is taking new forms to which this country has hitherto been unaccustomed. One of these forms is commonly known as propaganda, powerfully and deliberately directed, to promote the political and commercial influence of the national state. It has during the last few years been forged into a political weapon which is already exercising a potent influence in certain areas where British interests are directly concerned, and where they are visibly suffering as a result of this new impact.[25]

One of the first tentative British steps was to create the British Council in 1934 to conduct what in public was called cultural diplomacy, but in private was referred to more candidly as cultural propaganda.[26] Mussolini's Italy joined the attack with hostile anti-British broadcasts from Radio Bari, directed largely against British influence in the Middle East.[27] And in East Asia, where the Japanese were aspiring to a 'Greater East Asian Co-Prosperity Sphere', British interests were also challenged by short-wave radio.[28] By the mid-1930s, a full-blown global propaganda war was taking place, and Britain, as the one true global power, was its principal target. With its armed forces stretched to the limit after years of disarmament following the Great War, counter-propaganda suddenly became a more attractive, and cost-effective, means of ensuring that Britain's position and resolve were known and understood.

Although it could be argued that the 'projection of national culture' by organisations such as the British Council (funded partially by the Foreign Office) was a rather 'soft' way of dealing with mounting international tension following German rearmament, the Italian invasion of Abyssinia and the reoccupation of the Rhineland, it was a recognition that something had to be done in the field of propaganda to defend Britain's position in the world. In an increasingly militaristic environment, the British were attempting to promote an alternative, peaceful way in which international cooperation and mutual understanding were more acceptable futures than aggressive posturing or threatening behaviour. In retrospect, it might seem a rather limp response to the propaganda of the dictators. At the time, however, it reflected the philosophical nature of democratic thinking not only as a genuine ideological alternative to Fascism or Communism, but also about the need to engage in a campaign for hearts and minds on a global scale, which Britain would have preferred to avoid. As permanent secretary of the Foreign Office, Sir Robert Vansittart, stated in 1936: 'what is really and ultimately at issue in the world is dictatorship or democracy, liberty or the man-machine. I am not sure there will ultimately be room in the world for both, possibly not without a struggle of some kind, though it need not necessarily be a world-war again, or a war at all if democracy will show plainly that it can and will look after itself ....'[29]

If a modern, albeit nascent, mass democracy was to spend its valuable taxpayers' money on appealing to foreigners, how should this be done? On one thing, most were agreed: it should not be done in the manner of the dictators. Overseas propaganda needed to reflect the society from which it emanated and British society needed to set an example to the rest of the world that there were genuine and viable alternatives to extremism. One of the axioms of effective propaganda, however, was that image and reality should retain a high degree of synergy. Mussolini was to discover this to his cost.[30] But the British also understood George Canning's axiom that in diplomacy, threats should not be issued unless force was available to back them up. Until the various British rearmament programmes achieved sufficient maturity to put Britain in a stronger diplomatic position, the government had to pursue a policy of appeasement. And although, again in retrospect, it might appear that appeasement was borne of weakness, it had to be projected at the time as something quite different, as a policy which sought peaceful resolution to what might be legitimate grievances and as a policy which sought peace instead of war.

The outbreak of war in 1939 might therefore suggest not only a failure of appeasement as a policy, but also a failure on the part of the British propaganda that supported it. But would this be a fair assessment? British diplomats certainly felt that foreign propaganda was poisoning the atmosphere in which diplomacy was expected to function. This atmosphere had become a sign of the times, a product of the opening up – or greater accountability – of post-war democracy. Prior to the Great War, diplomacy tended to be conducted behind closed doors, far away from the prying gaze of the public. But that war was supposed to have ushered in a new period of 'open covenants, openly arrived at', not least because secret diplomacy was widely accredited as having contributed to the outbreak of hostilities in 1914. But in the 1930s, many felt that the trend had gone too far the other way. The new revisionist regimes seemed content to conduct their diplomacy in conjunction with presentation and at the expense of the ability to get things done without recourse to public opinion. It was all very well for the dictators to do this; they controlled their media. But for the democracies, greater public accountability, combined with a free and ever more curious news media, it seemed that they were at a disadvantage and correspondingly were always on the defensive. When, for example, Lord Halifax visited Hitler in 1938, his protests about the British government being unable to control the British press in their critical opinions of the Führer fell on incredulous ears. At least the British knew when they surveyed the German press that it was speaking for the Nazi government.

As such, therefore, the dictators recognised that in the 'age of the masses' propaganda and policy went hand in hand. The democracies, on the other hand, struggled with this new reality and, within the context of a free media and a general antipathy towards the very notion of propaganda, had to find means other than direct control if they were to compete on equal terms. The Chamberlain government proved particularly adept at evolving a typically British compromise.[31] Instead of control, it tried 'influence' on the principle that it was better to influence those few who were in a position to influence the many than to attempt direct appeals to mass opinion itself.

Although the Foreign Office was the first Whitehall department to establish a peacetime News Department, it was not until 1930 that Downing Street followed suite with a Press Office of its own.[32] Hence, a channel was established by the government to release information to the press – British and foreign – on a regular basis. This was a formal recognition of the need for government to inform the media more systematically than hitherto of its policies and of its thinking behind such policies. This superseded – though it did not replace – the time-honoured system of ministers meeting with editors and proprietors over dinner or in the gentlemen's clubs. But regular press conferences also provided ministers with the opportunity of influencing the media agenda. Persuasion rather than coercion was the democratic way. This system, in fact, placed the emphasis upon the journalists to verify that what they were being told by press officers was 'the truth', or at least 'their truth'. But it also made it essential for those press officers not to deceive the press. Thus was born, from both philosophical and pragmatic seeds, the tradition of 'information policy', which had the advantage of avoiding any charges that what was being done was in fact propaganda. Democratic politicians and their ministers issued 'facts and figures'. It was 'news' and it was for the free media to express their own views on the 'known facts'.

But no matter how skilful politicians became at media agenda setting, the news media could not be relied on uncritically to replicate the official line. Ramsay MacDonald and Stanley Baldwin were amongst the first prime ministers to address the public via the cinema newsreels, reaching almost half of the population with explanations about what the government was doing and why.[33] The national government established a very close relationship with the five newsreel companies, and the historical record shows a remarkable degree of synergy with the official line. Slightly less cooperative – but only slightly – was the BBC which, although enjoying a monopoly in the new medium of radio broadcasting, cherished its very independence from government interference.[34] That said, dissidents of appeasement, such as Winston Churchill, found it difficult to gain access to the airwaves, and when the government finally accepted that it would have to counter Italian and Nazi radio propaganda, especially in the Middle East and in Latin America respectively, it asked the BBC to launch its foreign language services in Arabic, Spanish and Portuguese in early 1938.

This was a clever move. The Foreign Office, or rather certain anti-appeasement elements within it surrounding Sir Robert Vansittart and Rex Leeper, had distrusted the BBC and had wanted to conduct these broadcasts themselves. They thought the BBC would be too independent and too resistant to influence in determining the content of the broadcasts, when what was needed was direct official refutation of German and Italian allegations. But the Chamberlain government decided that the overt independence of the BBC would be a useful quality in the struggle to persuade foreign listeners that the British were not afraid of 'the truth', thus enhancing the credibility of British broadcasts over that of their competitors. The same thinking prevailed during the Munich crisis when the BBC was asked to launch a service in German and in other European languages.[35]

Psychological Rearmament

The wave of popular and media relief which greeted 'Chamberlain the peacemaker' on his return from Munich would suggest that British public opinion was not psychologically prepared for war in 1938. Chamberlain had been cheered in Germany too, infuriating Hitler, which would suggest the same for German public opinion. After five years of intense nationalist and militarist propaganda, culminating annually in the spectacular party rallies in Nuremberg, this does not suggest a triumph for Nazi propaganda. The Nazis had walked a tightrope between rebuilding the nation's confidence – and its armed forces – while at the same time not provoking an anti-German alliance before they were ready for armed conflict. Since 1936, the Spanish Civil War had been raging under intense media coverage, and for cinema audiences newsreels depicted the horror of what future European war might be like when the new terror weapon of the bomber was unleashed on cities like Guernica.[36] During the Munich crisis, the Chamberlain government became alarmed that the German people might not have access to the 'true' picture of what was happening, and resorted to a covert – and probably illegal – operation involving buying airtime on Radio Luxembourg, which was capable of penetrating the German domestic wireless frequencies.[37]

After almost a decade of defence cuts following the Great War, the British had begun rearming since 1935. Again a policy-presentation tightrope was involved. Why should the largely peace-loving (or war-fearing) British public pay through increased taxation for rearmament programmes if there was at that time no obvious threat of war? Again the experience of 1914 suggested that arms races provoked rather than prevented war. The national government formed in 1931 to deal with the economic crisis developed the case that rearmament was for defensive reasons – the Nazis made the same case to the German people – especially against the threat of the bomber which, as Baldwin famously said, would 'always get through'. The emphasis was placed on fighter defence but, by the time of Munich, the rearmament programmes were far from complete. This was but one fact driving the policy of appeasement.[38] Lack of psychological preparation for war was another.

The final year of peace saw a concerted effort to address this shortcoming. Munich had established the framework into which national and international perceptions about the rights and wrongs of any future war would be located. If the Munich agreement held, then well and good. If it did not, Britain would need to be prepared both militarily and psychologically for the unthinkable: Guernica on a European-wide scale. Britain would also need allies. Flying back from Munich, Chamberlain and his adviser Horace Wilson discussed a plan to do with that famous 'scrap of paper'. They knew the world's media would be waiting for them at Heston airport (including live-television cameras)[39] and they decided to send out a clear message, not just to Hitler but to the rest of the world as well. When Chamberlain waved the agreement to the cheering crowds, he was effectively saying: here are the limits of German expansion. If Hitler honoured his word, then there would be 'peace in our time' (although Chamberlain later came to regret that phrase). If he did not, then the world would see who was responsible for unleashing a second major war in a generation. Careful scrutiny of the newsreel footage reveals Chamberlain looking up to the cameras. He knew that the Americans would be watching.

As efforts were made in early 1939 to firm up friendships, with a royal visit to the United States and an official visit by the French president to Britain, the British began seriously to address their preparations for war. Plans had been underway since 1935 to create a Ministry of Information in the event of war; the British would not start the next one as unprepared as they had been in the last one. Rearmament plans were accelerated, and the case was made for the fighter as a viable defence against the bomber. Newsreels ran special series on the formidable nature of French defences, focusing on the Maginot line, on the readiness of anti-aircraft defences, and on the strength of the army, navy and air force. Britain tried to line up the forces of European and North American democracy as a counterbalance to the Rome–Berlin Axis, which also existed more in image than in reality,[40] and went so far as to court the Soviet Union. The West lost that race when Germany and the Soviet Union signed a pact in August 1939, and it is a tribute to the ability of Nazi domestic propaganda – or perhaps its coercive control – that the German people accepted this apparent reversal of ideological thrust. In view of the fact that the pact came as a shock to the West, which had a pretty good track record of anti-Communist propaganda of its own, one wonders how western opinion would have greeted the news of an Anglo-Soviet alliance two years before Operation Barbarossa made it a reality.

The lines had, however, already been drawn. In March 1939, Hitler tore up the Munich agreement and invaded the rump of Czechoslovakia. This was, in fact, the first time that Hitler had incorporated non-Germans into the Reich and exposed as false his persistent line that he was merely attempting to redress the grievances of Versailles and pursue a policy of self-determination for all Germans separated from the Reich. Appeasement was dropped like a lead balloon, and guarantees were issued to Poland, Romania and Greece. The problem now was how to gear up for a war that threatened to take place on three fronts, in Europe, in the Mediterranean and in the Far East simultaneously. This was the nightmare scenario for British defence planners, especially following the anti-Comintern pact of 1937 consisting of Rome, Berlin and Tokyo. In reality, these three powers rarely coordinated their foreign policy in quite the way it was believed they did. They shared common enemies, and some of their ideologies, but that was about it. They certainly all gained from the appearance of acting in concert, and their propaganda skilfully exploited this. But they were equally capable of deceiving each other, as witnessed by the astonishment in Japan when the Nazi-Soviet pact was signed. And when war came in September 1939, both Italy and Japan stayed out, at least for the moment.

If wars begin in men's minds, then Chamberlain had his made up for him by the German invasion of Poland on 1 September. The guarantee to Poland had to be honoured; it would have been too humiliating after the failure to help Czechoslovakia in March and would have sent completely the wrong signals to the rest of Europe. Britain thus declared war on Germany knowing that there was little it could do for the Poles, but did so for 'just' reasons. As Chamberlain said, war was necessary because it would be 'evil things' that Britain would be fighting against, 'brute force, bad faith, tyranny and oppression'. As for the British people, they accepted the decision with a resignation that belied many of the hopes and fears of the 1930s. The Americans stayed out, but the bombers did not arrive for another six months, providing invaluable time to prepare both physically and mentally. The German people too accepted the war with nothing that could be remotely described as enthusiasm. Hitler had announced that Germany had been provoked following the death of two German radio operators in Danzig, an interesting twist in the role played by propaganda in the origins of the war.

Conclusions

Propaganda does not start wars, but it can certainly play a significant contributory role. During the inter-war period, state sponsored propaganda was used increasingly to supplement, and sometimes even substitute for, national and foreign policies. In the dictatorships, nothing was left to chance and it tended to be organised alongside rigorous state censorship and the use, or threatened use, of force. At home or abroad, it was the same. But their propaganda was never quite as coherent as they would have their opponents believe. Nazi propaganda for example was conducted from several, often rival, ministries. The British eschewed a dedicated peacetime ministry, but planned one for wartime and increasingly addressed the issue of media relations because they knew that public opinion now counted for something. After all, if war should come, ordinary citizens would be in the 'front lines', thanks to the advent of bombing as a weapon of war. The traditional gap between governors and governed, even in limited democracies like the Britain of pre-1918, could no longer be occupied by mass media operating with increased government 'guidance'. That guidance had to operate within a democratic context, a contract that was based upon certain principles including the requirement not to lie deliberately to either the media or to the people. That is what made democracy different from its rivals, and it was partly what gave democracy its moral justification. It was the British and French who, after all, declared war on Germany, not the other way around.

It would be difficult to argue that British propaganda prior to the outbreak of war contributed towards the heightening of international tension in the same way as that of Germany, Italy or Japan. Britain was always on the defensive, having relinquished its position of apparent strength at the end of the First World War. The Axis powers used propaganda to keep the British on the defensive by a combination of bluff, bluster and disinformation. But British strength was always more apparent than real, and it was exposed by the apparent three-theatre threat of the 1930s. Appearances would appear to count for much more in an age of mass media and the internationalisation of communications. Prior to 1939, appearances did count for a great deal, and Hitler, Mussolini and Stalin understood this only too well. For the British, however, the gap between the appearance of world power and its reality remained too wide for any amount of propaganda to fill. The best they could do was to hope for the best, prepare for the worst and try to ensure that their case was as credible as possible. To achieve the latter, they had to tell their truth while recognising that the whole truth about their real position could never be told.

When war was declared, Chamberlain announced the news on the radio. In Germany, the people were told that the *Wehrmacht* was invading Poland because it had been provoked by a (fabricated) attack on the German radio station at Gleiwitz, resulting in the death of one German and the wounding of another. On the opening night of the war, the Royal Air Force launched its first raid over German soil, dropping leaflets rather than bombs. In Britain, all the cinemas were closed for fear of the human devastation should German bombers arrive. In France, the people were told of the strength of their defences. In Russia, the people were not told of the secret clauses of the Nazi-Soviet pact providing for a Soviet invasion of Polish territory. The Second World War may have begun, but the 'age of illusions' was well and truly over.

Notes

1. Although this phrase is often attributed to Hiram Johnson, it has also been ascribed to Boake Carter, George Orwell, Arthur Ponsonby and Samuel Johnson.
2. R. Taylor, *Film Propaganda: Soviet Russia and Nazi Germany* (London, 1979); D. Welch, *Propaganda and the German Cinema, 1933–45* (Oxford, 1985), and his *Nazi Propaganda: The Power and the Limitations* (London, 1983); P. Kenez, *The Rebirth of the Propaganda State: Soviet Methods of Mass Mobilization, 1917–1929* (Cambridge, 1985).
3. P. M. Taylor, *The Projection of Britain: British Overseas Publicity and Propaganda, 1919–39* (Cambridge, 1981); D. Le Mahieu, *A Culture for Democracy: Mass Communication and the Cultivated Mind in Britain between the Wars* (Oxford, 1988); and M. Grant, *Propaganda and the Role of the State in Inter-War Britain* (Oxford, 1994).
4. T. Jeffrey, *Mass Observation: A Short History* (Birmingham, 1978).
5. P. M. Taylor, *British Propaganda in the 20th Century: Selling Democracy* (Edinburgh, 1999); D. Culbert, ed., *Film and Propaganda in America: A Documentary History* (New York, 1991); R. W. Steele, *Propaganda In An Open Society: The Roosevelt Administration and the Media, 1933–1941* (Westport, CT, 1985).
6. A. R. Pratkanis and E. Aronson, *Age of Propaganda: The Everyday Use and Abuse of Persuasion* (New York, 1992).
7. J. Ellul, *Propaganda: The Formation of Men's Attitudes* (New York, 1965), and his *The Technological Society* (New York, 1964).

8. Among the numerous conceptual discussions are J. Hawthorne, *Propaganda, Persuasion and Polemic* (London, 1987).

9. In particular Harold Lasswell, who wrote *Propaganda in the World War* as early as 1927. (See the reprint by MIT Press, Cambridge, MA, 1971.)

10. For further details, see M. L. Sanders and P. M. Taylor, *British Propaganda during the First World War* (Basingstoke, 1982).

11. G. Messinger, *British Propaganda and the State in the First World War* (Manchester, 1992).

12. This made it even harder for the British next time, between 1939 and 1941. See N. J. Cull, *Selling War: The British Propaganda Campaign Against American 'Neutrality' in World War II* (Oxford, 1995).

13. H. C. Peterson, *Propaganda For War: The Campaign Against American Neutrality, 1914–1917* (Norman, 1939).

14. General Erich von Ludendorff, *My War Memoirs*, 2 Vols (London, 1919).

15. A. Ponsonby, *Falsehood in Wartime* (London, 1928); J. M. Read, *Atrocity Propaganda, 1914–1919* (New York, 1972).

16. The modern history of British domestic wartime morale remains unwritten. In the meantime, see C. Haste, *Keep the Home Fires Burning* (London, 1977).

17. S. Badsey and P. M. Taylor, 'Images of Battle: The Press, Propaganda and Passchendaele', in P. Liddle, ed., *Passchendaele in Perspective* (London, 1997), pp. 371–90.

18. Anon, *The Times History of the War* (London, 1920).

19. S. Constantine, *Buy & build: The Advertising Posters of the Empire Marketing Board* (London, 1986).

20. The best works on this have never appeared in print. They are T. J. Hollins, *The Presentation of Politics: The Place of Party Publicity, Broadcasting and Film in British Politics, 1918–1939*, University of Leeds PhD thesis, 1981; and T. Ryan, *Labour and the Media in Britain 1929–1939: A Study of the Attitudes of the Labour Movement towards the New Media, Film and Radio, and of its Attempts to Use them for Political Purposes*, University of Leeds PhD thesis, 1986.

21. Z. A. B. Zeman, *Nazi Propaganda* (Oxford, 1973); R. E. Herzstein *The War that Hitler Won: Goebbels and the Nazi Media Campaign* (New York, 1987).

22. For a contemporary analysis, see M. Polanyi, *The Contempt of Freedom: The Russian Experiment and After* (London, 1940).

23. J. C. Robertson, *The British Board of Film Censors: Film Censorship in Britain, 1896–1950* (London, 1985); M. Bernstein, ed., *Controlling Hollywood: Censorship & Regulation in the Studio Area* (London, 2000).

24. Cited in J. Hale, *Radio Power: Propaganda and International Broadcasting* (London, 1975).

25. Public Record Office, Foreign Office papers, FO 395/534, P 823/160/150 (hereafter PRO, FO 371, etc.), memorandum by Kenneth Johnstone, 'Foreign cultural propaganda and the threat to British interests abroad', 19 February 1937.

26. F. Donaldson, *The British Council: The First Fifty Years* (London, 1984).

27. See C. A. MacDonald, 'Radio Bari: Italian Wireless Propaganda in the Middle East and British Countermeasures, 1934–38', *Middle Eastern Studies* 13 (1977), 195–207.

28. G. J. Kasza, *The State and the Mass Media in Japan, 1918–45* (Berkeley, 1988).

29. PRO, FO 395/541, P332/332/150, minute by Vansittart, 3 February 1936.

30. L. Quartermaine, *Mussolini's Last Republic: Propaganda and Politics in the Italian Social Republic (RSI) 1943–45* (Exeter, 2000); D. Thompson, *State Control in Fascist Italy: Culture and Conformity, 1925–43* (Manchester, 1991).

31. A. P. Adamthwaite, 'The British Government and the Media, 1937–8', *Journal of Contemporary History* 18 (1983), pp. 281–97; R. Cockett, *Twilight of Truth: Chamberlain, Appeasement and the Manipulation of the Press* (London, 1989).

32. J. Margach, *The Abuse of Power: The War between Downing Street and the Media from Lloyd George to Callaghan* (London, 1978).

33. N. Pronay, 'British Newsreels in the 1930s: 1 – Audiences and Producers', *History* 56 (1971), 63–72, and '2 – Their Policies and Impact', *History* 57 (1972), 63–72.

34. A. Briggs, *The History of Broadcasting in the United Kingdom, Vol. II, The Golden Age of Wireless* (Oxford, 1965).

35. W. J. West, *Truth Betrayed* (London, 1987).

36. A. Aldgate, *Cinema and History: British Newsreels and the Spanish Civil War* (London, 1979).

37. N. Pronay and P. M. Taylor, ' "An Improper Use of Broadcasting": The British Government and Clandestine Radio Operations against Germany during the Munich Crisis and After', *Journal of Contemporary History* 19 (1984), 357–84.

38. J. Ruggiero, *Neville Chamberlain and British Rearmament: Pride, Prejudice, and Politics* (Westport, CT, 1999).

39. K. R. M. Short, 'A Note on BBC Television News and the Munich Crisis, 1938', *Historical Journal of Film, Radio and Television* 9 (1989), 165–80.

40. D. C. Watt, 'The Rome-Berlin Axis: Myth and Reality', *Review of Politics* 22 (1960), 519–42.

Chronology

1918	11 November	Armistice ends fighting in First World War
1919	14 March	Britain and the United States offer to guarantee France against future German aggression
	28 June	Treaty of peace with Germany signed at Versailles
	19 November	US Senate fails to muster two-thirds vote for ratification of Treaty of Versailles
1920	19 March	US Senate again fails to ratify Treaty
1922	6 February	Four-, Five- and Nine-Power Treaties signed at Washington Conference
	29 October	Mussolini takes power in Italy after staged 'march on Rome'
1923	11 January	French and Belgian troops occupy the Ruhr industrial region of Germany
	24 July	Treaty of Lausanne between the Allies and Turkey completes the peacemaking
	8–9 Nov.	Hitler with General Ludendorf attempts *Putsch* in Munich, arrested, jailed, dictates *Mein Kampf* in Landsberg prison
1924	16 August	Allied and German delegates at London conference sign protocol that ends Ruhr crisis
1925	28 April	Britain returns to the gold standard
	16 October	Rhineland Pact signed at Locarno conference
1929	5 September	Briand, the French premier and foreign minister, at 10th Assembly of League of Nations, proposes European federation
	29 October	New York Stock Market crash
1930	17 May	Briand circulates 'Memorandum on the Organisation of a System for European Federal Union' to European members of the League of Nations
	14 September	National Socialists make large gains in Reichstag elections

1931	18 March	Austro-German customs union scheme revealed
	11 May	Crash of Kreditanstalt in Austria deepens economic crisis in southern Europe
	13 July	Bank holiday declared in Germany
	7 July	One-year Hoover moratorium on inter-governmental debt payments agreed by Britain, USA, France and Germany
	18 September	Japanese army commences its conquest of Manchuria
	21 September	Britain abandons the gold standard
1932	7 January	Secretary of State Stimson announces the American policy of non-recognition of the Japanese conquest of Manchuria
	28 January	Shanghai crisis begins
	2 February	World Disarmament Conference opens
	1 March	Japanese puppet state of Manchukuo established in Manchuria
	15 May	Assassination of Japanese Prime Minister Inukai signals end of party government in Japan
	21 July–20 Aug.	Britain negotiates preferential trade agreements with Dominions at Ottawa conference
1933	30 January	Hitler becomes chancellor of Germany
	24 February	The League of Nations Assembly votes to adopt the Lytton report on Manchurian conflict
	4 March	Franklin D. Roosevelt inaugurated president of the United States, declares national bank holiday five days later
	27 March	Japan leaves the League of Nations
	31 May	Sino-Japanese Truce
	27 July	World Economic Conference breaks down
	21 October	Germany leaves the League of Nations and disarmament talks
1934	26 January	German and Poland conclude a non-aggression pact
	17 April	France rejects further disarmament talks with Germany (April note)
	18 April	Japan claims the right to establish a 'Monroe Doctrine for East Asia'
	30 June	Night of the Long Knives in Germany, when Hitler eliminates potential opposition within Nazi party and others
	25 July	Abortive Nazi *coup* in Vienna
	18 September	The Soviet Union enters the League of Nations
1935	7 January	Mussolini and Pierre Laval, the French prime minister and foreign minister, conclude Franco-Italian Agreements
	9 March	Hitler announces the existence of the *Luftwaffe*
	16 March	Hitler orders conscription in Germany

	14 April	Stresa agreements adopted by France, Britain and Italy on German rearmament and *status quo* central Europe
	2 May	Franco-Soviet mutual assistance treaty signed
	16 May	Czech-Soviet mutual assistance treaty signed
	18 June	Anglo-German naval agreement signed in London
	August	Seventh Comintern Congress held in Moscow
	3 October	Italy begins its conquest of Abyssinia (Ethiopia)
	Nov./Dec.	Japan establishes an autonomous regime in North China
	8 December	Sir Samuel Hoare, the British foreign secretary, and Pierre Laval, for France, agree to a plan for restoring relations with Italy by largely accepting its conquest of Abyssinia
1936	6 January	Mussolini signals to Germany his disinterest in Austria
	26 February	*Coup* by the Japanese army's 'Imperial Way' faction fails
	7 March	German troops reoccupy the demilitarised zone of the Rhineland, contrary to Treaty of Versailles
	3 May	Popular Front parties gain victory in French parliamentary elections
	9 May	Italy annexes Abyssinia
	18 July	The Spanish Civil War begins
	2 August	France proposes non-intervention agreement on Spain
	14 October	Belgium reverts to a policy of neutrality
	25 October	Rome–Berlin Axis signed
	1 November	Mussolini announces the Rome–Berlin Axis
	25 November	Anti-Comintern Pact signed by Germany and Japan
	12–25 Dec.	The Xi'an incident, in which Chiang Kai-shek is held hostage by Chang Xueliang and the Chinese Communist party
1937	2 January	Anglo-Italian Mediterranean agreement
	28 May	Neville Chamberlain succeeds Stanley Baldwin as British prime minister
	4 June	In Japan Fumimaro Konoe forms his first government
	7 July	Marco Polo Bridge incident escalates into full-scale war between China and Japan
	5 October	President Roosevelt's 'Quarantine Speech' at Chicago
	3–24 Nov.	The League of Nations convenes a conference in Brussels to discuss the situation in China
	5 November	Hoßbach Conference at which Hitler divulges plans for aggression
	6 November	Italy joins the Anti-Comintern Pact
	11 December	Italy leaves the League of Nations
	14 December	Nanjing falls to Japanese forces
1938	20 February	Eden resigns as British foreign secretary, replaced by Lord Halifax
	11–13 March	Germany invades Austria and *Anschluß* declared
	16 April	Anglo-Italian agreement signed
	20–21 May	May 'Weekend' Crisis

	11 July	Japanese and Soviet forces clash at Changkufeng
	15 September	Chamberlain flies to meet with Hitler at Berchtesgaden to discuss his demand for the Sudetenland
	18 September	Anglo-French discussions in London on Berchtesgaden agreement
	21 September	Czech government accedes to German demands
	22 September	Chamberlain flies again to see the Führer at Godesberg; Hitler now demands the immediate occupation of the Sudetenland
	24 September	French army calls up reservists
	25–26 Sept.	Anglo-French talks in London
	26–27 Sept.	French army and British fleet mobilisation
	28 September	Hitler agrees to Mussolini's proposal for a conference
	29–30 Sept.	Munich Conference (Germany, Britain, France and Italy)
	30 September	Anglo-German declaration of 'peace in our time'
	5 November	Japan declares 'New Order in East Asia'
	9–10 Nov.	*Kristallnacht*: Nazis demonstrate systematic brutality to Jews in Germany and Austria
	6 December	Franco-German declaration
1939	15–16 March	Germany occupies the rump state of Czechoslovakia
	22 March	Lithuania cedes Memel to Germany
	31 March	French and British guarantees to Poland
	7 April	Italy seizes Albania
	13 April	Anglo-French guarantees to Greece and Romania
	14 April	France, Britain and the Soviet Union begin negotiations towards a triple alliance
	28 April	Hitler denounces German-Polish non-aggression pact and the Anglo-German naval agreement of June 1935
	May–Sept.	The Soviet Red Army inflicts crushing defeat on Japanese forces at Nomonhan
	3 May	Molotov replaces Litvinov as Soviet foreign minister
	22 May	Germany and Italy sign 'Pact of Steel'
	30 May	Soviet-German negotiations begin
	14 June	Japan blockades the British concession at Tianjin in China
	26 July	The United States abrogates its trade treaty with Japan
	11 August	British and French military delegations arrive in Moscow
	23 August	Nazi-Soviet Non-Aggression Pact signed in Moscow
	1 Septembe	Germany attacks Poland; Italy declares 'non-belligerence'
	3 September	Britain and France declare war on Germany
	10 September	Canada declares war on Germany
	17 September	Red Army occupies parts of eastern Poland
	28 September	Polish armed forces surrender
	4 November	United States amends neutrality legislation to permit 'cash and carry' purchases of war materials by the Allies
	30 November	Soviet Union attacks Finland

1940	20 March	Daladier resigns as French premier, replaced on 22nd by Reynaud
	30 March	Wang Jingwei's pro-Japanese government set up in Nanjing
	9 Apri	Germany invades Denmark and Norway
	10 May	German offensive in the west against Holland, Belgium and France begins; Churchill replaces Chamberlain as prime minister
	26 May–4 June	Dunkirk evacuation of British and French forces
	10 June	Italy declares war on France and Britain
	14 June	Paris declared an 'open city' to avoid destruction
	16 June	Reynaud resigns and Pétain becomes premier of France
	22 June	France and Germany, France and Italy conclude armistice agreements
	1 July	French parliament sitting in Vichy votes Pétain special powers, l'État Français supplants the Third Republic
	16 July	In Japan Fumimarō Konoe forms his second government with Yosuke Matsuoka as Foreign Minister
	17 July	Britain closes Burma Road supply route to China
	13 August	*Luftwaffe* begins the Battle of Britain
	27 August	United States Congress approves conscription by a one-vote majority
	3 September	United States exchanges 50 destroyers with Britain for the loan of British bases
	20 September	United States begins to break Japanese diplomatic code
	22 September	Japanese troops occupy northern Indochina
	25 September	United States offers China a $25 million loan
	27 September	Tripartite Pact signed between Germany, Japan and Italy
	7 October	German troops enter Romania
	28 October	Italy attacks Greece
	5 November	Roosevelt re-elected for a third term as president
	18 December	Hitler issues his directive for Operation Barbarossa (the attack on the Soviet Union)
1941	11 March	Lend Lease legislation passed in United States Congress
	6 April	Yugoslavia invaded by Germany
	13 April	Japan and the Soviet Union sign a neutrality pact
	22 June	Germany attacks the Soviet Union
	12 July	Britain and the Soviet Union conclude a treaty of mutual assistance
	23 July	Vichy agrees to allow Japan to occupy southern Indochina
	26 July	United States freezes Japanese assets
	9–12 Aug.	Roosevelt and Churchill sign Atlantic Charter at Argentia conference
	6 September	Japan decides on war with the United States and Britain, but to continue negotiations with Washington
	4 October	United States confirms the suspension of trade with Japan

16 October	Tōjō Cabinet formed in Tokyo
13 November	United States amends neutrality legislation
7 December	Japan attacks Pearl Harbor
8 December	Britain and the United States declare war on Japan
9 December	China declares war on Japan and Germany; Free France under Charles de Gaulle declares war on Japan
11 December	Germany and Italy declare war on the United States

Further Reading

The Treaty of Versailles

M. F. Boemeke, G. D. Feldman and E. Glaser, eds, *The Treaty of Versailles: A Reassessment after 75 Years* (Cambridge, 1998)

M. MacMillan, *The Peacemakers: The Paris Peace Conference of 1919 and Its Attempt to End War* (London, 2001)

A. Sharp, *The Versailles Settlement: Peacemaking in Paris 1919* (Basingstoke, 1991)

Nazi Germany

M. Burleigh, *The Third Reich: A New History* (London, 2000)

W. Deist, M. Messerschmidt, H. Volkmann and W. Wette, *Germany and the Second World War, Volume I, The Build-up of German Aggression* (Oxford, 1990)

K. Hildebrand, *The Foreign Policy of the Third Reich* (Los Angeles, 1973)

G. L. Weinberg, *The Foreign Policy of Hitler's Germany*, Volume I, *The Diplomatic Revolution in Europe, 1933–1936*, Volume II, *Starting World War Two, 1937–1939* (Chicago, 1970 and 1980)

Fascist Italy

S. Azzi, 'The Historiography of Fascist Foreign Policy', *Historical Journal* 36 (1993)

R. J. B. Bosworth, *Mussolini* (London, 2002)

M. Knox, *Mussolini Unleashed, 1939–1941* (Cambridge, 1981)

M. Knox, *Hitler's Italian Allies* (Cambridge, 2000)

D. Mack Smith, *Mussolini* (London, 1981)

R. M. Salerno, *Vital Crossroads: Mediterranean Origins of the Second World War, 1935–40* (New York, 2002)

Imperial Japan

M. Barnhart, *Japan Prepares for Total War: The Search for Economic Security, 1919–1941* (New York, 1987)

I. H. Nish, *Japan's Struggle with Internationalism: Japan, China and the League of Nations, 1931–33* (1993)

I. H. Nish and Y. Kibata, eds, *The History of Anglo-Japanese Relations: The Political and Diplomatic Dimension, Volume II, 1931–2000* (Basingstoke, 2000)

L. Young, *Japan's Total Empire: Manchuria and the Culture of Wartime Imperialism* (Berkeley, 1998)

Soviet Union

G. Gorodetsky, *Grand Delusion: Stalin and the German Invasion of Russia* (New Haven, 1999)

C. J. Haslam, *The Soviet Union and the Struggle for Collective Security in Europe 1933–1939* (Basingstoke, 1984)

C. J. Haslam, 'Soviet-German Relations and the Origins of the Second World War: The Jury is Still Out', *Journal of Modern History* 69 (1997)

G. Roberts, *The Soviet Union and the Origins of the Second World War* (Basingstoke, 1995)

France

A. P. Adamthwaite, *Grandeur and Misery: France's Bid for Power in Europe* (London, 1995)

M. Alexander, *The Republic in Danger: General Maurice Gamelin and the Politics of French Defence, 1933–1940* (Cambridge, 1992)

R. Boyce, ed., *French Foreign and Defence Policy, 1918–1940* (London, 1998)

R. J. Young, *France and the Origins of the Second World War* (Basingstoke, 1995)

Britain

A. Best, *Britain, Japan and Pearl Harbor: Avoiding War in East Asia, 1936–1941* (London, 1995)

D. Dutton, *Neville Chamberlain* (London, 2001)

R. A. C. Parker, *Chamberlain and Appeasement: British Policy and the Coming of the Second World War* (Basingstoke, 1993)

B. J. C. McKercher, *Transition of Power: Britain's Loss of Global Pre-Eminence to the United States, 1930–45* (Cambridge, 1999)

G. Post Jr., *Dilemmas of Appeasement: British Deterrence and Defence, 1934–1937* (New York, 1993)

The United States

R. Dallek, *Franklin D. Roosevelt and American Foreign Policy, 1932–1945* (New York, 1979)

W. Heinrichs, *Threshold of War: Franklin D. Roosevelt and American Entry into World War II* (New York, 1988)

C. A. MacDonald, *The United States, Britain and Appeasement, 1936–1939* (London, 1981)

D. Reynolds, *From Munich to Pearl Harbor: Roosevelt's America and the Origins of the Second World War* (Chicago, 2001)

Poland, Czechoslovakia and Eastern Europe

A. M. Cienciala and T. Komarnicki, *From Versailles to Locarno: Keys to Polish Foreign Policy, 1919–1925* (Lawrence, KS, 1984)

I. Lukes, *Czechoslovakia Between Stalin and Hitler: The Diplomacy of Edvard Beneš in the 1930s* (New York, 1996)

I. Lukes and E. Goldstein, *The Munich Crisis: Prelude to World War II* (London, 2000)

A. Prazmowska, *Britain, Poland, and the Eastern Front, 1939* (Cambridge, 1987)

A. Prazmowska, *Eastern Europe and the Origins of the Second World War* (Basingstoke, 2000)

The Neutrals

J. Hiden and T. Lane, eds, *The Baltic States and the Outbreak of the Second World War* (Cambridge, 1992)

P. Salmon, *Scandinavia and the Great Powers, 1890–1940* (Cambridge, 1997)

N. Wyllie, ed., *European Neutrals and Non-Belligerents During the Second World War* (Cambridge, 2002)

The Spanish Civil War

P. Preston, *A Concise History of the Spanish Civil War* (London, 1996)

P. Preston and A. L. Mackenzie, *The Republic Besieged: Civil War in Spain* (Edinburgh, 1996)

R. Radosh, M. R. Habeck and G. Sevostianov, eds, *Spain Betrayed: The Soviet Union in the Spanish Civil War* (New Haven, 2001)

China

P. Coble, *Facing Japan: Chinese Politics and Japanese Imperialism, 1931–1937* (Cambridge, MA, 1991)

J. W. Garver, *Chinese Soviet Relations 1937–1945: The Diplomacy of Chinese Nationalism* (Oxford, 1988)

D. A. Jordan, *Chinese Boycotts versus Japanese Bombs, 1931–1932: The Failure of China's Revolutionary Diplomacy, 1931–1932* (Michigan, 1991)
Y. Sun, *China and the Origins of the Pacific War, 1931–1941* (New York, 1993)

Political Science and History

C. Elman and M. Fendius Elman, eds, *Bridges and Boundaries: Historians, Political Scientists, and the Study of International Relations* (Cambridge, MA, 2001)
R. Jervis, *System Effects: Complexity in Political and Social Life* (Princeton, 1997)
K. Waltz, *Theory of International Politics* (Reading, MA, 1979)

Ideology

A. Cassels, *Ideology and International Relations in the Modern World* (London, 1996)
M. Knox, *Common Destiny: Dictatorship, Foreign Policy, and War in Fascist Italy and Nazi Germany* (Cambridge, 2000)
S. Payne, *A History of Fascism, 1914–1945* (London, 1996)

Economics

R. Boyce, *Capitalism at a Crossroads, 1919–32: A Study in Politics, Economics and International Relations* (Cambridge, 1987)
P. Clavin, *The Failure of Economic Diplomacy: Britain, Germany, France and the United States, 1931–1936* (Basingstoke, 1995)
B. Eichengreen, 'The Origins and Nature of the Great Slump Revisited', *Economic History Review* 45 (1992)

Peace Movements

P. Brock and T. P. Socknat, eds, *Challenge to Mars: Essays on Pacifism from 1918 to 1945* (Toronto, 1999)
M. Ceadel, *Pacifism in Britain, 1914–1945: The Defining of a Faith* (Oxford, 1980)
N. Ingram, *The Politics of Dissent: Pacifism in France, 1919–1939* (Oxford, 1991)

Armaments

T. C. Imlay, *Facing the Second World War: Strategy, Politics and Economics in Britain and France, 1938–1940* (Oxford, 2003)
J. Maiolo, *The Royal Navy and Nazi Germany, 1933–39* (Basingstoke, 1998)

E. R. May, *Strange Victory: Hitler's Conquest of France* (London, 2000)
A. R. Millett, and W. Murray, eds, *Military Effectiveness, Volume II, The Interwar Period* (London, 1988)
R. J. Overy, *War and Economy in the Third Reich* (Oxford, 1995)

Intelligence

A. Best, *British Intelligence and the Japanese Challenge in Asia, 1914–1941* (Basingstoke, 2002)
P. Jackson, *France and the Nazi Menace: Intelligence and Policy Making 1933–39* (Oxford, 2000)
E. R. May, ed., *Knowing One's Enemies: Intelligence Assessment before the Two World Wars* (Princeton, 1984)
W. K. Wark, *The Ultimate Enemy: British Intelligence and Nazi Germany, 1933–1939* (Oxford, 1986)

Diplomacy and Diplomatists

G. A. Craig and F. Gilbert, *The Diplomats 1919–39* (Princeton, 1994 edn)
M. Dockrill and B. J. C. McKercher, eds, *Diplomacy and World Power: Studies in British Foreign Policy, 1890-1950* (Cambridge, 1996)

The League of Nations

J. P. Dunbabin, 'The League of Nations Place in the International System', *History* 88 (1993)
F. S. Northedge, *The League of Nations: Its Life and Times, 1920–1946* (Leicester, 1986)
Z. S. Steiner, 'The League of Nations and the Quest for Security', in R. Ahmann, A. M. Birke and M. Howard, eds, *The Quest for Stability: Problems of West European Security, 1918–1957* (Oxford, 1993)
C. Thorne, *The Limits of Foreign Policy: The West, the League and the Far Eastern Crisis of 1931–1933* (London, 1972)

Propaganda

N. Cull, *Selling War: The British Propaganda Campaign Against American 'Neutrality' in World War II* (Oxford, 1995)
P. M. Taylor, *The Projection of Britain: British Overseas Publicity and Propaganda, 1919–1939* (Cambridge, 1981)
D. Welch, *The Third Reich: Politics and Propaganda* (London, 1993)

Notes on Contributors

P. M. H. Bell is Emeritus Reader in History, University of Liverpool. His many publications include *The Origins of the Second World War in Europe* (revised edn, 1997), *France and Britain, 1900–1940: Entente and Estrangement* (1996), *France and Britain, 1940–1994: The Long Separation* (1997) and *The World since 1945: An International History* (2001).

Antony Best is Senior Lecturer in International History at the London School of Economics. He is the author of *Britain, Japan and Pearl Harbor: Avoiding War in East Asia, 1936–41* (1995), *British Intelligence and the Japanese Challenge in Asia, 1914–41* (2002), and of a number of scholarly articles and essays on Anglo-Japanese relations.

Robert Boyce is Senior Lecturer in the Department of International History at the London School of Economics. He is author of *British Capitalism at the Crossroads, 1919–1932: A Study in Politics, Economics and International Relations* (1987), co-editor of *Paths to War: New Essays on the Origins of the Second World War* (1989), and editor and translator of *French Foreign and Defence Policy, 1918–1940: The Decline and Fall of a Great Power* (1998). He is completing a study of *The Great Crisis, 1928–1933: Watershed of the Contemporary World.*

Alan Cassels is Professor of History Emeritus at McMaster University, Canada. He has published widely on Italian foreign policy in the Mussolini period and on the ideology of Fascism. His most recent book is *Ideology and International Relations in the Modern World* (1996).

John Ferris is Professor of History in the Department of History at the University of Calgary. He has written widely on the history of British strategy, intelligence and diplomacy in the twentieth century. Among his publications are *The Evolution of British Strategic Policy, 1919–1926* (1989) and *The British Army and Signals Intelligence During the First World War* (1992).

John W. Garver is a Professor in the Sam Nunn School of International Affairs at Georgia Institute of Technology in Atlanta, and a specialist in

Chinese foreign relations. He is the author of *China and the Soviet Union, 1937–1945: The Politics of Chinese Nationalism* (1988), *The Sino-American Alliance: Nationalist China and U.S. Cold War Strategy in Asia* (1997) and *Protracted Contest: Sino-Indian Rivalry in the Twentieth Century* (2001).

John Gooch is Professor of International History at the University of Leeds and an authority on contemporary Italian history. His publications include *Army, State and Society in Italy, 1870–1915* (1989). He is completing a major research project on the history of the Italian armed forces under Fascism, 1922–1940.

Jonathan G. Haslam is Reader in the History of International Relations at Cambridge University, Fellow of Corpus Christi College, and the author of a three-volume study of Soviet external relations between the world wars as well as *The Vices of Integrity: E. H. Carr, 1892–1982* (2000) and *No Virtue Like Necessity: Realist Thought in International Relations Since Machiavelli* (2002).

Peter Jackson is Senior Lecturer in International History at the University of Wales, Aberystwyth, and *Chercheur Associé* at the Fondation Nationale des Sciences Politiques. He is the author of *France and the Nazi Menace* (2000) and a number of articles on international relations between the two world wars.

Robert Jervis is Adlai E. Stevenson Professor of International Politics at Columbia University. He is the author of numerous books, including *Perception and Misperception in International Politics* (1976) and *System Effects: Complexity in Political and Social Life* (1997).

Warren F. Kimball is Robert Treat Professor of History at Rutgers University in Newark, New Jersey, and Mark Clark Distinguished Visiting Professor at The Citadel, Charleston, South Carolina. He has written extensively about the international history of the Second World War, including most recently *Churchill & Roosevelt: The Complete Correspondence*, 3 Vols (1984), *The Juggler: Franklin Roosevelt as Wartime Statesman* (1991) and *Forged in War: Roosevelt, Churchill, and the Second World War* (1997, paperback 1998).

Christian Leitz is Associate Professor in the History Department of the University of Auckland. His many publications include *The Economic Relations Between Nazi Germany and Franco's Spain, 1936–1945* (1996) and *Nazi Germany and Neutral Europe during the Second World War* (2001). He is writing a new history of Nazi foreign policy.

Igor Lukes is Associate Professor of International Relations and History, Boston University, and an authority on the crisis in central Europe before and after the Second World War. He is the author of *Czechoslovakia Between Stalin and Hitler: The Diplomacy of Edvard Beneš in the 1930s* (1996) and co-editor of *The Munich Crisis, 1938: Prelude to World War II* (1999).

Joseph A. Maiolo is Lecturer in International History in the Department of War Studies, King's College, London. He is the author of *The Royal Navy and Nazi Germany, 1933–39: A Study in Appeasement and the Origins of the Second World War* (1998) and assistant editor of *The Journal of Strategic Studies*. He is writing a history of armaments competition and the origins of the Second World War.

Williamson Murray is Emeritus Professor of History at Ohio State University and currently Senior Fellow at the Institute for Defense Analysis, Washington. He has published widely on the strategic history of the 1930s and 1940s. His most recent publications include *The Luftwaffe: 1933–45* (1996), with Allen Millett *A War to be Won: Fighting the Second World War* (2000), and as co-editor *The Making of Strategy: Rulers, States, and War* (1994) and *The Dynamics of Military Revolution, 1300–2050* (2002).

Anita J. Prazmowska is Senior Lecturer in International History at the London School of Economics. She is the author of *Britain, Poland and the Eastern Front, 1939* (1986) and *Britain and Poland, 1939–43: The Betrayed Ally* (1995). Her most recent publication is *Eastern Europe and the Origins of the Second World War* (2000). She is writing a history of the origins of the Communist regime in Poland.

Philip M. Taylor is Professor of International Communications at the University of Leeds. His publications include *The Projection of Britain: British Overseas Publicity and Propaganda, 1919–39* (1981), *Munitions of the Mind: A History of Propaganda from the Ancient World to the Present Day* (1995) and *British Propaganda in the 20th Century: Selling Democracy* (1999).

Donald Cameron Watt is Professor Emeritus of International History at the University of London. His many publications includes *Too Serious A Business: European Armed Forces and the Approach of the Second World War* (1973), *Succeeding John Bull: America in Britain's Place, 1900–1975* (1984) and *How War Came: The Immediate Origins of the Second World War* (1989). He is also official historian of *The Central Organisation of Defence, 1945–1966* and Fellow of the British Academy.

Neville Wylie is Lecturer in Politics at the University of Nottingham. He is the author of *Britain and Switzerland During the Second World War* (forthcoming), editor of *European Neutrals and Non-Belligerents during the Second World War* (2001) and review editor of the journal, *Intelligence & National Security*.

Index